THE BRITISH GENERAL
ELECTION OF 1966

Other books in this series

THE BRITISH GENERAL ELECTION OF 1966

By

D. E. BUTLER

Fellow of Nuffield College, Oxford

and

ANTHONY KING

Senior Lecturer in Government, University of Essex

·MACMILLAN

London · Melbourne · Toronto

ST MARTIN'S PRESS

New York

1966

MACMILLAN AND COMPANY LIMITED
Little Essex Street London WC2
also Bombay Calcutta Madras Melbourne

THE MACMILLAN COMPANY OF CANADA LIMITED
70 Bond Street Toronto 2

ST MARTIN'S PRESS INC
175 Fifth Avenue New York NY 10010

Library of Congress Catalog card Number
66–28082

PRINTED IN GREAT BRITAIN

ACKNOWLEDGMENTS

ALTHOUGH these election studies are the responsibility of the authors whose names appear on the title page, they could not be prepared without the co-operation of a very large number of people. The Warden and Fellows of Nuffield sponsored and personally encouraged the work; those who planned and fought the election gave freely of their time in person and by correspondence; the press provided an ample record from which we have drawn freely; and pollsters made available their findings. We must once more set down our debt of gratitude to all those who have provided us with so much of our raw material.

It would be inappropriate to name personally the many people in the party organisations who have helped us so generously. But we must list some others who in diverse ways have made major contributions, in addition to those whose signed chapters represent only part of the help that they gave us:

Ann Bishop	Vera King	Mary Potter
Marilyn Butler	R. L. Leonard	Peter Pulzer
Andrew Duncan-Jones	R. J. May	Richard Rose
Anne Duncan-Jones	Anita Neville	Donald Stokes
Marjorie King	Herbert Nicholas	Philip Williams

Nuffield College, Oxford
July 1st, 1966

DAVID BUTLER
ANTHONY KING

v

CONTENTS

CARTOONS

PHOTOGRAPHS

DIAGRAMS

MAPS

PREFACE

ON March 31st, 1966, postwar British politics came full circle. Labour's triumph of 1945 had given way to the Conservative hegemony of the 1950s. For a time, between 1959 and 1961, it seemed that the Labour party was about to disintegrate or else go into a long secular decline. Now in 1966 Labour's recovery was complete. The party had won in peacetime what it had won only once before, in wartime twenty-one years earlier: a full hold on governmental power.

It is the purpose of this book to chronicle the post-1964 phase of Labour's recovery. If the book has a theme, it is that Labour's victory in 1966 was no more inevitable than its victory in 1964 — however much the outcome may have been foreseen during the few weeks before polling day. At times during 1965 it seemed that the fall of the Labour government was only a matter of weeks away. As late as January 1966 much of the press predicted that Labour would lose the Hull North by-election and that the government would run into serious economic trouble and have great difficulty holding on till the autumn. More than any other election since 1945, the 1966 election is in danger of being misperceived in retrospect.

Even the campaign, although it appeared to change few votes, is of great intrinsic interest. It found the two major parties simultaneously at a moment of transition. Labour was only slowly shedding the preoccupations of the forties and fifties; the Conservatives, fighting for the fourth consecutive time under a new leader, were attempting to reorient their policies and their whole approach to electoral politics. Neither process was near completion when the election intervened. The 1966 campaign also raised questions concerning the ability of parties to communicate policy during elections, the roles of journalists and broadcasters, and the functions, if any, of constituency organisations. 'Elections should be fun,' said Quintin Hogg. The 1966 campaign may not have been as much fun as some others, but it was none the less important for that.

This book follows in the tradition of the six earlier Nuffield studies. Its authors were conscious of an obligation to provide information comparable to that contained in earlier volumes. The following chapters thus include accounts of what the parties, the press, the broadcasters and the polls did centrally during the election; they also attempt to deal with some of the minutiae of electioneering as seen at the local level. Chapter I consists of an outline of the main political events between October 1964 and February 1966 and can probably be omitted by any reader already familiar with the period. But in addition this volume follows the 1964 study by examining in some detail the strategic and other problems that confronted each of the parties in the period before the campaign began. As in 1964 our account draws heavily on the press — whose coverage of British politics grows more thorough as each year passes — and on interviews with members of parliament and officials in all three parties. Our interviews began early in 1965, and almost every page that follows bears their imprint. Unfortunately the basis on which we gathered our information means that there can be no footnotes to our interviews, nor even any names in our list of acknowledgments. We trust that those who gave so freely of their time are already conscious of our gratitude.

One final point must be made. The Nuffield studies have never attempted to produce detailed explanations of why the electorate behaved as it did on particular occasions. Such explanations can only be based on meticulous and elaborate survey research of a type well outside the scope of the series. There is, however, a detailed survey study of the British electorate now in train. In the summer of 1963 and again in October 1964 David Butler and Professor Donald E. Stokes of the University of Michigan commissioned interviews with a sample of 2,000 electors in eighty constituencies. Many of the same voters were re-interviewed shortly after the 1966 election together with an additional sample. The results of this study, which is sponsored by Nuffield College, will be published late in 1967. It is hoped that it will yield new insights into how the British people perceived politics and politicians in the 1960s. The most that the present volume can do in the meantime is to draw on the available opinion poll data and to provide a full analysis of the published voting figures. If our conclusions are tentative it is because, for the moment, only tentative conclusions are possible.

BIBLIOGRAPHICAL NOTE

THE following list consists of a selection of books and articles on British elections and party politics published since the general election of 1964. A few books now in the press have also been included.

Abrams, Mark, 'Social Class and Politics', *Twentieth Century*, vol. CLXXIII, 1965, no. 1025, pp. 35–48.
Bagley, C. R., 'Does Candidates' Position on the Ballot Paper Influence Voters' Choice? — A Study of the 1959 and 1964 British General Elections', *Parliamentary Affairs*, vol. XIX, 1966, no. 2, pp. 162–74.
Bealey, F., Blondel, J., and McCann, W. P., *Constituency Politics: a study of Newcastle-under-Lyme*, Faber, 1965.
Beer, Samuel H., *Modern British Politics*, Faber, 1965.
Blondel, J., 'Towards a General Theory of Change in Voting Behaviour', *Political Studies*, vol. XIII, 1965, no. 1, pp. 93–5.
Blumler, J. G., and McQuail, D., *Election Television in the 1960s*, Faber, forthcoming.
Budge, Ian, 'Electors' Attitudes towards Local Government: A Survey of a Glasgow Constituency', *Political Studies*, vol. XIII, 1965, no. 3, pp. 386–92.
Butler, D. E., 'A Comment [on swing]', *Parliamentary Affairs*, vol. XVIII, 1965, no. 4, pp. 455–7.
Christoph, J. B., 'Consensus and Cleavage in British Political Ideology', *American Political Science Review*, vol. LIX, 1965, no. 3, pp. 629–42.
Deakin, Nicholas, ed., *Colour and the British Electorate 1964*, Pall Mall, 1965.
Epstein, Leon D., 'The Nuclear Deterrent and the British Election of 1964', *Journal of British Studies*, vol. V, 1966, no. 2, pp. 139–63.
Gallup Analysis of Election '66, published the *Daily Telegraph*, 1966.
Kahan, Michael, Butler, David, and Stokes, Donald, 'On the Analytical Division of Social Class', *British Journal of Sociology*, vol. XVII, 1966, no. 2, pp. 122–32.
Kaufman, Gerald, ed., *The Left*, Anthony Blond, 1966.
King, Anthony, 'Britain: the Search for Leadership', *European Politics I*, ed. by William G. Andrews, Van Nostrand, 1965.
King, Anthony, ed., *British Politics*, Hammond and D. C. Heath, 1966.
Lees, J. D., 'Aspects of third-party campaigning in the 1964 General Election', *Parliamentary Affairs*, vol. XIX, 1965–1966, no. 1, pp. 83–90.
Leonard, R. L., *Elections in Britain*, Van Nostrand, 1967.
McKenzie, Robert, 'Between Two Elections', *Encounter*, vol. XXVI, 1966, no. 1, pp. 11–21, and no. 2, pp. 21–9.
Mitchell, B., and Boehm, K., *British Parliamentary Elections*, Cambridge University Press, 1966.
Paterson, Peter, *The Selectorate*, MacGibbon and Kee, 1967.
Ranney, Austin, *Pathways to Parliament*, Macmillan and University of Wisconsin, 1965.
Rasmussen, J. S., *The Liberal Party: A Study of Retrenchment and Revival*, Constable, 1965.
Rasmussen, J. S., 'The Disutility of the Swing Concept in British Psephology', *Parliamentary Affairs*, vol. XVIII, 1965, no. 4, pp. 442–54.
Rose, Richard, *Politics in England*, Faber, 1965.
Rose, Richard, ed., *Studies in British Politics*, Macmillan, 1966.
Rose, Richard, *Influencing Voters: A Study of Campaign Rationality*, Faber, 1967.
The Times House of Commons 1966, published by *The Times*, 1966.
Watkins, A., *The Liberal Dilemma*, MacGibbon and Kee, 1966.
Windlesham, Lord, *Communication and Political Power*, Jonathan Cape, 1966.

CHAPTER I

THE SHORT PARLIAMENT

THE most remarkable thing about the 1964 parliament was that it lasted as long as it did. Harold Wilson had been asked on becoming leader of the Labour party what he would do if Labour had only a tiny majority after the next election. 'Oh,' he had replied, 'we don't discuss nightmares like that.' Later, as the results were coming in, a future cabinet minister maintained on television that, short of a coalition, no government could survive for long with a majority of less than about a dozen. In the event, however, Labour succeeded in governing for fully seventeen months with a majority over the Conservatives and Liberals that fluctuated between five and only one. And when the 1964 parliament was dissolved on March 10th, 1966, it was at a time entirely of the Prime Minister's own choosing.

It is easy in retrospect to assume that Mr. Wilson's decision to govern as though Labour had a larger majority was inevitable, and certainly it had come to seem so within weeks of his taking office. Yet the arguments for caution—for either forming a coalition with the Liberals or trimming the more controversial parts of Labour's programme—were strong. No party in Britain had ever attempted to govern alone with such a precarious majority; it was by no means clear that it was possible physically. Moreover, with a balance of payments deficit running at an annual rate of more than £700m., it seemed probable that any British government would shortly have to take economic measures that were bound to prove unpopular.

Mr. Wilson, however, did not hesitate. Once it was clear on October 16th that Labour would have even a tiny overall majority in the House of Commons, he accepted the Queen's commission to form a government. He did not consult the Liberals nor, so far as is known, his own colleagues. That evening he asserted his determination to govern in a television broadcast to the country.

'The first thing I want to say to you is that my colleagues and I pledge ourselves to do everything in our power to serve our country and our people. The government have only a small majority in the

House of Commons. I want to make it quite clear that this will not affect our ability to govern. Having been charged with the duties of government we intend to carry out those duties.'

He added:

'Over the whole field of government there will be many changes which we have been given a mandate by you to carry out. We intend to fulfil that mandate.'

Mr. Wilson's reasons for responding as he did are not entirely clear, possibly not even to himself. He must have recoiled instinctively from the idea of a formal coalition, which would have involved him in days, possibly weeks, of difficult negotiations and inevitably limited his freedom of manoeuvre. A short-term arrangement with the Liberals was not necessary, since no one doubted that Labour could carry on alone at least for a brief period,

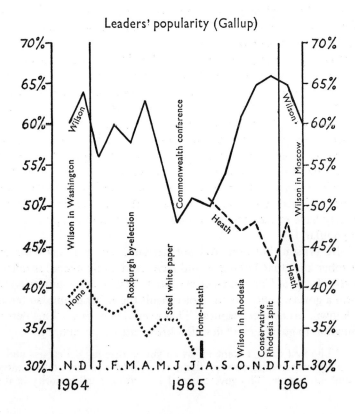

Leaders' popularity (Gallup)

and a long-term arrangement would have set up intolerable strains within his own party. His party would also have reacted against any announcement in advance that the Labour programme would be scaled down. If there were compromises to be made, they would be made most easily in the light of the developing parliamentary situation. In any case, Mr. Wilson was only embarking on an experiment; if the experiment failed, he could honourably go back to the country and ask for a proper working majority. It may be, too, that Mr. Wilson chose to govern because it had never occurred to him to do anything else. There were no signs in his behaviour that he had ever seriously envisaged the possibility of a small majority; he had not, as people were later to remark, done any contingency planning.

Voting intention (Gallup)

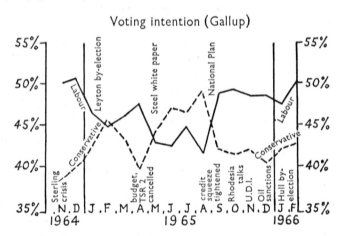

The period of the 1964 parliament can be divided into four phases, corresponding roughly with the fluctuations of the opinion polls (see chart). The first lasted from polling day in 1964 until the end of January; it was terminated by the Leyton by-election. The second lasted until May and saw a decline in Labour's lead in the polls. In the third phase, from May to early September, the Conservatives gained ground in the local government elections, in two by-elections and in the opinion polls; it seemed doubtful for a time whether Labour would survive. But the fourth phase, extending into the 1966 election campaign, brought a sharp increase in both the government's standing and Mr. Wilson's.

At all stages the opinion polls exerted a powerful influence on the three political parties and, although accurate measures are not available, the morale of M.P.s undoubtedly rose and fell in time with them. Incidents that were brushed aside when a party led in the polls assumed enormous significance when the same party was behind. The press, taking its cues from both M.P.s and polls, similarly fluctuated in its estimate of the government's prospects. In August 1965 *The Economist* likened the Prime Minister to Mr. Micawber 'left stranded on the sands of Scilly, waiting for something to turn up'. The same journal two months later wondered whether Mr. Wilson's position could really be as impregnable as it now seemed.

The first phase—the so-called 'hundred days'—was dominated by a balance of payments crisis which rapidly transformed itself into a major sterling crisis. The question of who was ultimately to blame will long be argued; it played a large role in political debate throughout the 1964 parliament, Conservatives asserting that the situation was well under control until Labour's rashness caused foreign holders of sterling to lose confidence, the Labour party arguing that they had inherited a balance of payments deficit so large that a crisis of confidence was inevitable once the facts became known. As late as March 1966 the Prime Minister could still cause Labour audiences to murmur with disapproval when he spoke of 'Labour's tarnished inheritance' or the 'Tory mess'.[1]

It had been known for some months that Britain would end 1964 with a large balance of payments deficit, and on the evening of October 16th the Prime Minister and his senior colleagues were apprised of the full magnitude of the problem. They decided against devaluation and opted instead for a surcharge on imports which was imposed on October 26th at the rate of 15%. At the same time the government announced that it was enquiring into ways of cutting expenditure. The surcharge was intended to be temporary but, even so, it attracted strong criticism from abroad, especially from Britain's partners in the European Free Trade Association, who had not been consulted. Conservative criticism

[1] For accounts of the crisis friendly to Labour, see Anthony Shrimsley, *The First Hundred Days of Harold Wilson*, Weidenfeld & Nicolson, 1965, and Peter Shore, *Entitled to Know*, MacGibbon and Kee, 1966, esp. Chapter VI. For a Conservative view, see Reginald Maudling's article, 'What Really Happened in 1964', *The Director*, June 1966. Cf. Henry Brandon, *In the Red: the Struggle for Sterling*, André Deutsch, 1966.

was tempered at first by the knowledge that the previous government had been preparing a similar scheme. Reginald Maudling, the ex-Chancellor of the Exchequer, using a phrase he was later to regret, commented in an immediate statement:

> 'It is true the Labour government have inherited our problems. They seem also to have inherited our solutions.'

On November 11th the new Chancellor, James Callaghan, introduced a special budget. Its total effect was meant, if anything, to be mildly deflationary. On the one hand, the budget raised pensions and provided for the abolition of prescription charges for drugs. On the other hand, it raised national insurance contributions and added 6d. to the duty on petrol. Breaking with precedent, the Chancellor announced that the standard rate of income tax would go up by 6d. in the spring, and that he would then introduce a capital gains tax and replace the existing income and profits taxes on companies with a corporation tax. The budget was designed to redeem Labour's election pledges on pensions and prescription charges; it was also designed as a gesture to the trade unions, to encourage them to co-operate in working out an effective incomes policy.

Neither the surcharge nor the budget, however, relieved the strain on sterling. They may even have increased it. According to the Conservatives, alarmist statements by senior ministers contributed to a general atmosphere of uncertainty. A consortium of central bankers made £142m. available to Britain on November 7th, but delays in introducing an expected rise in Bank rate caused further uncertainty, and on Friday, the 20th, sales of sterling reached alarming proportions. On Monday, the 23rd, Bank rate was raised from 6% to 7% — the first time it had been raised on a Monday since 1931 — but still the pressure on sterling continued. It was not until late on Wednesday, November 25th, that Lord Cromer, the Governor of the Bank of England, was able to report to the government that he had secured from foreign central banks pledges to support sterling amounting to £1,070m. The pound was safe, but Britain was deeply in debt.

By this time, too, something approaching a crisis had been precipitated in the aircraft industry. The government was determined to cut back on a number of 'prestige' projects, including the supersonic Anglo-French Concord and the TSR-2. Concord probably would have been cancelled but for the stiff French resistance encountered by Roy Jenkins, the Minister of Aviation, on a visit to Paris at the end of October. The final decision to proceed with the project was taken only in late January, and between February and April TSR-2 and two other military projects were abandoned and American planes ordered as replacements. Anxiety about the industry's future caused the government difficulties throughout the winter, and on January 14th ten thousand aircraft workers marched in protest through the centre of London. But the opposition gradually died away. Projects once cancelled could not be revived, and most of the workers made redundant quickly found jobs in allied industries.

Left-wing discontent with the government's performance inevitably developed, even in its early days. In an interview recorded before the election Mr. Wilson had said that the Labour party had something in common with an old stagecoach.

> 'I do not mean it is out of date, but if it is rattling along at a rare old speed most of the passengers are so exhilarated — perhaps sea sick — they don't start arguing or quarrelling. As soon as it stops they start arguing about which way to go. The whole thing is to keep it at an exhilarating speed.'

The sense of movement achieved by the government was considerable, but as early as November 1964 serious protests were lodged against the cabinet's refusal to accelerate payment of the increased old age pensions announced in the autumn budget; the sterling crisis forestalled any inclination on the government's part to meet the dissidents half-way. And in the following months the left became even more vocal, particularly over Britain's support for American policy in Vietnam. In March 1965, 49 M.P.s tabled a motion calling on the government to declare its inability to support U.S. policy. In June some fifty members wrote privately to Mr. Wilson warning of the dangers of escalation. In February 1966 nearly a hundred Labour M.P.s (joined by four Liberals) wired to Senator Fulbright in Washington protesting against the American resumption of bombing in North Vietnam.

Vietnam was the main object of left-wing protest, but there were others: American intervention in the Dominican Republic in April, the continuing presence of large British forces in Germany, the government's immigration white paper in August, and the omission of steel nationalisation from the second Queen's Speech in

November. In general the left had little success. They were naturally inhibited by the precariousness of Labour's majority, and Mr. Wilson had taken into the government most of those — Frank Cousins, R. H. S. Crossman, Anthony Greenwood and Barbara Castle — who might have been their natural leaders. Of greater long-term significance, however, was the fact that the old right–left pattern in Labour politics seemed to be breaking up. In the 1964 parliament a distinct left-wing element could still be identified; but on an increasing number of issues, notably immigration and the government's defence policy east of Suez, it found itself joined by many younger M.P.s who lacked the left's traditional commitments to nationalisation and nuclear disarmament.[1]

From the beginning the government's chief aim had been to restore Britain's balance of payments, if possible by the end of 1966. The import surcharge was one means towards this end. Another was the prices and incomes policy. On November 9th George Brown, head of the new Department of Economic Affairs, informed trade union leaders that he wanted agreement by Christmas to the principle that all wage increases should be related to productivity. On December 1st Sir Peter Runge, president of the Federation of British Industries, commented after a meeting with Mr. Brown that agreement before Christmas was possible. Eventually the Declaration of Intent on Productivity, Prices and Incomes was signed at Lancaster House on December 16th, ten days ahead of schedule. The government undertook to set up machinery to review the movement of prices and incomes. Management and the unions undertook to try to remove obstacles standing in the way of greater efficiency, and to assist the workings of the new prices and incomes machinery. The agreement existed only on paper, but it was one that had eluded the Conservatives.

During this period Labour led the Conservatives comfortably in all the major opinion polls. The electorate seemed content to

[1] One of the more remarkable features of the parliament was the almost total disappearance of the independent nuclear deterrent as an issue between the parties. The letting out of contracts for an additional nuclear-armed submarine was halted, but otherwise the government kept Britain's nuclear arm intact, saying only that it wished to join other NATO powers in an Atlantic Nuclear Force. The left made no serious protest despite its association with the Campaign for Nuclear Disarmament earlier in the decade. The reasons were probably the lowering of the international temperature, at least between the U.S. and Russia, the development of nuclear weapons by a fourth and a fifth power, France and China, the narrowness of Labour's majority, and Mr. Wilson's careful handling of the left.

blame the Conservatives for the crisis; according to the National
Opinion Poll, only one-third even of Conservative voters were
prepared to place the blame on Labour. Voters appeared to dis-
approve strongly only of the government's decision to introduce

'Down, dammit, down'

[*Guardian*, Apr. 20th, 1965]

sharp rises in M.P.s' and ministerial salaries; nearly two-thirds of
a Gallup sample thought the rises should be postponed. At the
New Year the government seemed to have established itself firmly.
The Conservatives had yet to find their way in opposition.

But then came the shock of Leyton. On January 21st Patrick
Gordon Walker, the Foreign Secretary, in a vain effort to re-enter

parliament after his defeat at Smethwick, lost to the Conservatives what had supposedly been a safe Labour seat. The swing against Labour was 8·7%. At Nuneaton the same day Mr. Cousins, the Minister of Technology, held the seat for Labour but again on a much reduced majority. In retrospect it seems probable that voters in both constituencies were protesting against the pushing aside of their former members, as it appeared, for newcomers. At the time, however, the results seemed to signal an abrupt decline in Labour support. Speaking two days later, Mr. Crossman, the Minister of Housing and Local Government, said the results could not be put down to special circumstances. He blamed the 'mass abstention by Labour voters' on the government's harsh measures to save the pound. The shock to Labour morale might have been even greater had it not been for the distraction of the illness and death in the same week of Sir Winston Churchill.

Leyton ended the parliament's first phase and opened its second, which lasted until roughly the beginning of May. The government absorbed the Leyton defeat surprisingly rapidly and, apart from a brief moment in February, Labour continued to lead in both major opinion polls. Swings to Labour were recorded in by-elections at Salisbury and Saffron Walden (the latter caused by the retirement from politics of R. A. Butler who, as Lord Butler, became Master of Trinity College, Cambridge). It was the Conservatives who suffered the only by-election upset of the period when on March 24th their candidate at Roxburgh, Selkirk and Peebles was beaten by a young Liberal, David Steel. The tendency in early 1965 for the weaker anti-Conservative candidate at a by-election to lose votes to the stronger led to speculation — later to prove unfounded — of a spontaneous 'radical alliance' in the constituencies. It was clear, however, that any ground being lost by Labour was not being made up by the Conservatives. Discontent with Sir Alec Douglas-Home, already present on the Conservative benches, began to make itself increasingly felt.

Having encountered resistance from the aircraft industry in its early months, the government now became embroiled with the doctors. On February 8th the professional review body awarded the general practitioners £5½m. instead of the £18m. for which they had asked. The government eventually conceded that the entire sum should be paid direct, rather than be used to reimburse doctors with special expenses as the review body had recommended, but in the meantime the British Medical Association had requested all 23,000 doctors in the health service to indicate their readiness to resign. A doctors' strike seemed conceivable for a time, but the temperature of the controversy was gradually lowered as negotiations between BMA and minister dragged on through 1965. It was not until after polling day in 1966 that something approaching a final settlement was reached.

Mr. Callaghan introduced his second budget, intended to be mildly deflationary, on April 6th. In addition to the 6d. on income tax already promised, the duties were raised on tobacco, spirits, beer and motor cars. The Chancellor delighted his own backbenchers by abolishing entertainment allowances for business men except when bona fide overseas buyers were being entertained. More important, a new capital gains tax was introduced, with a rate for 1965–66 of 30% for individuals and 35% for companies, and a corporation tax, which was not to come into effect until the following year. The Finance Bill, running to 226 pages, was published on April 27th, and the debate on it occupied much of parliament's time until well into July. Edward Heath enhanced his reputation on the Conservative side by organising a team of party spokesmen who opposed the bill clause by clause. The Conservatives objected particularly to the impact the corporation tax would have on industry. By the end the Conservatives had managed to defeat the government three times — all on the night of July 6th–7th — and Mr. Callaghan himself had introduced some 243 amendments.

Like the budget, the prices and incomes policy was intended to have a long-term, cumulative impact. The government had refrained from imposing an immediate wage freeze when it first came into office, fearing to forfeit the trade union support it needed. During the winter of 1964–65 Mr. Brown created the machinery mentioned in the Declaration of Intent and negotiated a norm for annual increases in incomes. On February 11th a white paper announced the setting up of the National Board for Prices and Incomes; a month later Aubrey Jones, a Conservative M.P., resigned his Birmingham seat to become its first chairman. On April 8th another white paper announced that the norm was to be 3–3½%. Five months of negotiation had ensured, however, that there would be numerous exceptions, which included provisions for increases in productivity and for employees whose wages fell behind those of others doing similar work. A specially convened conference of the Trades Union Congress ratified the white paper on April 30th, the Transport and General Workers' Union being the only major dissenters. The union's opposition to incomes policy embarrassed the government repeatedly during the rest of the year, and the Conservatives demanded in vain that Mr. Cousins, the TGWU general secretary who was also a member of the cabinet, resign one or other of his two offices.

Unfortunately for the government, Mr. Brown's efforts to achieve restraint on prices and incomes coincided with sharp increases in both. The index of retail prices, which had been fairly steady during the last half of 1964, rose by $2\frac{1}{2}\%$ in the first four months of 1965, increased taxes accounting for a large proportion of the rise. Mr. Brown brought increasing pressure to bear on firms and trade associations to hold prices back, and from May onwards he regularly referred increases to the Prices and Incomes Board. Partly as a result, the rate of inflation slowed markedly; the rise in the last eight months of 1965 was only 2%. Wage rates and earnings, however, continued to rise. On January 13th British Railways engineers received a 9% rise; on May 12th 200,000 Co-operative Society employees were awarded 6%; on May 28th London Transport offered its busmen a 7% increase; and only a week after the institution of the $3-3\frac{1}{2}\%$ norm the Postmaster General awarded rises substantially above the norm to 120,000 postmen. By the end of the year wage rates had risen by $4\frac{1}{2}\%$, earnings by considerably more. The tendency for earnings to rise faster than prices and for both to rise faster than production was to become a major theme of Conservative propaganda.

The first Queen's Speech in November 1964 had contained a daunting programme of legislation, but during its first few months most of the government's public activity lay in the fields of foreign policy and administration. Indeed, even its friends commented on how slow the government's major bills were in coming forward. The main reason was undoubtedly that most of Labour's proposals, however far-reaching, existed only in outline; it took ministers and civil servants time to spell them out in detail. This was particularly true in connection with housing and land, where the government was also inhibited by the continuing sterling crisis. Nevertheless, the flow began in the New Year. Following the passage of an interim Protection from Eviction Act in December, Mr. Crossman's Rent Bill appeared towards the end of March; its main purpose was to provide for the fixing of 'fair' rents for private tenants. In February Ray Gunter, the Minister of Labour, introduced legislation designed to reverse the decision in *Rookes* v. *Barnard*; the bill extended immunity from the law of torts to breaches of contract threatened in connection with industrial disputes. In April the same minister introduced a Redundancy Payments Bill in an effort to encourage the mobility of labour. All three measures had been enacted by the end of 1965.

Much the most controversial item in the Queen's Speech, however, had been the re-nationalisation of steel. The proposal was opposed not only by the Conservative party but by a number of Labour M.P.s of whom Woodrow Wyatt and Desmond Donnelly became the most vocal. They sought a compromise solution which would substitute government control and participation for outright state ownership; they also made clear their determination to refuse to support full nationalisation. The threats of both men had to be taken seriously. Faced in addition with evidence of public hostility (most polls showed less than one-quarter of the electorate in favour), the government hesitated. On the one hand, Mr. Wilson did not want to alienate his left wing or to seem to be succumbing to pressure. On the other hand, to proceed with the bill would clog the parliamentary timetable with an unpopular measure and run the serious risk of a Wyatt–Donnelly revolt. Accordingly, although a bill had been drafted by mid-February, the government postponed introducing it and instead announced its intention to publish a white paper.

After many delays, the white paper finally appeared on April 30th. It provided for the nationalisation of the fourteen biggest firms in the industry. The debate on it, on May 6th, was the most dramatic of the parliament. Efforts had been made beforehand to bring the rebels into line, but towards 10 that evening, after both Mr. Wyatt and Mr. Donnelly had spoken against the government, it seemed possible that both would abstain. Then, moments before the division was due, Mr. Brown, winding up for the government, declared that the government would listen to any proposals from the industry designed to secure state control short of 100% state ownership. Mr. Brown's intervention retrieved the votes of Mr. Wyatt and Mr. Donnelly — the government had a majority of four on the division — but incensed the left. Since the rebels were not threatening to do more than abstain, it was not clear what purpose Mr. Brown's initiative was intended to serve. Nor was it clear (nor did it become clear) whether Mr. Brown was acting on the Prime Minister's authority. What gradually did become clear, however, was that steel nationalisation was dead, at least for the life of the 1964 parliament.

The steel debacle almost certainly damaged Labour in the eyes of the public. It created the image, in Mr. Gunter's words, of 'a warring, bitter, divided party'. A Gallup poll taken at the end of May showed more than one-half of the respondents believing the party was 'at loggerheads' compared with less than one-third eighteen months before. More important, steel was probably one of the factors — what the others were it is hard to say — which caused a sharp decline in Labour's electoral fortunes. Both the by-elections held between May and July registered a swing to the Conservatives, and in the local government elections in May Labour suffered stunning reverses, the swing to the Conservatives since the general election being in the order of 6%. Labour's decline was registered by the polls too; the party fell behind in the National Opinion Poll only in August but trailed in Gallup consistently from May till September. Not surprisingly, Labour morale slumped badly.

During this third phase, which lasted from early May to early September, the balance of forces between and within the political parties seemed in flux. (These developments are discussed in more detail in the next three chapters.) In June Jo Grimond, the Liberal leader, indicated that the Liberals would consider joining Labour in a coalition on condition that 'a serious agreement on long-term policies' could be reached. He added that no overtures had been received, but with Labour's majority looking increasingly precarious the possibility of a Lib–Lab pact provided a staple of newspaper speculation until well into the autumn. Also in June, the discontent with Sir Alec Douglas-Home, latent since the Roxburgh defeat in March, erupted again, and rumours of Sir Alec's imminent departure persisted through July. Then, quite unexpectedly, on July 22nd he announced that he was going. He addressed that evening a subdued meeting of the 1922 Committee:

'I believe . . . that we are in a position now when a Conservative leader can lead the party to victory at a general election.

'All that being so, I come to two promises which I have always made to you. I have always considered them binding. The first is that I would never allow disunity in the party, least of all over myself; the second, that I would tell you when I considered that the time was right to hand over the leadership to another.'

He had asked Sir William Anstruther-Gray, the committee's chairman, to set in motion the new election procedures.

'I myself set up the machinery for this change and I myself have chosen the time to use it. It is up to you to see that it is completed swiftly and efficiently, and with dignity and calm.'

It was, and on July 27th Mr. Heath became to all intents and purposes the new Conservative leader. He was the first leader chosen while the party was in opposition since 1911 and at 49 the youngest leader since the middle of the last century.[1]

Mr. Heath's election was expected to open a new period in the Conservatives' fortunes. Apart from the attack on the Finance Bill, which Mr. Heath had led himself, the Conservatives' opposition to the government had been somewhat dispirited. With Labour usually leading in the opinion polls, this was hardly surprising; the Conservatives did not want to provide the Prime Minister with an excuse for a snap election, when he could accuse them — as he had already begun to do — of factious opposition. But the opposition's restraint disturbed its supporters in the country, and caused the press to focus even more attention on the government than it would have otherwise. The coming of Mr. Heath seemed to portend a change. The new leader was treated to the inevitable press and television publicity. He and his advisers began to put together for the party conference a new policy document, intended to erase the impression left by the last few years of Conservative rule. Above all, the Leader of the Opposition's standing in the opinion polls began to soar: in July, the last month of Sir Alec's leadership, the Gallup poll reported the proportion approving of the Conservative leader as 32%; in August, the first month of Mr. Heath's, the proportion was 51%. In August indeed the Leader of the Opposition's standing exceeded that of the Prime Minister for the first and only time in the parliament.

[1] Mr. Heath's leadership was confirmed at a party meeting on August 2nd. For details of the party's new election procedures, see below p. 48. For further details of Sir Alec Douglas-Home's retirement, see below pp. 45–52.

Mr. Wilson had had a difficult time at the Commonwealth Prime Ministers' conference in June. African Commonwealth leaders, mistrustful of Britain's intentions towards Rhodesia, sought assurances that any grant of independence would be accompanied by majority rule. In a cautiously worded final communiqué the conference called on Britain to summon all political elements in Rhodesia to a constitutional conference. President Nyerere, unable to accept Mr. Wilson's assurances, dissociated Tanzania from the communiqué. Controversy also raged around Mr. Wilson's proposal for a Commonwealth peace mission for Vietnam, especially the suggestion that he should lead it himself. In the end, the mission was formed, but neither China nor North Vietnam was willing to receive it. Abortive, too, was the despatch of a left-wing junior minister, Harold Davies, on a peace seeking trip to Hanoi. Both moves were greeted with derision by the opposition. At most they stilled for a time the left's protests about the government's Vietnam policy.

In August the government issued its white paper on immigration. The white paper, which restricted entry from the Commonwealth to 8,500 a year and proposed stringent deportation procedures, came as the climax to more than five years of debate. It marked the triumph of public opinion over the initial opposition of nearly all politicians to the imposition of controls, and also marked the final retreat of the Labour party from its opposition to the Conservative measure of 1962. Earlier in the year it had seemed that the Conservatives might try to outflank Labour on the issue. Sir Frank Soskice, the Home Secretary, announced tighter immigration controls in the House of Commons on February 4th, but Sir Alec Douglas-Home had already called for new legislation the day before, and on March 1st he and most of the shadow cabinet voted for Sir Cyril Osborne's restrictionist bill. In July Selwyn Lloyd called for a policy of 'one in, one out'. An all-party group, led by Roy Hattersley and Mrs. Shirley Williams on the Labour side, and Norman St. John-Stevas among Conservatives, attempted to halt the swing to the right on the issue, and Mr. St. John-Stevas may have had some success in his own party. But it was the government's own white paper which finally ended the controversy. A revolt at the Labour conference in September came to nothing.

By this time Labour morale in parliament had reached its nadir.

The pound had been under steady pressure through May and June, despite a series of speeches by the Chancellor and the Prime Minister categorically rejecting devaluation. In mid-July Mr. Callaghan told the House of Commons that he was 'resisting the temptation' to restrain the economy still further. But then on July 27th the axe fell. All forms of public investment were to be delayed or cut, many projects were deferred for six months, exchange control was tightened, the period for hire purchase repayments was cut. Labour M.P.s were aghast, especially when in August short-time working at Fords and Hoovers appeared to foreshadow a rise in unemployment. And still the pressure on sterling was maintained. The official figures computed the loss of reserves in July at £91m., in August at £140m.; unofficial estimates suggested that the losses were in fact much greater. When, on September 2nd, the Speaker of the House of Commons, Sir Harry Hylton-Foster, collapsed and died of a heart attack in a London street, it looked as though Mr. Wilson's government had come to the end of its tether.

What happened next is still something of a mystery. From May onwards both the Gallup poll and NOP had registered a fairly steady decline in support for Labour, and an increase in support for the Conservatives. They agreed on the trend, although they differed about its magnitude and NOP put the Conservatives ahead only in August (see p. 171). Suddenly in mid-September both polls put Labour back in the lead, Gallup by 6½%, NOP by 2·6%. The explanation probably owes something to the government's vigour in early September in persuading the bakers and building societies to peg their prices, and to Mr. Brown's activities at the Trades Union Congress. It may owe more to the fact that the August polls, taken shortly after both Mr. Callaghan's July measures and the election of Mr. Heath, had underestimated Labour's strength.

At the beginning of September, with Mr. Callaghan in the midst of negotiations for further credits to support sterling, Mr. Brown had his first major confrontation with the trade unions. It was believed that the American authorities had been promised a stiffening of the prices and incomes policy, and Mr. Brown sought to persuade the TUC at Brighton to accept a compulsory early warning system for price increases and wage claims. After twelve hours of heated debate, the general council accepted the scheme, but only on the understanding that a voluntary method of vetting wage claims by the TUC be attempted first. Even this compromise was adopted by the full congress by only 5,251,000 votes to 3,312,000. A fortnight later, on September 16th, Mr. Brown published his department's long-awaited National Plan. The plan, which envisaged an annual growth rate of 3·8% per annum over the six years to 1970 and a total increase in the national product of 25%, was denounced by Mr. Heath, even before it had been published, as 'the biggest publicity gimmick' the government had so far produced. Its press reception, however, was generally favourable, and a few days earlier the Bank of England had announced the success of Mr. Callaghan's negotiations. Ten foreign central banks had agreed to provide Britain with stand-by credits totalling £357m. Once again the pound was safe; once again Britain was deeper in debt.

Whatever the explanation for Labour's upswing in September, it ushered in the fourth and final phase of the 1964 parliament — the phase of undoubted Labour dominance. The government's majority remained tiny, and as long as it did the atmosphere of uncertainty could not be dispelled entirely. Early in 1966 the government was afflicted by disruptive gas cuts in the West Midlands, an overtime ban by London busmen, and a threatened rail strike. Nevertheless, the atmosphere of near-panic of the summer of 1965 never returned. Roderic Bowen, the Liberal M.P. for Cardigan, enabled the government to keep its majority of three by accepting the Deputy Chairmanship of Ways and Means (Dr. Horace King, a Labour member, succeeded the Conservative Sir Harry Hylton-Foster as Speaker). The Labour party led the Conservatives by wide margins in both polls from September until the eve of the campaign; NOP once showed Labour's lead at an implausible 19·2%. Perhaps equally significant, Mr. Wilson's standing with the public, having slumped during the summer, recovered and more than recovered: towards the end of 1965 the number approving of Mr. Wilson as Prime Minister almost matched the levels reached by Sir Anthony Eden and Harold Macmillan at the height of their power.

The rise of Mr. Wilson coincided with the acute phase of the crisis over Rhodesia. In May the Rhodesian Front government led by Ian Smith had won a sweeping victory in the Rhodesian elections. Ever since, Mr. Smith had been under strong pressure to declare the country independent, unilaterally if necessary. Britain, under pressure from African Commonwealth members, insisted on an improvement in the Africans' political status before independence, and on guarantees of unimpeded progress towards majority rule; any constitutional settlement must have the support of all Rhodesians, black as well as white. Talks at Downing Street in early October produced no result, and on October 25th Mr. Wilson himself flew to Salisbury. The Prime Minister ruled out the use of force but warned the Rhodesians of the economic consequences that would follow from a unilateral declaration of independence. The deadlock persisted, however, and finally on November 11th Mr. Smith broadcast to the Rhodesian people:

'We have struck a blow for the preservation of justice, civilization, and Christianity; and in the spirit of this belief we have this day assumed our sovereign independence.'

UDI confronted Mr. Wilson with the severest test of his political skill since he had come to office; 'my Cuba' he called it. He had to carry with him the British people, some of whom had relatives in Rhodesia and who could be expected to turn against any government which seemed bent — at great expense to Britain — on crushing a beleaguered British minority. At the same time, in order to keep the problem in British hands, he had to satisfy the African states, which were clamouring for action. He had to be responsive to both the Conservative opposition and his own left wing. His method was to impose sanctions slowly, indicating at each stage that any British government would have had no alternative. He repeatedly asserted his desire for negotiations provided only that Rhodesia returned to the path of constitutional development. On November 11th Britain banned all purchases of Rhodesian tobacco and sugar. On December 1st most other Rhodesian exports were embargoed and a squadron of Javelin fighters despatched to Zambia. A few days later the government assumed power over the Rhodesian Reserve Bank. An oil embargo followed on December 17th. By the end of January 1966 Britain had imposed a ban on all trade with the rebel regime.

Rhodesia split the Conservatives, recreating the tensions in the party which had existed throughout the long imperial retreat of the 1950s. Mr. Heath, who had been leader for only a short while,

supported the government, though increasingly critically; the
Conservatives had been as committed as Labour to resisting
Rhodesian independence on the basis of permanent white rule.
Mr. Heath deplored the UDI and either supported or did not
oppose the various sanctions as they were imposed, insisting only
that force should not be used, and that Britain should try to avoid
driving the white settlers to extremes. The failure of sanctions to

[*Evening Standard*, Nov. 25th, 1965
The Conservatives' Rhodesian Tightrope

have an immediate effect led the Conservatives early in 1966 to call
for the reopening of negotiations. Mr. Heath could not, however,
carry the right wing of his party with him. Lord Salisbury intervened in an acrimonious debate at the party conference in October,
and on December 21st in the House of Commons the Conservatives plumbed the depths of humiliation: at the end of the debate
on oil sanctions 50 Conservative members defied Mr. Heath's
advice to abstain and divided against the government, and 31 left-
wing Conservatives, seeking to counterbalance the right, voted
with Labour.

Fortunately for the Conservatives, most of the main decisions on Rhodesia had been taken by the end of the year and, although the issue remained open, the acute phase of the crisis had passed. Even so, January and February were not happy months for the party. Speeches by Mr. Maudling and by Enoch Powell, the party's most outspoken ideologue, revived the continuing debate on incomes policy, on which the Conservatives had been divided ever since leaving office; some wished to oppose Labour's administration of incomes policy while accepting the idea in principle, others to reject the policy entirely. More acutely embarrassing was an article by Angus Maude, a front bench spokesman on Commonwealth affairs, published in the *Spectator* of January 14th: the Conservative party was seen by the electorate at large, he said, as a 'meaningless irrelevance'. Mr. Maude was eventually forced to resign from the front bench but only after several days of intense publicity.

Although the government had had to postpone its plans for a guaranteed minimum income and the relief of mortgage holders, a number of its other major bills began to come forward. The Rating Bill, published on November 26th, provided rebates for domestic ratepayers with low incomes and enabled rates to be paid in instalments; it was intended to be an interim measure pending the complete overhaul of local government finance. The Land Commission Bill, published on December 22nd, provided for a commission to acquire land and to levy a charge on the development value of land disposed of for building. On January 26th came the National Insurance Bill, which provided for earnings-related benefit in the early months of widowhood, sickness and unemployment. Mr. Crossman's plan for housing, which had already appeared as a white paper in November, set up a target of 500,000 house completions a year by 1970; half the houses were to be provided by public authorities, half privately, and the system of subsidies for local authorities was to be rejigged. All of these measures were still pending when the campaign began.

The government's chief preoccupation, however, remained the economy. At the very least, Labour's ability to carry out its full programme would depend on the balance of payments and the strength of sterling. The Prime Minister described 1966 as the 'make or break year' for Britain. The government's economic measures were of two types. Some were designed to promote the modernisation and reorganisation of industry. The Department of Economic Affairs promoted regional economic planning, and industrial development councils ('little Neddies') were set up to facilitate co-ordination and the adoption of modern methods in particular industries. On December 16th the government received the Plowden report on the aircraft industry; it recommended that the state should acquire holdings in the two largest airframe firms. On January 25th it was announced that a new Industrial Reorganisation Corporation would be established, with power to initiate and finance industrial mergers and rationalisation. Other measures were designed — well or badly — to keep prices and incomes in check. The government sought to implement the Devlin report (August 5th) which castigated restrictive practices in the docks. Planning of the early warning system continued until the eve of the campaign. So did Mr. Callaghan's credit squeeze. On February 1st Lord Cromer advised the clearing banks to continue to exercise restraint in lending. A week later increases in hire purchase deposits were made mandatory.

Early in the New Year the results of the government's review of defence policy, which had been proceeding since Labour took office, began to appear. The government had already offended the opposition by cutting drastically the size of the Territorial Army. It now provoked fresh opposition by refusing to provide the Royal Navy with a replacement aircraft carrier for use in the 1970s. The First Sea Lord, Admiral Sir David Luce, resigned together with Christopher Mayhew, the Minister of Defence for the Navy, during the third week in February. In subsequent statements Mr. Mayhew indicated that he dissented not simply from the refusal to build an additional carrier but from the whole drift of the government's defence policy east of Suez. A section on the Labour benches, consisting mainly of the traditional left but including also a number of younger M.P.s, had criticised for some months the costs and risks of keeping large British forces stationed in the Middle and Far East. A number of Conservatives, notably Mr. Powell, the party's official spokesman on defence, shared their doubts, and it seemed possible that defence might play a large part in the general election compaign which was about to begin.

Speculation about an early election had been rife since the parliament began. It was particularly intense in the weeks following Leyton and again after the revolt on the steel white paper. Mr.

c

Wilson had repeatedly quashed such rumours, however, and on June 26th at Glasgow had stated that he had no intention of going to the country in 1965. But the possibility remained that the government would be forced into an election as the result of losing its majority in the House of Commons. This possibility, which had seemed real after Leyton, re-emerged on November 7th, 1965, with the death of Henry Solomons, the Labour member for Hull North. The seat was the most marginal to fall vacant during the life of the parliament: Labour had gained it in 1964 with a majority of 1,181, and a swing of only a little over 1% was needed to return it to the Conservatives. Newspaper reports from Hull suggested until the eve of poll on January 27th that Labour was likely to lose the seat. In the event, Labour increased its majority to 5,351 on a swing of 4·5% — the largest swing to the governing party in any by-election in a marginal seat since May 1924.

From Hull North onwards speculation in the press and at Westminster about an early election never ceased. The Prime Minister carefully avoided referring to the subject in his speeches, but his tone became steadily more aggressive. The death on February 4th of Harold Hayman, who was believed to have a large personal following in the marginal Labour seat of Falmouth and Camborne, underlined the continuing precariousness of the government's majority. By the time Mr. Wilson flew on an official visit to Moscow on February 21st, the bulk of the press and most M.P.s confidently expected polling day to be on March 24th or 31st. An atmosphere of electioneering had pervaded the whole of the 1964 parliament. Now, it seemed, the campaign itself was about to begin in earnest. How the parties reacted to the results of 1964, and how they developed their strategies for the general election of 1966, is the subject of the next four chapters.

CHAPTER II

LABOUR: POWER FOR HOW LONG?

IN the two years before the 1964 election the Labour party constructed an elaborate apparatus for the making of electoral strategy. It included the campaign committee, which remained continuously in being from 1962, the National Executive and its various sub-committees, and the publicity organisation under John Harris. This apparatus linked together the permanent staff at Transport House under the NEC, and the party in parliament. It had a single purpose: to win the coming election. The party leader, whether Hugh Gaitskell or Mr. Wilson, was the most powerful single person involved — no major decision could be taken against his will or without his being consulted — but to some extent the apparatus had a life of its own. Certain procedures were developed, and certain constitutional proprieties had to be observed. Even the leader had to work in harness with others.

These arrangements were completely transformed by Labour's victory at the polls. Men hitherto preoccupied with the party's election planning now became engrossed in the problems of government departments. Instead of merely responding to the decisions of others, they now assumed responsibility for taking the decisions themselves. Inevitably they became less single-minded. The hierarchy of civil servants replaced the hierarchy of party officials. The links between the parliamentary leadership and Transport House became more tenuous. Above all, the position of the leader was transformed. The responsibilities of government bore down more heavily on him than on any of his colleagues, and he was under constant pressure from his advisers. He could no longer, even if he wished, think and act chiefly as a party politician. Yet the precariousness of Labour's majority meant that questions of political tactics and strategy could never be wholly absent from Mr. Wilson's mind. He had invariably to consider the government's actions in the light of the parliamentary situation and, although events might conspire to remove the decision from his hands, he alone bore the responsibility of determining the date of the next election. The politics of the 1964 parliament can be seen in large part as the history of one man's strategic thinking.

It has often been said that Mr. Wilson had no long-term strategy, that he merely moved from one expedient to the next. Between 1964 and 1966 the incessant speculation surrounding his every move, and his obvious delight in playing the political game, lent support to this view. It was possible to class him 'as a superb tactician and operator in the short-term, but with a weak grasp for long-term political strategy'.[1] In one sense his critics were right. The Prime Minister drew most of his inspiration from the policies developed by Labour during the last few years of opposition. He gave no evidence of having, like a de Gaulle or a Johnson, a vision of the future. On the rare occasions when he spoke of his grand design, the phase sounded trite and empty of concrete meaning. But in another sense Mr. Wilson's critics were wrong. He did have a long-term political strategy for his government. Except possibly for moments during the first hundred days, he never lost sight of the need to create the conditions in which Labour could win a second, more convincing electoral victory. In pursuit of this goal he acted consistently, resolutely and far more long-sightedly than was often appreciated at the time.

The evidence for this view is ready to hand. Unlike many political leaders, who prefer to keep their strategic thoughts to themselves, Mr. Wilson during this period delighted in thinking aloud in the presence of journalists and M.P.s, and even on the air. Press reports of his reflections enabled him to communicate with his own party, especially when their morale was low. Kites could be flown, and trial balloons sent up. They also served to keep the opposition on edge since the Conservatives could never be sure which of his pronouncements to take at their face value; in this connection Mr. Wilson's reputation for deviousness — whether deserved or not — was probably an asset. In fact, his statements probably did generally reflect the current state of his thinking.

---

[1] This belief was attributed to most of Mr. Wilson's critics by James Margach, 'Mr. Wilson's Psychology of Power', *Sunday Times*, October 24th, 1965. Cf. an article written by Peregrine Worsthorne after an early interview with the Prime Minister, 'Wilson on His Hundred Days', *Sunday Telegraph*, January 24th, 1965: 'After the interview one naturally tried to discover some theme or pattern to give it coherence. None emerged. It was as if one had spent a fascinating hour talking to the captain on the bridge without ever really discovering where he was steering to.' Much the same point was made by William Rees-Mogg, 'What's Gone Wrong?', *Sunday Times*, June 6th, 1965.

He would not reveal short-term tactical manoeuvres, where surprise was of the essence, but there was no particular reason why he should not be candid about the more distant future.

The narrowness of the election result in 1964 took Mr. Wilson completely by surprise. He had planned to use the first and second years of a Labour government in putting the economy right; the third and fourth would then be used to fulfil the party's more ambitious election pledges. It may be that, like President Kennedy in the United States, he envisaged his first term of office mainly as a preliminary to a more creative second term. Instead, the narrow result meant that he would have at most two years, perhaps less, before having to return to the country; elaborate exercises in phasing were out of the question. It meant, too, that the electorate had less confidence in Labour than the polls had once suggested. Mr. Wilson had always known that, after thirteen years in opposition, the credibility of a Labour government would have to be established. It was now certain that the operation would be undertaken in the most difficult possible circumstances. It was still not clear whether Labour could control the House of Commons.

As if this were not enough, the government had to cope with the economic crisis. The first three months were taken up with a series of *ad hoc* initiatives and responses. There was little time for strategic thinking. It soon emerged that the government could control the House, but in the somewhat frenetic atmosphere of the hundred days mistakes were bound to be made. Leyton brought Labour up with a bump. A party official recalled:

> 'Leyton was a blessing in disguise really. The Prime Minister was becoming just a technician. Leyton forced him to remember that he was a political leader.'

Mr. Wilson later tried to rationalise the hundred days, claiming that the government had deliberately set out to take all of its unpopular decisions in a rush. He reminded his audiences of Lord Attlee's dictum that any new government should enact its most contentious measures first. In fact, this line of reasoning can only have been a consolation. Most of the economic measures taken by the government in its early days could not have been postponed. Moreover, the government behaved as though it did not realise that some of its measures — notably the increases in M.P.s' pay — were going to prove unpopular.

Nevertheless, by the end of January 1965 the Prime Minister had arrived at almost all of the strategic principles that were to guide him for the rest of parliament. He was determined above all that the government should try to remain in power for at least a year, preferably longer. Labour needed time more than anything else: time to restore the economy; time to become accepted as a national and not merely a sectional party; time for Mr. Wilson to establish himself as Prime Minister; time for other members of the government to emerge as national figures. Labour needed time above all to fulfil its election pledges. The Prime Minister feared the result of any election fought by the Conservatives on the slogan 'Labour's broken promises'. He may have had conscientious doubts about whether a party which had not acted on its pledges deserved to win; later on he certainly took pleasure in checking off for visitors the items in Labour's manifesto that were already in train. Until the very eve of the election, too, he believed that the British people were tired of electioneering and would turn against whichever party forced a dissolution.

Although the point cannot be proved, it is doubtful whether Mr. Wilson ever seriously considered going to the country between the general election and the autumn of 1965. Occasional hints in this direction were probably meant to unsettle the Conservatives. Quite apart from Mr. Wilson's general views, there was no time when he could be certain of winning; by-elections and local government elections consistently produced ambiguous results or conflicted with the opinion polls. But he never ruled out the possibility of a snap election entirely, and he never could rule out the possibility of Labour's losing its majority in the House of Commons. Minor defeats could of course be absorbed or reversed. What the Prime Minister obviously had to fear was a series of deaths or by-election defeats, or a back bench revolt, at a time when Labour was unpopular in the country. Mr Wilson sought above all to avert an early election; but he also sought to ensure that, if there were one, Labour would be in a position to win it. To a remarkable extent the same means served both ends.

The chief of these was to make a virtue of Labour's unpopular decisions in terms of the country's need for firm government, while at the same time constantly seeking to discredit the Conservative leadership. The Prime Minister sought in effect to immunise the electorate both against unpopular government actions and against any Conservative effort to capitalise on these. He juxtaposed in the public mind the spectacle of a Labour government, tough, determined and purposeful, with the spectacle of the Conservatives, who had bequeathed to Labour one of the largest balance of payments deficits in Britain's peacetime history, and who even now constituted a fractious, irresponsible and divided opposition. Mr. Wilson took up the themes of the 'Tory mess' and the '£800m. deficit' early in the parliament and reiterated them constantly. How much success he had it is hard to be sure, but the opinion polls continued for much of the parliament to report a higher proportion blaming the Conservatives than Labour for the economic crisis. As time went on a good deal of discussion was focused on the question of how long the charge could be made to stick.

Especially in the early months, Mr. Wilson's attacks on the Conservative leaders were incessant. He blamed them for the crisis and rebuked them for harassing the government's efforts to deal with the crisis. The Prime Minister asserted his claim to national leadership, not by eschewing controversy in the manner of President Eisenhower, but by going out of his way to attack the Conservative leaders as unworthy, even unpatriotic. The fact that Sir Alec Douglas-Home's position was insecure, with other leading Conservatives vying for the succession, made his task all the easier. Mr. Wilson was undoubtedly motivated partly by outrage at the government's economic inheritance, but his main purpose was clearly partisan. His attacks delighted his own followers. They seemed bound to have some effect in the country. They kept the Conservatives on the defensive, especially in the House of Commons where Mr. Wilson was frequently at his most aggressive. Mr. Wilson wished to deter the Conservatives from forcing an election. He also wished to ensure that, if they did force one, it would be a very awkward one for them to fight.

But of course the Prime Minister was not completely in control of events. The parliamentary timetable could be determined only within the limits of what bills were coming forward from departments. Measures had to be taken to support sterling and to deal with the economy. Moreover, the government might lose support in the country as the result of causes which it could not control. Death or misfortune might deprive it of its majority at any time; the possibility of parliamentary revolts could never be entirely discounted. For all these reasons Mr. Wilson had to consider, in addition to the general political climate, the particular circumstances in which Labour might be defeated. Much of his strategic thinking was devoted to trying to structure the parliamentary situation so as to minimise both the chances of defeat in the lobbies and its possible electoral consequences.

It was in this context that he had constantly to be looking ahead. The steel debacle in May 1965 led him to ruminate throughout the summer on how the problem of the Liberals should be dealt with. Concern for the future of Mr. Brown's early warning legislation was probably a factor in his final decision to go to the country in 1966. Apart from foreseeing possible sources of trouble, the Prime Minister sought to ensure that legislation which he believed to be popular — on housing, rates or land — would always be either just passed, or before the House, or in immediate prospect. Ministerial speeches constantly referred to the government's legislative plans for the coming autumn or spring. The stream of white papers was similarly intended to create an impression of continuous activity. In the spring of 1965 Mr. Wilson contemplated running the unpopular steel nationalisation bill through the House of Commons in double harness with a more popular measure, possibly one on land. If the opposition defeated the government on steel, he could go to the country complaining that the whole of Labour's programme had been placed in jeopardy. If the opposition, fearing to be placed in this position, relaxed its pressure on steel, then so much the better.

A factor consistently reinforcing the Prime Minister's confidence was his sense of the Conservatives' weakness. At various stages it looked as though the Conservatives might win an early election, but Mr. Wilson sensed, probably rightly, that the Conservatives themselves never quite believed it. Except possibly for a few weeks in June and July, opposition pressure in the House of Commons was never continuous; ambushes and the like were hardly ever resorted to. Losses at by-elections rather than defeats in the House were the Prime Minister's main worry. Since by-election defeats were likely to come at a time when it would be hard for Labour to win a general election, much thought had to be given to whether Labour should remain in office even if it lost its parliamentary majority. Here again the problem of the Liberals presented itself. In this connection, as in all others, Mr. Wilson was determined to keep open as many options as possible. The future being unpredictable, he had to ensure that anything he said or did in the present did not limit his subsequent range of action. He felt this need particularly during the summer of 1965 and again in the weeks when his decision on the election date was hardening. A large element of choice was not only desirable in itself; it introduced a large element of uncertainty into Conservative and Liberal thinking and would maximise the Prime Minister's bargaining strength if the need for an arrangement with the Liberals ever arose.

Other elements in Mr. Wilson's strategy can be stated more briefly. He wished to preserve party unity, partly because his own long-term future depended on it, partly because displays of disunity could only harm the party in the country. He took pains to include (some said entrap) as many left wingers as possible in the government and to try to reassure the left on matters of policy. Equally, however, he was concerned to establish Labour as a tough party whose leaders could not be pushed around, and as a patriotic party concerned to preserve Britain's power and standing in the world. The Prime Minister took care therefore never to succumb to left-wing pressure, especially when it was expressed publicly, and to resist the left, particularly on matters of foreign policy. In his dealings with business, the professions and the trade unions, he sought to appear independent of sectional interests. On matters of home policy he was largely content to follow up Labour's manifesto. He had helped to devise it and believed it was popular. Its proposals were modified only on administrative grounds, as in the case of the Land Commission, or as the result of intense political pressure, as with immigration and steel.

Finally, Mr. Wilson had one other important item of political capital: his own reputation. It was essential to him that he not only be, but also appear to be, a master of political tactics. Partly it was a matter of *amour propre* and of a long-standing sense that the Labour party valued him most for his political adroitness. But in the circumstances of the 1964 parliament his reputation was of more immediate value. It undoubtedly daunted the Conservatives, who felt they had no one to match him. Fear of Mr. Wilson's tactics as well as the tactics themselves kept the Conservatives off balance; with another Labour leader, for example, they might not have been so apprehensive of a snap election. In the end Conservative Central Office appointed a journalist, T. F. Thompson, as 'special adviser on tactics' especially to keep the Prime Minister in check. The Conservatives' unease in Mr. Wilson's presence reassured his own supporters, who came in time to have an almost touching faith in his ability to extricate them from tight situations. Mr. Wilson husbanded his reputation with great care. The steel debacle infuriated him particularly because it might seem to others that he had lost his touch.

In all of the Prime Minister's electoral thinking, the National Executive and the party staff at Transport House played very little part. To some extent this was inevitable. The size of Labour's majority meant that ministers' political attention had to be focused primarily on parliament. There was little incentive for new policy thinking, given the scale of the party's programme and the uncertainty about the future. The pressure on the Prime Minister's own time was bound to be enormous. Even so, a leader other than Mr. Wilson might have tried to preserve closer contacts with the party. Mr. Wilson probably wished to deny any large role to a body which could potentially cut across his own lines of authority. He cannot have overlooked the influence on the NEC of the left and the trade unions. Perhaps he felt that Transport House had little to offer him. In any case, he could always address the party directly in speeches and broadcasts.

Whatever his reasons, the sudden divorce between government and party was felt keenly on the party side. The NEC never adjusted to its new role. Ministerial attendance was erratic, and NEC members outside the government never felt they were taken into confidence. At the March 1965 meeting John Boyd, the Amalgamated Engineering Union representative, complained about the lack of consultation on incomes policy, labelling Aubrey Jones, the new chairman of the Prices and Incomes Board, 'an enemy of the working class'. Mr. Brown was expected to justify the policy at the April meeting, but the division bell rang before the matter was raised.[1] NEC indignation reached its peak in July, following the announcement of the Chancellor's restrictionist measures. It was largely to assuage this feeling that a joint NEC-ministerial meeting was arranged for later in the year; it eventually took place, after several postponements, at Chequers in mid-

[1] 'Confusion on Role of Labour's Executive', *Guardian*, April 29th, 1965.

February 1966. In the meantime, it had been agreed that Executive meetings should be divided into two parts, the first devoted to sub-committee reports, the second to ministerial expositions of government policy.

Such liaison as was effected between party and government took two main forms. The first was an Officers' Committee created during the week of Leyton to replace the pre-election campaign committee. Intended to link the cabinet with both the NEC and back benchers in parliament, it appears to have met fortnightly at first but then increasingly irregularly. Various members of the Executive complained that the committee was usurping functions that were properly the NEC's, including the arrangement of party political broadcasts. What precise functions, if any, it performed is not clear.[1] The second group, intended to co-ordinate government and Transport House publicity, had a similar career. It included Percy Clark, the Labour party's director of publicity, Terry Pitt, the research director, a deputy whip and, at first, George Wigg, the Paymaster General. For some months it met on Wednesday evenings to co-ordinate the next week-end's speeches. In September, however, Mr. Wigg was replaced by Mr. Crossman, a member of the Executive. Despite the publicity surrounding Mr. Crossman's appointment, this aspect of his duties largely fell into abeyance.

The divorce between government and party was felt nowhere more keenly than among the permanent staff in Transport House. Three senior department heads departed with the election, two into the House of Commons. Those who were left suffered a drastic decline in their status. From being an essential part of Labour's election machine, in close contact with the party's leaders, they found themselves cut off from the government and without anything very important to do. One official complained to a journalist about 'the impenetrable brick wall presented by the civil servants'. The malaise extended to questions of pay and

---

[1] The members of the Officers' Committee were the Prime Minister; Mr. Brown, the party's deputy leader; Edward Short, the Chief Whip; Herbert Bowden, the Leader of the House of Commons; Ray Gunter and Walter Padley, the party's chairman and vice-chairman; Dai Davies, the treasurer; and Len Williams, the general secretary. Members of the NEC complained that Mr. Davies and Mr. Williams were the only members of the committee not in the government. Mr. Short and Mr. Bowden were there to represent the state of feeling on the back benches. The Officers' Committee, like at least three other committees, was sometimes known as the 'liaison committee'.

working conditions, and led in the autumn of 1965 to the launching of a 'Plan for an Efficient Party' campaign.[1] It affected particularly the Research Department, which was largely shorn of its policy-making functions and forced to spend even more of its time than before preparing party speeches and propaganda. Labour's victory would have reduced the department's policy role in any case; the imminence of another election made it almost impossible to think of the longer-term future.

The malaise affected the party's publicity operations rather less. The success of Labour's pre-1964 advertising had persuaded the party of the need to make use of professional advisers. Indeed, one advertising executive complained that Labour had come to have an almost magical belief in the power of publicity; 'it was a sort of cargo cult,' he said. In the weeks after Leyton the professional advisory group — reconstituted after 1964 but still functioning much as before — had to resist strong party pressure to mount some kind of campaign.[2] The group felt that the events leading up to Leyton were not the sort that could be conjured away by propaganda; whatever was wrong would have to be put right on the government's side. The group also resisted Transport House pressure to present the impending May 1965 local elections, which they knew were certain to embarrass Labour, as a vote of confidence in the Labour government. In the end the only cam-

---

[1] 'No Overhaul of Labour's Party Machinery', *Guardian*, November 25th, 1965; cf. *Plan for an Efficient Party Campaign*, the campaign's manifesto signed by the editors of four Labour journals representing the whole ideological range of Labour journalism, and the issues of its *Campaign Newsletter*. Jim Northcott, the campaign's organiser, had helped to prepare a special supplement, 'Our Penny-Farthing Machine' for the October 1965 number of *Socialist Commentary*. Cf. Richard Rose, 'Doubts over the Role of Transport House', *The Times*, March 6th, 1965; Gerald Kaufman, 'Transport House: the Truth', *New Statesman*, May 7th, 1965.

[2] The group consisted of outside volunteers from advertising and market research agencies. It had been reorganised after the 1964 election so that it now consisted of an inner cabinet or 'planning group' and a series of satellite groups concerned with such matters as public relations, education, publications and 'women'. The leading figures, as before, were David Kingsley, Mark Abrams, Miss Ros Allen, Brian Murphy and Percy Clark, the party's publicity director. The group apart from Mr. Clark preserved its complete independence of the official party organisation, maintaining that its advice was more likely to be accepted if it were seen to be completely detached. The major problem was liaison. Like almost everyone connected with the party after 1964, the members of the group felt that they did not know who they were dealing with, and that it was impossible to get anyone to take decisions. In the space of eighteen months, four different M.P.s, three of them ministers, were deputed to act as links with the government. In the circumstances threats of resignation were bound to be frequent.

paign launched during the parliament was the 'In a go-ahead Britain, you need Labour' campaign of the summer of 1965, aimed mainly at party workers. The publicity group came into its own only on the eve of the election early in 1966.

It worked throughout without the aid of market research. Mark Abrams and others were drawn on for advice, but the continuing study of public opinion carried out for the party by Dr. Abrams before the 1964 election lapsed completely. The main reason was probably that the party felt it had learned all it needed to know before 1964. As one senior official put it:

> 'I was in favour of polling, but I don't suppose there was a great deal to add to what Abrams found before the election. Those polls then were prodigiously influential — though of course no one will admit it now.'

Market research encountered hostility from party officials who felt their own expertise was being impugned, and also because Dr. Abrams was still felt by some to have been over-involved in the Gaitskellite controversies of 1960–61. It may be, too, that the Prime Minister was reluctant to share his sources of information with others and preferred to rely on his own channels. He consulted unpublished data from the regular polling organisations and continued to receive some material from Dr. Abrams. Committees at Transport House considered various alternative schemes at various times, but nothing came of any of them. 'They were not so much rejected,' said one supporter of Dr. Abrams, 'as just shunted aside.' The only polls conducted for Labour during the 1964 parliament were a small-scale series on two by-elections, Erith and Crayford, and Hull North.

The defeat at Leyton brought Labour up with a bump, but ministers had already expected some decline in Labour's popularity. Conservative opposition in the House was bound to intensify as the election receded, and some of the government's deflationary measures introduced in the autumn — the increases in national insurance contributions, for example — were not due to take effect till the spring. Leyton redoubled Labour's determination to blame the Conservatives for the country's economic difficulties. Even so, the Leyton and Nuneaton by-elections, together with a Conservative upswing in the opinion polls, ruled out whatever possibility there had ever been of an early election.

A decision to fight in March would have had to be taken within three or four weeks of Leyton while the country was still in mourning for Sir Winston Churchill. Instead, the Prime Minister reiterated his intention of staying on at least till the autumn and probably beyond. He held out hope of getting steel and land out of the way in the present session, and of moving on in the autumn and winter of 1965–66 to deal with popular matters like rates, leasehold reform, mortgages and possibly even the minimum income guarantee. By then the economy would have begun to right itself, and the Labour government would be accepted as part of the natural order of things.

The serious problem remaining, however, was steel. Back bench opposition to any attempt to pass a steel bill in the first session built up in the weeks immediately after Leyton; according to one report, nearly two-thirds of the parliamentary party was uneasy. Only the left remained enthusiastic. On March 18th the cabinet decided to proceed with steel but to preface the actual bill with a white paper. The aim was probably to placate the left (in the cabinet as well as on the back benches) while at the same time testing the mood of the country and the rest of the parliamentary party. If the debate on the white paper went well, the government might be emboldened to introduce its bill. If it went badly, the left might come to accept the impossibility of carrying steel on a majority of three. In the event the debate went badly, and memories of it facilitated the omission of steel from the Queen's Speech in November. The left made only a token protest.

Like Leyton, the steel debate and the local elections that followed ruled out any chance of an early election. Labour retained its lead in the National Opinion Poll, but the Conservatives moved ahead in Gallup in the middle of May. After Leyton Mr. Wilson had deferred the prospect of an election indefinitely. This time he indicated that his sights were set on the end of October. Governments traditionally benefited from the holiday months, with parliament in recess, and the Prime Minister was not sure that he wanted to risk another winter. The government was safe until October, with the third reading of the Finance Bill the only high hurdle remaining, and by then an even longer list of domestic reforms would be ready to go forward: land reform, the National Plan, a two-tier system for mortgages, rating reform, higher unemployment and sickness benefits. Even if an election did not come in the autumn, such a programme ought to tide the government over into 1966. The Prime Minister probably talked in this vein partly to reassure his own supporters; their confidence had been very badly shaken by the events of May, and they needed to be reminded that the government had the most popular part of its programme still in train. More important, he almost certainly wished to open up the October option, to create an atmosphere in which he could call an autumn election if he chose without surprising the country or being accused of running away.

If these were his motives, something happened during the next four weeks to change his mind; for on June 26th, speaking at Glasgow, Mr. Wilson gave his most categoric pledge of the parliament:

> 'It is not my intention to recommend a dissolution of parliament this year. I have made it clear throughout that provided we are able to get our essential legislation through parliament, we intended to stay and see the job through. . . .
> 'I thought it better to say this and to end uncertainty and speculation by a straight statement, than to play the silly "Will it be June? — Will it be October?" game with the British people and British industry, which did so much harm last year.'

What happened was mainly the announcement on June 15th that Britain's trade gap had widened during May to £109m. In the face of a nervous stock exchange and renewed pressure on sterling, the Prime Minister felt compelled to try to introduce an element of stability into the situation. The need was already apparent for sterner economic measures, which would in any case rule out an election in the autumn. Possibly, too, the prospect of some kind of Liberal–Labour arrangement, which was then being talked about seriously for the first time, made the future seem more secure.

Some feeling in favour of talks with the Liberals had been expressed on the Labour back benches as early as the week after Leyton, but Mr. Wilson appears not to have shown any particular interest until about mid-May. A report at that stage suggested that the government would probably in future show Mr. Grimond 'more respect'.[1] Then in June Mr. Grimond himself took the initiative. In a widely quoted article in the *Sun* he wrote:

[1] James Margach, 'Mr. Wilson Learns a Lesson', *Sunday Times*, May 16th, 1965.

'If you are living on a small majority it is common sense either to approach the Liberals . . . with proposals for active cooperation, or at least to concentrate your proposals within a range where their support is likely.'

He repeated the point in a party political broadcast on June 23rd and again in an interview with the *Guardian* published the next day. He was anticipating the day when the Liberals might find themselves holding the balance of power in the House of Commons.

Speculation about the Prime Minister's attitude persisted for the next five months. In fact, Mr. Wilson appears to have altered his views hardly at all between June and October, and he may even have formed them in anticipation of Mr. Grimond's initiative. He remained firm on two points. The first was that nothing approaching a formal pact could be entered into. The Labour party would not accept it, and there were indications that negotiations would split the Liberals; neither leader could be confident of delivering the support of his own followers. The second was that some modification of the next session's programme would have to be considered. It was by no means clear that the government could struggle on through another winter in the face of combined Conservative–Liberal opposition. The debates on the Finance Bill were seriously straining the health of some M.P.s, and the Conservatives continued to gain ground in the opinion polls. In July the Chancellor's measures ruled out any immediate prospect of reduced mortgage rates or increases in welfare benefits. In August Mr. Wilson began to allude to 'a new dimension' in politics to be introduced after the summer recess.[1]

The Liberals, provided they could agree among themselves, had ten votes to offer the government. What had Mr. Wilson to offer the Liberals? One possibility was electoral reform. The subject had already been referred to a Speaker's Conference, and hints that the government might consider the alternative vote favourably began to appear in the first week of June. Gerald Kaufman, apparently on the basis of an interview with the Prime Minister, aired the question at some length in the *New Statesman* in August.[2] Without in any way committing himself, Mr. Wilson does seem to have taken the possibility quite seriously. The Research Department at Transport House prepared a memorandum

---

[1] Nora Beloff, 'Lib–Lab Breeze from Scillies', *Observer*, August 8th, 1965.
[2] 'Towards a Lib–Lab Arrangement', August 6th, 1965.

in the course of August, and several academics believed to be interested found themselves approached. But the general view seemed to be that the alternative vote would hurt Labour; in particular, an article by Henry Durant of the Gallup poll in September suggested that it would have cost Labour the 1964 election.[1] The government continued to keep the issue alive — Mr. Short referred to it in a speech in October — but from September onwards the government probably would not have considered introducing it except as a last resort.

The contents of the Queen's Speech, however, could still be adjusted. Many items in the programme for the second session were expected to appeal to the Liberals in any case: rating reform, leasehold enfranchisement, and the creation of an Ombudsman. More important was the possibility that steel might be dropped. Despite the white paper affair, the government continued to insist until well into July that a steel nationalisation bill would be introduced, if not in the first session, then in the second. Mr. Wilson gave assurances to the Durham miners' gala on July 17th. But as the summer wore on the dangers of proceeding with steel impressed themselves increasingly on both the Prime Minister and his supporters in parliament, and any doubts lingering in ministers' minds were stilled by the death of the Speaker in early September, with its threat to their majority. The Queen's Speech was expected to refer to steel but in a way to suggest that there was no intention of proceeding with a bill. In the end, it was omitted entirely. The omission was undoubtedly intended in part as a gesture to the Liberals.

The prospect of a formal pact had already been foreclosed by the Prime Minister in his speech to the Labour party's annual conference. Labour, he said, had not been approached by any other party with a view to a pact or coalition.

> 'We are clear what our mandate means in terms of our parliamentary programme and in terms of executive government. I hope that others will feel able to support these measures which we put forward because we believe them to be in the national interest. If they can, we shall welcome their support. If they cannot, we shall have to go on without them.'

A fortnight later, however, in an interview with the *Guardian* the Prime Minister indicated that, at least for the immediate future,

[1] *Sunday Telegraph*, September 19th, 1965. This view was not held universally; cf. Michael Steed, *New Outlook*, Nov.–Dec. 1965, p. 4.

D

Labour would continue to adjust itself to the Liberal presence. The Liberals could not ask for a veto over Labour measures.

> 'But a wide field of our legislative programme ought to — and will, I think — fit in with the doctrine, enunciated by the "Guardian," of "parallel courses".'

At the time of the general election it was still too early to say what the long-term course of Liberal–Labour relations would have been.

In the autumn of 1965, although no one knew it at the time, the parliament was entering its final phase. The number of ministers favouring an early election gradually increased, and the improvement in Labour's standing in the opinion polls inevitably led to renewed speculation in the press. But for the moment Mr. Wilson held firm. He retained his conviction that the country did not want an election and his desire to complete Labour's programme. His belief in the government's ability to carry on was reinforced both by the finding of a solution to the problem posed by the Speaker's death and by the fact that the legislation planned for the second session, which included a number of popular measures, would be hard for the Conservatives and Liberals to oppose. It seemed at this stage that the 1966 budget could be a mild one. Perhaps most important, the advocates of an early election overlooked the imminence of the Rhodesian crisis. No Prime Minister could seriously contemplate a four weeks' election campaign in the midst of delicate diplomatic negotiations which could quite possibly split the country. In any case, Mr. Wilson had ruled out an election before the end of the year in his Glasgow speech.

Very gradually, however, during the winter of 1965–66, the arguments in favour of an election in the spring began to accumulate. The Prime Minister had always known how lucky the government had been that two Labour members had not died simultaneously during a parliamentary session; the death of Mr. Solomons and the illness of Mr. Hayman were reminders that this good luck might not hold indefinitely. The array of problems facing the government was daunting: the danger of inflation, which from mid-December onwards seemed to dictate a deflationary budget; mounting industrial unrest, especially among the railwaymen and seamen; the Rhodesian crisis, which threatened to flare up at any time; difficulties with Labour backbenchers and the unions over Mr. Brown's early warning legislation. Any one of these could cause a sharp decline in Labour's popularity at any moment. Conversely, the Conservatives' position seemed bound to improve. Mr. Heath might begin to make an impact, the Conservatives could be expected to launch a major advertising campaign during the summer, and the local elections were certain to give a fillip to Conservative morale following on Labour's spectacular gains in 1963. Above all, the prospect that Mr. Wilson had always held out — that Labour would have substantially completed its programme by the end of the second session — was fast receding. Parliamentary time was too short, and the state of the economy still would not permit such measures as the minimum income guarantee. Thus, one of the major elements in the logic of waiting till October 1966 was removed.

If the risks of waiting were great, so were the positive temptations to go. For the first time, in January 1966, the Prime Minister could seriously consider an early election at a time when all the indicators suggested that Labour would win it. By mid-January Labour had led the Conservatives by handsome margins in both main polls for the past four months. One of the two autumn by-elections had resulted in a slight swing to the Conservatives, but the figure was well below that normally suffered by the party in power. Mr. Wilson's own standing with the public was at its height. Moreover, an election fought on a fresh register would almost certainly benefit Labour, owing to the Conservatives' greater success in organising postal votes and tracing removals.[1] All these considerations told in favour of March or April. They also increased Mr. Wilson's personal risks in waiting. Some ministers and backbenchers had felt for months that the Prime Minister had missed two earlier opportunities — in March and October 1965 — of going to the country. If he now insisted on carrying on and Labour were subsequently defeated, all of the blame would be his. If he now went to the country and

---

[1] For a persuasive statement of the case for an early election, see R. L. Leonard, 'Why It Should Be March', *Guardian*, January 3rd, 1966. Mr. Leonard laid particular stress on the fresh register. He also pointed out that, once having committed himself to October, the Prime Minister could be accused of hanging on for partisan reasons if, when October came, he held back from having an election because it looked as though Labour would lose.

Labour lost, at least others would be implicated in his error.

Nevertheless, there can be little doubt that Mr. Wilson was powerfully torn. On the one hand, he recognised all the arguments in favour of March or April. On the other hand, to go to the country at a time when Labour could still command a majority in the House of Commons would be to fly in the face of both his

"HA-HA, OLD WILSON'S IN AN AWFUL DILEMMA!"
[*Evening Standard*, Feb. 8th, 1966

repeated public statements, and his rooted belief that the government should carry on. There was a calculating element in the Prime Minister's thinking; if he went to the country in March, he risked the Conservative accusation that Labour was running away from a tough budget, and also that Labour voters, not wanting an early election, might stay at home. But there was also an emotional element; having convinced himself as well as others of Labour's capacity to govern, he almost certainly felt that he would be going back on himself if he called an election before either it was unavoidable or Labour had completed its programme. The belief that, despite its small majority, his government had not shirked tough decisions was not merely a part of the Prime Minister's rhetoric. It had become part of his nature.

In addition, the danger that Labour might lose an early election, remote as it seemed, could not be discounted entirely. Other Prime Ministers — Disraeli and Baldwin, for instance — had gone to the country at a time they believed to be favourable, only to be defeated. Industrial unrest or some major government blunder could lead to disaster. So could massive apathy among Labour voters. It was just possible that the Conservatives might suddenly seem attractive. Moreover, even if a Labour victory seemed certain, the risks of defeat were enormous. Defeat in an election provoked by Labour, at a time when the party had not completed its programme and when the country still faced an economic crisis, could completely undermine Mr. Wilson's personal position and leave Labour to languish in opposition, perhaps for a generation. No Labour Prime Minister could forget 1931 or 1951. Others could give Mr. Wilson advice; the responsibility was his alone. It is scarcely surprising that he took some time to make up his mind.[1]

Opinions differ about whether Mr. Wilson first began to think seriously of a spring election before or after Christmas. Some party officials remarked afterwards that their first inklings came in December. In any case, the impending by-election in Hull North would have forced the Prime Minister to consider the spring, whatever his inclinations. The loss of Hull would make it almost impossible for the government to continue, while victory would lead to renewed pressure for an early election. Much thought was given to the timing of the by-election. The approach of Christmas ruled out December, but the choice still lay between January and late February or March, after the new register had come into force. The local Labour party favoured March but was eventually over-ruled; a local by-election in Hull produced a good result for Labour, and the government did not want the seat to remain vacant any longer than necessary. Equally important, advancing the date would give Mr. Wilson some indication of the state of public opinion, while leaving open the option of a general election in March.

What the Prime Minister would have done if Labour had won

[1] It is still not clear which ministers were pressing the Prime Minister in which direction. For a list of the advocates of an early election, see James Margach, 'April Election is Now Almost a Certainty', *Sunday Times*, February 6th, 1966. Most of the arguments advanced by his colleagues, with the possible exception of Treasury economic forecasts, must have been familiar to Mr. Wilson. He probably heeded them only in so far as they weighed in his calculation of the personal risks of staying on.

only narrowly at Hull remains a matter for speculation. Even after Labour's sweeping victory, he seemed reluctant to commit himself finally to March or April. In a speech at the Albert Hall three days later, he did not rule out an early election (as he had done so often in the past); but privately he still appeared to hanker after completing Labour's programme. A colleague commented after Hull: 'It's ideal for Harold, because it justifies him in not making up his mind on the election.'[1] But during the following week his determination hardened. The death of Mr. Hayman on Friday, February 4th, may have helped remove any last lingering doubts. Two days later James Margach noted in the *Sunday Times* that pressures were building up irresistibly on the Prime Minister to end all political and economic uncertainty by getting the election over in the spring. He added: 'And these pressures are likely to prove in harmony with his own thinking.' When the joint ministerial-NEC meeting convened at Chequers that week-end, Mr. Wilson said nothing of his decision, but few present can have doubted the way his mind was moving.

From then until the end of the month, it was a matter of keeping the Prime Minister's options open, and of creating an atmosphere in which an early election would not seem unnatural or rushed. The heading off of the threatened national rail strike on February 9th undoubtedly increased Mr. Wilson's determination. Leaks to the press became increasingly frequent. On February 12th Emanuel Shinwell, the chairman of the parliamentary Labour party, called for an early election in a speech at Easington; he was almost certainly speaking at the Prime Minister's behest. On the 16th Mr. Wilson's staff let it be known that Mr. Bowden and Mr. Short had presented him with the case for going in the spring. On the 17th Mr. Bowden announced in the House of Commons that the government proposed to hold debates during the next ten days on the welfare state and on leasehold reform. At the same moment March 31st began to be spoken of as a near certainty. Mr. Wilson would probably have preferred to wait until after the budget; a standstill budget could have been got through by agreement. But

---

[1] Quoted by James Margach, 'Wilson Mopping Up the Centre', *Sunday Times*, January 30th, 1966. On January 30th the reports of all the leading political correspondents suggested that the Prime Minister was edging away from a spring election. It is possible, of course, that Mr. Wilson was merely trying to find out how strong a reaction they would provoke. At this time, too, much was made of Mr. Wilson's alleged indecisiveness; see e.g. Alan Watkins, 'Lord Protector Wilson', *Spectator*, February 4th, 1966.

the timing would have been difficult, and the pressures for a deflationary budget were once again building up.

By the time the election was announced on February 28th, the Prime Minister's initial hesitancy had long since given way to confidence and the desire for battle. He had taken a great risk in October 1964 in determining that Labour, with a majority of only five, should govern as if it had been returned with the full confidence of the nation. He had taken even greater risks in the ensuing months, in refusing to hold a snap election and in moving forward with almost the whole of Labour's legislative programme. Now, on the eve of the campaign, it seemed all but certain that Mr. Wilson's patience was about to be rewarded.

CHAPTER III

CONSERVATIVES: RE-FORMING UNDER FIRE

EVEN before Labour's victory in 1964, Mr. Wilson had been acutely conscious of the advantages accruing to any government simply from the fact of its being in power. The personal authority of the Prime Minister of the day usually far exceeds that of the Leader of the Opposition. He alone determines the date of the election. Because the Prime Minister and his colleagues control the parliamentary timetable and the timing of official announcements, their power to command public attention is almost unlimited. By contrast, the opposition is seldom in a position to do much more than respond to government initiatives. Whereas the government can perform, the opposition can only promise. It will have difficulty communicating its policies to the public. It is always in danger of appearing negative and carping, particularly since a party out of power is deprived of all access to official information and the advice of the civil service.

The move from government to opposition must be difficult for any party. For the Conservatives, after thirteen years in power, it was peculiarly so. Many of the party's leading figures had had little experience of opposition, except possibly for a few months during the dying days of the postwar Labour government, and it took some of them months to adjust to their new situation. The Conservatives had also been badly demoralised by the events of the preceding three years. The sense that the party had lost its way would not have disappeared entirely even if the Conservatives had won the election; defeat merely reinforced it. But perhaps the Conservatives' greatest difficulties stemmed from the very narrowness of Labour's victory. If Labour had won decisively, the Conservatives could have gone on in their own time to solve the various problems confronting them. Instead, they had to act rapidly and in the knowledge that every decision they made could be overtaken by an unexpected election. They could neither pause to reflect nor consistently take a long view. The party was, in the phrase of Lord Blakenham, 're-forming under fire'.

The Labour party had only one central strategic problem: how to time the next election so that Labour could win it. And only one man, Mr. Wilson, could solve it. The problems confronting the Conservatives were more numerous and, by their nature, involved different sections of the party and different individuals. The question of the party leadership presented itself, the problem of reorganising Central Office, and the need to rethink the party's policies. A number of senior officials felt that the Conservatives had lost touch with the thoughts and feelings of ordinary voters, and during the 1964 parliament they persuaded the party to embark on an ambitious programme of market research. In addition, the party had at each stage to consider its strategic objectives in relation to the coming election. Many of these activities were closely related in Conservative planning, but here it seems best to treat each of them in turn.

Sir Alec Douglas-Home emerged from the 1964 election with his reputation in many ways enhanced. His selflessness and integrity had won him the affection of almost the whole of his party, and the Conservatives under his leadership had, apparently against overwhelming odds, all but won the election. Nevertheless, his leadership had always had a temporary air about it. The extraordinary circumstances of his emergence in 1963 continued to cast doubt on the legitimacy of his position. More important, Sir Alec simply seemed unsuited to the kind of political warfare that the two major parties were now engaged in. He knew nothing of economics and little of the worlds of industry and commerce; he seemed to belong more to the Conservatives' patrician past than to their technocratic future. In the House of Commons he could often make a well-reasoned speech, especially on foreign affairs; he left a strong impression of straightness and decency. But he was no match for Mr. Wilson, and the bulk of his party knew it. Sir Alec also failed to make any deep impression on the public. Throughout the 1964 parliament his standing in the public opinion polls trailed far behind that of the Prime Minister (see chart, p. 2).

For all these reasons the question of Sir Alec's retirement tended to be discussed — by all but his most ardent admirers — more in terms of when than of whether.[1] It was a difficult question.

---

[1] Gerald Kaufman was probably characterising opinion accurately when he wrote shortly after the election: 'Sir Alec is widely deemed to have fought a

No consensus on an alternative leader had developed by October 1964, and none showed any sign of developing during the ensuing months. This fact greatly inhibited the Conservatives, who feared above all else a repetition of the unhappy struggle for power of 1963. The adoption of a new method for electing the leader in February 1965 lessened the difficulty but did not remove it. The party was also inhibited by the likelihood of an early general election; no one wanted to fight an election under an entirely new leader, and when any wounds opened by a succession struggle would not have had time to heal. Moreover, many Conservatives, although aware of Sir Alec's limitations, were also conscious of the debt the party owed him and had no desire to see him let down publicly. As a result, and because there was no accepted procedure for getting rid of an unwanted leader, strong pressure against Sir Alec took some months to develop.

Sir Alec had no illusions about his position. He wished to remain leader, but he knew that a time might come when the costs of remaining, both to the party and to his own reputation, would far outweigh any possible benefits. He emphasised his willingness to retire when the time came, partly because he did not want to be seen to be driven out. Perhaps more than anyone else, Sir Alec was conscious of the need for a successor to have emerged before he retired; he did not wish it said that he had bequeathed to his successor his own inheritance of bitterness and distrust. Whether Sir Alec hoped that Mr. Heath would emerge as his successor must remain a matter for conjecture. It seems highly probable that he did. In any case, from January 1965 onwards Sir Alec made no secret of the fact that he was prepared to consider retiring. In late March a newspaper report appeared of a conversation between him and a senior Conservative:

> 'Weighing everything together, he was still, at that moment, convinced that although in some respects he might be considered to have become a liability, it would be quite wrong from the party's point of view to go until there is a manifest consensus on the successor.'[1]

---

doughty election campaign, and it is today as difficult to find leading Conservatives who will say that he should not have led the party last month as it is to find members of the shadow cabinet who insist that he must lead them next time.' 'Choosing a Tory Leader', *New Statesman*, November 20th, 1964.

[1] Quoted by Nora Beloff, 'If Butler Had Been There After Roxburgh', *Observer*, March 28th, 1965.

Such conversations embarrassed the whips since they could only have the effect of further undermining Sir Alec's leadership.

Press reports of discontent with Sir Alec have to be treated with caution, since it was in the interest of his more active critics to have it believed that the party was seething with unrest. Nevertheless, a good deal of unhappiness does seem to have been expressed just before and during the first Christmas recess. The Conservative attack had not been pressed in the House of Commons, and the number of Conservatives believing that perhaps Sir Alec's government did bear some responsibility for the country's economic difficulties was growing. In mid-January the whips felt compelled to make plain that Sir Alec would remain as leader and to reassure M.P.s that the front bench would be much more aggressive when parliament reassembled. In a speech in Lincolnshire Joseph Godber, the former Minister of Labour, went out of his way to try to stabilise the position:

> 'When Parliament reassembles next week, it will be seen once more, just as it was seen before Christmas, that Sir Alec has the complete confidence of Conservative M.P.s. . . .
> 'We look for Sir Alec Douglas-Home to go on leading us now and we shall be happy to follow him into the next general election.'

Sir Alec asserted his own determination to carry on in a speech at Hampstead on February 3rd.

The post-Christmas wave of discontent coincided with the enquiries of the party Chairman, Lord Blakenham, into the method of choosing the party leader. Criticism of the old evolutionary method had persisted ever since the events of 1963, and shortly after the election Sir Alec had announced that the system would be reviewed. The major problems concerned the composition of the electoral college and the type of ballot to be used. Despite resistance from the National Union, the principle had been accepted by late December that, although the usual process of ratification would be retained, the decisive vote would take place only among members of the party in the House of Commons. The problem of the ballot proved more difficult. The party was unwilling to commit itself to Labour's straightforward majority system, believing that the method adopted should aim to produce a broad consensus. The alternative vote was ruled out on the ground that it did not allow for the nomination of compromise candidates after the first ballot. The system eventually adopted — providing for three ballots if necessary — was promulgated by Sir Alec on February 25th.[1]

Sir Alec made it clear that he rejected the suggestion that he should retire and offer himself for re-election. The attractions of such a procedure were obvious; even if someone stood against him, Sir Alec would be bound to win the election, and his victory would consolidate his authority, at least temporarily. But the objections were equally obvious. If no one else came forward, the press would claim that the election had been rigged, and in any case criticism of Sir Alec would persist. If another candidate appeared and got only a derisory vote, it could always be claimed that members had voted for Sir Alec only out of loyalty. If the other candidate got a large vote, then of course Sir Alec's position would soon become untenable. Either way a victory for Sir Alec in the spring would have limited his room for manoeuvre if he had decided in the autumn that he wished to retire. The re-election proposal was seriously considered but, for all these reasons, eventually rejected.

At this stage it seemed that Sir Alec was secure. A poll of Conservative M.P.s published in the *Sunday Times* on February 7th indicated that three out of four were broadly satisfied with his leadership; the poll also showed that neither Mr. Maudling nor Mr. Heath was emerging clearly as his successor. But in late March a second wave of discontent followed the Conservative defeat at Roxburgh, in the Homes' own backyard. The critics blamed Sir Alec in part for the defeat and also for the Conservatives' failure to improve their position in the opinion polls despite the government's errors. On this occasion the bickering became public. Patrick Wall, the M.P. for Haltemprice, on April 1st re-

---

[1] For the full text of the new procedure, see *The Times*, February 26th, 1965, or Anthony King, ed., *British Politics*, D. C. Heath and Hammond, 1966, Documentary Appendix. Under the new system, a candidate would be elected on the first ballot only if he both received an absolute majority and secured 15% more votes than his nearest rival. If the first ballot failed to produce a winner, a second ballot would be held for which new nominations could be made. To be elected on the second ballot, a candidate needed only an absolute majority. If no one obtained an absolute majority on the second ballot, then a third and final ballot would be held. The names on the ballot paper would be those of the three leading candidates on the second ballot. Voters would be required to indicate their second as well as their first preference. The candidate with the smallest number of first preferences would be eliminated and his second preferences distributed between the other two. On the third ballot, one candidate would, in the nature of the system, have to achieve an overall majority.

buked Iain Macleod for not following Mr. Maudling's example in pledging his loyalty to Sir Alec. The next day another back-bencher, Humphry Berkeley, turned on Mr. Wall:

> 'I hope that none of my colleagues will copy the conduct of Mr. Patrick Wall, who, under a guise of slobbering loyalty to Sir Alec, promotes the claims of his own candidate and seeks to denigrate another.'

More significant, some of the critics tried to use the press as a means of spreading the idea that Sir Alec could not remain for long. It was put about that only a 'Bishop of Bradford' was needed to precipitate the abdication.[1]

The post-Roxburgh flurry quickly subsided — the possibility of an election in May or June precluded any immediate change — but each wave of criticism left Sir Alec's position a little weaker than before. In addition, the idea gained currency that the time for Sir Alec to go would be on the eve of the summer recess. The aim may have been to stave off a leadership crisis but the effect was to make one almost inevitable in June or July. A change of leader during the summer would enable Sir Alec's successor to appear at the party conference and also give him three or four months to establish his position in the event of an autumn election. The change would almost certainly have to occur while parliament was in session, since otherwise the new electoral procedure would be almost impossible to put into operation. From March onwards Conservatives spoke of the leadership problem 'resolving itself' sometime in the early summer.

Some party officials had favoured a change ever since the election, and a majority of the shadow cabinet probably felt the same way. What caused Sir Alec's position to deteriorate during the spring was the mounting evidence that his support among the constituency associations was being eroded away. His speeches to party workers in the country no longer evoked the same warm response, and their lack of enthusiasm communicated itself to

---

[1] See Alan Watkins, 'Tory Rumblings', *Spectator*, March 26th, 1965. The allusion was to the sermon by the Bishop of Bradford which first brought the abdication crisis into the open in 1936. For a description of the dissidents' efforts to exploit the press, see 'The Birth of a Campaign to Oust Sir Alec' by *The Times* political correspondent, April 5th, 1965. The writer reported that someone had tried to persuade him to develop the Bishop of Bradford analogy, and added: 'for what it is worth, I held it better to deal with the speeches of those involved and with events rather than to be the manipulator of speeches and events.'

members of parliament. As a member of the shadow cabinet put
it afterwards:

> 'Usually these waves of feeling move outwards from the House
> to the constituencies. This time it was the other way round. Sir Alec's
> support stayed reasonably firm among the members, but they kept
> coming back with stories of how unhappy their people were. It was
> worst among the Young Conservatives and business men — business
> men especially.'

The feeling in the constituencies almost certainly weakened Sir
Alec's will to remain, since he had always regarded the constituency
rank and file as the basis of his support. The number of M.P.s
seeking a change gradually increased during the spring, and also
the intensity of feeling among Sir Alec's persistent critics. If anything, the party's improved standing in the opinion polls did him
more harm than good by drawing attention to the steady decline
in his own popularity.

Towards the end of June, following Mr. Wilson's announcement that there would be no election in 1966, the final crisis began. On the 27th a report in the *Sunday Express* claimed that
fully one hundred M.P.s now wished Sir Alec to give way to Mr.
Heath. Although it certainly exaggerated the number of Sir Alec's
active opponents, the report led four days later to the leadership's
being discussed for the first time at a meeting of the 1922 Committee executive. At a second meeting, on July 5th, the executive
appears to have been evenly divided despite the reading of a
statement by Sir Alec that he had no intention of resigning. Supporters of Mr. Heath were particularly vocal at the meeting but,
according to later newspaper reports, they were joined by almost
all of the younger members present.[1] How concerted the efforts to
remove Sir Alec were remains in dispute; a large number of
members were undoubtedly relieved when it looked at last as
though the issue were going to be forced. But for the moment Sir
Alec remained firm. He was prepared to retire when the time
came, but he and his advisers were determined, above all, that
he should not be driven to resign.

There the matter might have rested but for three events during
the following ten days. On Tuesday, July 13th, a report in *The*

---

[1] See 'Insight on the Tory Leadership', *Sunday Times*, July 25th, 1965. This
is the fullest account of Sir Alec's retirement so far published and, as far as the
present authors have been able to check it, appears to be largely accurate.

Times made public the proceedings in the 1922 Committee. Two days later the fortnightly National Opinion Poll published in the *Daily Mail* reported an increase in Labour's lead from 2·0% to 4·6%; more important, it showed that over a wide range of qualities, including 'sincerity', the general public clearly preferred Mr. Wilson to Sir Alec. Finally, on July 18th, the *Sunday Times* published a long article by its political editor, William Rees-Mogg, entitled 'The Right Moment to Change'. The writer referred to the debates in the 1922 Committee, to Sir Alec's loss of support among the party in the country, and to the NOP. Sir Alec had not proved as bad a leader as he and others had feared, but he had not been anything like as good a leader as his original supporters had hoped.

> 'He has in fact played the sort of captain's innings one used to see in county cricket before the war. There were then in most counties good club players, often fresh from the university, who were appointed captain because they were amateurs. They lacked the professional skills and they never had very high averages. But occasionally, when the wicket was taking spin at Canterbury or Weston-super-Mare, they would come in when their side had scored thirty-seven for six and by dint of concentration and a well-coached forward prod survive to make twenty runs or so and see their side past the follow-on.'

The time had come, Mr. Rees-Mogg concluded, for Sir Alec to go.

These events affected members of parliament. A procession of M.P.s voiced their anxieties to the whips during the next few days. They also affected Sir Alec. Although shaken by the opinion poll, he probably travelled that week-end to The Hirsel, his country home in Scotland, intending to stay on. But, apparently after reading the newspapers on Sunday, he changed his mind and returned to London on Monday all but determined to resign. According to newspaper reports, he was persuaded by William Whitelaw, the Chief Whip, and Edward du Cann, Lord Blakenham's successor as party Chairman, to pause before taking any decisive step; but on Tuesday July 20th, following a foreign affairs debate in which Sir Alec performed poorly, his decision became irrevocable. Sir Alec had indicated that he would remain only if his advisers insisted that his resignation at this juncture would be a disaster for the party. This they could not claim. Accordingly, at the regular meeting of the 1922 Committee on Thursday, July 22nd, Sir Alec announced that he was stepping down. Although the event had been anticipated for more than nine months, when it came it took both the party and the public completely by surprise.

Was Sir Alec forced to retire? The short answer must be yes. There can be no doubt that his resignation in July 1965 was entirely voluntary. He could have resisted back bench pressure and remained party leader for some months to come. But, as his advisers pointed out to him at the time, sooner or later a public row would have become inevitable. Sooner or later one of the younger Conservative members was bound to get up and say: 'Sir Alec must go. We all admire him for his virtues, but he is just not the man to be leading the party in the twentieth century.' When that time came, Sir Alec's position would become untenable. These considerations figured largely in the conversations between Sir Alec and those nearest to him. In the end, he had to chose between retiring voluntarily at once, or staying on only to be forced to retire at some time in the future. He chose to go at once.

The leadership election which followed, far from proving the nightmare which many Conservatives, remembering 1963, had feared, proceeded smoothly and uneventfully. Sir Alec's resignation had been perfectly timed; it enabled the party to reach its decision with parliament still in session but allowed for a week-end in which M.P.s could consult their constituents away from each other and from enquiring reporters. Mr. Maudling and Mr. Heath were nominated at once and were joined on Sunday, July 25th, by Enoch Powell. Most reports suggested a narrow win for Mr. Maudling, but a number of newspapers — including *The Times* and the *Daily Mail* — supported Mr. Heath editorially, and correspondents in the constituencies suggested that Mr. Heath was preferred by the Conservative rank and file. On Tuesday, July 27th, the day of the first ballot, both NOP and the *Daily Express* poll reported a substantial preference among the electorate for Mr. Maudling. When the results of the first ballot were declared that afternoon, however, it was Mr. Heath who had pulled ahead. He had 150 votes compared with 133 for Mr. Maudling and only 15 for Mr. Powell. Mr. Maudling at once stood down and, when nominations closed on July 28th without new candidates appearing, Mr. Heath became in effect leader of the Conservative party. He owed his victory, it would seem, largely to the sense that he, more than Mr. Maudling, would provide the Prime Minister with vigorous and unrelenting opposition.[1]

Few in the upper reaches of the Conservative party mourned Sir Alec's departure, but even his detractors conceded that in his twenty-one months as leader he had performed certain valuable services. One was to pull the party together in the aftermath of Harold Macmillan's last months in office. Another was to produce a new method for electing the party leader. A third was to initiate a major re-examination of the party's organisation and policies. This re-examination began while the question of Sir Alec's leadership was still open and tended to be overshadowed by it. It also failed in the short run to produce electoral results. Nevertheless, it represented one of the most ambitious efforts at internal reform ever undertaken by a British party and deserves to rank with the modernising era of the Conservative party after 1945.

The first reforms came almost immediately after the election. On October 22nd it was announced that Sir Michael Fraser, director of the Conservative Research Department since 1951, had been appointed Deputy Chairman of the party and secretary to the shadow cabinet. Although the title of Deputy Chairman was old (three men had held it before), the post was largely new. Hitherto no one in the party had played a role analogous to that of the managing director in a private firm. The part-time Chairman and Vice-Chairman worked directly with the professional heads of departments; the General Director functioned mainly as the administrator of Central Office. The new Deputy Chairman, who was vested with considerable authority in his own right, was meant to act as a link between the Chairman and the full-time officials and also to co-ordinate policy and organisation. The idea of creating such a post was Lord Poole's and had been adopted before the election despite some slight misgivings in Central Office. Considerable power could be amassed by a Deputy Chairman, particularly if his background were that of a permanent official.

---

[1] No systematic evidence exists either about which M.P.s voted for which candidate or about the criteria they used in making their selection. Mr. Heath's candidacy almost certainly benefited from the activities of a 'Young Turk' campaign organisation led by Peter Walker (Worcester), Anthony Kershaw (Stroud) and Peter Emery (Reading). For the fullest available accounts of Mr. Heath's election, see Alan Watkins, 'How Heath Pulled It Off', *Spectator*, July 30th, 1965; and James Margach, 'The Bloodless Victory that put Heath on Top', *Sunday Times*, August 1st, 1965.

E

At the same time it was announced that the Deputy Chairman would become responsible for the Research Department. This body, which had led a semi-autonomous existence since its creation in 1929, was to be more fully integrated into Central Office. The change was largely formal but had the effect of abolishing the office of chairman of the Research Department, which had been held by R. A. Butler concurrently with the chairmanship of the Advisory Committee on Policy ever since 1945. Mr. Butler had irritated a number of party leaders by his indiscretions during the election, and they were undoubtedly glad of an opportunity to have him removed. The change also ensured that the two chairmanships could not be used as the basis for independent power in the party. Five months later, in March 1965, the Conservative Political Centre was also integrated into Central Office. The aim was to involve party workers in the country more closely with policy making. Between January and October 1965 the number of CPC discussion groups in the constituencies grew from just over one hundred to well over three hundred.

All of the new party officials were younger, some of them much younger, than their predecessors. Sir Michael Fraser was 49 when appointed. Brendon Sewill, the new director of the Research Department, was 35; David Howell, the new CPC director, only 29. And on January 21st, 1965, Lord Blakenham was succeeded by Edward du Cann, the member of parliament for Taunton and at 40 the youngest party Chairman since J. C. C. Davidson in 1926. Mr. du Cann's appointment came as a total surprise. He was relatively unknown in the party, having been only a junior minister in the Conservative government, and the names of both Selwyn Lloyd and Ernest Marples, the ex-Minister of Transport, had been mentioned for the job. Mr. du Cann was probably appointed partly because he was younger than the others, but mainly because his business experience — he was managing director of several unit trusts — brought him into contact with sections of the community which the Conservatives feared they had alienated.

By this time there existed in Central Office a community of view about the party's chief priorities. They were three in number. The first was to make the whole organisation much more 'political' than it had become. Party officials felt that during the party's years in power the organisation had become preoccupied with routine mechanics, in the case of the agents on the one hand, or with purely social activities, in the case of some constituency associations and the Young Conservatives on the other. The functions of political education and propaganda tended to be neglected. The second priority was to introduce into the party modern business ideas and techniques. The Conservatives had fallen behind Labour in the field of market research and behind most efficient businesses in the recruitment and training of personnel, in publicity, and in finance. The third was the stream-lining of Central Office itself and the improvement of the professional staff in the country. The party organisation had not been reviewed for a generation; out-of-date practices went on unchecked, and a few officials believed that there was serious over-manning. In essence, as one of the younger men put it, it was a question of 'putting the right people into the right jobs at the right salaries'.

While Lord Blakenham was still Chairman, two committees, under Lord Chelmer and Mr. Macleod, were established to investigate the status and remuneration of constituency agents, and the Young Conservatives. The Chelmer report recommended higher salaries and an improved training scheme for agents, and a system of subsidies for highly marginal constituencies to enable them to attract the better agents from safer seats. It also laid great stress on the need to raise the status of the agent *vis-à-vis* the M.P. or candidate and the constituency chairman; in a circular letter to Conservative area chairmen Mr. du Cann recommended that agents 'should be regarded as the equivalent of a managing director of the local organisation'. In future agents were to be 'educated' as well as 'trained' and fitted to take a leading part in political discussion. Although the Chelmer report was never published, most of its main findings were in the course of being implemented by the time of the 1966 election. The Macleod report, which appeared in early December, also emphasised the need to foster serious political discussion and recommended that the Young Conservatives be organised so as to take a more active part in general community affairs. It suggested that the upper age limit be raised to 35 'so that we can develop special activities for the 25–35 age group which has hitherto been comparatively neglected by our party and which, in consequence, has tended to drift away from us'.[1] The Macleod proposals were under consideration when the election intervened.

[1] Conservative and Unionist Central Office, *The Macleod Report*, 1965.

One aspect of the party's work that caused considerable trouble was publicity. On October 30th, 1964, within a fortnight of the change of government, Roger Pemberton, a former Colman, Prentice and Varley executive, succeeded George Hutchinson as Chief Publicity Officer. During the next few months steps were taken to reorganise the department into four sections — broadcasting, press, editorial, and layout — and to begin to recruit an outside advisory group on the model of the Labour party's. But Mr. Pemberton suffered from persistent ill health and, after one holiday to recuperate, finally resigned towards the end of June. From then until late November the party was without a publicity head. A number of possible candidates were approached, one of whom accepted the position tentatively only to inform Central Office six weeks later that he was unable to leave his present employment. The party found it almost impossible to persuade men of ability to leave the highly competitive world of advertising and public relations for the requisite period of two or three years. In the end, Gerald O'Brien, the party's press officer who had acted as publicity officer since Mr. Pemberton's departure, was confirmed in his place. At the same time C. Austen Barnes, a marketing executive, was appointed part-time 'adviser on planning and development in the field of communications'.

It is open to question whether the hiatus made much difference. The Conservatives had found before the 1964 election that it was extraordinarily difficult to mount a successful publicity campaign unless it could be extended over a long period, tied to a number of policy themes, and designed to strike in the public mind a chord that already existed. In 1963–64 the party's efforts had been bedevilled by the struggle over the leadership and then by the difficulty of evolving consistent themes; the party had spent almost £1m., apparently to no great effect.[1] In the early part of 1965 the leadership question remained open, and later in the year the Rhodesian crisis intervened. In any case, the party had no confidence that the public was yet in a mood to respond favourably to anything it had to say. Whether a campaign should be launched in the summer of 1966 was still under discussion when the election came. No plans had been made, but the postponement of the

---

[1] Richard Rose, 'Pre-Election Public Relations and Advertising', *The British General Election of 1964*, p. 374. His figure of £992,000 apparently underestimated the party's total publicity expenditure.

revenues declined, while at the same time more money was needed for higher salaries, market research and equipment. The Conservatives believed they suffered from the fact that most party members, believing the party to be rich, were not sufficiently money-conscious. In February Robert Allan, one of the party's joint treasurers, submitted a report recommending the doubling of constituency contributions to Central Office, a rise in the annual subscription and the setting up in each constituency of a special fund-raising committee. In May an urgent appeal for funds was circulated to constituency treasurers; it set £300,000 as a target for contributions to the centre, more than half as much again as the previous year's. In October at the party conference Mr. du Cann and Lord Chelmer, the new party treasurer, launched a 'Ten Shilling Unit' campaign. Efforts were set in train at the same time to make more efficient the raising of funds from private individuals and companies. Central Office officials felt they had made some progress by the time of the election but that much remained to be done. 'I want to see finance put right,' a senior official commented, 'before I die.'[2]

[1] The Conservatives' problem was summed up by one man who said: 'It's much harder to re-launch an old product than to market an entirely new one.' For a critical commentary on Conservative publicity efforts, see a series of articles, 'The Party Persuaders', *Crossbow*, January–March 1966.

[2] What little information appeared in print about Conservative finance was almost entirely the work of Ian Waller, political correspondent of the *Sunday Telegraph*; see 'Money Shock for du Cann', February 14th, 1965, 'Cash Drive by Tories', May 23rd, 'Fighting Fund Plea by Tories', August 1st, and 'Appeal to Rich Tories', August 22nd. After the election, on May 22nd, 1966, the *Sunday Telegraph* published a report of a private speech by Mr. du Cann to the 1922 Committee concerning party finances. Subsequently the paper stated that, in publishing the report, it had not wished to reflect on the competence and integrity of the Conservative officials involved. During the 1964 parliament Central Office officials were often at pains to claim that the Labour party, with an assured income, was actually better off than the reputedly wealthy Conservatives.

Two further reforms were instituted to co-ordinate more closely the activities of Central Office and the party in parliament. Shortly after Mr. du Cann became Chairman the liaison committee, which had met weekly during the Conservative period in office, was replaced by a daily meeting in Smith Square. The meeting took place at 9.30 each morning in the Chairman's office and discussed both day-to-day tactics and long-term party strategy. It was attended, in addition to Mr. du Cann and Sir Michael Fraser, by the heads of Central Office departments, the Chief Whip, the chairman of the 1922 Committee or his representative, and a representative of the leader, usually his parliamentary private secretary. Attendance at the meeting was sometimes erratic, and on some mornings little was achieved; but most of those who attended claimed that it was of great value. A member of the shadow cabinet said in June 1965:

> 'I've been to every daily meeting so far, and it's well worth an hour of my time. The point is that it makes it possible to "co-ordinate the orchestra" — not just occasionally but right the way through.'

In addition, Mr. du Cann established a general election committee which had always before it a twenty-section plan containing complete administrative arrangements for a campaign. The committee met weekly at first, then less often, then weekly again as the election approached. It consisted of Mr. du Cann, Sir Michael Fraser, the heads of departments and a representative of the leader, in the case of Mr. Heath usually John MacGregor, the head of his private office.

The effort to modernise the party extended to questions of parliamentary candidatures and the leadership of Conservative associations in the constituencies. The aim was to bring the party in the constituencies into much closer touch with the leadership — in hopes that the leadership could thereby be brought into closer touch with the electorate — and also to ensure that local candidates and party officers accurately reflected the social composition of their communities. Sir Alec Douglas-Home and Lord Blakenham had concluded, even before Mr. du Cann became Chairman, that the proportion of peers, landowners and retired business men and service officers among the party's candidates and leaders should gradually be reduced. Suggestions to this effect were circulated to the constituencies beginning in November 1964, and early in 1965 the list of approved parliamentary candidates was completely overhauled. These efforts not unnaturally aroused a certain amount of antagonism. A question that remained unanswered at the time of the election was whether the post-1964 wave of reforms, unlike the wave after 1945, would create serious, perhaps disruptive, tensions within the Conservative party.[1]

But the aspect of the party's re-examination most affected by the uncertainty about the election date was undoubtedly the review of policy. There was general agreement that such a review should be undertaken; the party had shown signs of exhausting its ideas during its last years in office, and new themes were needed to give coherence to party propaganda (just as after 1945, in the words of one party official, 'we had to train them to say boo all at the same time when they heard the word "controls"'). It was clear, however, that the review would have to be conducted at far greater speed than in the postwar period. The next election could not be delayed beyond about two years, and at any given moment some new items of policy would have to be available for inclusion in an election manifesto. Policy thinking, too, would have to keep pace with changes in the Labour party's own policies and decisions. For all these reasons, many of the ideas thrown up by the review were bound to prove ephemeral.

Mr. Heath, on becoming chairman of the Advisory Committee on Policy on October 24th, 1964, assumed overall direction of the policy review. He chose to eschew a re-examination of the party's general aims and philosophy in favour of a detailed examination of specific areas of policy. Concentration on particular subjects would ensure that material would be available for a manifesto; it would also avoid the kind of ideological controversy that had bedevilled Labour after 1959. Mr. Heath also believed that the enquiry should not be restricted to a small core of party officials but should enlist the services of M.P.s, business and professional men, and

[1] One other reform should be mentioned although it was carried out largely independently of Central Office. In March 1965 the Scottish Unionist Association adopted a pattern of organisation modelled along English lines. The eastern and western divisional councils were abolished and replaced by five regions under agents responsible to the Scottish party Chairman. The association at the same time changed its name to the 'Scottish Conservative and Unionist Association'. The Scots refused to follow English practice in one respect, however; the regions were to be called regions and not, as in England, areas. For a brief description of the reorganisation, see ' "Super Agents" in Scots Unionist streamlining', *Guardian*, March 6th, 1965.

university teachers. The scale of the operation, and the speed at which it would have to be conducted, dictated the involvement of a fairly large number of people. In addition Mr. Heath shared the view generally held in the party that the Conservatives must re-forge their links with the non-political world. How much Mr. Heath's leadership aspirations influenced his choice of methods it is impossible to say; given the extent to which he had to co-operate with others, they cannot have been particularly important.

Accordingly, during the first Christmas recess, some twenty advisory groups were established, each consisting of eight to twelve members, about half of them M.P.s; only the group on the economy, with eighteen members, was larger. The number of groups and sub-groups gradually multiplied over the winter and spring until there were 36. They were normally chaired by a front bench spokesman and included M.P.s who were also members of the appropriate subject committee in the House of Commons. Over-lapping membership was kept to a minimum although a few individuals sat on two groups in closely related fields. A Research Department official normally acted as secretary. Regular contact was maintained with the Advisory Committee on Policy and, through the group chairmen, with the shadow cabinet.[1] Mr. Heath himself read each group paper as it emerged — 'a terrible week-end's work'. At the outset the problems to be studied were divided into two categories: those arising out of existing policy and in urgent need of review or amplification, and those requiring longer-term consideration. But as time went on this distinction became blurred. Among the subjects included in the original priority list were the modernisation of the economy, land, social insurance, trade union reform, rates and immigration.

---

[1] The main function of the Advisory Committee on Policy was to ensure that representatives of every section of the party had a voice in policy making at a fairly early stage. According to a Research Department official, it had the advantage of making it impossible for the views of specialist groups to get out of line with the thinking of the ordinary man. The Committee in 1965 consisted of Mr. du Cann, Mr. Heath, Sir Edward Boyle, the vice-chairman, two representatives of the party in the House of Lords (Lord Carrington and Lord Colville), five representatives of the 1922 Committee (Sir William Anstruther-Gray, Miss Harvie Anderson, John Hall, Sir Ian Orr-Ewing and William Roots), eight representatives of the National Union (Sir Max Bemrose, Lord Chelmer, Lady Davidson, Mrs. Charles Doughty, Sir John Howard, Sir Dan Mason, Dame Margaret Shepherd and Sidney Chapman, the chairman of the Young Conservatives) and three co-opted members (Sir Michael Fraser, David Howell and Michael Noble). The secretaries were Brendon Sewill, the director of the Research Department and James Douglas, another Research Department official.

Mr. Heath sought to have an 'approach document', based on the groups' preliminary reports, ready for the party conference in the autumn. In the meantime, an outline manifesto had to be kept ready in case of a spring or summer election. On joining the CPC in December, Mr. Howell prepared an 8,000-word document which was circulated for comment and, in a revised version, accepted by Sir Alec at a meeting at The Hirsel in January. Mr. Howell also attempted to fill the gap left by the decision not to publish any major document till the autumn by commissioning a series of pamphlets entitled 'Conservative New Tasks'. The pamphlets — designed in part *'pour épater les bourgeois'*, as one of Mr. Howell's colleagues put it — gave the younger generation of party intellectuals a chance to project their ideas, and also sketched in some of the broader themes that had not had time to emerge from the subject groups. Although the pamphlets varied in approach, all their authors laid stress on the need to encourage and reward efficiency and enterprise.[1]

Few doctrinal differences impeded the progress of the review (although Mr. Powell's ideological sorties often embarrassed the party in public). Instead, Mr. Heath and his younger colleagues found themselves, as they saw it, having to shift a heavy weight of inertia both in the shadow cabinet and on the back benches. The intensity of their concern about the British economy and the country's standing in the world was not universally shared. William Rees-Mogg, who was close to many of the reformers, vented their frustration in a newspaper article in early July:

> 'Inevitably . . . there are many Conservatives who cannot see what the whole fuss is about, who feel that the country is really doing well enough, if only the wrong chap had not slipped into Downing Street. Any major party will have its full share of people who are either complacent or timid, and they comprise a soft centre which gives a spongy and indeterminate resistance to most proposals for change, and to all proposals for radical change.'[2]

The ex-ministers in particular were often closely wedded to the policies they had administered in office. As far as possible they were given new subjects to deal with in opposition, but even so

---

[1] There were twelve pamphlets in all, published by the Conservative Political Centre between March and June. Many of the same ideas were expressed in a Bow Group symposium published at about the same time: Michael Wolff, ed., *The Conservative Opportunity*, B. T. Batsford and CPC, 1965.

[2] 'The Radical Centre', *Sunday Times*, July 4th, 1965.

they tended to return to their old positions when matters came up for collective decision. One M.P. engaged in the review remarked:

> 'It's hard to make them see where their own particular groove came from and where it's going, quite apart from getting them to move into new grooves.'

Inevitably the review generated tensions analogous to those created by the party reorganisation. The sharpest conflicts, according to one of the younger men, were between the generations; the young in the party, he said, often treated the old 'very brutally'.[1]

Late in the spring the groups were instructed to submit preliminary reports in the course of July. The new policy document would take account of the findings of committees whose work was well advanced. Some subjects would have to be glossed over; in other cases details would be held back deliberately for publication (if at all) nearer the election. The document was intended to form the basis of a manifesto for an autumn election; alternatively it could be used to help the Conservatives project their new policies during the winter. During July the reports were considered in groups of four or five by the Advisory Committee. Approval by the party leader was not required since by the end of the month Mr. Heath himself had become leader. Mr. Heath did not, however, wish to impose the new policies on the party and was determined to try to carry the shadow cabinet with him. This he did without great difficulty in a series of meetings during September. Numerous alterations were incorporated in the first draft, largely prepared by Mr. Howell, but only the section on the trade unions was revised substantially. At the party conference in October the document, by now entitled *Putting Britain Right Ahead*, received a warm reception, though it was merely 'commended' to the conference and no votes were taken.

Putting Britain Right Ahead embodied radical proposals in four fields of policy in particular.[2] The first was taxation. The document asserted that existing taxes bore too heavily on 'the very people . . .

---

[1] Much was also made in the press about back bench complaints over the fact that the membership of the policy groups was being kept secret. The complaints may have done Mr. Heath some harm, but it is doubtful whether his critics were numerous; some of them were probably aggrieved at not having been included in the review. The names of members were kept secret, partly to ensure that they were not lobbied, partly because some of the non-M.P. members did not wish their participation to become public.

[2] In this connection, see Anthony King, 'New Stirrings on the Right', *New Society*, October 14th, 1965.

upon whose vigour and initiative' the country's prosperity depended. It admitted that immediate tax cuts might not be possible but pledged the party to the creation of 'new incentives' as soon as the state of the economy permitted. It proposed the transfer of a proportion of the cost of the social services from the Exchequer to the employer; an increase in indirect taxation of this type would enable individual and company taxes to be lowered and place a premium on the efficient use of labour. In the second field, Europe, the document reasserted the Conservatives' commitment to enter the Community, which had tended to be passed over before and during the 1964 election campaign. It spoke of Britain taking 'the first favourable opportunity' of joining. In the meantime British entry was to be made easier by a gradual changeover in agriculture 'from the present system of deficiency payments to a controlled market with levies on imports'.

The third field was the trade unions. *Putting Britain Right Ahead* called for an extension of productivity bargaining and for the setting up of a new range of industrial courts. 'These would concentrate on the settlement of industrial disputes — including disputes arising out of dismissals, disputes between trade unions and their individual members and appeals against decisions of the Registrar [of Trade Unions and Employers' Associations].' Certain types of collective agreements, notably those on procedure, the document said, should be made enforceable. In the fourth field, social security, the Conservatives went further than their 1964 manifesto in trying to move beyond the Beveridge insurance principles. They advocated the concentration of welfare provisions on those most in need, the setting up of a new Department of Health and Social Security, and the extension of occupational pension schemes to cover the whole of the working population. 'Under this new plan, the present State graduated pensions scheme would become a residual State scheme for those relatively few who would not otherwise be covered.' In addition, the document proposed a twelve-point housing programme, including accelerated planning procedures, a limited form of land levy (which had already been announced in March), and an obligation on local authorities to operate differential rent schemes.

Putting Britain Right Ahead was also characterised by two striking omissions. The party's manifesto in 1964 had declared that an effective incomes policy was 'crucial to the achievement of sustained growth without inflation'. The new document mentioned the subject only briefly in connection with the need for more competitive efficiency and incentives. Some Conservatives, notably Mr. Maudling, continued to press the claims of an incomes policy but, partly owing to the apparent failure of the government's policy, opinion in the party had hardened against it since the election. The new document also omitted any mention of national economic planning, although the Conservatives had established the National Economic Development Council and their election manifesto had lauded 'the democratic concept of planning by partnership'. The document's authors did not reject planning entirely — Mr. Howell referred on another occasion to the need for 'a general chart of the future of the economy' — but, like incomes policy, the subject had become controversial within the party. Mr. Powell had denounced NEDC as 'a Trojan horse' and the so-called little Neddies as 'little Trojan horses' and this view was held by others in the party, though usually in a less extreme form.[1]

Assessments of *Putting Britain Right Ahead* differed even within the party. A member of the Advisory Committee wondered how much the policy groups, working on their separate subjects, could achieve in the absence of common philosophical 'points of reference'. But the majority view was that it had been a remarkable achievement to agree on so much policy in such a short time. Perhaps most important, *Putting Britain Right Ahead* and later the election manifesto evinced a willingness to break away from Conservative policies of the 1950s and to think through problems afresh. Many of the themes advanced in the two documents — efficiency, incentives, competition, action rather than exhortation, managerial and trade union reform, the move into Europe — would almost certainly remain staples of Conservative thinking for some years to come.

The policy review could be expected to serve two distinct purposes. On the one hand, it could provide the party with policies

---

[1] The extent of Mr. Powell's influence on Conservative thinking during this period will long be debated. Anthony King's article cited on p. 62, n. 2 probably exaggerated it. Although Mr. Powell was liked by almost all of his colleagues, he was regarded, angrily or tolerantly, as an irrelevance by most of them. His detractors noted the failure of his thinking to advance beyond negative criticism and the inconsistency between his statements in opposition and his own actions in government. Cf. John Wood, ed., *A Nation Not Afraid: the Thinking of Enoch Powell*, B. T. Batsford, 1965.

for when it came to power. Some critics of the review doubted whether policies evolved in opposition could ever be useful to a party in government, but they were in a minority. On the other hand, the new policies might help to return the party to power. The advisory groups were strictly instructed to treat all issues on their merits in the light of Conservative principles, but Central Office and the party leaders were obviously conscious of the need to make the new policies palatable to the electorate. In order to discover what was palatable, or what might be made palatable, the party had to discover what the tastes of the electorate were. For this purpose, the Conservatives undertook a programme of survey research far more ambitious than anything attempted by either party before. The surveys were kept strictly apart from the policy review, and there is no evidence that the findings of the research in any way influenced the policies adopted. As one of the officials most deeply engaged in the research put it:

> 'We're very old-fashioned about these things. We decide what the right policy is, and then we look at the research simply to see how best to present it.'

Well before the 1964 election a number of Conservative officials had decided that something should be done, whether or not the party were returned. They felt that the party was failing more and more to communicate with the uncommitted; they also had to take into account the widespread belief that the social base of the party was tending to narrow. Many Conservatives were continuing to address themselves to an electorate which in terms of social experience, class and age was rapidly ceasing to exist. Research was needed not merely to discover the truth but to make it possible for the truth to be impressed on others. Several senior officials felt, too, that Labour had put them on their mettle by moving so far into the research field after 1959. They were inclined to attribute much of Labour's success to the party's having learnt the lessons taught by Dr. Abrams.[1]

Opposition to research was not as powerful as it had been in the Labour party. The Conservatives had used surveys before 1959, and again on a rather larger scale between 1962 and 1964. But the studies so far had been commissioned on an *ad hoc* basis, sometimes to provide a retrospective explanation of some recent

[1] *The British General Election of 1964*, pp. 66–71.

disaster. There was no continuing flow of research information. As long as the party was successful, additional information about the electorate hardly seemed necessary. Research could be very expensive. In addition, few leading Conservatives understood the technical aspects of surveying or appreciated the uses to which it could be put. The reluctance of the leadership — in the National Union as well as in parliament — stemmed partly from lack of understanding, partly from a diffuse sense that for a political party to commission surveys would be somehow immoral. The feeling that there was nothing new to be learned by these means was also widespread.

Nevertheless, the aftermath of the 1964 election brought new men into positions of influence, and in the winter of 1964–65 a number of studies were arranged. National Opinion Polls continued to be used for data on specific, limited subjects.[1] More important, the party commissioned one of the largest private market research organisations to try to find out in detail the demographic pattern of support (or non-support) for the three parties, and also to discover how and why voters regarded the parties as they did. The firm was asked not to produce a single massive report but to analyse its data part by part in response to party requests; it was the intention that some of the interview respondents should be contacted again. It was hoped that this long-term research — described by one Central Office official as an attempt 'to build a model' of the electorate — would complement a programme of short-term surveys started late in 1965. A senior party officer commented:

> 'If I can use this metaphor, I think of the one operation as a "library" which we can go to for reference from time to time when we want to look things up. The other operation is a matter of taking quick "snapshots" of the electorate. One is as important as the other, but they serve very different purposes.'

The short-term surveys arose out of a combination of circumstances. T. F. Thompson, the party's 'special adviser on tactics'

---

[1] A report in the *Sunday Times* (December 27th, 1964) suggested that the Economist Intelligence Unit had been commissioned to do market research. In fact, the Unit was asked to undertake a series of international studies of how particular substantive problems were handled in other countries. Like the policy review generally, this work was completely divorced from the survey research.

appointed in April, had been responsible on the *Daily Mail* for working with National Opinion Polls. He had come into frequent contact with Humphrey Taylor, an NOP executive who also dealt with the surveys commissioned by the Conservatives. The two men complained to each other after the 1964 election about the party's failures in the survey field. During the summer and autumn of 1965 Mr. Thompson and other officials were urging the party to expand its research operations, and Mr. Taylor leapt at the chance to move into this new field. In the end it was decided that Mr. Taylor should establish his own market research firm, with the Conservative party, at least at first, as his major client. The firm was set up under the name Cozreledit Ltd. in November 1965 (the name was later changed to Opinion Research Centre), and from December onwards Mr. Taylor worked for the party almost full-time. By contrast with the usual political polls which, since they aim to predict the outcome of elections, use large samples and relatively short questionnaires, Mr. Taylor sought to interview a small number of people at much greater length. His firm also sought to work extremely rapidly; a report on a party political broadcast in the evening could be ready by lunchtime the next day.[1]

The research programme as a whole had three main purposes: to provide the Conservatives with an image of themselves, to identify the 'target voters' with whom the party ought to be trying to communicate, and to educate the party itself into an understanding of electoral behaviour. The third of these purposes had only begun to be fulfilled at the time of the election. Mr. Heath, Mr. du Cann and their immediate colleagues were all receptive — indeed several of them had initiated the project — but both the need for research and some of its specific findings had to be communicated outwards to members of the shadow cabinet, the 1922 Committee, the Advisory Committee, and to the rest of Central Office. The research could have its maximum impact only if it reached all fifty or so of the party's senior figures. In particular, the findings were needed as a counterweight to the information about the electorate emanating from Conservative agents and active workers. Some of the information coming up through the party was accurate, but much was distorted by the local workers'

---

[1] The one press report concerning Mr. Taylor's activities appeared in the *Sunday Times*, 'A Private Tory Pollster', November 28th, 1965.

partisan preconceptions. A younger Central Office re-marked:

> 'When the old-timers talked nonsense before, all you could do was say "Rubbish," and they'd just say "Rubbish" back. Now you can produce some evidence.'

The image of the party reported by the surveys was not re-assuring. In some respects it was positive; the Conservatives were seen as the party of experience and education and as being more competent at dealing with foreign affairs. But the general im-pression was negative, even among many Conservative voters. The party was thought of as out-of-date, stale and lacking in ideas and dynamism. The reports brought out the extent to which voters regarded the Conservatives as the party of the upper classes, out of touch with ordinary people. What emerged most clearly was the degree to which the party still suffered from the events of 1961–64. The image of the party in many voters' minds was a compound of Mr. Macmillan, the pay pause, unemployment, neglect of educa-tion and the social services, and Profumo. These findings, more than any other single factor, caused the Conservatives largely to ignore the past and to concentrate on their new leaders and new policies in their propaganda.

The Conservatives defined 'target voters' in a slightly different way from Dr. Abrams. Whereas he had concentrated on marginal seats and included all Liberals, the Conservatives conducted their surveys in all types of constituency and included in their definition all voters who, in response to a battery of 'party identification' questions, did not seem to be firmly committed to any party. The target voters tended to be young and to be concentrated in the lower-middle and upper-working classes. Most of them, as Dr. Abrams had discovered, were less well educated than the com-mitted party supporters, less interested in politics, and less well informed about public affairs. The Conservatives found, to a greater extent than Dr. Abrams, that the target voters' views on policy were hard to disentangle from the views of the committed partisans. Dr. Abrams had found them occupying a roughly 'middle' position; the post-1964 research found them holding middle views on some issues but views in line with one or other political party on others. Both parties' research showed that on a wide range of issues there was a broad consensus cutting across party lines. The Conservatives reckoned the number of target voters — one M.P. used the phrase 'T.V.s' — at between 5 and 5½ million.

These findings had begun to have a considerable impact on Conservative thinking by the early months of 1966, but not all of the reports were in, and much of the material took some time to assimilate. The 'library' aspect of the research, especially, had yet to come fully into operation. Someone lamented afterwards:

> 'If only we'd had nine more months, the Conservatives would have been in a position to launch one of the best researched and best thought out propaganda campaigns in the history of British politics.'

The research had, however, a fourth purpose: to provide the party with a continuous flow of information about public attitudes towards issues and personalities. Mr. Taylor began to work in this field in December and continued throughout the election. Much was done during the Hull North by-election. But the maximum impact of survey research was felt only in February and early March, on the eve of the election campaign.

By the time Mr. Heath became leader the Conservatives had been in opposition for nine months. Apart from brief periods of euphoria in early March and early May, it had not been a happy time. The party in parliament was under constant pressure from the constituencies to harass the government, but Sir Alec and the whips recognised that they had to tread warily. They had no desire to provide the Prime Minister with an excuse for going to the country at a time when Labour was popular, and they feared that excessively vigorous opposition might rebound in Labour's favour; the electorate was believed to feel that Labour should be given a chance. As a result the party had to seem to be exerting considerable pressure, in order to satisfy Conservative activists, while at the same time avoiding giving offence to the general public. In early February Mr. Grimond taunted the Conservatives in the House:

> 'Nothing terrifies the opposition Chief Whip more than if he thinks there is going to be a division. He rushes out and people are locked in the lavatories.'

F

The Times parliamentary correspondent commented in August:

'The fact is that during this first session, notwithstanding the spate of censure motions, they have avoided victory like the plague.[1]

In mid-summer, however, the position seemed to be about to change. Mr. Heath's election coincided with a slump in both Labour's standing in the opinion polls and the party's morale in

[*Guardian*, Mar. 21st, 1966]

parliament. The Conservatives recognised that, bar an autumn election, one of their main problems during the coming months would be to project the new leader. Mr. Heath spent part of August at Villefranche in the south of France — where he was photographed swimming and romping with his host's children — and September in steering *Putting Britain Right Ahead* through the shadow cabinet and in a short tour of the Highlands of Scotland. Some in the party later regretted the French and Scottish diversions; Mr. Heath's initially favourable reception by the public

[1] 'Parliament at a Watershed', *The Times*, August 5th, 1965.

was not sustained. They conceded, however, that the new leader needed a holiday after the gruelling debates on the Finance Bill. Mr. Heath felt that it would be unfortunate to begin his period in office by cancelling the first visit by a Conservative leader to the Highlands for many years. In any case, there were three seats there that the party hoped to recapture.

Three important strategic decisions were taken at about this time. The first was to revive Labour's charges about 'the Tory mess' and 'the £800m. deficit' in order to try to refute them. At least one Central Office official believed that the Conservatives had blundered seriously under Sir Alec in not replying to these charges, that in the absence of Conservative replies the public had come to accept them as true, and that it was not too late to repair the damage. Accordingly Mr. Heath counterattacked at the party conference in Brighton (which, breaking with precedent, he attended throughout), in a speech at Bristol later in October, and on a party political broadcast in December. The arguments were complicated, but it was hoped they would spread outwards from opinion leaders to the rest of the community. The party's research indicated that they were making some impact. But, although Mr. Heath continued to refer to the subject, the effort was not seriously sustained into the New Year.

The second decision concerned how the Conservatives should deal with Mr. Wilson. The party had, of course, realised from the beginning that the Prime Minister, with his tactical skill and his favourable public image, constituted one of their major problems. He could hardly be ignored, but persistent attacks on him, as before the 1964 election, appeared only to add to his public stature. It was largely to think this problem through that Mr. Thompson was hired from the *Daily Mail* in April. When Mr. Heath became leader, the question arose whether he should try personally to destroy Mr. Wilson's credibility, by attacking him persistently and directly, or whether he should concentrate on policy, thereby hoping to establish in the public mind a contrast between Mr. Heath, the man deeply concerned with the country's problems, and Mr. Wilson, the mere political tactician. The decision was taken that the new leader should leave it up to other members of the shadow cabinet to try to deal with the Prime Minister directly; it was felt that the electorate would react against any party leader seen to be using 'bear garden' tactics. In the event, although the decision was not held to completely (Mr. Heath often attacked Mr. Wilson, especially in the House, and his speeches in the autumn contained a number of strong attacks on individual Labour ministers), some Conservatives felt that the case against the Prime Minister had been allowed to go by default. Mr. Macleod's speeches had been little reported, Mr. Maudling's scarcely at all; 'Reggie is just not good at that sort of thing.' The third decision was closely related to the first two. It was that Mr. Heath should devote the autumn and winter to projecting the party's new policies. As well as wanting to turn the electorate's mind away from the past, the Conservatives recognised that they had only a short time, perhaps less than a year, in which to make the public familiar with a wide range of new ideas. But then came Rhodesia, the surge in the Prime Minister's popularity, and the Conservative split. January brought the Maudling–Powell debate on incomes policy, the furore over Mr. Maude, and the Hull North by-election. Partly for these reasons, the effort to project policy did not begin properly until February. On February 5th Mr. Heath spoke in Birmingham on the social services, his remarks, later vehemently attacked by Mr. Crossman, becoming known as the 'Birmingham manifesto'. On the 10th he spoke at Hammersmith on housing. On March 5th, with the election campaign already under way, he spelled out Conservative policy on the trade unions at Southampton. But for the election, the speeches would have been linked to other initiatives designed to project the policies still further.

Mr. Heath's own standing in the opinion polls meanwhile steadily declined. In February it was lower in the Gallup poll than Sir Alec's fourteen months before. Although he had been leader for only six months, murmurings against him were already being heard. Party workers and M.P.s complained increasingly of his coldness, his failure to hold the party together over Rhodesia, his excessive reliance on a group of youthful advisers, and his apparent inability to communicate with the general public.[1] In January and early February Conservative morale reached almost its lowest point since the election.

It was at this moment that it became clear that Mr. Wilson

---

[1] These thoughts were uttered privately far more than publicly. For a summary of the dissidents' views, see two articles by Alan Watkins in the *Spectator*, 'The Troubles of Mr. Heath', October 15th, 1965; and 'The State of the Tories', January 7th, 1966.

would call a general election in the spring. The Conservatives'
policy review, their reforms at Central Office and in the constituencies, the programme of survey research — all were about
to be tested, long before they had been completed, before some of
them had even been properly begun. As Mr. Heath and his
advisers made last-minute preparations for the forthcoming campaign, there was at stake not merely the outcome of the election
but to some extent, too, their own vision of the Conservative party
and their own reputations.

CHAPTER IV

THE LIBERAL PREDICAMENT

AT the first Liberal assembly which Mr. Grimond addressed as leader, in the autumn of 1957, he asserted that the party had passed the point of no return:

> 'In the next ten years, it is a question of get on or get out. Let us make it get on.'

Mr. Grimond sought to give the Liberals a new purpose in the aftermath of Suez. He envisaged the creation of a new radical party comprising Liberals, the moderate wing of the Labour party, and some of the more progressive Conservatives. How the new party would come into being could not be foretold. The Liberals might form its nucleus, or they might merge their identity into a broader coalition. It was only after the 1959 election that the way forward became clear. The disruption of the Labour party made it seem inevitable that Labour would disintegrate or else suffer catastrophic electoral defeat. In either case the Liberals could emerge, probably in alliance with the Labour moderates, as the most powerful party of the left.

The election of 1964 dashed these hopes, at least in the short term. The Liberals increased their vote from one and a half million to more than three million and gained two additional seats. But Labour won the election. Liberals could no longer count on Labour splits or be certain of a Labour election defeat sufficiently cataclysmic to cause the party to break up. The Liberals thus found themselves in the 1964 parliament having to decide, day by day, how to vote in the House of Commons, what the general tenor of their relations with the government should be, how they could maximise their votes and seats at the next election, and what, if any, should be their new long-term strategy. No satisfactory answer to the strategic problem was ever produced. A member of the party executive commented shortly after two heavy by-election defeats:

> 'Our trouble is simply that we need a strategy and don't have one. The party's principles aren't precise enough to tell us what to do

without one, and without a strategy you're bound to get muddle. Why don't we have one? Because we were deprived of our traditional strategy by Labour's winning last autumn, and because the party hasn't been able to agree on a substitute. Most Liberals really have no very clear idea of where the party should go from here.'

For the first six months of the new parliament, the Liberals were not under heavy pressure. Mr. Grimond had promised the day after polling day that the Liberals would do everything possible to ensure that stable government continued 'for a reasonable period of time'. In fact the government did not rely on Liberal votes; it commanded an absolute majority in the House and, although Liberal voting intentions attracted a good deal of interest, the government could survive unaided. The Liberals chose to approach each issue 'on its merits' as it arose; apart from taking account of constituency interests, they do not appear to have voted tactically. Up to the end of May 1965 the Liberals had voted with the government 40 times, against the government 85 times, and had abstained on three occasions. During this period the Liberal share of the vote dropped at five of the eight by-elections the party fought, but never by more than a few points. More important, the Liberals improved their second-place position at East Grinstead in February and captured Roxburgh, Selkirk and Peebles from the Conservatives in late March. It seemed for a time that the radical alliance which had eluded the party at Westminster was being forged spontaneously in the constituencies.

The Liberal posture in the House of Commons was one of complete independence. If the Prime Minister had approached Mr. Grimond with an offer of a coalition or working agreement in October 1964, the party might have responded. But he did not, and there could be no question of the Liberals either making overtures themselves or voting consistently with the government in the absence of an arrangement. The question of an alliance with the Conservatives never arose. Independence appealed to many Liberals for its own sake, but the party had no real choice. It had little to bargain with at this stage, since the government did not need its support, and any policy of siding with one party or the other would have both weakened the Liberals' future bargaining position and antagonised Liberals in the constituencies. The party hoped that its independence would be recognised and appreciated by the electorate.

This posture was not, however, entirely comfortable. Although the Liberals did not fall back substantially in by-elections, they made little progress either, except in the somewhat special circumstances of East Grinstead and Roxburgh. In May and June, with the government's popularity rapidly declining, there was a danger that opinion would begin to polarise between the government and the chief opposition party; the Liberals would seem increasingly irrelevant. The party in parliament came under pressure from Liberals in the constituencies, who exaggerated the extent of Liberal support for the government, and apparently believed, despite the government's absolute majority, that the Liberals were keeping Labour in.[1] Some in the party feared that the Liberal M.P.s would be swept away on an anti-Labour tide. The M.P.s themselves were caught in a dilemma. On the one hand, they were increasingly critical of Labour's performance and wished to dissociate themselves from the government. On the other hand, most of them had no desire to see the Conservatives returned to power and recognised that their own seats might be in danger if any swing to the Conservatives was too large.

Mr. Grimond probably felt this dilemma more acutely than anyone else. His radicalism made him more hostile to the Conservatives than many of his colleagues; the same radicalism heightened his disillusionment with the Labour government. In speeches and in private Mr. Grimond grew increasingly impatient with the government, especially after the introduction of the Finance Bill at the end of April. He was also particularly sensitive to two other considerations. First, he believed that the chances of Labour's losing its majority during the coming autumn and winter were very great. The Liberals would then be forced to choose for the first time between sustaining Labour in office and precipitating a general election. Unless the party was made to consider this choice in advance, there was a serious possibility of a split when the time came. Secondly, Mr. Grimond realised more than most Liberals that the policy of independence in parliament was neither a long-term strategy nor likely to develop into one. Either the

---

[1] This belief mystified and annoyed many of the Liberal M.P.s. They could not understand how Liberals in the constituencies could so misread the parliamentary situation. To some extent the party workers were merely transmitting the views of ordinary voters and asking that the party in parliament assert its independence of the government more forcefully. But it was still not clear how the ordinary voter had come to have such a false picture. Many Liberals believed that it was being deliberately fostered by Conservative canvassers.

party must content itself with building up support gradually in the constituencies while waiting for Labour to decline — processes which might take many years — or it must come to some agreement with Labour. The prospect of holding the balance of power presented the Liberals with their most serious threat, and also with their greatest opportunity.

Mr. Grimond did not arrive at these views suddenly. As early as March 8th he gave an interview to *The Times* political correspondent in which he dwelt on the possibility that the Liberals might find themselves holding the balance at a time when the Conservatives were determined to throw the government out:

> 'Then my view is that either we must have some reasonably long-range agreement with the Government or a general election. We must have an agreement for a few months on some purpose we both want.
>
> 'I should be very much opposed to going back to the 1929 system, in which the Labour Government and the Liberal Party made practically daily *ad hoc* decisions on the business of Government.
>
> 'I should be very much inclined to say: "We are in this difficult situation. Here are certain things both parties want to get through. We will support you on all issues, however minor, until that is done." '[1]

A series of *ad hoc* bargains would bring parliament into disrepute and probably subject the unity of the Liberals to intolerable strains. Mr. Grimond was conscious, moreover, that it would not be enough for the Liberals to give the government 'general' support: short of a binding agreement, the Liberals would be bound sooner or later to bring the government down, possibly over an objectionable clause in a particular bill, more probably on a censure motion affecting some deeply held matter of conscience. Mr. Wyatt subsequently pointed out to the Labour conference that the government would need Liberal support on every issue: 'when we are wrong as well as when we are right, because anybody can support us when we are right; it is when we are wrong that we need the backing.'

Mr. Grimond's views attracted little attention when they were first published; the discussion at that stage seemed academic. But his article in the *Sun* in early June (see pp. 35–6) was widely publicised, and Mr. Grimond seems to have concluded that the time had come to air the matter publicly. The party had to be educated

[1] 'Mr. Grimond's Terms for Helping Labour', *The Times*, March 8th, 1965.

and its views solicited, and Mr. Grimond wished to make it clear to the Prime Minister that any agreement would have to be worked out well in advance of need; the Liberals refused to be jockeyed into a position of either maintaining Labour in power against their will or being blamed for making stable government impossible, possibly at a time of crisis. Accordingly, Mr. Grimond stated his position at length in an interview with the *Guardian* published on June 24th and again in a party political broadcast. He made it clear that he did not propose to approach Mr. Wilson but was merely setting out his views in very general terms. Before acting, he consulted his parliamentary colleagues, receiving enthusiastic support from some, rather less enthusiastic support from others.[1]

The publication of the interview, with its headline 'Coalition offer to Labour by Mr. Grimond', caused the greatest furore in the Liberal party for many years. The views of Liberals in the country cannot be estimated precisely, but they probably mirrored those of the party in parliament. These ranged from full agreement with Mr. Grimond (David Steel and Jeremy Thorpe), through acquiescence (Russell Johnston, Eric Lubbock, Alasdair Mackenzie and George Mackie), to outright disagreement (Peter Bessell and Emlyn Hooson). Lord Byers, the party Chairman, was also dubious. Some Liberals objected instinctively to the idea of a pact with one of the party's two hereditary enemies; they feared that Liberalism might be swallowed up in the Labour party. Mr. Hooson, Mr. Bessell and others believed that the Liberals could continue to make slow headway in terms of seats, that speculation about a Liberal–Labour alliance would cause marginal Liberal voters to switch to Labour or the Conservatives, and that sooner or later one or other of the two major parties would disintegrate leaving the field clear for the Liberals. The opponents of a pact were clear that the Liberals would have to join the Conservatives in defeating the government as soon as Labour lost its absolute majority. Both they and the supporters of Mr. Grimond doubted

[1] The whole of the subsequent debate was conducted in public, and the press reported the views of almost all of the Liberal M.P.s during the latter half of June. For Mr. Grimond's initiatives, see 'Coalition Offer to Labour by Mr. Grimond', *Guardian*, June 24th, 1965; and 'Liberal Terms for Alliance with Labour', *The Times*, same date. Mr. Grimond revealed on a television programme on the day his interview was published that he had consulted his colleagues. Cf. a useful *Guardian* pamphlet, 'The Liberals and the Government', 1965.

whether a pact could in fact be negotiated; but whereas Mr. Grimond regretted the fact, the others were delighted by it.

Those hostile to the idea made their opinions known at once. On June 27th in a speech to the party executive Mr. Hooson, the M.P. for Montgomery, dismissed the idea that either Labour or the Conservatives were likely to modify their programme to meet Liberal demands:

> 'Over the next few weeks it will become increasingly clear that there is only one course open to the Liberal Party; that is to soldier on in complete independence of any arrangement with Conservative or Labour and to press for policies in which we believe.'[1]

Mr. Bessell, the member for Bodmin, went further, dismissing talk of a Liberal–Labour pact as better suited to cloud cuckoo land than to twentieth-century Britain. The debate, which raged on through the summer and into the autumn, was sometimes presented as a controversy between the party's right and left wings. Some credence was lent to this view by the fact that the three leading proponents of a pact, Mr. Grimond, Mr. Steel and Mr. Thorpe, were all, by any measure, members of the party's radical wing. But Mr. Hooson and Mr. Bessell, especially Mr. Hooson, held left-wing views on some issues, and in general the debate was probably more one of strategy than of ultimate aims. The same seems to have been true in the constituencies, with Liberals in seats where the party was second to the Conservatives most enthusiastic about an arrangement.

The debate never got down to details. Mr. Grimond mentioned several topics — restrictive practices, incentives, regionalism, the reform of government and electoral reform — in his *Guardian* interview, but obviously the Liberals were not going to spell out their position at length in advance of negotiations. Nor did either side alter its position substantially. The only immediate effect of the debate was to draw attention to Liberal differences in the House of Commons — reports of a right-wing revolt appeared in the press in early August — and to confuse and demoralise much of the party in the country. Moreover, despite a brief flurry of speculation following the death of the Speaker, no concrete response was forthcoming from the Prime Minister. Mr. Grimond's enthusiasm for an agreement on policies never diminished, but he

---

[1] 'Sir Alec's Position Again at Issue', *Guardian*, June 28th, 1965.

became increasingly concerned to warn Mr. Wilson that in the absence of an agreement the government could not rely on Liberal support. In a newspaper article in September he repeated that the terms of any agreement would have to be worked out in advance:

> 'I believe we could find common aims behind which a majority could unite and for which there will be real enthusiasm. But their formulation will take time. The parliamentary situation will not give us the time. The throwing of life-belts to a sinking Government is not a job I would welcome.'[1]

The Liberal assembly, coming before it was known that Mr. Bowen would accept the Deputy Chairmanship, generated a good deal of excitement, but in fact it was largely an anti-climax. With only a few weeks remaining before the second Queen's Speech, it was clear that no Liberal–Labour pact was possible, at least in the short term. There had never been any question of a formal coalition or of an electoral arrangement in the constituencies; too little time was now left for the necessary policy discussions. In two speeches to the assembly Mr. Grimond was mainly concerned to preserve the parliamentary party's freedom of manoeuvre in the event of its holding the balance, and also to convey to the party his sense that Liberalism's potential influence had never been greater:

> 'We are now in a position of power. . . . We intend to exploit it — in the national interest, and not for the benefit of either the Tory or Labour parties.'

He hoped that the party would agree to support the Liberal M.P.s in voting according to their consciences. He indicated that this might mean an early election. The only decision of importance taken during the assembly was to refrain from opposing the second reading of the government's Land Commission Bill. Although the parliamentary party objected to the proposed Land Commission, it supported the levy on development charges that went with it.

In the event, the Liberals never did hold the balance of power in the 1964 parliament. How would they have behaved if they

---

[1] Jo Grimond, 'The Liberals and the Government', *Guardian*, September, 20th, 1965. Much the best account of Liberal thinking at this time is to be found in Alan Watkins, 'Mr. Grimond Spells It Out', *Spectator*, September 24th, 1965. The writer stressed how little Mr. Grimond's views changed. He also pointed out that Mr. Grimond was prepared to see the Liberals merging with the Labour party; many of his colleagues were interested only in replacing Labour.

had? Much would have depended on the state of public opinion. If it looked as though an early election would return the Labour party, the government would have had no incentive to approach the Liberals and an early election probably would have been inevitable. If a Conservative victory seemed probable, Mr. Wilson might well have sought an arrangement and some Liberals, at least, would have been anxious to do business with him. Whether a satisfactory agreement could have been reached is another question, especially since two other factors pulled in opposite directions. On the one hand, the Liberals knew that their potential power was at its maximum in a closely divided parliament and that any election would be likely to produce a working majority for one side or the other. On the other hand, an important section in each of the Labour and Liberal parties would almost certainly have objected strenuously to any agreement acceptable to the other. The Liberal M.P.s would have hesitated to precipitate an election if many of their seats seemed in danger, but in the winter of 1965–66 the great majority of them believed their seats to be safe. It is hard to escape the conclusion that, if Labour had lost its majority, the Liberals would have been compelled within months, possibly weeks, to join with the Conservatives in forcing an appeal to the country.

Although the 1965 Liberal assembly took no major decisions, it was the first to meet following a drastic overhaul of the party's central organisation. The Liberals had suffered for many years from a lack of coherence and liaison among the party's numerous components: the Liberal Central Association, the parliamentary groups in the two Houses, the Welsh and Scottish Liberals, the Women's Liberal Federation, the Young Liberals. The structure was exceedingly complex, with few clear lines of authority. The headquarters staff suffered particularly since they never quite knew who they were working for or to whom they were supposed to report. Various reform schemes were suggested, the one finally adopted resembling the new organisation in the Conservative party. Timothy Beaumont, a wealthy clergyman who had been active in Liberal affairs for some years, became Head of the Party Organisation. Like the Conservative Deputy Chairman, he was meant to act as 'chief of staff' and to provide a formal link between the party officials and the politicians. The intention was that Mr. Beaumont, working for only a nominal salary, should develop the office so that someone else could take over in two or three years' time.

There was also created a new post of party Chairman, again on the Conservative model, though the Liberal Chairman had significantly less power. His role, which was entirely extra-constitutional, was to act as chief party co-ordinator. His authority would derive partly from his frequent contacts with the leader, but mainly from any sense that might develop that the party needed to work more closely together. Frank Byers (he became Lord Byers in December 1964) had played this role informally since well before the 1964 election, and he was confirmed as Chairman in April 1965. From then on he held a Chairman's meeting each alternate Monday afternoon. It was attended by the heads of departments at headquarters, a representative from the Central Association, the chief whips in the two Houses, a representative from the candidates' association, and usually two or three others *ad hoc*. It discussed, as one regular attender put it, 'everything under the sun but especially election plans'. At the time of the 1966 election it was still too early to say whether the experiment of having a Chairman was succeeding. Some Liberals despaired of ever eliminating the jealousy among the party's various components and of making them work together.[1]

The progress of organisation in the constituencies was also not as rapid as most Liberals would have liked. Communication between London and the constituencies was improved, with the institution of a regular 'campaign bulletin', but the number of full-time agents — roughly eighty in 1964 — declined, and the activities of too many local associations remained sporadic and inefficient. Edward Wheeler, the chief agent, voiced his concern in a speech at Manchester in April:

'We have been told that some of the Labour Party staff are very concerned about the state of their organisation, and that they want another Wilson report. It was his famous report which referred to their organisation as "penny-farthing".

'I think, and I am going right out on a limb here, that in some cases — not all — Liberal organisation does not even come up to

[1] Other changes during the 1964 parliament included the enlargement and strengthening of the Organising Committee, the reorganisation of headquarters into four divisions (Research, Organisation, Administrative and Finance, and Press and Publicity), the appointment of panel chairmen to speak for the party on various aspects of policy, the creation of a Publicity Review Group, and the moving of Liberal headquarters from Victoria Street to 36 Smith Square.

that. It is more like a certain sedan chair — no wheels at all. It would not be so bad if the front and back chairmen were walking at the same pace but, unfortunately, they are not and the ride sometimes gets very uncomfortable indeed.'[1]

Organisation improved substantially only in some of the designated 'special seats', where the Liberals had a reasonable chance of winning, but even there the party's financial difficulties prevented the giving of aid on the pre-1964 scale. Mr. Thorpe remained chairman of the special seats committee. As a member of the Organising Committee he announced at the September assembly a three-stage plan for recruiting new party members and workers. Like so much else, it had scarcely got under way when the election intervened.

More progress was made in the field of finance where, after the general election, the party's chronic difficulties had grown acute. The local associations remained reasonably self-sufficient, but the headquarters' bank overdraft grew alarmingly; the figure of £20,000, cited by Mr. Beaumont at the assembly, was almost certainly an underestimate. Sir Andrew Murray, the treasurer, came increasingly under attack for, among other things, failing to try to raise money from private industry. He was said to have warned a private session of the assembly that, if the party wanted 'dirty money', it had better look elsewhere for its treasurer. In a contest for the treasurership Sir Andrew was defeated by Mr. Thorpe, who objected particularly to the party's heavy dependence on the annual assembly appeal. By the time of the election the overdraft had been cut to less than £10,000. Even so, the new Liberal headquarters in Smith Square were proving a considerable burden.

But perhaps the Liberals' most serious problem lay in sustaining morale and enthusiasm. The 1964 results had impressed out-side observers but had left most party workers somewhat dispirited after the heady days of Orpington and West Derbyshire. The victory at Roxburgh acted as a tonic, but then came Mr. Grimond's Liberal–Labour initiative and dissension both nationally and in the constituencies. In January 1966 further depression was caused by reports that Mr. Grimond was considering resignation. He had been leader now for nine years, was growing weary of incessant campaigning, and had been discouraged by the confused reception

[1] 'Liberal Organisation Criticised', *Guardian*, April 9th, 1965.

accorded his overtures to Labour. He was growing impatient, too, with some of his followers, who often appeared little interested in exerting real political influence and sometimes seemed wilfully to refuse to understand the party's position in parliament.[1] It was galling that Mr. Bowen, a Liberal, should have restored the government's majority by accepting the Deputy Chairmanship, thereby depriving the Liberals of a rare opportunity for power. During the Christmas recess Mr. Grimond discussed his position with Lord Byers, Mr. Thorpe and Mark Bonham Carter, but in the absence of an obvious successor it was decided that he should stay on at least until after the next election.[2]

The eve of the campaign thus found the Liberals in less good heart than seventeen months before. Three by-election results during the winter of 1965–66 intensified the decline in party morale. At each the Liberal vote dropped sharply; at Erith and Crayford and Hull North it fell by more than half. Nevertheless, the party by now occupied a distinctive place in British politics, with an apparently expanding core of committed voters. The Liberals had suffered a slump before both of the previous elections only to see the opinion polls move in their favour once the campaign began. With six weeks remaining till polling day, there remained a quite reasonable hope that, although the 1966 election might result in a reduced number of Liberal votes, it might also lead to an increased number of Liberals in parliament.

---

[1] Mr. Grimond himself and others close to him were continually frustrated by what they considered to be the naïvete of most Liberals confronted with a sophisticated political situation. For example, the same Liberals who campaigned most ardently for proportional representation were often the most ardent opponents of any arrangement with either of the other parties. Yet proportional representation almost certainly could not be achieved without the aid of another party. And, if it were achieved, the Liberals might frequently find themselves holding the balance of power in the House of Commons, in which case some arrangement with another party would be inescapable. Mr. Grimond accepted the case for proportional representation on its merits, but the political problems bound up with it caused him to campaign less enthusiastically for it than he might have otherwise. It did not, for instance, rate high on his list of priorities for the kind of interim Liberal–Labour arrangement which he envisaged in the 1964 parliament.
[2] Mr. Grimond subsequently issued a statement asserting his determination to stay until after the next election, but stating also that, if either party secured a working majority, he might reconsider his position; he intended in any case to remain member for Orkney and Shetland (*The Times*, January 3rd, 1966).

CHAPTER V

ON THE EVE

By late February it was clear to all three parties that polling day would come towards the end of March. Everyone had expected an election some time in 1966, but there had been so many false alarms that when it finally came it took almost everyone by surprise. The Conservatives, in particular, had persuaded themselves that Mr. Wilson would hold off till the autumn. Quite late in February leading Conservatives still seemed convinced that rumours of an early election were unfounded. Even Labour was caught somewhat off balance; the Prime Minister conveyed his decision to only a limited circle at first, and Transport House could not make overt preparations for fear of alerting the Conservatives. In all three parties election planning began in earnest during the second or third week in February and had been all but completed by the end of the month.

Labour did not want too quiet a campaign. Its one great fear was the apathy of Labour voters, who had to be given some positive reason for going to the polls. The Conservatives therefore were to be attacked continuously: for their failure to do more while in power ('thirteen wasted years'), and for their irresponsibility in opposition. They were also to be portrayed as threatening the welfare state. In a speech at Enfield on February 9th Mr. Crossman went out of his way to attack Mr. Heath's 'Birmingham manifesto' and to accuse the Conservatives of seeking to abandon all-in social security in favour of a return to the means test state. At the same time Labour wished to be perceived as a responsible party of government. It was going to the country only for a fuller mandate to complete its programme. The party was determined not to appear flamboyant and not to raise any new issues which would give hostages to fortune and be open to attack by the Conservatives. In particular, Labour was determined not to find itself in the position of constantly replying to Conservative charges. It was for this reason that the party sought to come first in the series of press conferences and that the Prime

Minister refused to appear on television, except on his own initiative.[1]

Mr. Wilson originally intended to remain aloof from the campaign until the last week, but pressure from the party and consciousness of the risk he was taking finally led him to accept speaking engagements for every evening from March 11th onwards. He nevertheless wished to remain prime ministerial, to be seen governing during the day and to avoid becoming embroiled in partisan exchanges. It was essential to him not to dissipate the fund of good will built up during the Rhodesian crisis. The Prime Minister was also determined, as in 1964, to avoid any anti-climax; if the campaign was to have a climax at all, it was to come at the very end. Mr. Brown volunteered to repeat his arduous speaking tour of 1964, and responsibility for the press conferences went naturally to Mr. Callaghan. It was arranged that Mr. Wilson should appear at the press conferences only in the last week. Liaison was to be effected informally through Mr. Callaghan and Mr. Crossman. Otherwise Transport House was left largely to run itself. The general secretary's meeting — attended each morning by Messrs. Williams, Gunter, Crossman, Callaghan, Pitt and Clark, and by Miss Doreen Stainforth and Tom Driberg from the television committee — would execute the Prime Minister's decisions and deal on a day-to-day basis with the press conferences and television.

Thanks to the publicity group, a campaign theme was already available. Over the Christmas recess, when it was clear that an election was bound to come in 1966, the group prepared two contingency plans. For an autumn election it proposed to mount a publicity campaign during the spring and summer concerned

---

[1] The story of the timing of the press conferences is curious. The Newspaper Society became involved in the negotiations because of the newspapers' irritation at the facilities granted to the television networks in 1964. Some British newspaper men had also been annoyed by the active presence of large numbers of foreign journalists. These problems were largely resolved — each party dealt differently with the foreign journalists — but no agreement was ever reached on the order in which the press conferences should come. In the end Labour and the Conservatives both opted for 11 a.m., the Liberals for 10.30. Furious protests from the journalists failed to budge the Conservatives but the Liberals eventually agreed to move to 11.30 leaving 10.30 free for Labour. Labour also agreed to admit a Liberal observer, while the Liberals received no reply to their similar request to the Conservatives. Afterwards all three parties claimed to have been delighted with the arrangements as they worked out. Labour came first as it wanted; the Conservatives, coming second, were in a position to reply to Labour; the Liberals, coming third, attracted all the journalists who had attended the first two.

mainly with the government's record. A spring election, however, would rule out a sustained campaign; a theme was needed that could be projected in three weeks. Hundreds of slogans were put forward, discussed, and rejected. Finally Peter Davies, a member of the group, suggested 'Labour government works' to which David Kingsley, the chairman, added simply 'You know'. The slogan was intended to sum up the government's achievements, past and future, to discourage marginal Conservatives from voting and to encourage marginal Labour supporters, to win the tacit support of Liberals, and to contrast Labour's effectiveness in government with the Conservatives' ineffectiveness. It was colloquial and, in the words of one of its proponents, 'the kind of phrase that has people "nodding with it"'.

Mr. Brown and Mr. Gunter approved 'You know Labour government works' on Friday, February 18th. The Prime Minister gave his consent during a visit to Transport House the next day. At first Mr. Wilson hesitated — the proposed slogan was vaguely reminiscent of 'In your heart you know he's right', the theme of Barry Goldwater's disastrous campaign in America — but in the course of the day his enthusiasm grew. He also approved of the device of a rondel, designed by Rosemary Oxley, another of the group's members (see photograph following p. 108). Like the slogan, the rondel was meant to be used as much on television as on the hoardings. Some disagreement developed between the group and one or two of the party's other advisers about television. The group wished to use plain backgrounds and strident, arresting music in the party political broadcasts; the others desired something more elaborate. In the end the group largely got its way. It had been agreed from the beginning that the Prime Minister should take the first and last broadcasts. Otherwise the general secretary's meeting was given a fairly free hand.[1]

The manifesto caused more trouble than anything else. Although others had been informally involved at every election, the manifesto in normal circumstances would have been prepared mainly under the aegis of Mr. Brown, the chairman of the NEC's home policy sub-committee, and Mr. Pitt, the head of the Research Department. The need for speed, however, and the Prime Minister's determination to keep matters under his own control complicated the process further. Among those enlisted at various

---

[1] On television see also below pp. 134–36.

stages were Peter Shore, who was both Mr. Wilson's parliamentary private secretary and Mr. Pitt's predecessor; Thomas Balogh, one of Mr. Wilson's economic advisers; Mr. Crossman, who had largely drafted the 1964 manifesto; and Gerald Kaufman, the Prime Minister's political press officer. In January Mr. Shore, Mr. Pitt and Mr. Balogh prepared a document on domestic policy for the joint ministerial-NEC meeting at Chequers on February 6th; copies of the document were numbered and later retrieved. As one of the participants remarked:

> 'It had to be a draft manifesto but in a form that wouldn't be seen as a manifesto if it leaked. It was called "The Next Five Years" but it was really the last sixteen months plus the next year.'

After the Chequers meeting Mr. Brown was charged with producing a full manifesto, and a draft entitled *Time for Decision* was eventually ready for the National Executive meeting on March 7th, though not before lines of authority had got seriously crossed and tempers frayed.[1]

Three areas of policy were particularly controversial. On Mr. Brown's Early Warning Bill, where strong trade union resistance was expected, the manifesto said simply that the government would 'seek such developments in the early warning system as are necessary for the [Prices and Incomes] Board to do its job properly'. On Europe *Time for Decision* stated:

> 'Labour believes that Britain, in consultation with her E.F.T.A. partners, should be ready to enter the European Economic Community, provided essential British and Commonwealth interests are safeguarded.'

It was said afterwards that this passage in the draft was the only one to provoke a formal vote. On the docks, partly as the result of considerable left-wing pressure, Labour promised to 'reorganise and modernise the nation's ports on the basis of a strong National Ports Authority and publicly owned Regional Port Authorities'. The manifesto contained a number of new proposals: the creation

---

[1] The versions of what happened are almost as numerous as the participants. Matthew Coady reported in the *New Statesman* on February 25th, 1966 ('On the Starting Line') that Mr. Brown was affronted at the prominent role being played by Mr. Shore and Mr. Crossman: 'He felt that he was being by-passed and he said so — in that way which he has made so peculiarly his own — proving yet again that there is never a dull moment in that band of brothers the Parliamentary Labour Party.'

of a National Freight Authority, the rationalisation of the aircraft industry 'on the basis of public participation', legislation to curb the powers of the House of Lords. But for the most part *Time for Decision* consisted of a defence of Labour's record and an extension of the plans put forward in *The New Britain* eighteen months before.[1]

The Liberals opted to fight again as they had in 1964. Mr. Grimond, Mr. Thorpe, Lord Byers and Mr. Bonham Carter would speak widely in the country, with Lord Byers taking most of the morning press conferences in London. Three or four party leaders, including Mr. Grimond, were to lunch together on Sundays to discuss campaign tactics. Their main problem was to demonstrate to wavering voters that the Liberals were still relevant. It was decided to assume that the country did not wish to return the Conservatives, to state publicly that Labour would win the election, and to argue that only the Liberals could act as a radical 'brake on socialism'. The phrase was suggested by Ludovic Kennedy, who volunteered to manage the party's television, but it had long been implicit in Liberal thinking. Whereas the Liberals in 1964 had concentrated their fire on the Conservatives, it was clear that now they would have to be equally critical of Labour.

The Liberals were also concerned to field at least three hundred candidates. It had been recognised for some months that the party's total would probably fall below the 365 of 1964 but, coming unexpectedly, the election announcement caught a large number of associations without candidates and caused some to threaten to withdraw. At one time it appeared that the party might fall fifty below its target. Three days of telephoning by Lord Byers and others were needed to retrieve the position. The Liberals seemed best placed in Scotland with 24 candidates adopted and a long-term plan for capturing the North East (Banff, West Aberdeenshire, and North Angus and Mearns) coming to fruition. M.P.s discussed policies for the election at a week-end meeting in Oxfordshire on February 5th–6th, and an outline manifesto was ready by the 22nd. Entitled *For All the People* it proposed site-value taxation, a withdrawal from East of Suez, motorway tolls and a non-discriminatory immigration policy.

[1] The full texts of all three party manifestos can be found in *The Times House of Commons 1966*.

The Conservatives, whose plans had advanced far enough for Mr. Heath to outline them to the 1922 Committee on February 17th, had two main aims. The first, a corollary of their earlier decisions, was to fight a positive campaign and to concentrate on the party's new policies. The Conservatives believed on the basis of their survey research that the target voters disliked perfervid partisanship. They also wished to erase memories of 1961–64 from people's minds and to direct their thinking to the present and future. Thus, although they would attack the Labour government's record, they intended to avoid being drawn into a debate about the 'thirteen wasted years' and the record of Conservative administrations. As one member of the shadow cabinet explained it:

> 'I remember when I became a parliamentary candidate after 1945. Labour then kept the Tories at bay by constantly reminding people of the unemployment of the thirties. We won in 1950–51, not by answering Labour's charges about the thirties, but by providing new answers for the problems of the late forties. That's what we're trying to do now for the late sixties.'

In the short term, a policy-centred campaign seemed to offer the best chance of winning the coming election. In the long term, such a campaign seemed best calculated to leave a lasting impression in the minds of opinion leaders and ordinary voters, and to impress Mr. Heath's stamp on the Conservatives themselves.

The second aim, not stated publicly, was of course to project the new leader. Mr. Heath had so far made little impact on either the public or his own party. If his leadership were not to be challenged in the event of a Conservative defeat, he had to succeed during the next few weeks in making an impression on both. Mr. Heath's shyness and frequently strained appearance were undoubtedly handicaps, but his advisers hoped that he would gain self-confidence as the campaign went on and that his obvious command of policy would carry conviction. After nearly two years of Sir Alec, the object was to persuade the public that in Mr. Heath the Conservatives had a vigorous leader and a man of action. The slogan 'Action not words' — 'Deeds not words' had been the original suggestion — was chosen to reinforce this side of the leader as well as to convey the Conservatives' sense that Labour had consistently shirked action in favour of exhortation. In the minds of some Conservatives the slogan was too 'opposition' in tone but, they claimed, it already rang a bell with a section of the target voters.

The plans for Mr. Heath's campaign, most of which had been prepared months in advance, were meticulous. So that he could meet the party, much of it for the first time, ticket-only meetings were arranged for him in almost every provincial centre. Sundays were omitted and also three days in which he intended to prepare for broadcasts. Only towns which had a live television link to London were chosen. Mr. Heath would organise each speech so that the first few minutes would be suitable for broadcast on the television news; another section would be aimed at the press; a third, the bulk of the speech, would consist of a general review of policy and be aimed at his party audience. Mr. Heath, like Mr. Wilson in 1964, chose to take the press conferences himself. He asked Mr. Macleod, one of the party's most experienced broadcasters, to assume responsibility for television, and Mr. Maudling to stump the country. Arrangements were made for effecting liaison among the three men, but little was planned in the way of positive co-ordination.

In addition to the speeches and press conferences, Mr. Heath sought to keep the central direction of the campaign in his own hands. It was planned that he would confer with Mr. du Cann, Sir Michael Fraser and anyone else who was called in both before and after the morning press conference. Following the practice of 1964, the Chairman's meeting was moved from early morning to lunchtime; it was intended to execute Mr. Heath's decisions and to provide an informal means of exchanging information and discussing tactics. The membership of the meeting remained much the same except that Mr. Whitelaw remained in his constituency and Humphrey Taylor joined the group. The speed of the campaign — Mr. Heath travelled mainly by helicopter and car — was subsequently dwelt on in the press, but most of his advisers maintained that the speed in fact left time for thinking and working. Much of the staff work devolved on to Robert Allan, the former party treasurer who acted as chief of staff, and on to John MacGregor, the head of the leader's private office.

The decision to concentrate on policy implied the selection of a limited number of themes. In the end five were chosen, according to varying criteria: (1) The economy. It was a central problem which could hardly be avoided. The Conservatives were convinced that the economy would run into trouble in the autumn and that therefore some of their longer-term measures, notably reductions in direct taxation, would have to be postponed in favour of steps to meet the crisis. Some in the party believed that emphasising the economy would impress the electorate, which was thought to be apprehensive already; others feared that it might only remind voters of 'the Tory mess'. (2) Europe. This, too, was a central issue, especially if the economy were to be put right. It was an issue with which Mr. Heath had long been identified, which divided Labour, and which appealed to the bulk of the press. Although the target voters did not feel strongly about Europe, those with views tended to favour the Conservative position. (3) Trade union reform. The party believed it had a distinctive policy and that, like the economy and Europe, the issue was of central importance. The target voters favoured reform and, although most of them believed that the problem could best be handled by Labour, they recognised that the Conservatives had a policy, which they tended to view sympathetically. (4) Social services. Again the Conservatives had a distinctive policy on a subject which they believed to be important. They believed that the idea of concentrating welfare benefits on the most needy appealed to the electorate, although in advocating the restoration of prescription charges they knew they were running a risk. (5) Housing. This was selected partly because the Conservatives had developed policies, but also in hopes of neutralising Mr. Crossman's propaganda. It was also an issue which all the opinion polls suggested was regarded as important by the electorate. What remained to be seen was whether the Conservative policies could be made to seem sufficiently distinct from those of Labour.

In choosing their five themes, the Conservatives were swayed by the intrinsic importance of the issues, by their belief that votes could be swayed by them, and by the extent of the policy groups' progress in producing detailed plans. Transport and technology were omitted, for example, partly because the requisite detailed work on them had not been completed. A number of other issues — Rhodesia, defence, immigration, nationalisation, and (at least as a separate issue) the cost of living — were assigned lesser importance in the belief that they could no longer sway votes.[1]

[1] For a voter to be influenced by an issue, he must perceive that it is an issue, he must distinguish between the parties' policies, and he must perceive one of the parties as having a position nearer to his own than that of the others. Even

Education was not included in the five partly because surveys indicated that the target voters, although not much moved by the issue, were largely in favour of comprehensive schools. Crime was similarly excluded; voters held strong (often disturbing) views on the subject but believed that it should be left out of party politics.

Mr. Du Cann's briefing is said to have been "the most scientific appraisal of a political battle " ever given on the eve of an election campaign.

[Garland, *Daily Telegraph*, Mar. 10th, 1966

Having chosen the main themes, the party was determined not to be deflected from them. Only a limited range of policy could be conveyed to the electorate; there was a danger with some of the other issues of dividing the Conservatives.

A draft manifesto, based on *Putting Britain Right Ahead*, had

---

then, the voter may not be influenced if, for example, the issue is of no particular importance to him. The Conservatives appear to have recognised these points and to have based their calculations in part on them. In the case of the cost of living, the discovery was made late in the day. As late as the Hull North by-election the Conservatives seemed determined to make the cost of living a major campaign issue. They were subsequently persuaded that neither party was perceived by any significant number of target voters as being more capable than the other of keeping the cost of living down.

been in existence since December. It concentrated on three themes, housing and trade union reform later being separated out to form the five. With the election believed to be imminent, a series of meetings was held to bring the draft up to date, first among Mr. Heath and his advisers and then with the shadow cabinet. The document that eventually emerged was entitled *Action Not Words* and consisted of an introduction covering the five themes and 131 briefly stated proposals for action. Tax reform played as prominent a part in the manifesto as in *Putting Britain Right Ahead*, but the emphasis on competition was less heavy; the younger Conservatives had found that a number of concepts they used among themselves — competition, enterprise, the pace-makers, the new competitors — were coolly received by the electorate. In addition to repeating many of the points in the earlier document, *Action Not Words* pledged the Conservatives to build 500,000 houses a year, to transfer £100m. from local rates to the Exchequer, to retain the Territorial Army, and to maintain Britain's commitments East of Suez.

At a number of briefings in late February and early March, Mr. Heath and Mr. du Cann explained their election strategy to the party and attempted to buoy up the Conservatives' sinking morale. Mr. du Cann summoned the party's market research findings to his aid. On March 8th he informed the opposition front bench that 'the most scientific appraisal of a political battle' ever made on the eve of an election campaign showed that the party could win the election. Nevertheless, as the Conservatives prepared to do battle, they reminded onlookers of the army of King Harry on the eve of Agincourt. Their spirits were low, the odds against them heavy.

CHAPTER VI

THE CAMPAIGN

THE study of elections by pollsters and academics has steadily eaten into the idea that campaigns change votes. The myth that elections are like trials in which the voter listens like a juryman to the evidence and then makes up his mind was, perhaps, always a myth. But general recognition of the fact that most elections are decided long before a parliament is dissolved is relatively recent. It becomes reasonable to ask why, if campaigns do not decide elections, so much energy is put into them by politicians, and why observers think it worth while to chronicle them in detail.

In part the answer lies in the fact that there is no proof that campaigns are invariably ineffective. Some people plainly do change their minds about how to vote or whether to vote. In one post-war election (1951) the Gallup poll recorded a fairly massive movement of opinion, and in three of the last six contests the margin was narrow enough for a very small movement indeed to have reversed the outcome. Moreover, parties care not only about winning a parliamentary majority but also about getting the maximum number of seats. The politician has every incentive, like the league footballer, to play hard till the final whistle, whatever the score may be.

But campaigns have functions, quite separate from their immediate impact on voters' preferences. They involve the whole community in the process of government. The rituals of electioneering are not empty forms if they contribute to the citizen's sense that he has been consulted, however obliquely, about the men and the policies that will shape his conditions of life. While elections may divide people into opposing camps at the same time they unite them in a common activity. The mere fact that elections take place is one of the major elements contributing to our sense of national community.

But the content of elections is still more important. Many people's ideas about the contemporary problems of government are derived during their exposure, often reluctant, to campaign arguments. What the parties say may not sway many votes, but some of it is remembered and shapes the climate of public opinion in the years that follow. A campaign may contribute more to political education than to electoral choice.

Elections, of course, educate politicians far more than voters. Fears of the next contest, often illusory ones, continually shape their conduct. The campaign itself, with its face to face contacts and its evolving themes, must leave its mark on the participants. The promises made on the hustings trouble those who make them far more than their audiences realise. The obligation to fulfil the undertakings given in a party manifesto is, whether for reasons of ethics or expediency, taken surprisingly seriously.

Elections too, may be fought with almost as much of an eye on internal party politics as on floating voters. Party leaders know that their standing with their supporters turns on the way in which they conduct the battle. The style of defeat — or of victory — may be more important than its size.

An election campaign, then, whether or not it succeeds in swaying votes, merits detailed attention both as a significant historical event and as an important part of the political process. But, it may be objected, the party strategists are not so high minded. Do they have any such long-term goals or general ideas in mind when they plan their campaign? How, in fact, do they see their problem? Most would answer in simple terms 'to win the election' or 'to get as many votes and as many seats as possible'. But most would qualify their desire for immediate success by a longer-term caution '. . . without making too many commitments that could be embarrassing later'. Parties limit their election promises not just for fear of being shown up during the campaign, but also for fear of being shown up years later. In the 1966 campaign, more than any of its predecessors, both sides clearly shaped their campaign with an eye to the future.

Just before 6 p.m. on Monday, February 28th, it was formally announced from 10 Downing Street that parliament would be dissolved on March 10th and that polling would take place on March 31st. It was the first election since universal suffrage to take place during the traditional budget period between the end of February and late in May. But the 31 days' notice — 11 more than the legal minimum — was in accord with precedent: in each of the previous five elections the Prime Minister had announced polling day between 28 and 35 days in advance.

The election was announced with Labour 4 to 1 on favourites with the bookmakers and 9% ahead in the Gallup poll. Since the advent of polls no party had ever dissolved with such a lead.

Year	Party in power	Gallup lead at dissolution	Final outcome party lead (G.B. only)
1945	Conservative	13% Labour	9·5% Labour
1950	Labour	2½% Conservative	3·7% Labour
1951	Labour	8% Conservative	1·5% Labour (Cons. won election)
1955	Conservative	4% Conservative	2·0% Conservative
1959	Conservative	5½% Conservative	4·3% Conservative
1964	Conservative	5% Labour	1·8% Labour
1966	Labour	9% Labour	7·3% Labour

The probability of a comfortable victory for one side was far more widely accepted than ever before, for in pre-war days the absence of polls meant that the most inevitable of landslides were not generally foreseen. This time the size of the lead in the polls, in conjunction with the growing credence given to such evidence, set the election in a novel context; the widespread sense of inevitability affected both the conduct and the reception of the campaign.

The battle started at once — on the air and in parliament. Immediately upon the announcement, each of the three leaders was interviewed in turn by the BBC and ITV. Mr. Heath, seeming strained, accused Mr. Wilson of trying to cash in on the favourable opinion polls before the economic situation got more difficult. Oddly enough, Mr. Heath did not challenge the findings of the polls, although unless he discredited them he could hardly convince people that he was going to win; he refrained, partly perhaps because it would be disingenuous, and partly because if, as he expected, the polls turned his way, he would soon want them to be believed.

Mr. Wilson in his interviews justified calling the election on the ground that 1966 was 'make or break year' and he needed a majority adequate to guarantee the passage of essential legislation — although he added that in the past 500 days they had got through more essential business than the Conservatives had in their 5,000 days of office.

For the first time since 1955 the House of Commons continued to sit after the announcement of polling day, and it was very much in an election mood on March 1st when the Chancellor of the Exchequer produced his economic statement or 'little budget'. He gave a relatively buoyant report on the condition of Britain's gold and dollar reserves and then announced a scheme of tax rebates for lower paid mortgage holders; the £50 million cost would be more than met by a proposed 2½% tax on gambling stakes. He also announced that Britain would convert to decimal currency in February 1971. Mr. Callaghan's speech evoked great Labour enthusiasm, especially his assurance that, although he must 'keep the position open', he did not foresee the need for severe increases in taxation in the spring budget. Despite the inevitable charges of electioneering, his proposals were such that the Conservatives could hardly declare outright opposition to them on the eve of the contest.

The remaining ten days of the parliament's life were largely devoted to clearing routine legislation out of the pipeline; but question time and formal debates on broadcasting and on defence gave M.P.s the opportunity to try out election speeches and the Speaker needed a firm hand to control party turbulence. On March 2nd Mr. Crossman had to face a vote of censure for his handling of a re-development scheme in Islington, and on March 8th Charles Pannell, the Minister of Public Building and Works, was caught out threatening retrospective penalties on those who ignored building restrictions. The government, for its part, made a number of cheerful and conceivably vote-winning announcements in addition to Mr. Callaghan's 'little budget': a Ministry of Social Security was to be created; leasehold enfranchisement was to go ahead; school building was to be increased; and — a sop to a very special pressure group — government documents were probably to be made available to historians after only 30 years.

After the initial salvos there was something of a pause in Smith Square as the parties organised their leaders' campaign tours and the publication of their manifestos. In the constituencies the candidates and agents, severely restricted in their election expenditure, made preparations in private. On March 7th the National Executive of the Labour party met to endorse the manifesto and the final list of candidates; there was no last-minute gathering of candidates.

Mr. du Cann gave his market research briefings not only to the opposition front bench but also to the 1922 Committee on March 3rd and to candidates on March 6th.

One issue enlivened the early days of March. On February 28th, in answer to an interviewer's question, Mr. Heath had challenged Mr. Wilson to confront him on television. When he renewed the challenge in a letter on March 3rd, Mr. Wilson replied suggesting a three-way meeting with Mr. Grimond. Mr. Heath said that he was not interested in a 'tea-party discussion' and pointed out that in 1964 Mr. Wilson had wanted a direct two-way confrontation with Sir Alec Douglas-Home. Mr. Wilson said that his original proposal in 1964 was for a tripartite confrontation and that he was not in any case prepared to forgo the advantage of the last word; he asked why the Conservatives had not raised the matter earlier in the inter-party discussions on election broadcasts and suggested that negotiations might proceed through the 'usual channels'. But the whips failed to meet. On March 17th Mr. Heath again wrote to Mr. Wilson proposing a series of three two-way confrontations so that each of the three party leaders could meet the others face-to-face. In reply Mr. Wilson repeated his position: why hadn't the matter been raised earlier and why didn't Mr. Heath answer Labour's challenges on the cost of his programme?

At this stage two Independent Television companies offered facilities, and one of their proposals was accepted by the Prime Minister and Mr. Grimond, but not by Mr. Heath. On March 21st the BBC sent a proposal for a 65-minute programme that would involve both two- and three-way confrontations. This was more acceptable to Mr. Heath but by inadvertence the BBC letter was delayed in transit. However, the whole proceedings were now being treated by the press as openly farcical. The Prime Minister plainly was not going to agree to a direct confrontation: although he might outpoint Mr. Heath, he had much more to lose. But just as Mr. Wilson, being far ahead of the Conservatives, had no reason to share a platform with Mr. Heath so Mr. Heath, being far ahead of the Liberals, had no reason to share a platform with Mr. Grimond. To appear with Mr. Grimond would be somewhat to diminish his own status; there was also the danger that Mr. Grimond might combine with Mr. Wilson against him. Mr. Wilson might appear disingenuous in moving away from a position he had himself taken in 1964 but Mr. Heath was put in the equally adverse position of offending all Liberally-inclined people by denying Mr. Grimond a look-in. Mr. Wilson was determined not to appear on Mr. Heath's terms, but Mr. Heath had perhaps more to gain, and some of his advisers thought he was mistaken in his entirely personal decision to refuse the three-way confrontation he could have had.

On March 10th, the fourth parliament of Queen Elizabeth II was prorogued. Nineteen government bills died uncompleted, among them the Land Commission Bill and the Building Controls Bill; another casualty was Humphry Berkeley's Sexual Offences Bill. Little time was spent on mourning the passing of this House of Commons: its achievements were exaggerated or belittled in a partisan way and the hope was generally expressed that its successor would have a more decisive majority.

The campaign itself was void of sensational incident.[1] It was not only that no news broke to give a fresh direction to it, but there was also no slip of the tongue or rash pledge comparable to Mr. Gaitskell's taxation pledge in 1959 or Mr. Wilson's Hardy Spicer remarks and Mr. Hogg's 'bonkers' in 1964. When on Turnham Green on March 19th Mr. Hogg exuberantly used an antique walking stick against Labour banners which were waved in his face, he gave the photographers some splendid pictures. When, at Slough on March 22nd, Mr. Wilson was hit painfully in the eye by a stink bomb, he got all the morning headlines and his immediate remark 'with an aim like that, the boy ought to be in the England eleven' did him no harm (although the youthful culprit later denied that the Prime Minister was his target). The nearest thing to a serious slip of the tongue was in fact Mr. Heath's best joke of the campaign. At Cardiff on March 18th he mocked Mr. Wilson's publicised entertainment of television stars, and referred to the giant panda just sent to Moscow for mating. 'In a month's time we will be reading that Mr. Wilson is having tea at No. 10 with a pregnant panda.' Even on a day when the leaders' brush over Europe was providing important copy, most papers found prominent space for Mr. Heath's assumption that Mr.

[1] The election took place in calm weather, meteorologically and internationally. In the whole of March the only extraneous stories that did much to steal the headlines were two air crashes in Japan, the protracted team assault on the North Face of the Eiger, the theft of the football World Cup, the Dutch Royal wedding, the Archbishop of Canterbury's visit to the Pope, a child care scandal, and an American space flight.

Wilson would still be in Downing Street a fortnight after polling day.

The campaign lacked form and to recount its development in narrative form is more or less impossible. There was no evolving argument; no speech stood out as a landmark. In a higgledy-piggledy way, the party leaders put forward their pre-chosen arguments for selective reporting by the press and on television. But there was no clear sequence and the story of the campaign can only be told by looking at the main utterances on the main themes.

The Conservatives received credit for being first in the field with their manifesto and for timing its publication to get full coverage both in the Sunday papers of March 6th and in the dailies on Monday. (The only snag in this was that Mr. Heath's major speech at Southampton on March 5th, launching Conservative trade union policy, was somewhat blanketed.) *Action not Words* had on the whole a favourable reception for both its format and content. It was, for one thing, much shorter than usual (3,000 words compared with 7,000 in 1964 and with 10,000 in the Labour manifesto). *The Times* welcomed the grasping of the trade union nettle but was sceptical about where the money was coming from for the other proposals. The *Daily Mirror* observed:

'Not a bad start for Ted Heath and his Shadows — not a bad start at all. He was quick off the starting line. His election Manifesto is punchy and brief.'

Labour's manifesto, *Time for Decision*, which appeared two days later, was less kindly received, being regarded as a relatively verbose restatement of the 1964 manifesto. As Mr. Wilson said, 'There are no surprises in this document.' The promises of a National Freight Authority and of state participation in the aircraft industry were regarded as the biggest innovations; the diminished attention given to science and technology drew some sardonic comment. *The Times* observed:

'It is noticeable that the boyish enthusiasm about the wonders of science which pervaded the 1964 production has been exchanged for the role of statesmanlike sobriety in the face of harsh reality.'

The Liberals' *For All the People* did not emerge until March 10th. Its reception was more cursory and its distinctive proposals attracted scant attention.[1]

The themes stressed by the parties in their manifestos were of

[1] On manifestos see also above pp. 87–9 and 93–4.

H

course largely echoed by their candidates throughout the country. But there were differences in emphasis. The table opposite shows the issues touched on in election addresses; most of these were prepared hastily in the first weeks of March and too much should not be read into the figures. Yet, especially in the contrasts with 1964, they contain some fascinating indications of what the election was about in the eyes of the contestants. The economy, housing, education and pensions continued to be most mentioned by all parties. But all parties had stopped talking about nuclear policy while the Conservatives had discovered crime and Europe. No member of the Labour cabinet mentioned Europe or trade union reform. Nationalisation and the level of employment had greatly receded in prominence and so had overseas aid, the United Nations and the Commonwealth. Future historians may be struck more by these non-issues than by the subjects that were more prominently discussed. The Conservatives would claim that they did in fact deal with most of the non-issues. However, in the course of the campaign nationalisation and nuclear weapons never hit the headlines. Education only received intermittent discussion, the Conservatives having decided not to put the comprehensive school issue in the forefront of the battle. Housing, though intended as one of the Conservatives' five main themes, never developed as an issue; even though Mr. Crossman and Mr. Boyd-Carpenter dutifully clashed on the housebuilding statistics and Selwyn Lloyd suggested that Labour would force mortgage rates up to 8%, in fact party policies seemed insufficiently differentiated to sway votes.

The campaign argument focused mainly on the state of economy, on joining the Common Market, and on the trade unions: these were the pegs on which the parties attempted to develop the classic theme of every election: 'Look what we have done and will do — and think of the mess the others have made and would make.' The Labour campaign, though a routine and deliberately low-keyed affair, centred on two slogans that exemplified this idea: 'You know Labour government works' and 'Thirteen wasted years'. The strategy was that these should sink in through repetition without being swamped by any new extraneous argument; the Labour party was to deploy its case cautiously and unprovocatively and Conservative challenges should in general be brushed aside since headline-making clashes were to be avoided.

Subjects mentioned in candidates' addresses (1964 percentages in brackets)	Cons. %	Lab. %	Lib. %
General			
Mention of own party leader . .	19 (41)	47 (8)	16 (31)
Attack on Con. misrule up to 1964 .	— (—)	32 (24)	30 (26)
Attack on Lab. misrule 1964–66 . .	56	—	33
Slogan: 'Action not words' . .	47	—	—
'You know Labour government works'	—	69	—
Social Questions			
Education	66 (89)	71 (93)	60 (90)
Health — general policy . . .	25 (55)	42 (58)	14 (30)
Abolition of prescription charges . .	— (—)	40 (50)	— (—)
Reintroduction of prescription charges .	9	—	—
Pensions	70 (90)	86 (86)	56 (87)
Housing — general policy . . .	74 (85)	87 (90)	60 (74)
Rents, Rent Act	29 (10)	79 (86)	33 (87)
Home ownership	40 (33)	74 (86)	46 (57)
Immigration	11 (8)	— (14)	— (3)
Crime	40	—	2
Reintroduction of capital punishment .	6	—	—
The Economy			
Prosperity, cost and standard of living .	69 (89)	69 (65)	67 (51)
State of economy, exports, trade . .	53 (60)	73 (69)	67 (31)
Employment, unemployment . .	8 (63)	16 (30)	5 (10)
Taxation, rates	77 (60)	42 (41)	67 (64)
Nationalisation	14 (63)	13 (27)	33 (30)
Trade unions, industrial relations. .	62 (24)	8 (5)	44 (24)
Monopolies, restrictive practices . .	27 (22)	6 (34)	39 (56)
Transport	29 (49)	21 (49)	26 (33)
Agriculture	20 (34)	11 (30)	26 (41)
Regional development . . .	21 (26)	26 (39)	60 (50)
Co-ownership	— (—)	— (—)	52 (80)
World Affairs			
Nuclear weapons policy . . .	6 (83)	2 (58)	7 (60)
Negotiation of test-ban treaty . .	5 (31)	14 (—)	19 (—)
Other defence	38 (14)	35 (50)	44 (62)
Europe	50 (11)	9 (8)	67 (38)
Aid to developing countries. . .	2 (20)	10 (27)	1 (15)
United Nations	6 (8)	23 (43)	30 (55)
Commonwealth	5 (35)	2 (37)	— (31)
Rhodesia	44	15	21
East of Suez	11	1	31
No mention of foreign affairs . .	15 (7)	48 (22)	1 (52)

This table is based on an analysis of the addresses of Conservative, Labour and Liberal candidates from a random sample of one-fifth of the constituencies in England, Scotland and Wales. A simple mention of any of these topics, however brief, was recorded.

The Conservatives, as intended, focused their campaign around the party's new policies. Labour's failings were castigated but there was no major emphasis either on broken promises or the unfitness of Mr. Wilson for his office, nor was there any major effort to refute 'Thirteen wasted years'. Although Labour observers may not have recognised it, the Conservatives were intent on a positive campaign, a demonstration that they had well-thought-out and new remedies for the nation's problems.

Mr. Heath was necessarily the main vehicle for carrying this message to the electorate. At the daily press conference, in his nightly speeches and on three of the party's five TV broadcasts, he expanded the Conservative package of five related themes. He had, of course, to sell himself as well as his policy and his use of helicopter and plane to get to the provinces every afternoon conveyed a sense of up-to-date hustle. Many of the party faithful in his ticket-only audiences were seeing him as leader for the first time. Mr. Heath was not a phrasemaker; his two most remembered slogans were '9–5–1' which, as discussed below, was double-edged, and 'Vote now — pay later' which he ruined in delivery. As the campaign went on, some observers felt that he grew in oratorical skill — but, except perhaps in his final TV performance, there was no evidence that he made any great breakthrough in communicating to his audiences.

As usual the onset of an election gave new prominence to the Liberal party. The broadcasting authorities felt compelled to give it proportionate coverage. Much of the national press attended its news conferences, more readily following the party's move in 1965 to Smith Square. Since the party's problem has long been to establish its credibility as a serious force, this increase in attention at so critical a moment is disproportionately valuable.

Mr. Grimond from the outset ostentatiously predicted a Labour victory and argued that a large Liberal vote and a large Liberal contingent in parliament could do far more than the Conservatives to restrain Labour excesses. He made effective jabs at the follies of left and — even more — of right, and Lord Byers' press conferences provided one of the fresher running commentaries on the campaign. But it would be hard to point to a great Liberal impact on the battle. Mr. Ludovic Kennedy's assault on Mr. Wilson on March 15th certainly provided one of the most effective of election broadcasts — but it is unfortunately true that the death of Mr. Grimond's son a week before polling day drew headlines to him and his party in a way that no political event could have done.

Apart from this the party attracted most comment for its advice to Liberals, given by Mr. Grimond on March 25th, to write Liberal on their ballot papers in seats where no Liberal was standing if the Conservative and Labour candidates were equally unacceptable by Liberal standards. The idea of spoiling ballot papers was sententiously condemned by Mr. Callaghan, Mr. Heath and a number of newspaper editorials. Lord Byers stressed that it was advocated only as a last resort (a resort in which some, though not many, Liberals took refuge; see p. 263).

When nominations closed on March 21st, it was plain that the battle lines were much as in 1964.[1] Apart from the Speaker's seat and eight Ulster constituencies, the Conservative and Labour parties faced each other everywhere. The Liberals finally fielded 311 candidates, 54 fewer than in 1964, but the Communists increased their challenge from 36 to 57 seats and the Scottish Nationalists from 15 to 23. The usual scattering of Independents attracted little note, apart from the uncle of a murdered girl who stood against the abolitionist Sydney Silverman; and Sir Oswald Mosley who, 48 years after his first entry into parliament, stood in the East End for his Union Movement. A militant motorists' organisation failed in its quest for a woman named Barbara Castle willing to confuse the electors of Blackburn by standing against the Minister of Transport.

In terms of action the pattern of the campaign was clear. The Labour and Conservative leaders spent the morning in London and travelled out each afternoon to make a major speech; Mr. Wilson had at least one meeting every night from March 11th until polling day. Mr. Heath took Sundays and three other nights off, usually when he had broadcasts. The morning press con-

---

[1] A minor complication in the election timetable was discovered in mid-March. St. Patrick's Day, March 17th, is a public holiday in Northern Ireland. Any day which is a public holiday in any part of the United Kingdom is a *dies non* for the purposes of electoral administration. The Home Office therefore belatedly advised returning officers that nominations made on March 17th might be invalid. Although this ruling was challenged by some experts, returning officers throughout the country refused to accept nominations; in a few cases candidates who had gone through the procedure were nominated again on March 18th to make quite sure that their nominations were valid.

ferences were handled by Mr. Heath and Mr. Callaghan, although Mr. Maudling once stood in for Mr. Heath and Mr. Jenkins and Mr. Brown once each for Mr. Callaghan; Mr. Wilson took over the Labour conference for the final three days. The whistle-stop tours of the country which used to be required of the leaders were undertaken by Mr. Maudling and Mr. Brown and attracted

Dates of Mr. Wilson's and Mr. Heath's main campaign speeches.

oddly little national publicity. Occasional excerpts appeared on the television news, but Mr. Maudling issued few handouts and Mr. Brown's words were only spasmodically reported. Neither contributed any memorable phrase — still less any memorable gaffe — to the national campaign. The main function of these ritual journeyings was plainly to enhearten the local faithful and to attract local publicity.

Newspapers and television editors in search of colour paid a lot of attention to hecklers. Mr. Heath usually had decorous, ticket-only meetings, though even there hecklers made an appearance; sometimes, it seems, they were planted by his own side as they discovered that he performed better under fire. Mr. Heath also spoke at less formal meetings out of doors. Mr. Wilson made a point of addressing open meetings and night after night the television audience saw demonstrations of his virtuoso skill in dealing with interrupters. Only once or twice in the middle of the campaign did his touch with hecklers falter. He did not crush the man at Dunstable who cried 'That was last night's speech'; and a persistent youth at Reading, who had wrecked a central passage in the discourse, scored again by thanking the Prime Minister for his courtesy in dealing with him. The main impact of the heckling was indeed to focus news coverage on Mr. Wilson's skilful but partisan retorts at the expense of the more prime ministerial parts of his speeches. But the Prime Minister's easy assurance in dealing with a riotous audience (bent on revenge for the celebrated shouting down of Sir Alec in 1964) at the Rag Market in Birmingham attracted a good deal of favourable comment.

Mr. Brown encountered some rough treatment on his tour and, although his voice gave way, he throve on the heckling. He complained at what he saw as 'organised' interruption by schoolboys, and he did bring into the open the extent to which rowdiness was encouraged by the presence of TV cameras. He protested at the planting of interrupters by a producer doing a film on heckling (for American consumption) — but there were many cases of spontaneous exhibitionism fostered by the swivelling of cameras and spotlights.

The press conferences, which had been accidently established as a feature of electioneering in 1959, produced no sensations, but they remained a focal point of the campaign. At each press conference the principal spokesman made an opening statement lasting five minutes or so and then responded to twenty minutes of questions. All those who participated expressed some frustration both at the quality of the interrogation and still more at the patchy and unpredictable coverage of what was said. It is arguable that the press conferences, although providing useful copy for the midday news bulletins and the evening papers, had a distorting impact. The assembly of the cream of the political writers every day in the same place produced something of an in-group atmosphere; the nuances of campaigning in Smith Square were far removed from the realities of everyday electioneering in the constituencies.

Certainly Smith Square was more influenced than other places by the opinion polls and by their failure, discussed on p. 173, to show any developing trend; the reiterated report of Labour's handsome lead continued to damp down the campaign. However, Conservative scepticism grew, for neither canvass returns nor meetings gave any indication of the landslide the polls presaged. Even Labour leaders and officials saw little to indicate the 5% or 6% swing that NOP and Gallup were showing. Moreover, local elections in the West Midlands and Ealing on March 17th were not very good for Labour. But the polls indisputably affected the ever more publicised betting odds. The odds against the Conservatives moved from 3 to 1 at the outset to 20 to 1 a few days before the poll, and from 100 to 1 against a Labour majority of over 150 to a mere 2 to 1.[1]

The campaign began in earnest with the appearance of the three leaders in the BBC 'Election Forum' (see p. 132). But for the first week of the campaign proper the Cowley 'noose trial' filled the headlines. On March 9th a worker at the Q block in the British Motor Corporation factory in Oxford described how on March 4th he and seven others were 'tried' before several hundred colleagues and fined £3 apiece for failing to take part in an unofficial strike; a noose had been hanging over one of the rafters in the canteen where the trial had taken place. The Minister of Labour, Mr. Gunter, immediately asked for a report on the affair, and the Transport and General Workers' and Amalgamated Engineering Unions set up enquiries. For several days the story was kept alive by new revelations, and denials, of intimidation of the eight men; one was found wandering in a daze and others went sick from nervous exhaustion. Shop stewards said that there had been no more than skylarking and that the noose had been in the canteen for months. A dossier of an alleged secret 'M6 Cabinet' that controlled the 600 workers in Q block was produced and a Cowley employee wrote to the Liberal party protesting at the absurdity of his being paid £30 a week for 30 hours of unskilled work.

On March 13th a second workers' 'kangaroo' court at another BMC factory, at Theale near Reading, came into the news:

---

[1] Of the two largest London bookmakers Ladbroke's handled over £1,622,000 of bets on the election and William Hill £496,500.

[*Keystone*

Mr. Brown and the Declaration of Intent

[*Daily Express*

Mr. Gordon Walker loses
Leyton

[*Associated Press*

Mr. Steel wins Roxburgh

[*United Press International*

Sir Alec Resigns

[*Keystone*

Mr. Wilson and Mr. Smith,
October 8th, 1965

[*Central Press*

Conservative Conference 1965. Macleod, Thorneycroft,
Maudling, Douglas-Home, Fraser, du Cann, Heath

LABOUR SPOKESMEN

[Keystone

Mr. Williams, Mr. Wilson and Mr. Gunter
outside Transport House

[Press Association

Mr. Wilson at Hammersmith

[East Anglian Daily Times

Mr. Callaghan at Ipswich

[Central Press

Mr. Wilson, Mr. Brown, Mr. Callaghan present
Labour Manifesto

[Central Press

Mr. Brown in North Kensington

[United Press International

Mr. Wilson in Huyton

[*Sports & General*

Conservative Press Conference

[*Sports & General*

Mr. Heath goes on tour by
helicopter

[*Keystone*

Mr. Hogg lashes out

[*Keystone*

Mr. Maudling in the country

[*Tom Smith, The Observer*

Mr. Macleod on TV

[*Associated Press*

Mr. Heath at Lewisham

[*Central Press*

Heckling Mr. Heath

[*Associated Pres*

Mr. Grimond

[*Universal Pictorial*

Lord Byers at Liberal Press
Conference

[*Daily Expre*

Smethwick: Mr. Griffiths defeated by Mr. Faulc

[*Hornchurch Upminster Echo*

Mr. Macleod at Hornchurch

[*Press Associat*

Mr. and Mrs. Wilson leave Transpe
House on election night

fifteen workers had been fined the previous November for failing to support a dispute. On March 15th the shop stewards repaid the fines on instructions from higher authority in their unions, although in this case the dispute had been official and the fines had been levied after a more formal procedure (but in defiance of the AEU executive). Other similar stories were heard from Lincoln, Newcastle and Birmingham.

These episodes, reported with much highly coloured detail, inevitably provided the text for a lot of political speeches, especially as both Oxford and Reading were highly marginal seats. Mr. Hogg asked the Attorney General what action he would take and was rebuked for writing an article on the subject in the *Sunday Express* of March 13th when the matter was *sub judice*. Sir Keith Joseph and Mr. Heath argued that Conservative trade union proposals 'would end intimidation'. Mr. Heath, on March 13th, said that the episodes were only the tip of the iceberg 'and other things are now beginning to emerge'. Labour spokesmen, while dissociating themselves from the Cowley and Theale affairs, attacked managements for letting such conditions arise and the Conservatives for their political exploitation of industrial trouble. Mr. Paget amused himself by asking the Attorney General for an enquiry into other private courts such as those held by the Stewards of the Jockey Club or the Committee of the Stock Exchange.

Mr. Wilson kept silent about the matter until March 17th, when he condemned what had happened at the factories but pointed out that, while the Minister of Labour and the Attorney General had taken immediate action, the Conservatives had not been prepared to leave the matter to the machinery of the law but 'with open delight' had used it for electioneering purposes. At the same time he attacked Conservative trade union policies; they ignored the fact that industrial relations were human relations and sought to have everything settled by lawyers and industrial courts. Why if Mr. Heath wanted to reform the unions had he refused to set up a Royal Commission in 1960 when he was Minister of Labour?

By the end of the week the press had got tired of the issue and gave little publicity to the charges that the victims of nervous breakdowns had been harried by reporters far more than by their workmates. Mr. Urwin, who conducted the TGWU enquiry, said on March 16th that the press had blown up the affair out of all proportion for political purposes. There had been some unconstitutional action, but something much less sinister than an Oxford debagging ceremony had been turned into a trial with the aid of cheque book journalism. Mr. Maudling commented, 'It is the old story. First you blame the wicked Tories and then the newspapers. . . . It is a good thing that the press are so alert to examples of petty tyranny in this country.'

The Conservatives had naturally seized on the 'noose trial' as a peg on which to hang their radically new trade union policy. Later they came to have some doubts about whether luck had really favoured them, for they would have liked to talk about unions later in the campaign and in a different vein; as it was, the focus of the story was on civil liberties rather than on economic efficiency. The press became bored with union matters and it was hard to get much printed about the positive side of Conservative trade union policy, although the party still thought it topical enough to make it the theme of their second TV broadcast on March 17th.

The Labour party had been worried at first when the story seemed to mushroom out of control. Later they came to think that its consequences were less unfavourable; it had consolidated some trade union support and the hostile publicity died away quicker than expected. Indeed some people in Transport House thought that, in specially scheduling a TV press conference by Mr. Gunter on March 16th, they had made a mistake, keeping the issue alive longer than necessary, and that Mr. Wilson's speech on March 17th had compounded the error. Nevertheless one leading figure commented: 'It's good tactics to let a cavalry charge over-reach itself before counterattacking.'

In all his early speeches and press conferences, Mr. Heath had spoken of joining Europe and on Tuesday, March 15th, he welcomed the meeting of Western European Union ministers in London by repeating the Conservatives' firm commitment to enter the Common Market. Mr. Brown on tour at Stowmarket responded immediately: 'Going into the Common Market is not an issue between us. What is an issue is whether one does it rationally or in a headlong manner.'

The matter really came to life the next day when Michael Stewart, the Foreign Secretary, announced at the end of the meeting of Western European Union that the French now favoured British entry into Europe (it later emerged that the French delegate had in fact exceeded his brief and that no real change of attitude had taken place). The Foreign Secretary's statement led Mr. Heath immediately to challenge the government to say what it would do now. Speaking at Norwich he pointed out that without a change in agricultural policy British entry was impossible; Conservatives were ready to make the change but Labour was not. At his press conference the next morning, March 17th, Mr. Callaghan emphasised Britain's willingness to join but stressed the need to negotiate; Mr. Peart (who was present to speak on the new farm price review) took the opportunity to reindorse British agricultural policy and to attack the increase in food prices which, he said, the Conservative plans to meet European agricultural policies would involve. Mr. Heath pointed to Labour's smugness and inconsistency about the new situation: until they were ready to announce their acceptance of the Treaty of Rome there could be no entry. Mr. Callaghan accused Mr. Heath of rushing his fences as he had done in the 1962 negotiations and of being willing to write a blank cheque without regard to the interest of farmer or housewife, of the Commonwealth or EFTA. But detailed Labour comment was curtailed by the announcement that Mr. Wilson would deal with the matter at length in his speech the following day, although Mr. Jay, reputed to be one of the most anti-European members of the cabinet, said at Oxford that to enter the Common Market unconditionally, as Mr. Heath proposed, would 'cripple our chances of economic recovery'.

At his morning press conference on Friday, March 18th, Mr. Heath suggested that Mr. Wilson should stop Mr. Peart and Mr. Jay from wandering around the country proving that it was impossible for Britain to enter the Common Market — but it had 'always been known that Mr. Wilson has been anti-European'. He argued that the Conservative agricultural proposals would increase the weekly family budget by only 6s. 3d. a week, not the £1 a week that Labour had suggested. While Mr. Heath said that a Conservative government would send its Foreign Secretary at once to the Six to set up a timetable for negotiations, Mr. Callaghan warned against thinking that the French had made a new initiative: 'We must beware of falling over ourselves at the slightest lifting of the skirt of the Common Market.'

Although rumour had suggested that Mr. Wilson was going to make some dramatic announcement in his speech at Bristol, in fact he said nothing new but he said it dramatically. 'Given a fair wind we will negotiate our way into the Common Market, head held high, not crawl in.' He mocked Mr. Heath for 'rolling on his back like a spaniel at any kind gesture from the French'.

Mr. Heath was provoked by this to a premeditated but well-timed explosion to reporters at Cardiff airport. He described parts of Mr. Wilson's speech as 'poisonous' and 'filthy' and 'too sordid for words'. He observed that Mr. Wilson seemed to be going out

"Ha, Mr. Heath! You're just De Gaulle's spaniel!"
[*Daily Express*, Mar. 21st, 1966

of his mind and that his remarks amounted to a flat refusal to go into the Common Market.

Mr. Wilson's speech got a bad press, but Conservative research suggested that his cautious approach had gone down well with the electorate. Moreover, he had set the tone for Labour, which now had a line on which to meet the Conservative attacks. Mr. Jenkins, the most European of ministers, taking the next day's press conference, wholeheartedly endorsed Mr. Wilson's line and accused Mr. Heath of 'still living in his Brussels world of 1962'. However, Mrs. Castle could not be restrained from an attack on the free movement of labour and capital that a merger with the Six would involve. Speaking at Hartlepool that day she said: 'I don't know how many of you are prepared to uproot yourselves and get jobs in France and Germany. I thought you wanted them in the North East.'

Mr. Maudling, taking the morning press conference for Mr. Heath, attacked the Prime Minister for facing both ways at once: 'You cannot have the Common Market in its present form and reject the idea of agricultural levies.' But Mr. Heath, apart from a reference to cabinet divisions, did not dwell on Europe in his speech at Nottingham that evening and thereafter the issue receded in prominence. There were Labour-inspired rumours that a Minister for European Affairs would be appointed after the election, and speculation tipped Mr. Gordon Walker for the post. Pointing out that Mr. Gordon Walker had been particularly hostile to the Brussels negotiations, Mr. Heath saw 'no point in Mr. Wilson having a Minister for European Affairs when he is laying down conditions that make it impossible to start negotiations'.

The Conservatives did not drop the European issue but they made little attempt to thrust it back into the headlines; they did not even exploit seriously one of the most intriguing side issues, the argument between Mr. Wilson and Mr. Macmillan. At Bristol Mr. Wilson had said that the French refusal to allow Britain into the Market in 1963 was due to Conservative duplicity. 'In meetings with de Gaulle at Rambouillet [in December 1962] they failed to deal straight with him. They failed to tell him that, following the breakdown of the disastrous Tory Skybolt policy, they were about to go to the United States for Polaris submarines. It was the Nassau agreement that slammed the door of the Common Market in Britain's face.' The next day Mr. Macmillan issued a statement flatly denying the accusation, insisting that he was at no time guilty of failing to 'deal straight' with the French President.

The Conservatives, although they had been consulted about it in advance, made little play with Mr. Macmillan's counterblast. It was only on March 28th that Mr. Wilson was drawn out on the subject at his first press conference: he had checked the Rambouillet record and found only a very small reference to doubts about Skybolt; he suggested that perhaps Mr. Macmillan had communicated his plans without the use of words. Mr. Wilson's remarks provoked Mr. Macmillan again:

'It is a matter of regret that the elucidation had to be forced out of him by the press. What is even more regrettable is Mr. Wilson's fall from the level of standards normally expected from a Prime Minister. . . . The record shows that I gave [President de Gaulle] all the facts in my possession.'

Mr. Heath also issued a statement: President de Gaulle had confirmed only four months earlier that Mr. Macmillan had given him the relevant facts at Rambouillet.

On March 28th Mr. Wilson also referred to his plans to appoint a Minister for Europe. The final flurries on the subject came the following day when the National Farmers' Union issued a statement critical of European agricultural policy and Mr. Heath replied defensively, 'The intention of the Labour party has been to mislead and it seems as if they have succeeded in this case'; the Conservatives would not enter the Market unconditionally, but he was sure that the great majority of British farmers had much to gain by joining.

There was some debate about whether the Conservatives had handled the Common Market issue correctly. Some felt that there were few votes in it and that talking of it actively annoyed some loyal supporters. Others felt that it should have been run harder and longer. The press was, apart from the *Express*, strongly pro-European and would have been ready to carry on with the story after March 19th; the *Mirror–Sun* group in particular might be wooed by the issue towards, at the least, electoral neutrality; moreover, since it was a matter on which the cabinet was known to be divided, the longer the story ran the more the speeches of ministers would reveal their split. It is hard to disentangle where the advantage lay. One leading Conservative remarked: 'After Wilson's speech, we couldn't go on (even if we should have, which I doubt) because we would really have seemed like spaniels, cringing to get in regardless.' However, although the mass public was perhaps unmoved, the stress on Europe may have helped in winning an influential minority of Liberals and middle-of-the-road people. Another Conservative remarked: 'In an election it's always a mistake not to go on riding a theme that the press likes and is covering sympathetically.'

The Unilateral Declaration of Independence by Rhodesia had marked a turning point in British politics in the autumn of 1965, but it did not loom very large in the election. Selwyn Lloyd had brought back from his visit to Salisbury in February a unifying theme for the Conservatives — 'talks now' — and this was dutifully echoed in leaflets and speeches. Sir Alec Douglas-Home and Selwyn Lloyd both attacked Mr. Wilson's handling of the situation and Mr. Heath said on March 14th that the Rhodesian issue could not be swept under the carpet; although Mr. Wilson had completely misjudged the effectiveness of sanctions, they should be continued. The Liberals were implacable: 'We don't believe it is possible or right . . . to talk with the Smith regime until they have come back to constitutional government,' said Lord Byers on March 14th.

Mr. Wilson only turned to the subject on March 20th. He argued that there could be no compromise on accepting an illegal revolt; the Smith regime had been holding on in the hope of a Conservative victory; the Conservatives, to pacify their extremists, had abandoned their support of a national policy on Rhodesia; their 'unparalleled irresponsibility' had done great harm — it had aided and abetted rebels. Mr. Heath replied bitterly at his press conference on March 21st that Mr. Wilson's speech had broken any remaining national unity: he had smeared Mr. Lloyd's mission as purely political; he had not got a policy and all he could do was to slander his opponents. 'We do not need lessons in loyalty from Mr. Wilson.'

On March 28th Mr. Heath was led to reiterate his belief in talks, without any prior commitment on either side, by a letter to *The Times* from the leaders of the white opposition in Rhodesia which criticised the Conservative approach. He denied that the Conservatives would give ground on points on which Labour would not budge: all that they wanted was talks. In the 1950s Labour had always argued for talks in any difficult situation but now they would not follow such a course in Rhodesia, their own direct commitment. Mr. Wilson used *The Times* letter to reassure people who were worried lest the government planned to use force:

> 'We keep on getting this. I have just denied it afresh. We have no intention of using force in Rhodesia.'

There was in fact no evidence in the constituency reports or the opinion polls that Rhodesia was a vote-changing issue. Those who were most passionately on Mr. Smith's side were certainly not going to vote Labour. The middle mass of the electorate seems to have had little interest in the issue but, on the whole, some faith in Mr. Wilson's handling of it.

The social services provided one of the Conservatives' chosen themes. But the publicised argument seldom centred on them, although on March 22nd and 23rd they were the subject of one of the sharpest direct clashes of the campaign. The Labour party devoted their third television programme to deploying their own promises on the subject and to demolishing the Conservative approach; it was the 'knocking copy' that made an impact. The suggestion by the Ministers of Pensions and of Health that the Conservatives would apply the means test to pensions and to prescriptions was tellingly made. Mr. Robinson suggested that the Conservatives would put prescription charges up to 5s. The Conservatives, who had scrapped a TV programme on defence and foreign affairs with Mr. Powell and Sir Alec Douglas-Home, used the time to refute what they regarded as a monstrous slur; they put up Mr. Macleod and Mr. Heath to make a decisive reply. But, as many Conservative candidates testified, the part of the Conservatives' new social policy that was most understood was the reintroduction of prescription charges, a move which, as Conservative market research suggested, even middle-class people disliked. The sophisticated Conservative case — that prescription charges would only be paid by those who could afford them and that they would make possible accelerated hospital building — did not get across to many people.

One issue in the early skirmishing concerned the cost of the proposals in the Conservative manifesto. The Conservatives put it at £200–£250m. Mr. Callaghan put it at £850m. On March 13th the Conservatives made play with an error in a BBC advance press transcript of Mr. Wilson's first television broadcast which said '£1,000 million' rather than 'hundreds of millions'. On March 15th Mr. Callaghan challenged Mr. Heath in a set of questions to say what he would do to raise the money. If public expenditure was too high, why did he propose to spend an extra £800 million? Mr. Callaghan invited Mr. Macleod to come to the Treasury and have his programme costed in detail and on March 17th in an Independent Television encounter Mr. Callaghan, by general consent, came off best in a rather barren argument on whether the Conservative programme would cost £350 million or £800 million.

On March 16th, after an intervention by Mr. Wilson, the Minister of Agriculture announced that the terms of the annual farm price review had been agreed. Subsidies went up £23 million and the National Farmers' Union described the settlement as 'just, but only just'. For the Conservatives Mr. Godber commented:

'the review is substantially less harsh than last year. The farmers have had a better deal than they would have had if it had not been election time.'

On March 21st Mr. Callaghan announced the existence of a Treasury committee to review methods of controlling public expenditure half an hour before Mr. Heath unveiled a plan by Ernest Marples, the former Minister of Transport, to save £400 million by the cost-effectiveness budgetary approach developed in America. On television on March 24th Mr. Marples staked his reputation on the success of a cost-effectiveness department in reducing government expenditure drastically. At Slough on March 22nd Mr. Wilson mocked such plans saying that Labour was already fulfilling them. In real terms the increase in government estimates for 1966–67 was the smallest for very many years — only 1·8%.

The immigration issue which played so significant a part in 1964 was very much muted. Correspondents dutifully wrote up the contests in Southall and Eton and Slough and, above all, Smethwick. But the subject only hit the headlines twice. Early in the campaign Donald Finney, who had played a part in Mr. Gordon Walker's defeat in 1964, offered his support to the Conservative candidate in West Bromwich, who was thought to have a chance of defeating Maurice Foley, the minister concerned with immigrants. After some delay and some representations from above, Mr. Finney's help was rejected. Mr. Heath was more explicit on such matters than Sir Alec had been in 1964. He said firmly, 'I do not approve of any racialist organisation in this country and I would not accept help from anybody like that.' If a Conservative accepted racialist help, Mr. Heath would 'make the position plain'. On March 25th, Indian, Pakistani and West Indian immigrant leaders in Birmingham advised their communities to abstain from voting in the marginal seats on the ground that Labour had joined the Conservatives in 'compromising with racialism'. Their advice was widely reported and widely deplored: there is no evidence that it made much difference.

Defence, too, loomed less large in the campaign than had been expected. Mr. Mayhew had, after all, resigned in protest against the defence white paper only a month before, while, owing to French policy, the future of NATO was in confusion. But little was made of the cancelled aircraft carrier. On March 19th, Mr.

I

Wilson in a major speech at Plymouth (where in 1964 he had advocated an expansion of conventional forces) stressed that Labour was spending more on naval construction than its predecessor while using cost-effectiveness techniques to keep down total defence expenditure. In another speech at Preston on March 25th he militantly defended the cancellation of the TSR-2 aircraft. Mr. Heath reiterated the counter-challenges about broken faith and running down our defences in his Plymouth and Chatham speeches.

On March 15th Mr. Heath expressed some sympathy with General de Gaulle's attitude to NATO and Mr. Powell criticised British subservience to America. But these issues too attracted little campaign argument. Mr. Healey, although Secretary of State for Defence, went almost unreported in the national press apart from his sharp reaction towards the end of the campaign to Mr. Powell's suggestion that there were contingency plans for sending British troops to Vietnam. Accusing Mr. Powell of extreme anti-Americanism, he denied flatly that there was any truth in his allegation.

It was generally agreed by the leader writers and the politicians that the key problem facing the nation was the state of the economy, and that it should be the key issue of the election. Both in public estimation and in the space devoted to it by politicians it did loom largest — though whether it swayed many votes is open to question.

'The economic situation' is a far-ranging term. It could refer to the cost of living, or to the level of employment, or to the rate of growth. All these are, of course, interrelated, but each has a different impact on the voter and each can be separately presented. During the election, the arguments were put forward in a diffuse way. Except on the cost of Conservative proposals, it could hardly be said that the arguments of the two sides met head on.

Indeed it was notable that the economic indicators — the ordinary share index and the international price of the pound — slipped only a little during the election. The £ in New York stood at $2·79⅞ on February 28th and at $2·79‑5/16 on March 31st. The *Financial Times* ordinary share index stood at 347·7 on February 28th and 344·9 on March 31st. The stability may have been helped more by the regular trade and price figures published during March than by any political self-restraint. London and overseas financial centres, as their behaviour after the election showed, had fully 'discounted' a Labour victory. On March 12th (two or three days earlier than usual) the February trade figures were published showing a record £431m. of exports and a gap of only £5m. between imports and exports. Plainly such statistics were not going to do the Labour campaign any harm.

On March 10th *The Times* produced a sententious leading article on 'Why the £ is weak' with 27 points on the lines of

'. . . because Britain is living beyond her means;
because when even the mildest deflation begins to work, it is discontinued because extra leisure is put before extra effort by too many people in all classes;
because no government has been prepared to bring [the trade unions] under reasonable control;
because the world knows that, however slow the descent, the abyss is at the end of the road.'

The leading article was reprinted in full in other national newspapers and aroused wide comment and correspondence. Its publication coincided with Mr. Heath's first press conference at which he said that, since the election would be primarily fought on the state of the economy, sterling as a factor in it was bound to be part of the public debate. Mr. Wilson replied in the BBC 'Forum' broadcast that night

'I hope no one is going to bring sterling into this election. There are signs of it, but sterling should be above politics.'

Although Mr. Heath stressed that he was against all talk of devaluation, he argued that the strength of sterling flowed out of the general economic situation which must be discussed in any election. Mr. Callaghan in his first press conference on March 11th remarked:

'I am glad that Mr. Heath has denied that he had any intention of knocking the pound in his television broadcast ["Forum" March 9th]. He has said that he wholeheartedly supports sterling and will go on doing so. However desperate he may feel about the prospects of his party, I hope that from now on he will dry up on this subject.'

The Times political correspondent remarked on the thin soil in which the first myth of the campaign had established itself: no one, and certainly not Mr. Heath, had in fact uttered a word that could damage sterling.

In a television interview that evening Mr. Heath replied:

'I don't think we should dry up. I think that the economic affairs of this country should be discussed openly.'

And Mr. Callaghan repeated:

'I am the guardian of sterling for the time being. I can only give it as my considered view on a non-party basis that statements which are inimical to the strength of sterling are not warranted and damage the position of the currency.'

The issue of sterling did raise its head again briefly on March 15th, when Mr. Grimond observed in Kirkwall that a case could

"Marvellous! My popularity among the passengers isn't sinking!"

[*Daily Express*, Mar. 11th, 1966

be made out for devaluing the pound, and two days later when Mr. Layton (a Liberal party spokesman on economic affairs) argued on television that devalution should be discussed openly. When the question was raised at the Liberal press conference on March 18th Lord Byers effected a speedy retreat, pointing out that Mr. Grimond had never envisaged an immediate forced devaluation. The patriotic element in Mr. Callaghan's protests seemed to show that sterling was still an ungentlemanly subject — perhaps the last untouchable left from the Imperial tradition.

On March 10th Mr. Heath launched one of the most remarked on slogans of an election that notably lacked memorable phrases. At his first press conference he summed up the trouble with Britain's economic position as '9–5–1', referring to the 1965 figures of a 9% increase in wages, a 5% increase in prices, and a 1% increase in production. He made '9–5–1' the theme of his major speech at Bexley on March 12th — complaining that the government was concealing the truth about our economic ills. The propaganda effect was double-edged, as the Conservatives fully realised in their advance discussions on whether to use it. The production index was, after all, only seen as an abstract statistic while for wages to rise twice as fast as prices was surely to the advantage of the party in power. It was commented how few people would realise the economic dangers implicit in '9–5–1' compared to those who would appreciate the government's success in holding down prices in a year of rising wages.

The Labour answer to '9–5–1' lay in pointing out that the wage increases of 1965 contained a large once-for-all element with the introduction of the 40-hour week; they also stressed the fact that the price increases had come largely in their first months in office before their policies had begun to bite. In the ten months since the Prices and Incomes Board was set up in April 1965, prices had risen only 4d. in the £, compared to a 10d. rise in Labour's first six months and an 8d. rise in the last ten months of Conservative rule. The February retail price index, announced on March 23rd, rose by only 0·1% and Mr. Callaghan contrasted the headlines given to Mr. Heath's charges of prices being out of control and the actual announcement of the latest figures. Mr. Brown attacked Mr. Heath's 1% figure for the rise in productivity: the true figure was 2½%:

> 'If ever a wrong figure is quoted, you can be sure that Mr. Heath will get hold of it and hang on to it. . . . How Mr. Heath has the nerve to say that we are hiding figures I find it difficult to understand. . . . He sat on all the facts and figures month after month before the last election.'

Early in the election Mr. Cousins was made the target of Conservative attack. On March 8th, the Transport and General Workers had refused to co-operate with the Prices and Incomes Board on an enquiry into busmen's wages. Did Mr. Cousins, as a cabinet minister, approve of his union's stand? Did he support the incomes policy? And if not, where was collective responsibility? On March 13th he replied slightly equivocally: he and his union supported planned incomes growth but it had to be fair. Mr. Brown kept reminding everyone that 'an incomes policy to be successful must cover profits and dividends'.

In fact the incomes policy, despite its importance in the politics of the preceding year, never came to the centre of electoral controversy. The Conservatives, though they did not believe in the policy, at least in its present form, were reluctant to attack something that was plainly popular. They were also reluctant to propound the leading alternative to an incomes policy — throwing men out of work. On March 12th in Belper Mr. George Brown challenged the Conservatives to say if they believed in a rise in unemployment as a solution to the overheating of the economy. The challenge was not answered, nor was there a follow-up when on March 27th Mr. Heath said:

> 'The first thing would be to get some of the steam out of the economy and to get the number of vacancies more in line with the number of unemployed. It would not be a bad thing if the number of vacancies in industry were brought down below the number of unemployed.'

At Glasgow on March 23rd Mr. Heath, likening the situation to 1938, argued that the nation was facing the greatest threat short of war — the threat of national bankruptcy. Mr. Callaghan retorted the next day that if Britain repaid all her short-term loans the reserves would still be higher than when Labour took over from the Conservatives.

> 'A period of silence on Mr. Heath's part, or at least an admission of guilt would be more worthwhile than tired sermons about the bankruptcy of Britain. It is all very well invoking the situation in 1939, but Mr. Heath is no Winston Churchill; he is a Neville Chamberlain.'

One or two newspapers took up a classic example of the outmoded election 'scare' using material provided by Mr. Hogg on the eve of poll: he revealed an AEU summons to its members to attend an election meeting under threat of a fine. The AEU branch replied that the summons was to an ordinary branch meeting (at which the Labour candidate happened to be speaking) and that the fine, which had been in the rule book for generations, was, of course, never enforced because 99% of members never turned up to branch meetings. None the less photostats of the summons were distributed by Conservative Central Office and reproduced in a number of newspapers on polling day.

In the last week of a campaign parties continue to fire challenges at each other but they seem to do so as a matter of form: there is a strong sense that such skirmishing can no longer inflict serious casualties or decide the outcome. But in the last three elections the final television appeals of the party leaders have assumed ever greater significance, at any rate in the minds of the party strategists. In 1966 a cruel blow of fate deprived Mr. Grimond of his opportunity; Lord Byers substituted for him competently while Mr. Grimond attended his son's funeral. Mr. Heath, whose campaigning and television performance had been the subject of some criticism, came through his test successfully, achieving a new spontaneity in his delivery.

> 'I want to talk to you quietly tonight, as we get near the end of the election, about things which are very important to me . . . my fears . . . my hopes.
>
> The British . . . are slow to see danger and slower still to change . . . in the long run, we shall not survive if, from some failure of will, we let ourselves drift slowly backwards into industrial failure and out-of-date technology.
>
> You should believe the party which is prepared to take on the hard jobs. We are prepared to reform the trade unions; the Labour party is not. We are keen to enter Europe; the Labour party is not. We are willing to take tough measures to put the economy right. Mr. Wilson will not tell you the truth about the economy at all.
>
> . . . if change is difficult it is also vital.
>
> We want to make changes in favour of personal freedom; the Labour party want to make changes in favour of state control. Both parties want to move, but the Labour party seems to us to be moving in the wrong direction.
>
> . . . there is a role for Britain to play which will take all we can give it for the rest of the century. That role is Europe.
>
> I want young people to be able to build in marble when my generation can only build in brick. I want them to see a strong economy and a United Europe as a starting point for their lives and ambitions. For us the exciting business of laying these foundations for a new society and a richer culture. For them the even more exhilarating thrill of building upon these foundations.
>
> I shall be proud of my own work if we can get started on that. We will get started — all of us — and I believe that we should start now, with a Conservative government.'

Mr. Wilson showed his accustomed mastery in his final appeal — no partisan gibes but only the apotheosis of his family doctor manner:

> 'It's a choice between parties, the record of each and the policies of each. But going even beyond policy, is the vision that each party offers you for the future. The kind of Britain we want to see — the kind of Britain in which we want our children to grow up. The

opportunity they will have in life, and the influence that this new Britain can have in leading the world to peace. There are those whose horizons for Britain are confined to company reports and the counting house. Do we want to see Britain no more than a glorified supermarket? We want a Britain which tempers economic efficiency and strength and independence with compassion, for those among us who most need our help but with respect for their human dignity.

For two years and more before 1964, Britain had no government. Their vision for Britain whatever it may have been had withered and perished. But for 17 months now, Britain has had a government. . . . We have neither feared electoral unpopularity, nor have we been pushed around by any vested interest however powerful.

. . . It is the economic challenge which dominates the whole life of the nation. I've described 1966 as make or break year, and that is one reason why we can't afford another six months or more of electioneering. Or of a parliament with urgent tasks before it, paralysed and frustrated month after month by an inadequate majority.

. . . We have been brought to the brink because for thirteen years British industry has lost ground in the world.'

Mr. Wilson then listed government achievements, the National Plan, the rise in pensions, the Rent Act, leasehold enfranchisement and he concluded:

'There are too many people prepared to write us off abroad, and even nearer home. Let them realise that the nation they saw, or thought they saw, in those thirteen years, is not the real Britain. We face a tremendous challenge and we have not at any time during these 17 months or in this election period sought for one moment to conceal the fact that a hard road still lies ahead of us. But all our history proclaims that there are deep reserves of strength and power which are brought out to the full when Britain has a government prepared to tell the people the facts, to tell the people what has got to be done. So this Thursday can mark a new stage in the partnership between the people of Britain and their government — a government which is prepared to say, and to mean: "This is your country — now let us join together to work for it".'

One of the supreme ironies of the 1966 election was that the final emphasis of the Conservative leader was on the need for radical change and of the leader of the Labour party on the need for patriotism and stability.

CHAPTER VII

TELEVISION AND RADIO

By Martin Harrison

EVEN in the brief period between the 1966 election and its predecessor, broadcasting had had time to change and develop. For the first time the proportion of the population in homes equipped with television had risen to over 90%, leaving television only fractionally short of the universal coverage of radio. Current affairs broadcasting continued its steady increase in output and importance. With the introduction of a largely revised structure of programmes, the BBC was now devoting about 10% of its evening output to politics. The new situation was well exemplified when Sir Alec Douglas-Home was replaced by Mr. Edward Heath. Both the outgoing and incoming Conservative leaders spent entire evenings journeying from studio to studio to explain their positions for the different networks, and during the contest itself Mr. Heath staged a picnic in a seaside carpark, while Mr. Maudling produced a family game of football for the benefit of the cameras. Clearly television was having its impact on political ritual.

In contrast to the heated controversy over its activities in 1964, broadcasting's place in the 1966 campaign was more generally accepted and understood. Nevertheless, the campaign was preceded by a clash between broadcasters and politicians when the committee on party election broadcasts met to discuss election arrangements. Confronted with BBC–ITA proposals to cut party television broadcasts from thirteen (shared 5:5:3) to ten (shared 4:4:2), all three parties closed ranks to defend the *status quo* — conveniently for the Liberals, since the smokescreen behind which they had been concealing a drop in their candidacies might have been inadequate to protect their allocation from attack by their rivals. Eventually a compromise was reached, maintaining thirteen programmes but cutting the time allotted to them by forty minutes —giving a mixture of ten- and fifteen-minute broadcasts. The Welsh and Scottish Nationalists were for the first time allotted five minutes on regional radio and TV if they contested a fifth of their region's seats (as they subsequently did). Later, under the standing rules, the Communists qualified for five minutes on national radio and television by nominating over fifty candidates.

Communists and Nationalists alike complained bitterly at these arrangements, decided as usual in their absence; as in previous elections both broadcasters and politicians declined to accept responsibility and the broadcasting committee itself went into recess for the duration of the campaign. Yet while the criteria for allocating time to minor parties is inevitably a matter of dispute, on procedure and timing at least their complaints seemed cogent. The insistence on transmitting their programmes at 6.30 p.m. rather than 9.10 p.m. cut their audiences sharply (p. 143) and weighted them unduly with people too young to vote. The BBC contended that schedules which had been revised for thirteen programmes could not be touched again, and that 6.30 p.m. was a 'recognised time' for political programming. Clearly a less negative approach to minor party time might appropriately be evolved for future elections; since so few parties could possibly qualify it would be simple enough to ascertain their intentions in advance and make provisional bookings for them during the general revision of schedules, which would also allow them the publicity in programme weeklies they were denied in 1966.[1]

Surprisingly, the broadcasting committee never discussed whether the party leaders should meet in televised 'confrontation'. Apparently it was felt that the issue was closed by what had happened in 1964. In 1966 it was only raised when ITV interviewers extracted agreement in principle from the three party leaders on the evening the election was announced. Although a Gallup poll during the campaign showed 69% favouring a televised confrontation between leaders, with so much at stake neither major party showed real enthusiasm. Both, however, deemed it politic to appear willing and indeed Mr. Heath issued repeated challenges. Negotiations bogged down: Mr. Wilson insisted that Mr. Grimond must be included, Mr. Heath rejected any triangular 'tea-party' with Mr. Grimond an equal, and Mr. Grimond

---

[1] Minor party broadcasts were not listed in the programme weeklies on the ground that they could not be officially settled before nomination day. The Communists in fact announced their intention to qualify for air time at their national congress in November 1965. Though their TV broadcast was listed in daily paper programme guides, not a single morning paper except the *Daily Worker* listed their radio broadcast.

refused any formula which demoted the Liberals. Late in the day, the BBC and the ITV companies advanced a series of proposals designed to overcome the parties' contradictory stipulations, but without success. Though the chances of achieving confrontation never seemed bright, they were scarcely enhanced by the broadcasters' rather casual approach, and by the two television networks' self-defeating and somewhat inappropriate jockeying for position.

Nominally, the 'rules' or customs regulating political broadcasting remained as in 1964: there were to be no politics on Sundays; bookings of people appearing as party spokesmen were to be made through headquarters and subject to their veto; there were to be consultations over constituencies to be surveyed, and no programmes with live audiences. But the 'rules' had in practice become almost a vestigial formality, which rarely set any significant restraint on programmes — though a few producers felt intensely frustrated by the parties' ban on live audiences, which derived from a feeling that audiences drawn equally from all three parties produced an excessively partisan situation with two-thirds of those present vocally hostile to any speaker. In the light of the judgment on the Communists' unsuccessful petition to unseat Sir Alec Douglas-Home in 1964 the law was not viewed as so restrictive. The broadcasting authorities now felt free to use candidates in their programmes providing they were 'recognised front-bench spokesmen'; this opened the way to a string of confrontations between ministers and shadow ministers while in a host of minor ways, particularly in news coverage, the decision eased the broadcasters' nervous preoccupation with possible legal pitfalls.[1]

When the election came there was the usual flurry of cancelled or postponed programmes — BBC-1's satirical series 'BBC-3', a radio portrait of Lord Morrison of Lambeth, and an instalment in ITV's 'The Power Game', which included a short scene casting a slur on the Conservative party (ironically 'balancing' a comparable slur on Labour outside the campaign period). BBC-2 hastily cancelled a late evening discussion of electioneering abroad on the

[1] The decision (cf. *The British General Election of 1964*, p. 159) essentially brought within the law any programme of balanced discussion using candidates which was designed to educate or inform the electorate. The lawyers' limitation of its benefit to 'recognised front-bench spokesmen' seemed unduly cautious, and the term had in any case little meaning in relation to the Liberals. The lawyers' ruling was frequently stretched in practice, particularly in the regions.

curious ground that somebody might inadvertently refer to a British politician.[1] ITV dropped 'Hallelujah', a religious programme, because of two politically oriented songs, but let an ex-Communist, Douglas Hyde, explain in another religious programme why Communism and Christianity do not mix. However, in the face of press ridicule, the BBC rapidly rescinded a decision to postpone a children's puppet show simply because its title was 'You Too Can Be Prime Minister'. Trivial though such incidents were, they were symptomatic of the jittery readiness to play unnecessarily safe with which the broadcasting authorities still greeted the announcement of an election.

It was news coverage which brought the campaign most constantly to the widest audiences. Radio bulletins followed the development of each exchange between the parties throughout each day and summarised them nightly in round-ups of excerpts in 'Radio Newsreel' and 'Ten O'Clock', while evening television news was expanded on both channels to cover the campaign more competitively and expensively than in 1964.[2] ITN gave the election an average of six minutes in its fifteen-minute bulletin at 8.55 p.m. and the BBC 5¾ minutes out of a nominal twenty at 8.50 p.m. On many evenings election reports were running simultaneously on the two channels, while later on ITN's 'Election '66' often overlapped with BBC-1's 'Campaign Report'. For apolitical viewers escape from the campaign must have seemed a little difficult at times.

The relatively leisurely approach of television reporting in 1964 had now given way to fiercer competition for up-to-the-minute news. While the morning press conferences and the leaders' tours had provided the core of the evening bulletins in 1964, attention was now concentrated on the evening meetings. But the BBC ruled out live relays from meetings disliking the lack of editorial control, and ITN used them only twice — providing the most memorable single moment of the campaign on television when it imaginatively

<hr/>

[1] Apart from the inescapable minimum of news and party broadcasts BBC-2 ignored the election.

[2] About 28% of the population over five hears a sound bulletin during the day, while TAM data (p. 144 n.) shows an average audience of 4,400,000 and 7,300,000 homes respectively for the main BBC-1 and ITN bulletins during this period.

Throughout all figures are based for radio on bulletins at 8.00 a.m., 1.00, 6.00, 8.30 p.m. and 'Ten O'Clock'; for ITN on the 8.55 p.m. bulletin and 'Election '66', and for BBC-1 on the 8.50 p.m. bulletin and 'Campaign Report'. News interviews are included but discussions are excluded.

led its main bulletin with 4½ minutes of live coverage of the Prime Minister facing hecklers in Birmingham.

As always television excelled at conveying the differing campaigning styles of the principal actors, and provided a very different perspective from that revealed in party broadcasts. More tellingly than the daily press it caught the boyish zest of Mr. Hogg waving his walking stick, revelling in being an 'election character', and Mr. Brown's weary croak as he pugnaciously stumped the provinces, sparring with housewives and schoolboys. Conventional 'tight' shots of politicians were more readily discarded for livelier views including audiences, improvised platforms, market towns, shopping centres and factories. However, at times an editorial fondness for colour and conflict could lead to the coverage of heckling incidents going well beyond their intrinsic significance, though with his tendency to play audiences for reactions in order to bring his meetings to life and let him demonstrate his mastery of repartee, Mr. Wilson himself did in fact cut down the occasions when he was seen to make positive and constructive points.

Late evening coverage differed markedly on the two networks. While ITN's 'Election '66' adopted a 'hard news' approach, presenting twenty-five minutes of extracts from speeches supplemented by interviews, the BBC's 'Campaign Report' was more of a magazine, with feature items, discussions, interviews and analyses of the polls overshadowing straight reporting. Although 'Election '66' was lucid and workmanlike it proved hesitant about providing analysis and tended to equate reporting with anthologising passages from speeches. 'Campaign Report', presenting more varied fare, was more inclined to assume that the campaign was so fully reported elsewhere that the day's speeches could be taken as a peg for discussion. Despite the controversy it stirred (discussed below) 'Campaign Report's use of its more liberal and elastic time was in fact neither notably resourceful nor adventurous. Between the two approaches of straight reporting and of commentary with analysis, television had still to find an ideal balance in communicating the substance of campaign arguments while scrutinising and advancing them. Nevertheless, 1966 saw the most active and extensive broadcast coverage of an election yet produced in Britain.

Since news values have to be tempered by political 'balance' the parties' share of news time was much as it had been in 1964 (figures in brackets):

	Con. %	Lab. %	Lib. %	Other %
ITN . . .	43 (44)	40 (40)	16 (16)	1 (..)
BBC-1 . .	39 (42)	42 (41)	16 (17)	2 (..)
Radio . . .	36 (41)	46 (39)	17 (20)	.. (..)

Apparently the BBC editors seemed to feel that a government in power was on the whole more newsworthy, while ITN coverage reflected a judgment that the Conservatives made rather more of the running. The Liberals' slight loss of ground was probably due to Mr. Grimond's enforced absence from the campaign. The minor parties received fractionally greater attention: 'Campaign Report' interviewed the general secretary of the Communist party, while ITN gave several brief excerpts from Communist speeches and cast a fleeting glance at the Scottish and Welsh Nationalists. But despite expanded coverage the range of information remained surprisingly limited. The circle of politicians quoted in national

Politicians quoted in news coverage

	Times quoted				Times quoted		
	ITN	BBC-1	Radio		ITN	BBC-1	Radio
Wilson . .	49	31	69	Heath . .	54	44	115
Brown . .	20	19	15	Maudling .	9	5	9
Callaghan .	5	7	50	Hogg . .	9	4	6
Gunter . .	2	5	7	Powell . .	6	3	7
Healey . .	5	2	5	Macleod . .	3	3	5
17 Labour . .	16	12	35	13 Conservatives .	17	8	25
2 Communists .	6	1	2	Grimond . .	21	17	35
				Byers . .	19	8	47
4 Others . .	4	0	1	Bonham Carter .	8	2	10
				7 Liberals . .	10	2	15

bulletins actually shrank from sixty-one in 1964 to fifty-six. Mr. Wilson, Mr. Heath and Mr. Grimond were in fact quoted more often than all others combined. Indeed, if one measures time rather than quotations, Mr. Wilson and Mr. Heath alone had 53% of all news time given to politicians of all parties. Both dominated their own party's coverage — Mr. Wilson with 56% of Labour time, and Mr. Heath with 70% of Conservative time (largely because he took his party's press conferences).

Thus broadcast news presented a strikingly 'presidentialised' campaign. This was partly because the parties themselves often failed to give adequate notice of their other spokesmen's engagements. Again, commitment of teams to follow the three leaders everywhere lest a major story broke dug heavily into the broadcasters' resources. Perhaps more important was Mr. Wilson's practice of choosing to speak just before the main evening bulletins went on the air. This meant his meetings had to be covered with electronic cameras rather than the slower film camera coverage — and balance naturally required similar handling of Mr. Heath. Since electronic relays cost some £1,300 against £300 for film, editors understandably tended to let sequences run on to 'get their money's worth', crowding out lesser figures. But even radio, where such considerations were less relevant, 'presidentialised' its presentation to a large degree. This tendency for a narrow circle of politicians, and most particularly these two men, to reappear in bulletin after bulletin was not simply politically or constitutionally questionable; the sight of those same few faces night after night could help to explain the complaints of 'too much politics' on the air which arose in the campaign's closing stages.[1]

However, it was probably more important *what*, rather than *who*, was selected from the torrent of campaign comment, proposals and invective, since it shaped progressively impressions of what the election was about. As this table shows, radio and TV

Rank order of prominence given to selected issues in news and party broadcasts

	ITN	BBC-1	Radio	Party broadcasts*		ITN	BBC-1	Radio	Party broadcasts*
State of Economy .	1	1	2	1	Confrontation .	9	9	4	..
Europe . .	2	3	1	6	Social Services	10	6	..	2
Housing, Rates	3	4	8	5	Nationalisation	11	..	..	9
Prices, In-comes .	4	7	7	4	Agriculture .	11	11	13	9
Foreign Affairs	5	8	6	7	Cost of Con. Programme .	13	10	8	9
Rhodesia .	6	5	5	—	Education .	..	..	10	8
Defence .	7	..	12	—	Immigration .	—	—	11	9
Trade Unions	8	2	3	3	Transport .	..	..	..	—

* All major party broadcasts, radio and TV.
.. Indicates very brief coverage.
— Indicates no coverage.

[1] It also created problems for the politicians. Mr. Heath ruefully complained that extended coverage meant that his jokes were killed if he used them a second time.

alike presented the state of the domestic economy as the key campaign issue. Thereafter there were some intriguing variations in editorial selectivity. Thus ITN placed one of the two great topical issues (Europe) second by a large margin, while the other (the unions) was put in the same position by BBC-1. Five topics (the economy, the unions, Europe, housing and foreign affairs) took up half the time broadcasting gave to covering issues. ITN editors seemed more receptive to defence and foreign affairs news; those at the BBC to items on the social services. Radio's priorities differed from TV's mainly because of daytime coverage of the parties' news conferences. But despite these varying emphases all channels showed considerable agreement in identifying the chief issues, and in holding a balance between the major parties' stronger and weaker points. Their coverage was not too dissimilar from the preoccupations of the parties themselves, so far as these were revealed in the election broadcasts.[1] Nevertheless, the range of issues, as of men, that broadcasting could present was inherently limited. Matters like education almost certainly received greater attention in the country than on television. It appeared that those who criticised the campaign as 'tawdry' and 'unworthy' — and who could only have derived general impressions from the mass media — failed to allow for this inevitable selectivity. Despite the enhanced importance of the mass media in modern campaigns, they can only present a restricted daily anthology of encapsulated highlights. Invaluable though this is, the tendency to confuse the campaign itself with its reflection in the media must be resisted.

The pattern of other election programmes showed that tradition (or routine) was taking hold.[2] The BBC again presented 'Election Forum' with the three party leaders appearing in turn on three evenings before the dissolution to answer questions from over 12,000 submitted by viewers and listeners. The BBC's other main contribution 'Question Time' which was presented twice in every region, with party representatives submitting to questioning, also followed a 1964 formula. While the BBC prescribed 'Question

[1] In fact the party broadcasts' principal theme was the virtues and vices of the parties themselves, but this does not lend itself to extensive news coverage. It is not of course suggested the 'ideal' news coverage would exactly match the themes of party election broadcasts.

[2] For information about regional programmes I am indebted to Alan Angell, Michèle Blondel, Peter Fletcher, Wilfrid Harrison, Wendy Harrison, Vera King, Doreen Marshallsay, Douglas Nobbs, Cornelius O'Leary, Peter Richards, Donald Southgate, Jeffrey Stanyer and Frank Stacey.

Time' uniformly for all its regions, ITV regional output depended on the initiative of the programme companies. Some did nothing, arguing there was already enough political programming, but most made at least a nominal contribution. Several, such as Grampian, Southern and Scottish TV, followed the same formula as 'Question Time', while others adopted variants: Anglia had three programmes with party representatives questioned by the local and farming press; two 'ABC Hearings' were devoted to fairly extended interrogation in turn of party spokesmen on housing and the economy, while Tyne-Tees had editors of local papers putting their readers' questions. Television Wales and West with 'Fighting for Wales' and Ulster TV with 'Party Platform' both made their programmes more colourful by filming questions on location and taking additional questions at the studios during transmission. (There were some 2,000 calls for the TWW programme.) As always the success of these programmes turned mainly on whether the regions had any social reality. Granada, running its 'Marathon' programme for the third successive election, remained the only company which set out systematically to give ordinary candidates their moment on the air.

Coverage of the election in radio and television regional news and news magazines declined compared with 1964. What there was tended to be anecdotal and folksy rather than highly political, producing such thumbnail sketches as, 'The Republican candidate for Derry does all his campaigning on a bicycle, and spent eight years in gaol as a political prisoner.' The now traditional constituency surveys remained staple fare, focusing particularly on marginal seats. Anglia produced an enterprising variant by linking constituency reports and discussion of specific issues — Grantham and farming, Grimsby and fishing (but Kettering and steel nationalisation ran into a Labour veto); yet five minutes for travelogue and policy combined was scarcely serious. The flat or cosy approach of regional programmes could easily be patronised, but they did give minor parties a chance.[1] The Communists qualified in both Wales and Scotland, and the Scottish Nationalists,

---

[1] While the minor parties continued to protest at their allocation of broadcasting time, if they nominated candidates for one-fifth of the seats in a region, they obtained full equality in all programmes featuring party representatives; moreover, since Scotland was counted as one region, the Communists were included in Grampian and Border programmes although they had candidates in less than one-fifth of the seats.

K

Plaid Cymru and the Irish Republicans also received time, resulting in four-way discussions in Ulster and five-way ones in Wales and Scotland. If the result was sometimes unwieldy, these less familiar views often proved stimulating for both audiences and participants.

The most noteworthy national contribution came from the two weekly programmes 'Panorama' and 'This Week'. 'Panorama' tackled incomes policy, social welfare and Rhodesia, while 'This Week' dealt with strikes, the economy and education. The decision of 'Panorama' to give its full fifty minutes to one theme showed courage in a medium so frequently tyrannised by the stopwatch. It gave time for a thoughtfully provocative film survey of the chosen problem which pointed out some of its thorniest difficulties, and for a broad discussion between a minister and a shadow minister. The result was a valuable and rare blend of explanation and genuine discussion which both illuminated issues and clarified the differing party viewpoints.

In fact, broadcasting produced its best and its worst during the campaign. At worst it trivialised politics, as when Mr. Grimond, spurred on to keep the questions moving, managed to dispose of 46 questions in a 25-minute 'Election Forum', while Mr. Heath and Mr. Wilson were close behind with 58 and 43 respectively in 40 minutes. Again 'This Week' allowed a Callaghan–Macleod confrontation on the economy to degenerate into an acrimonious wrangle which totally obscured the issues and helped explain why 'politics' is at times a term of abuse. Despite their criticism of politicians and the party broadcasts, professional broadcasters showed at times that they, too, could abuse the medium and debase politics — and with less excuse. (A prime example was 'The World at One's repeated dismissal of the election as boring and trivial.) But at its best, broadcasting gave the major issues the spacious treatment they merited or promoted a dialogue which would otherwise not have taken place. Moments like 'This Week's moderate and courteous discussion on education between Mr. Crosland and Sir Edward Boyle both elevated politics and illuminated what was at stake.

Despite the extended news coverage, the official election broadcasts remained a focal point in the parties' planning. Labour decided as early as the spring of 1965 not to commission a film unit to put material 'in the can', but to aim for a fresh and topical series. Opinion among professionals advising the party had swung against unduly elaborate visual aids; moreover, in 1964 only about £50 worth of film out of the £6,000 worth shot had actually been used. As the 1966 election approached, the first and last television broadcasts were assigned to the Prime Minister, leaving the rest to be settled at short notice by the daily general secretary's meeting. Producing his own scripts, speaking from behind an

LABOUR TELEVISION BROADCASTS

'You <u>know</u> that Labour government works'

I. Wilson, at desk to camera. Explains why election necessary; asks for mandate to overcome obstruction, modernise Britain, speak with authority abroad and complete programme. Proposals all costed, realistic. Plans for rates, mortgages, leasehold, housing. Must judge parties on records and policies — contrasts these. Calls for clear decision to end electioneering for five years.

II. Theme music, Trevor Evans (*Daily Express*), John Bourne (*Financial Times*), Alan Watkins (*Spectator*) question Gunter on productivity, Royal Commission on Trade Unions, overmanning, union injustices, proposed labour courts and industrial relations.

III. Theme. Voice: You <u>know</u> Labour government works. Still of Labour manifesto. Hand turns to health section. Robinson: deterioration of NHS under Tories, prescription charges, Labour record. Hand indicates manifesto's 'full employment' section. Marsh contrasts Labour efforts on redundancy, retraining with Tory record. Pencil underlines 'social security' section. Herbison in Edinburgh attacks Tory pension schemes, recalls Labour's. Labour created welfare state, Tories would destroy it. Pencil underlines 'fair rents and mortgages'. Crossman warns Tory proposals would raise rents. Sums up contrasting party positions. Voice: Time for decision; theme, slogan.

IV. Theme. Slogan. Brown at desk, camera closes in. The economy the decisive issue. Reviews achievements, proposes elimination of deficit, surplus from 1967. Government actions and proposals on efficiency, productivity. Need to end inflationary spiral. Contrasts Tory and Labour approaches, achievements in incomes policy. Appeals for good majority so Britain can advance. Theme as 'Vote Labour' gradually fills screen.

V. Caption: 'The Prime Minister'. Wilson at desk, curtained window behind, camera closing to head and shoulders. Need for government, action and leadership, dangers of drift. Economic challenge dominates life of nation. Outlines achievements. Government forcing change, tackling unofficial strikes, problem industries, National Plan. Need for civilised society tempered with justice, compassion, e.g. housing, rents policy. Tasks worthy of great people. Achievement possible with united people when divisive clamour dies. Call for new stage in partnership between government and people. Let us join and work together. This is your country.

imposing desk, the Prime Minister's primary concern in both his broadcasts seemed to be to promote his 'family doctor image'.[1] Soft in voice, sober in dress and serious in mien he appeared the personification of respectability and responsibility. Partisanship was muted; his two programmes contained 42 mentions of 'Britain', 39 of 'government' and none whatever of 'Labour'.

Though different in style the three 'Transport House' programmes also tied in with the campaign theme 'You know that Labour government works' — which was blazoned on a rondel filling the screen as the programme opened and closed. A jauntily assured musical theme was also used. In the second broadcast the morning meeting decided to provide a topical and lively programme which would also bury the 'noose trial' issue, presenting the Minister of Labour questioned live by independent journalists. Unfortunately the questioning was weak and the answers diffuse, while faulty co-ordination among the performers, combined with lethargic production, brought the programme jolting to a halt half a minute early.

Originally the third programme was conceived as a series of progress reports by ministers on their achievements, but after considerable debate the statesmanlike approach was cast aside in favour of hitting the Conservatives where they were thought most vulnerable. Consequently a series of ministers (introduced by an unseen actor rather than an 'anchor man') came in turn before the camera to deliver a highly polemical indictment of the Tories as 'wreckers' of the welfare state. Then in the fourth programme, presenting George Brown on the domestic economy, both speaker and subject had selected themselves. Mr. Brown's subdued performance was very different from his larger-than-life presentation in 1964, but this was due less to the responsibilities of office than to his manifest physical weariness; his voice was husky after a long speaking tour and a doctor attended him in the studio.

The Conservatives were preoccupied with finding a campaign style appropriate to opposition. Realising they could expect little advance warning of the election, and could not base film pro-

---

[1] Mr. Lemass, the Irish Prime Minister, reported that Mr. Wilson 'expressed to me the opinion that a political leader should try to look, particularly on television, like a family doctor — the kind of man who inspires trust by his appearance as well as by his soothing words, and whose advice is welcomed — and he gave me to understand that he measures his own not inconsiderable success on television by the extent to which he projects his family doctor image'. *Guardian*, April 30th, 1966.

grammes on their achievements, they decided to rely on their regular publicity staff and not to engage an outside producer. Early in the year Mr. Heath assigned political control of the series to Mr. Iain Macleod, who himself acted as 'anchor man' in the

---

CONSERVATIVE TELEVISION BROADCASTS

'Action not words'

I. 'Action not words' says Heath as film shows him addressing rally. Cut to speeding train, then Heath in train explaining he cares about people; wasted opportunities make him angry. Cut back to meeting. Heath declares faith in welfare, attacks unofficial strikes. Three 'ordinary' Conservatives hail Heath's leadership. Cut back to meeting. Heath welcomes support of all supporting Tory ideals, leaves hall to warm applause, shaking hands. Five mins. to camera promises to tell people truth: not paying our way, must attack restrictive practices, modernise social services, join Europe.

II. Film of city crowds. Macleod introduces Crawley on how nationalisation and union failings converted him from socialism. Macleod introduces Hogg: union problem can't be swept under carpet or left to Labour, need comprehensive code for unions. Crawley advocates industrial courts. Hogg explains how these might work. Macleod summarises proposals, introduces Maudling (five mins. to camera) on fundamental question — compulsion v. individual responsibility, e.g. in incomes policy, crime, strikes, half-baked management. Must choose path Britain will take.

III. Still of Heath. Macleod introduces Walker recalling Labour 1964 appeal to youth, attacking failure to keep pledges, promises mortgage help, lower taxes. Macleod uses chart to show accuracy of Maudling's 1964 prediction of higher taxes under Labour. Summarises issues, introduces Heath (five mins. to camera). Socialists dare not face future on production, prices, unions. Social services must concentrate on those with greatest need. Labour European policy is double talk. Tories would get economy right, reform unions and welfare state, build houses, get us into Europe: Labour couldn't.

IV. Peggy Fenner: disgust at Labour attacks; Tories look to future. Macleod introduces her, Boyle, Marples, Maudling, denies Labour allegations on prescription charges; five-point outline of welfare proposals. Boyle criticises universal comprehensivisation, outlines Tory education plans. Macleod introduces Maudling attacking Labour economic record, explaining 1964 deficit; calls for incentives, competition, end to restrictive practices. Macleod introduces Marples on proposals for cost-effectiveness department. Macleod: it's the future that really matters.

V. Heath introduced at desk, profile first then closing to head/shoulders shot. Dangers from resistance to change, industrial failure and outdated technology. Must take grip on our century. Tories would tackle tough decisions: Labour wouldn't. Need to reform unions, management, law courts, old universities, parliament and parties. Britain must not slip back. New role in Europe. Need to work for next generation, get economy right, go into Europe. Start now with a Conservative government.

central three programmes. Though sceptical about the potentialities of the party broadcasts, Mr. Macleod's primary aim was to
give heart to Tory supporters, and thereafter not to antagonise
anyone else, though the broadcasts were also to be framed for
undecided and intelligent floating voters. One urgent priority was
to put over Mr. Heath personally, particularly with his own party.
Yet since reaching the leadership his television performances had
been extremely disappointing. This made it risky to open with a
straight soliloquy to camera, while the impossibility of procuring
professional interviewers for party broadcasts ruled out the
'tough' interview. Accordingly, the first programme presented
Mr. Heath in conveniently short sequences in a variety of situations and included enthusiastic tributes from loyalists to cheer the
faint-hearted within the party's ranks. This, though somewhat
disjointed, did at least prevent the damaging of morale by a poor
opening performance. Then, like Labour, the Conservatives
examined the problem of the unions, from the viewpoint of an
ex-Minister of Labour, an ex-Labour M.P. and a lawyer. Though
union reform was a major Conservative campaign theme and
highly topical, it was felt that the subject could not sustain a full
fifteen minutes, and Mr. Maudling was brought in to attack
Labour's economic performance. Originally the third broadcast
was to have featured Mr. Macleod attacking Mr. Wilson, but it
was thought that Ludovic Kennedy's opening Liberal broadcast
had done this already and the emphasis was switched to domestic
policy, with speakers chosen for their 'dynamism'. The aim was to
appeal particularly to people who might be disillusioned by Labour
failure to fulfil 1964 promises. In their next programme, stung by
Labour's onslaught on their social policies two nights earlier, the
Conservatives dropped plans to cover defence, Rhodesia and
foreign policy. Instead they made a determined rebuttal of
Socialist 'smears', while also preserving a positive approach, particularly with Mr. Marples, hotfoot from his travels in America
and Japan, enthusiastically expounding cost-effectiveness.

But the fifth and final broadcast stood in contrast with its four
straightforward but unremarkable predecessors. Unlike recent
Conservative leaders who confided production of their final appeals
to Mr. Norman Collins of ATV, Mr. Heath thrashed out his script
on the last Sunday of the campaign in close collaboration with his
BBC producers. The result was a quietly impressive and revealing

broadcast in which Mr. Heath was relaxed and assured, adopting
a simple and direct style in talking about subjects about which he
seemed genuinely to care. Whatever its effect on the wider
electorate, it did much to strengthen his position within his own
party.[1]

Liberal planning began shortly before the election when a seven-
man committee headed by Mr. Grimond decided to build the
television series around Ludovic Kennedy, Jeremy Thorpe
and Mr. Grimond himself. Mr. Kennedy in fact conceived,
scripted and presented the opening attack on Mr. Wilson as an

---

LIBERAL TELEVISION BROADCASTS

I. 'The True Story.' Darkened studio, two silhouettes. Lights up to
reveal L. Kennedy, Wilson photo. Kennedy: the true story of Wilson
the man, not the father figure. Long sequence of quotes from Wilson's
pro-nationalisation statements read over his photo and text on screen.
Wilson's belief in nationalisation had been stopped in last parliament
only by Liberals. With large majority would bring plans out of cold
storage. Only way of stopping this was to elect larger band of Liberals.
What happens depends on *you*.

II. 'This Won't Do.' Fanfare, swirling globe fills screen. Camera swings to
Kennedy: days of British imperial greatness gone, but too many
politicians don't realise it. Introduces Thorpe on defence costs as map
illuminates bases and costs, band plays Colonel Bogey and siren whoops.
World policeman role was bleeding economy, over-stretching forces.
Kennedy introduces Steel on restrictive practices, illustrated by film of
new and restrictive operations in newspaper plant. Need to make industry more efficient. Other parties unable to tackle union problem;
co-partnership the solution. With map Kennedy says future lies in
Europe. Thorpe summarises distinctive Liberal policies, appeals for
massive Liberal vote.

III. Kennedy explains Grimond's absence, introduces Byers, to camera.
Byers. When electioneering over still many jobs to be done, challenges
met. Industry: misuses of manpower, need for co-ownership, greater
competition, ban on restrictive practices, spur of Europe. Attacks
living beyond means at home, abroad. Labour with large majority
might waste time with nationalisation. Only Liberals could keep Labour
on right lines. Only insurance against complacent government.
Would see things that matter were done. Kennedy: last time you gave
Liberals three million votes; this time give them many more. Grimond
poster with slogan, 'Jo Grimond leads the Liberals'.

---

[1] Just before the final appeals NOP asked: 'Which of the three party leaders
do you think is most impressive on TV?' The replies were: Wilson 49%,
Heath 19%, Grimond 12%, Don't know/No TV 20%. Most significantly, 27%
of Conservative voters chose Mr. Wilson but only 5% of Labour voters thought
Mr. Heath most impressive. Though the ultimate effect is incalculable, as in
1964 the Conservatives' lack of confidence in their leader's appeal on TV had a
discernible impact on morale in the party organisation.

arch-nationaliser (with ammunition culled from the 1964 *Conservative Campaign Guide*). Technically skilful, the broadcast was politically remarkable for attacking Mr. Wilson personally rather than his party, and for candidly assuming a Labour victory. Both this programme and the second reflected Mr. Kennedy's belief that viewers' attention must be seized and held. The first opened melodramatically with the Prime Minister and Mr. Kennedy silhouetted in a manner reminiscent of a popular ITV crime series; the second employed a swirling globe and an illuminated map to put over the themes of over-commitment abroad and inefficiency at home. Though Mr. Kennedy had produced a synopsis for this programme while on location in the Orkneys, ingredients and performers were in fact not brought together until transmission day. As with so many Liberal broadcasts this one was put 'in the can' only a few minutes before recording time expired. Then, with Mr. Grimond unable to give his final appeal, the party turned with some apprehension to its chairman, Lord Byers. Mr. Kennedy explained Mr. Grimond's absence and introduced Lord Byers because the opening minutes would have been 'killed' if Lord Byers had made the explanation himself. Though there had been fears in the party that he might be over-aggressive Lord Byers made a positive and sympathetic case for Liberalism strongly infused with a 'plain man's' appeal to those who were wearied with 'politicking'.

Making the Communists' first ever television election broadcast Mr. John Gollan must have surprised many viewers as he paced a distinctly 'bourgeois' living-room decked with flowers and well-stocked bookshelves. He set out to present the Communists as the only party offering a real choice, indicating nationalisation, incomes policy, social services and foreign policy as areas where they had distinctive views. His soft-sell approach was underlined by his closing slogan, 'For a new Britain, for a people's Britain — go one better — Vote Communist'. Despite jumpy editing Mr. Gollan proved a pleasant-voiced, relaxed and bland performer; five minutes could scarcely have been used more effectively. Mr. W. C. Wolfe for the Scottish Nationalists and Mr. Gwynfor Evans for Plaid Cymru (speaking in English) both made simple appeals for their parties as the only ones dedicated to fighting for national causes.

The 1966 party broadcasts were markedly different from those in 1964. Learning from criticism and changed conditions, the major parties had abandoned complicated gimmickry in favour of a direct, almost austere style. Yet some old faults still remained — notably the tendency to overload programmes with too many speakers, too many points and too many changes of pace. Over-compression frequently led to stilted scripts which defied natural delivery. More than one broadcast became a procession of performers reciting lifeless prose with eyes glazed through excessive rehearsal or preoccupation with the 'Auto-cue'. Perhaps it is asking too much to expect politicians to be able to switch abruptly from partisan harangues on the hustings to the wholly different style and tone required for a televised talk to a family by their fireside. The Liberals, nevertheless, did grasp the need to hold their audiences, to put over a limited number of points, and to back arguments with evidence rather than *ex cathedra* assertions. Yet while Labour and the Conservatives still often lacked respect for the medium and ignored basic communication skills, in their differing ways Mr. Wilson, Mr. Gollan and Mr. Heath in his final broadcast all showed they could use television effectively.

Radio broadcasts were even simpler and more direct than those on television: no music, no slogans, at most two speakers reading a script. Even more than on television Labour set out to present the picture of a government getting on with the job, with only in-direct rebuttal of Tory attacks. Mr. Wilson opened in much the same terms as on television; Miss Lee gave a progress report on her efforts for the arts, and Mr. Cousins outlined his ministry's promotion of modernisation and efficiency. The three five-minute broadcasts were also 'governmental' and topical: Mr. Peart on food and farm prices in the wake of the annual price review; Mr. Crossman explaining the new system of rates rebates and Mr. Houghton recapturing the style of his old 'Can I Help You?' broadcasts with an outline of social welfare proposals. It was left to Mr. Jenkins rather than the party leader to close the campaign by meditating on the need to use prosperity to produce a more civilised community.

The Conservatives followed a slightly different pattern. In the ten-minute broadcasts Mr. du Cann outlined their challenge and key proposals; Mr. Arthur Jones and Mrs. Jill Knight spoke on rates and education; and Mr. Thorneycroft discussed crime and immigration in a manner that was somewhat less liberal than the official Conservative line. Two of the five-minute broadcasts were given to Sir Donald Kaberry and Mr. Charles Curran for rather idiosyncratic polemics. Finally Mr. Heath himself took both the last ten- and five-minute broadcast to drive home his principal arguments.

For the Liberals James Davidson opened with an attack on both the big parties, which was continued with customary relish by Lady Violet Bonham Carter in a shorter broadcast later. The Liberals' other short broadcast was a skilful and well-delivered appeal by Richard Wainwright to people who felt 'taken for granted'. Finally Mr. Grimond was able to close the radio campaign in person, reiterating the party's chief election themes.

Often given by second-rank figures, sober and austere in presentation, the radio broadcasts almost all appealed to an audience accustomed to something more than 'audible wallpaper'. But despite their sustained seriousness the level of performance was often well below what listeners were accustomed to in 'Radio Newsreel' and 'Ten O'Clock'. The 'good enough for radio' spirit seemed to creep in at times. Yet, while the radio audiences of 640,000 at 6.40 p.m. and 340,000 at 10.10 p.m. were tiny by television standards, by any other political yardstick they were a big enough section of the electorate to merit better production than at times they received.[1]

Nevertheless, the party broadcasts played a useful role. Here alone the parties had an untrammelled forum for presenting the themes and personalities they judged most important. It would in fact have been extremely difficult for Labour to communicate effectively its basic campaign argument that Labour government worked, or for the Liberals to show the relevance and effectiveness of a third party, within the conventional framework of current affairs programmes. Within the parties there was certainly little disposition to let the broadcasts go, even before the Labour party's clash with the BBC, which must have hardened the resolve to continue them. But in an election with no deeply felt issues all parties found it hard to fill their fifteen-minute programmes; there was some feeling that it would be preferable to have more, shorter broadcasts of five minutes, as ideal for holding the attention of an

---

[1] Audiences at 10.10 p.m. were fractionally up on 1964; those at 6.40 p.m. were 160,000 down, due to a general decline in the Light Programme audience and the shift from 7 p.m., preceding 'The Archers' rather than following it.

audience. The former outright hostility of many professional broadcasters to the party programmes had also moderated; the case for 'party time' was now readily admitted — if only from the realisation that they were the price that had to be paid for the relative independence enjoyed in other current affairs programmes. After the heated controversy over the party broadcasts in 1964, the only serious bone of contention seemed to be the practice of transmitting them simultaneously on all channels in peak time — tenaciously clung to by the parties, but never publicly defended.

The campaign ended amid widespread complaint about 'too much politics' on the air. There was in fact more political television than ever before; in the nineteen days before the poll BBC-1 and ITV jointly offered northern viewers some fifteen hours of politics (excluding news and 'Election '66') between 6.30 and 11.30 p.m. compared with only nine hours in 1964. For six hours the two channels offered political fare simultaneously. Combined with news coverage this might well have sated the less politically interested viewers. Nevertheless, no firm evidence emerged of whether 'too much politics' was a genuine reaction or a stereotyped reflex akin to the tendency to brand all campaigns 'boring'. Nor was it clear whether complainants felt there was altogether too much politics, or simply too much of certain types of programme. While Mr. Callaghan and Mr. Selwyn Lloyd admitted there were too many party broadcasts, Mr. Wilson put the blame on the additional programmes provided by the broadcasters.

Audiences for party television election broadcasts

	% of population aged five or over (BBC)	% of sets in use (TAM-rating)		% of population aged five or over (BBC)	% of sets in use (TAM-rating)
Conservative			Labour		
March 14th .	32·6	74	March 12th .	28·6	71
March 18th .	29·5	73	March 16th .	27·9	71
March 21st .	30·4	74	March 22nd .	34·2	79
March 24th .	31·9	75	March 25th .	30·7	74
March 28th .	30·7	77	March 29th .	35·6	78
Average .	31·0	75	Average .	31·5	75
Liberal			Communist		
March 15th .	35·5	79	March 23rd .	15·9	65
March 23rd .	29·7	73	Scot. Nat.*		
March 26th .	23·3	72	March 25th .	n.a.	68
			Welsh Nat.*		
Average .	29·5	75	March 25th .	n.a.	59

* BBC data not available. TAM estimate for, respectively, TWW and Border, Grampian and STV service areas.

Audience data for the political programmes in fact suggest little evidence of viewer fatigue.[1] Indeed, viewing figures for the party television broadcasts were the highest ever — with 85% of the electorate claiming in a post-election NOP survey to have seen one or more — due chiefly to the programmes' being put out at 9.10 p.m. (rather than 9.30 p.m.), and because, being shorter, they were less likely to be switched off.[2] The mildly 'captive' audience thus produced may perhaps explain why audience reactions were generally less enthusiastic than in 1964 — within the customary pattern of each party's supporters preferring their own side's programmes. (Whatever the critics may say about the programmes, the BBC's audience research panels assessed them as much of a muchness; none of the individual broadcasts was judged notably successful or signally inept.[3])

Generally competing with lighter fare, current affairs programmes were usually successful in attracting and holding

---

[1] Audience data is published with grateful acknowledgment to the BBC and Television-Audience Measurement Ltd., particularly for making additional calculations. BBC Audience Research figures are based on interviews with a random sample of the population aged five or over (50 millions). They are recorded as viewers/listeners if they saw/heard half or more of a programme. Audience reaction is gathered from voluntary viewer and listener panels.

TAM-ratings show the percentage of sets in a sample of homes receiving both BBC and ITV which were switched on during a broadcast, on the basis of minute-by-minute metered records. The two series measure different things and are not comparable.

[2] Size of audience for any individual programme largely reflected the day of the week and the pull of adjacent programmes — which also seemed the greatest influence on the degree to which broadcasts held their audience. With shorter programmes the 'drop-out' rate was appreciably lower. Shorter programmes may also explain why simultaneous transmission of party broadcasts on all channels tended to depress the total viewing audience by only a seventh, compared with a quarter in 1964.

[3] Mean reaction indices for the three series of television broadcasts were:

	Sympathisers	Opponents	Uncommitted
Conservative	65	38	48
Labour	67	38	48
Liberal	66	50	55

Reactions to the sound programmes were very similar to these.

The BBC's audience panels apparently judged Liberal broadcasts marginally more favourably; an NOP survey of March 26th produced a similar impression, as the proportion judging the Liberal programmes best slightly exceeded the party's opinion poll rating but those judging the Conservative or Labour programmes best fell far short of their party's opinion poll support. Asked 'Which party do you think has produced the best TV programmes during the last few weeks?', the response was, Conservative 16%; Labour 28%; Liberal 8%; Don't know/No TV 48%. However, this question is imprecise and was asked before the closing appeals; and respondents were less immediately focused on individual broadcasts than the BBC panels were.

audiences as large as might be expected for serious programmes at the time of day they were produced. 'Election Forum' at the beginning of the campaign and 'Question Time' at the end all had rather larger audiences than in 1964, while the main news bulletins and 'Election '66' all held their audience ratings without flagging right through to polling day. The greatest demands on viewers' stamina were made by 'Campaign Report', a long programme running each weekday evening. Though its audiences fell below normal figures for the regular 'Twenty-Four Hours', this was primarily due to starting later and running longer, and they showed no signs of wilting as the campaign went on.[1] In fact, with successive TAM-ratings of 20, 18 and 15 for its election editions, 'Panorama' was almost the only exception to the general pattern — but it was competing with a phenomenally successful new ITV series about a charlady turned tycoon. Possibly *any* politics was too much for a proportion of viewers, who contracted out of the election from the start, leaving a relatively interested audience; certainly there is little evidence in the audience figures of any 'backlash' from that appreciable section of the viewing public which was prepared to watch some politics — though anyone sifting through audience reaction data must be left with an impression of mitigated enthusiasm. Perhaps, with a relatively unexciting election, viewers came to feel that the broadcasters had a duty to present political programmes, and they had a duty to watch them, but that performing this duty was a matter more of endurance than of enjoyment.[2]

As current affairs programmes have expanded since the fifties, the points of possible friction between broadcasters and politicians have steadily multiplied. Yet, even considering that both sides have had time to recognise the inherent tensions of their relationship and live with them, however uneasily, there were remarkably few complaints of irresponsible broadcasts or party obstruction.

[1] Combined BBC radio/TV audiences for 'Election Forum' were: Mr. Grimond 7·1 million; Mr. Heath 8·15 million; Mr. Wilson 10·3 million. 'Question Time' had audiences of 4·5 million and 4·4 million. 'Campaign Report' had an average audience of 4·7 million (BBC) — TAM-rating 13, about 1·9 million homes.
[2] When NOP asked on April 7th 'How disappointed would you be if there were no party political broadcasts?', respondents replied: Very disappointed 10; quite disappointed 19; not very disappointed 22; not at all disappointed 44; Don't know/No TV 5.

One grave exception to this general harmony became public the day after polling, when Mr. Wilson snubbed the BBC by refusing an interview. While no official catalogue of grievances emerged during the ensuing flurry — the lengthy but varying list published in the press apparently emanated from one of his advisers — there was no doubting his personal displeasure.

The storm had been brewing well before the election. There had been a clash at the 1965 Labour conference when the Prime Minister summoned a senior BBC producer to his room because a dissident trade unionist had been invited to air his views on incomes policy — and this was only the most widely publicised and denied of a series of Labour attempts to get both networks to keep non-conformists from both wings out of programmes. Further ill-feeling arose from a complicated argument over the terms on which Mr. Brown appeared to present the National Plan on television; this gave birth to a Labour suspicion that the BBC was discriminating against them by changing long-standing rules for 'ministerial' broadcasts and the right of reply. Then a series of incidents during the campaign hardened Mr. Wilson's conviction that if the BBC was not being positively unfair it was at least failing to show the respect due to any government. Some of the blame undoubtedly lay with Labour's own chronically unco-ordinated internal communications and with the ill-advised activities of some of the Prime Minister's associates. But over a number of sensitive questions such as the confrontation issue and the arrangements for broadcasts on the day and evening after the poll, individual members of the BBC acted in a tactless and unimaginative way which produced resentment against the entire Corporation. Trivial incidents which would normally have been forgotten overnight fed the sense of grievance.

But resentment went beyond matters of protocol, etiquette and public relations. With its inferiority in solid press support Labour had come to count heavily on broadcasting to reach the voters. The trend away from straight reporting of political events towards a mixture of news, analysis and discussion stirred mounting disquiet. There was a fear that the party's case might be buried or obscured by the interplay of producers' interests and priorities (rather than any crude party bias). This had been discernible in Labour's reaction to 'This Week's approach to the 1964 campaign, but now came out more strongly in their reception of the

BBC's nightly 'Campaign Report'[1]: here a questioning, probing style and a preoccupation with the topical clashed with Labour's determination to fight a low-key campaign based largely on the themes of 1964. Some Labour tacticians apparently felt that any attempt to reach outside the range of issues they themselves had chosen was necessarily prejudicial to them and therefore unfair: conscious of Labour's governmental dignity they were reluctant to accept that it normally falls to the opposition to make the running at elections. The problem was exacerbated by the fact that the two issues that developed in response to news stories, the union question and Europe, were ones that Labour wanted to avoid.

In fact, though pushed by pure 'news' criteria towards giving Conservative issues greater play, or at least reflecting Conservative timing, 'Campaign Report' retained a remarkably fair balance, despite Labour campaign tactics which did little to help attain it. Yet one may sympathise with Mr. Wilson's irritation when a major speech at times became merely a peg on which to hang studio discussion by lesser lights: however 'balanced' the discussion, it stirred his fears of producers substituting 'their' election for the 'real' one. For while parties were plainly not entitled to regard the current affairs programmes as, in effect, supplementary party broadcasts, it was legitimate for them to challenge 'Campaign Report's tendency to assume that the campaign had been fully enough reported elsewhere to justify a concentration on comment and analysis. Equally questionable was the assumption implicit in some current affairs coverage that it is up to the parties to produce a steady succession of newsworthy themes — the 'issue-a-day' approach to electioneering. This assumption might well lead to campaigns that would confuse the public and undermine the long-term educational function that elections can fulfil. While all these fears and conjectures are highly questionable, at the core of Mr. Wilson's complaint lay a plausible fear that the pressure of media coverage could distort campaigning patterns for the worse.

Despite a few dark hints that a new watchdog body might be set up to oversee both ITV and the BBC, the public storm rapidly subsided and no formal action was taken. But the suspicions kindled on both sides would be slow to die. Such friction could

[1] 'Campaign Report' was especially exposed to criticism because, together with ITN's 'Election '66', it was for many politicians, who were making speeches and canvassing till late, their only exposure to election television.

always recur. Governments traditionally desire quiet elections, while oppositions normally want to raise the political temperature. Naturally broadcasters, for their part, always react favourably to those who provide fresh copy; it is, indeed, their duty to look for it, since the electorate is entitled to have the issues fully discussed. Despite Labour's irritation in 1966, the time may come when the party once more has cause to welcome the fact that political broadcasts are no longer passive and neutered, but have a more active and enquiring role: politicians will have to learn to bear any discomfort that it causes them. Producers, too, have ground for reflection. Their argument that elections are for the electors rather than the parties can be a cloak for considerable professional arrogance. As broadcast coverage steadily extends, the collective activities of producers may shape more and more the way in which voters see the campaign, and politicians' anxieties about the implications of this cannot be dismissed as irrational. There is much more to the problem of creative and responsible political broadcasting at elections than holding a mechanical balance between parties and issues.

In the 1966 campaign broadcasting made its most valuable contribution yet to electioneering. But the controversy which followed the campaign suggested that, after the years in which the primary problem was enlarging the area of the broadcasters' freedom, there was now a need for more serious consideration of the uses to which that freedom could most profitably be put.

CHAPTER VIII

THE PRESS

By Colin Seymour-Ure

NEWSPAPER men found the election rather tiresome; and some of the reasons for their feeling make the press in 1966 an unusually interesting subject of study. Certainly few changes of importance had occurred since 1964 within the industry. The pattern of circulation and readership remained much the same (see table). So did the pattern of ownership. But certain disadvantages — some familiar, others new — faced newspapers in their role as media of communication. And in their other role, that of active champions of one or other political party, there was less wholehearted commitment even than seventeen months before. The *Daily Mirror* and *Daily Express*, which between them reached two-thirds of the electorate, both found themselves awkwardly caught between cross-pressures that distorted their traditional loyalties.

Certainly being a channel of communication cannot have been much fun. The actual substance of the 1966 campaign was not, of course, a repeat of 1964. But, as the *Daily Mail* put it a week before polling day, the British public had been

> 'half-prepared for another election and been exposed to an electioneering atmosphere for seventeen months. So the contest, now it has come, is merely a continuance of what had gone before.'

The election was thus bound to lack freshness for the press. Moreover, not only had the press heard it all before: it was not, the *Mail* went on to imply, worth hearing anyway:

> 'Every issue has already been canvassed and discussed to the point of tedium. . . . Little is left but abusive exchanges of personalities, which disgust many people, and rival promises, some of which can never be kept.'

Other papers felt the same. On March 23rd *The Times* announced that it had had enough:

> 'The election campaign is a tawdry business. It drags its slow length through a mass of mediocrity. The time is overdue for some

Name of paper Proprietors Editor Preferred result on March 31st	Circula-tion[1] (1964 in brackets) '000	Reader-ship[2] '000	% of its readers in social class:[3]				Mean number of pages, 1–31 March	N c st e N
			AB	C1	C2	DE		
Daily Mirror International Publishing Co. (Cecil King) Lee Howard Labour win	5,019 (5,085)	15,061	5	13	47	35	29	
Daily Express Beaverbrook Newspapers (Sir Max Aitken) Derek Marks Conservative win	3,987 (4,190)	12,169	14	22	36	28	20	
Daily Mail Associated Newspapers (Lord Rothermere) Michael Randall Conservative win	2,464 (2,400)	6,584	18	24	33	25	16	
Daily Telegraph Telegraph Newspapers (Michael Berry) Maurice Green Conservative win	1,337 (1,324)	3,279	42	32	19	7	29	
Sun International Publishing Co. (Cecil King) R. Dinsdale Labour win	1,274 (1,450)*	4,739	4	11	46	39	15	
Daily Sketch Associated Newspapers (Lord Rothermere) Howard French Conservative win	844 (847)	3,035	7	14	44	34	22	
Guardian The Scott Trust (Laurence P. Scott) Alastair Hetherington Labour win; more Liberals	270 (278)	948	48	26	16	10	20	
The Times Times Publishing Co. (Gavin Astor) Sir William Haley Unclear; more Liberals	254 (255)	876	50	23	18	8	21	

Notes:
  [1] ABC figures for second half of 1965 and of 1964, except for *Sun* in 1964.
  [2] Institute of Practitioners in Advertising figures, Jan.–Dec., 1965.
  [3] IPA definition classifies estimated population 16 and over as follows: AB — 13%; C1 — 18%; C2
DE — 32%.

political leader to take it by the scruff of the neck and lift it onto a plane worthy of its argument.'

This view, not surprisingly, was challenged by the parties. Len Williams, Labour's general secretary, wrote to *The Times* about its leading article, and Mr. Heath and Mr. Hogg complained when the *Mirror* reprinted part of it.

Another reason for the press's ennui was the ever-increasing dominance of television as the chief medium of communication at elections. Not only was TV able to report the progress of the campaign and provide a forum for participants: it also enabled

...ber ...ding ...es on ...ion, ...I ...ch	Number of constituency reports, 1–31 March	Own opinion polls	% of election coverage (column inches in brackets) given from March 11–31 to:						
			Speeches, Conferences, Handouts, Manifestos, etc.				TV programmes and 'Confrontation'	Constituency reports and polls	Other: features, leaders, notebooks
			Con.	Lab.	Lib.	Mixed			
	None	No	7 (294)	13 (519)	2 (68)	1 (52)	4 (169)	4 (154)	69 (2,870)
	36	Yes	15 (683)	8 (380)	2 (85)	3 (155)	4 (176)	25 (1,145)	43 (2,013)
	7	Yes	12 (483)	7 (262)	1 (46)	2 (77)	4 (179)	20 (800)	54 (2,150)
	72	Yes	15 (999)	9 (588)	5 (338)	6 (390)	5 (304)	26 (1,680)	34 (2,194)
	11	No	11 (459)	11 (440)	3 (143)	6 (263)	4 (152)	18 (754)	47 (1,950)
	None	No	18 (409)	13 (303)	4 (89)	2 (49)	7 (173)	8 (185)	48 (1,126)
	87	Yes	7 (572)	10 (845)	7 (552)	9 (742)	4 (341)	24 (1,931)	39 (3,137)
	69	No	8 (414)	10 (494)	3 (141)	5 (237)	3 (148)	38 (1,834)	33 (1,603)

first leading article where more than one.
...udes regional reports and 'marginal' polls.
...visional figure. *Sun* started only in September 1964.

politicians to carry on a dialogue with the press. Mr. Wilson replied on the 'Election Forum' to the *Daily Mirror*'s attack on Mr. Cousins' presence in the cabinet; Mr. Heath similarly replied on the air to the *Mirror*'s strictures against the level of the campaign. In addition, the development of election television had reached the point where it was itself a subject — as well as a source — of news. For example, the confrontation debate between the party leaders was front-page news throughout the early part of the campaign.

But by far the most important and interesting effects on the press were caused by the spread of opinion polls. These have transformed the style of much election journalism. Aneurin Bevan, the story goes, complained that the polls take the poetry out of politics. Journalists could well agree. Polls undermine the journalist's traditional function of gauging the effects of the unfolding campaign and of forecasting the result. They are a blow to his pro-

Subjects of Lead Stories on the

	11	12	14	15	16	17	18	19	21
Daily Mirror	—	Ban on P.M.'s doodles	'Noose trial'	'Noose trial'	—	—	—	EEC	—
Daily Express	'Noose trial'	Opinion poll	'Noose trial'	'Noose trial'	'Noose trial'	Wilson speech	TV	Opinion poll	—
Daily Mail	Trade figures	'Noose trial'	'Noose trial'	'Noose trial'	Liberal broadcast	Opinion poll	—	EEC	—
Daily Telegraph	Sterling	'Noose trial'	Con. costs clash	'Noose trial'	'Noose trial'	—	EEC	EEC	—
Sun	—	'Noose trial'	—	'Noose trial'	EEC	—	TV	EEC	—
Sketch	—	Ban on P.M.'s doodles	Education	—	'Noose trial'	—	—	EEC	—
Guardian	Sterling	Trade figures	'Noose trial'	—	NATO	EEC	EEC	EEC	—
The Times	—	'Noose trial'	'Noose trial'	'Noose trial'	Heath press conf.	—	Nominations hitch	EEC	—

fessional expertise.[1] In the old days a journalist savoured the constituencies like a wine-taster, making his forecast on an impression of flavour and bouquet. (Lord Beaverbrook raised an *Express* reporter's salary by £10 a week for predicting the Conservatives' majority in 1935 to within 44.) Until recently *The Times*

[1] The most striking test of the rival claims of polls and journalists occurred before the general election, at the Hull North by-election. Almost all of the journalists in Hull predicted, or at least suggested, that the Conservative would win. The two polls conducted during the campaign, by the *Evening Standard* and by NOP for the *Daily Mail*, both predicted a comfortable victory for Labour. The polls were right; the journalists were wrong. For an analysis of the press's coverage of Hull North, see Leslie Stone, 'Hull: Where the Press went wrong', *Socialist Commentary*, March 1966.

gathered forecasts from each constituency and did a mammoth eve-of-poll sum to produce its overall prediction. But what, journalists must have felt in 1966, was the point of chronicling grassroots activity, trailing party leaders round the country and Smith Square — indeed of covering the campaign at all — when the polls showed a remorseless Labour lead in double figures? Not

Election, March 11th–31st, 1966

22	23	24	25	26	28	29	30	31	
—	Stink bomb	Leading article	—	—	—	—	Leading article	Pictures and exhortation	*Daily Mirror*
Economy	—	Heath speech	Opinion poll	—	—	Press conf.	Steel price rise	Poll	*Daily Express*
—	Stink bomb	Opinion poll	Opinion poll	—	Powell speech	Opinion poll	—	Poll	*Daily Mail*
Leaders' speeches	—	—	—	—	—	Macmillan/Wilson clash	Heath speech	Heath speech; poll	*Daily Telegraph*
—	Stink bomb	Grimond son dead	Leading article	—	—	Bets on Labour	Wilson on TV	Trade figures	*Sun*
—	Stink bomb	—	—	—	—	Poll night soccer	Steel price rise	Leading article	*Sketch*
GATT reviewed	Stink bomb	State of the parties	Heath speech	Wilson speech	—	Press conf.	Wilson on TV	Trade figures	*Guardian*
—	Stink bomb	Leaders' speeches	Immigrants urged not to vote	Wilson speech	—	EEC	Wilson on TV	Steel price clash	*The Times*

only was the function of prophecy gone: even the feeling of excitement mounting to a climax was missing. For newspapers, though, as distinct from journalists, the polls were of course prestigious and were presumably reckoned, like football results, to sell extra copies.

All of these factors affecting the scale and type of election coverage could be classified as 'external'. That is, they were governed by the general environment in which all newspapers operated: the balance of parties, the competitive position of the press in relation to TV, and the estimated state of public opinion. But other, 'internal', factors deriving from the characteristics of each particular paper also had an influence. Of these, a paper's readership profile and its corresponding criteria of news value were bound to be fundamental. For instance, the *Financial Times*, neither merely a specialist newspaper nor quite a national daily, had the approach of a quality daily to its election coverage — constituency reports and so on — but not the scale. And however much the *Mirror* might inveigh against the low level of the campaign, the fact of its predominantly lower middle-class, working-class readership prohibited it from reporting the election in any breadth or depth. On March 24th the *Mirror* complained: 'Nobody will ever say of the general election of March 31, 1966: "This Was Our Finest Hour".' Its own contribution to raising the campaign's level on the same day was a centre-page interview with Mrs. Wilson by Marjorie Proops. At that stage, the election had been headline news in the *Mirror* only three times since the dissolution (apart from two tangential stories on the 'noose trial'): once for Mr. Wilson's Bristol speech on the Common Market, a subject the *Mirror* felt passionately about; and once each for two of the prize trivia of the campaign: the ban on an exhibition of Mr. Wilson's doodles, and his being hit by a stink bomb during a speech at Slough.

A second major internal factor is the direction and intensity of a paper's party commitment. This may lead to bias in the presentation of stories and a partisan choice of stories to present. The extreme example in 1966 was of course the *Daily Worker*, whose relationship to the Communist party led it naturally to highlight the progress of Communist candidates. Lastly, the extent of a paper's financial resources must not be overlooked. The *Guardian*, for instance, probably weighed this fact with especial care when deciding whether to commission its eight A. J. Allen polls. *The Times* presumably considered sponsoring a poll and may well have been deterred by the cost.

The effects of these internal and external factors overlapped. The growing sophistication of election analysis led some papers to hire outside 'experts' as consultants, others to run their own polls. Richard Rose of Manchester University, co-author of the 1959 Nuffield election study, advised *The Times*. The chief authors of this book advised the *Sunday Times* (David Butler) and the *Observer* (Anthony King). Henry Durant and Mark Abrams wrote about polls, as well as producing them, for the *Daily Telegraph* and the *Observer*. Three papers — the *Telegraph*, the *Mail* and the

Express — had long been publishing polls regularly. The *Guardian*, faced with three polls sponsored by wealthy competitors, yet feeling that comprehensive election coverage required the use of surveys, commissioned a relatively new firm, A. J. Allen and Associates, to carry out eight polls in selected marginal constituencies. The *Sunday Times* and several provincial dailies also commissioned surveys in marginal seats. The *Observer* sponsored both a national poll and one in the South East region.

This left *The Times* and the *Sun* alone of the non-tabloid national dailies without some sort of poll. *The Times* reported as news the findings of NOP and Gallup after they had appeared in the *Mail* and the *Telegraph*, and its articles by Richard Rose were based regularly on Gallup data. Otherwise *The Times*' reaction to the polls was quite different from the *Guardian*'s. Neither paper abandoned constituency reports, traditionally the staple diet of the quality press; indeed *The Times* reports were carefully planned so that the twenty seats each party needed to win for a working majority were covered, plus several where the Liberals were strong and a few seats made interesting by special local factors. But *The Times* did not confine itself to 'geographical' constituencies: under the heading 'Types of Voter' it described various 'social' constituencies — housewives, agricultural workers, and so on. The result was a series of lively articles and vignettes, beginning with sentences like 'My husband says that if I vote for Harold Wilson he will divorce me.' The effort was thus to show how the campaign looked to individuals and to particular parts of the population, rather than to try to predict the result. On the face of it this looked like a conscious reaction to the precise opinion-sounding of the polls. In fact it was a straightforward attempt to find the best journalistic approach to the election. One wonders, though, whether *The Times* will remain content to be the only quality daily without its own poll. On the other hand, the *Guardian* in retrospect may feel that its polls contributed less than had been hoped to the effectiveness of its coverage. The *Sun*, the other non-tabloid without a poll, was presumably inhibited mainly by lack of money. It printed eleven constituency reports, concentrating on interesting seats, such as one where two of the candidates were women.

The extent to which the papers publishing polls also used

traditional methods varied, the two extremes being the *Telegraph* and the *Mail*. The presence of the Gallup poll had no apparent effect on the *Telegraph*'s organisation and treatment of its constituency reports. These were grouped regionally, with marginal seats picked out for emphasis, and a series was devoted to seats where immigration might be an issue. The *Mail*, in contrast, headlined its polls and printed only a scattering of constituency reports. The *Guardian* like the *Telegraph* retained its conventional reports; these reinforced its polls rather more effectively than the *Telegraph*'s since the polls were at the constituency level. The *Express* headlined its polls as often as the *Mail*, but unlike the *Mail* also ran regular reports on marginals ('Key Seat Close Ups') averaging two a day.

The *Mail* had claimed that long before the campaign began every issue had been 'canvassed and discussed to the point of tedium'. How far did this mean that the issues were not reported and discussed in the press during the election? In simple quantitative terms, the extent of coverage can be measured by calculating the amount of space given to election news other than constituency reports and polls: to speeches, features, leading articles and so on. Although the totals in the table (p. 151) are large — and the manifestos were reported as fully as ever — it does seem true that there was less discussion than in 1964 outside the leader columns. *The Times* ran nothing similar to its 1964 'Election Papers'. The *Telegraph* and *Express* ran centre-page features on policy, but as part of their partisan activities to be discussed below. The *Mirror*, given the limitations imposed by its readership, did undertake to discuss the issues and devoted its two centre pages to the purpose on half a dozen occasions. One week it assessed the Labour party ('Wilson's Wonder Boys', 'The Misfits and Flops', and 'Wilson at Number Ten'); the next it considered the Conservatives. Contributions by, or long interviews with, the three party leaders were features of the *Mirror*, *Sketch* and *Sun*; 'I also believe in cutting out the guff,' wrote Mr. Heath, suiting his style to the *Mirror*'s. The *Daily Mail*, apart from its columns by Iain Macleod and Bernard Levin, had no features at all examining policy. In fact the only paper to set out the background to a number of issues and to present the parties' policies so that readers could judge for themselves was the *Sun*. It ran a series of 'Probes': on modernisation, the cost of living, etc. There was an element of irony here since no national paper has a higher proportion of politically committed readers than the *Sun*.[1]

The effects of a paper's partisanship can emerge in various ways. One is through bias, in the sense of slanted headlines and the interpolation of comment into news stories. This can be tested impressionistically by comparing reports of particular speeches. A good example was one of the noisiest meetings of the campaign, Mr. Wilson's visit on March 16th to the Birmingham Rag Market where Sir Alec Douglas-Home had been shouted down in 1964. The *Express* apart, the impression left of who won the battle between Mr. Wilson and the hecklers varied distinctly according to a paper's political leanings. The *Worker*'s headline read 'WILSON GETS THE BETTER OF TORY HECKLERS'; the *Sketch*'s 'HECKLERS DROWN WILSON'. The *Sketch*'s story, beginning 'Mr. Wilson's big Birmingham rally ended in a shambles last night', left no doubt that he had not coped with the hecklers very successfully. The *Daily Telegraph*'s headline was emphatic — 'BIRMINGHAM YOUTHS HOWL WILSON DOWN' — but the story was neutral and took care to claim that Labour supporters made as much noise as the Conservatives. All the Labour papers made out that Mr. Wilson had emerged victorious. So did *The Times* ('Mr. Wilson giving as good as he took, finished by scoring a personal triumph in the way he stood up to the barrage of noise, chanting and cat calls') and the *Express* ('. . . within 20 minutes he had emerged as a cheeky chappy who, by sheer effrontery, had overcome an energetic and determined offensive against him'). The Labour papers were even more glowing: 'a superbly cool and talented theatrical performance' (*Guardian*); 'kept his head and won the battle hands down' (*Mirror*); 'flayed the Young Conservatives who were heckling him' (*Sun*).

The papers also assigned the story widely varying degrees of prominence. The *Express*, at one extreme, made it its front-page lead story ('WILSON: 15,000 IN BIG RIOT'). The *Mail*, at the other, gave it a short paragraph on page one headed 'MRS. WILSON HIT BY PAPER DART'. The *Mail* led that day with the latest National Opinion Poll and a speech by Mr. Heath on Europe. In between, *The Times*, *Telegraph*, *Sun* and *Worker* featured the story prominently on the front page, though not as the lead story. The

---

[1] The *Sun* largely inherited the readership of the Labour *Daily Herald*, which it replaced in September 1964.

Sketch and *Guardian* gave it full coverage on their back pages and the *Mirror* led its election news page with it.

But a more important effect of partisanship may be the choice of stories to report. This raises the important question of the uses to which press partisanship is put, since newspapers not only act as channels of communication but themselves participate in the electoral struggle. Their participation can be direct and explicit, in the form of editorial advocacy in the leader and feature columns, or indirect through careful selection of which news to emphasise or ignore. From this point of view, the most fascinating aspect of the press in 1966 was the way some of the most partisan papers were embarrassed by their opinions on subjects they wanted — or felt obliged — to stress, and by the implications of their opinion polls.

The Times was one of the few papers without a firm partisan allegiance. It had come out definitely if unenthusiastically for the Conservatives in 1964. This time it was equivocal. Faced with an election it did not want, the paper found it easy to say what the campaign ought to be about: 'Nothing matters to Britain so much as her economy' (March 1st). But it continued thoughtfully, 'It is quite another thing to guess how it will turn out.' By the 10th, after the appearance of the manifestos, it was evidently turning out all wrong. In a psalm-like leading article running to a full column, *The Times* chorused 27 reasons 'Why the £ is Weak'. (The article was reprinted, as from holy writ, by the *Mirror*, *Mail* and *Evening News*.) The 27 ranged from complaints about the inefficiencies of management to alleged defects in the national character ('Too many working hours are turned into gambling hours'). The final verse concluded:

> 'The £ could be strong if the British people had the ears to hear, the eyes to see, and the will to recover their native sense and energy. They have done it time and again in wars; why can they not do it just once in peace? That is what the General Election should be about.'

In its comment on specific issues *The Times* showed little enthusiasm for either party. In the end it stayed on the fence, preferring Mr. Heath on three of what it considered the five major issues — trade union reform, the social services, and Europe — and Labour marginally on the other two — enforcing competition, and building a society 'in which the individual's opportunity for fulfilment, which is the key to a happy life, will prevail'. As in 1964, *The Times* emphasised the need for as large a Liberal vote as possible.

The *Guardian*'s support for Labour was even more consistent than in 1964. It smiled warmly on the Liberals from time to time — 'without its Liberal members, Parliament would be a poorer place' — but its support was even less ardent than *The Times*'. On most issues the paper's preference for Labour was clear: housing, the social services, defence, economic growth (Labour's aims had 'a degree of detail' that carried conviction), and Rhodesia. Particular attention was paid to Rhodesia as a matter of policy; the paper crossed swords on the issue with Selwyn Lloyd, who claimed on March 18th that it had misrepresented his position. Mr. Wilson sometimes seemed 'in danger of becoming the best conservative Prime Minister of this century', but the *Guardian* felt that his social conscience had not been submerged. Given a five-year term, he was likely 'to take us some way towards a more just and civilized Britain'. The paper's main disappointment with Labour was over the Common Market: 'One toe in the Channel' was the headline to its comment on Mr. Wilson's Bristol speech. Even so, it found Labour's stand on the matter just as acceptable as the Conservatives'.

Little need be said of the editorial policy of the *Sun*, the other non-tabloid supporting Labour. Its final decision to support Labour was completely predictable, though it pretended to be dealing out impartial justice and delayed its verdict until the Friday before polling day. During the following week it elaborated its views in long front-page leading articles propounding Labour's superiority in economic, social and overseas affairs. But it did aim at coaxing Labour along on the issue of joining Europe; Mr. Wilson's Bristol speech it found 'lukewarm' and 'lamentably hesitant'. Of the *Sketch*'s editorial policy, still less need be said. It maintained its usual staunch Conservative line. The most important issue, it felt, was 'which party can take Britain into Europe'; and the one bright spot of the 'scrappy campaign' was the 'emergence of Mr. Heath'. The *Financial Times*, despite its Conservative tradition and close City connections, found the choice between the parties not at all clear cut. It finally plumped for Mr. Heath 'on a presidential basis' but it looked forward to Labour's return without misgiving, provided the majority was not too large.

On the Conservative papers which sponsored polls, the leader writers had a frustrating time. If their function was to rally support, they could week by week plot their failure. The position was particularly uncomfortable since the polls carried some prestige. Even the *Express*, which had always regarded its own poll as 'a useful guide' but not infallible, could not help admitting that it was 'noted for the success of its final predictions in both the last two General Elections'. Early in the campaign, the *Express, Telegraph* and *Mail* naturally tried to be optimistic. The *Express* commented: 'On the experience of past General Elections the polls are likely to change during the course of the campaign — perhaps in favour of the Opposition.' The *Telegraph* on March 14th thought that 'the tide of public opinion may already be turning', but a week later it gloomily confessed that the polls contributed strongly 'to a sense of helpless predestination'. The *Mail* reacted more in anger. 'What HAS gone wrong?' a leading article asked on March 17th; the steady Labour lead was 'unprecedented, unnatural and absurd'. Only on the 19th did it follow the *Telegraph* and concede that: 'For all the good it has done Mr. Wilson's critics it seems that the General Election campaign need not have taken place.' The *Express*, too, went on nibbling crumbs of comfort for as long as possible. With Labour's lead at $12\frac{1}{2}\%$, it announced on March 12th that polls 'do not always reflect special local situations'. On the 19th, with Labour's lead now $15\frac{1}{2}\%$, it drew attention to the Conservatives' success in local elections. But on the 25th, when Labour's lead dropped slightly to $13\frac{1}{2}\%$, although the headline read cheerfully 'TORIES CATCHING THE TIDE,' the leader-page comment was bewildered. 'Only one thing is sure,' it concluded limply, 'as in life, so in politics, there is no such thing as certainty.' Unlike the *Telegraph* and the *Mail*, the *Express* persistently cast doubt on the validity of its own poll.

With the polls lodged uncomfortably in their bosoms, the *Telegraph* and the *Mail* followed an unswerving Conservative line. Every day from March 21st (and often before that) the *Telegraph* argued the Conservative case in leader-page feature articles. Twice it gave up space to Labour, with contributions from Denis Healey on defence and Mr. Brown on the economy. But the *Express* was in a more difficult position. On the one hand, its philosophy prevented it from being too gloomy about the state of the country. 'Don't sell Britain short' was its reaction to *The Times'* sententious leader:

> 'This newspaper firmly places its faith in the future of Britain on the facts of twenty years. For they tell a proud and joyous story.'

On the other hand, the *Express* did not want to place its faith in a Labour government. It therefore concentrated in leaders and feature articles on anti-Labour issues — Rhodesia, defence ('where Britain is drifting into greater dependence on American arms and American policy'), and education — which were consistent with its basic optimism. But the Common Market complicated the position even further. Anyone who thought the *Express*'s attitude would change after the death of Lord Beaverbrook was mistaken. On March 19th it announced that 'the *Daily Express* must register anew its determined opposition to the Market, whether it comes stealthily through Mr. Wilson or bluntly through Mr. Heath'.

The *Mirror*'s problem was exactly the reverse: a pro-Labour paper, it inclined towards the Conservatives on Europe. In one sense it had an easier task. It was trying to persuade a party to adopt a policy rather than reject one; and it was not hampered by having to publish polls which indicated that it was failing to make headway. But in another sense the *Mirror*'s task was harder. Unlike the *Express*, which chose largely to avoid the European issue, it was determined to campaign on Europe; it was the only paper apart from the *Daily Worker* to wade into the election avowedly as one of the fighters. It sought to persuade not so much its readers as the leaders of the Labour party. At the same time, however, the *Mirror* did wish to go on supporting Labour. The paper thus found itself in the awkward position of urging its readers to vote for Mr. Wilson even though it disagreed with Mr. Wilson on the very issue in the campaign it deemed the most important.

Its response to this dilemma was summed up in the refrain 'First the Inquest — Then the Verdict'. The plan was first to clear away any disagreements with Labour and then to support the party against the Tories. At the outset therefore it took up a startlingly independent stance. The state of the economy, it felt, was much too serious for political bickering: 'What is needed, and urgently, is LEADERSHIP, GUTS and AUTHORITY at the top.' The question the *Mirror* asked of the manifestos was 'How much is statesmanlike realism, how much is political guff?'; and it was impatient with the shadow boxing of the party leaders on the two crucial problems of the balance of payments and the Common Market. The paper found the Prime Minister's Bristol speech a bitter disappointment: 'Not Wilson at his best (which is splendid) but Wilson at his worst (which is frightening).'

The failure of the Common Market to emerge as an issue till mid-March delayed the opening of the second phase of the *Mirror*'s campaign. By the 25th the paper's attitude was arousing comment among its contemporaries. Was it trying to exact a price for supporting Labour? Was it going to support Labour because of its readership but despite its feelings? When the final verdict did come therefore, on March 28th, the writer of the leading article seemed a little defensive. The paper denied any threats to withdraw support from Labour. 'The Mirror does not issue threats,' its leader concluded:

> 'It does not jump on bandwagons. It tries to give both sides in any major dispute. But it isn't, never has been, and never will be, a tin can tied to a political party's tail.'

If anything, the *Mirror* sounded a little too anxious to protest its independence. Perhaps it liked Mr. Heath and the Common Market but not the Conservative party; perhaps it liked Labour but not Mr. Wilson. 'GIVE WILSON A GOOD MAJORITY' was the headline on polling day, but the paper added: 'So that, this time, there can be NO ALIBIS.'

How were these explicit views reflected in the various papers' handling of news? There were the usual instances of slanted headlines. The *Telegraph*'s main headlines in 1964 had been consistently slanted. This time they were not, but bias could sometimes be seen on the campaign pages. More striking was the bias to be found in the *Mail* and the *Guardian*. 'TOUGHER SQUEEZE IS ON THE WAY' (*Mail*) and 'TRADE FIGURES GIVE LABOUR TIMELY BOOST' (*Guardian*) both referred to the same story, the publication of the February trade figures. The *Guardian* gave a neutral headline to its lead story on Labour's manifesto — 'THE POUND COMES FIRST ON LABOUR'S LIST' — but heralded the Conservative manifesto 'TORY MANIFESTO "DRIVEL" SAYS MR. BROWN'. Slightly different were the echoes of bygone scare techniques of which the *Sketch* in recent years has been the only exponent. 'ENOCH: BRITAIN FACES FLOOD OF $2\frac{1}{2}$ MILLION IMMIGRANTS' was the headline on a speech by Mr. Powell in his constituency; the story made it clear that the figure referred to the end of the century. On polling day the *Sketch* headline read 'WHAT WILL YOUR PAY BE WORTH IN 1970?' — a vital question every reader should face up to before he voted.

The figures reported by the opinion polls had one clear implication for Conservative newspapers: they must find an issue that would bring the campaign to life. The *Telegraph*, reacting to the Gallup poll on March 14th, thought 'the kangaroo courts — which the polls pre-date — may turn out to be just the issue needed to highlight and contrast the difference between the parties'. The paper therefore linked the 'noose trial' clearly to the campaign. The *Mail* was quite evidently frustrated by the lack of material on which to bite. 'LIBERALS SHOW TORIES THE WAY' was the headline on March 16th above a lead story by Walter Terry:

> 'Almost for the first time there was a show last night of real fight in the General Election campaign. It came not from the Tories but the Liberals. In their first TV broadcast they delivered a lesson in how to sustain a strong attack on Mr. Wilson.'

Once or twice the campaign seemed to be coming alight: during the exchanges on Europe, for example, and on March 28th when the *Mail* led with a speech by Enoch Powell headlined 'POWELL MAKES THE SPARKS FLY'. But on polling day Walter Terry summed up his feelings in a lead story beginning:

> 'This, for me, has been the My Dear Ted election: an excruciating and dull affair in which the political master, past and present, has been teaching the pupil, perhaps with a future, his lessons.'

With livelier headlines, the *Express* also tried to breathe life into the campaign. On March 15th: 'Mr. Quintin Hogg, thundering his old battle-cry of "Bonkers!", emerged explosively last night as the first major controversial figure of the election . . .' From time to time the paper detected 'head-on rows' between the party leaders: over television (the 18th), Rhodesia (21st) and in the press conferences (30th). The *Express* produced particularly rousing stories reporting Heath's speeches, for example '"BRITAIN AWAKE!" HEATH'S CALL' on March 24th.

The reflection of the press's political views was interesting in connection with two issues in particular: the so-called 'noose trial', and Europe. The incidents at Cowley and elsewhere were good stories by any standards, dramatic and full of human interest. But they had in themselves no direct political and hence electoral significance. The question was, then, which papers would seek to establish a connection between the incidents and the policies of one or other party in order to make political capital. The papers that did were, as one might have expected, all Conservative; Labour papers tended to report the story straight, recognising, as the *Guardian* put it on March 14th, that the trade unions were 'Labour's time-bomb'. The only paper to try to make capital openly was the *Telegraph*. On Monday the 14th a short, front-page story headed 'TORIES PLUG AWAY AT UNION "TRIALS"' began:

> 'The Conservatives intend to keep hammering away at "workers' courts" and "kangaroo justice" as an election issue. They will use it as evidence of the need for speedy implementation of their policy for trade unions law reform.'

The *Telegraph* hammered away with news stories too; something on the trials appeared every day, often on the front page, between the 10th and the 21st. Labour leaders' condemnations were printed fairly, though a defensive impression was bound to be given by stories beginning, for example:

> 'With Mr. Gunter, Minister of Labour, putting up a rearguard action against the Conservative offensive on trade union "kangaroo courts," Mr. Heath yesterday switched his attack to a new front. . . .'

The *Telegraph* was quick to pick up new allegations of similar incidents and was still finding them on the 19th — a case at London airport — after the other papers had given up.

Other Conservative papers were slow to make any explicit connection between industrial evils and their party's demand for reform. The *Express*, for instance, reported the stories plainly, giving space to Labour denunciations. Its first comment, on the 14th, was neutral, concluding: 'Mr. Wilson! Mr. Heath! here in this single issue is a test of your political courage and capacity to lead the nation.' Next day it denied Mr. Wilson's claim that the affair was a red herring and called for:

> 'a clear pledge from the Unions and from both parties that the so-called "courts" will be suppressed, and that un-British methods will no longer stand in the way of production.'

Alongside its leader, the paper published a feature by Trevor Evans headed 'DEALING WITH THE UNIONS' and beginning: 'Mr.

Edward Heath has been presented with a bonus by the Oxford shop stewards who fined seven men for refusing to join an unofficial strike.' Thereafter the *Express* showed little interest in the strike, turning its attention to Rhodesia and the Common Market.

The *Mail* did not start headlining the story until the 12th. One of its political staff then noted that:

> 'the "Noose Trial" is rapidly turning into an election issue. While all three parties condemned it Labour, with its strong union ties, seemed in some embarrassment about its approach to the whole question.'

A leading article after the week-end argued that these aberrations should not be made an election issue: 'They will exist regardless of the party in power until we modernise our thinking.' Like the *Express*, therefore, the paper followed the ramifications of the story fully, but without apparently trying to keep it alive or find new examples of intimidation. Two feature articles on the 16th gave a sober background to the story and an analysis of union disciplinary regulations. The *Sketch*, finally, gave good space to the story, although not often on the front page. But it made no comment until after the Amalgamated Engineering Union report. It then attacked the union's attitude to the affair and applauded the Conservative proposals.

A second example of the press's partisanship influencing its news coverage was the Common Market. It involved the papers that held strong editorial views on the subject: the *Mirror*, *Sun* and *Guardian* in favour of entry, the *Express* against. An early test of interest was reactions to the party manifestos, which did not put primary emphasis on Europe. The *Express*, for example, headlined its story about the Labour manifesto 'WILSON'S TERMS FOR EUROPE' and drew attention to Mr. Heath's comment that these terms would make entry impossible. The *Mirror* headed its report of the Liberal manifesto 'LET'S PUT OUR MONEY ON EUROPE, SAY THE LIBERALS' and picked out for comment the sections on Europe in all the manifestos. Otherwise the papers with passionate feelings on the Common Market did not start to vent them until the campaign got under way. From then on, however, the *Mirror* made a point of highlighting stories about Europe. Its election-page lead story on the 15th, for instance — 'HEATH'S BATTLE CRY IS — "INTO EUROPE"' — singled out remarks in Mr. Heath's first

M

TV broadcast which less ardent papers paid no particular attention to. Next day the equivalent story was headed, 'HEATH AND BROWN CLASH OVER THE MARKET'. The *Sun* went one better, leading the paper with the same story headed 'EUROPE: IN OR OUT'. The main columns of the *Guardian*, however, were still filled with the 'noose trial' and Rhodesia; it would be against the paper's principles to conduct a partisan campaign in its news columns. The *Express* was also absorbed in the same two subjects.

The big story about France withdrawing her veto against British entry broke on March 17th, though the *Mail* had a small scoop on the 15th — a technical scoop since the story was not splashed — when it published a short front-page item headed 'FRANCE GIVES BRITAIN A MARKET INVITATION'. The story reported comments by M. Couve de Murville in a *Le Monde* supplement on Britain. Reports of Mr. Stewart's press conference on the 17th clashed with an American space probe and Mr. Wilson's reception in the Birmingham Rag Market, and the only papers to give it front-page treatment were the *Mirror*, the *Express* (saying sourly 'EUROPE: LABOUR GETS INTO THE ACT'), the *Mail* and the *Guardian*. The *Guardian* actually made Europe the lead story and, rather overestimating the significance of Mr. Stewart's statement, was at its most European over the next few days. Mr. Wilson's announcement that he would declare his position on the 18th meant that that day the *Guardian* and the *Mirror* both featured Europe prominently. The *Telegraph* also featured the story that day but for rather different reasons, reporting that 'HEATH POINTS TO LABOUR SPLIT'. The next day, the 19th, the press came nearer than at any other point during the campaign to having a common lead story. Only the *Express* banished the Prime Minister's speech to a single column on the left of the page, leading instead with its latest poll.

On the Labour side, Mr. Wilson's Bristol speech disposed of Europe as an issue. How far did the press feel the same way about it as a news topic? Most papers made no special effort to keep the issue alive. The *Express*, despite its views, seemed quite happy all along to wage its war in the leader and feature columns. It continued, however, even after the 19th to emphasise stories with an anti-Common Market angle, for example about the only anti-European Independent, Mr. Christopher Frere-Smith in Marylebone. The *Mirror*, too, continued to give prominence to stories about the Market: another of Mr. Heath's television broadcasts, for example, and Labour's rumoured plan for a Minister for Europe. Both stories received little if any attention from other papers except the *Sun*. These three papers, in fact, were the only ones to extract as much news as they could from the European issue to support their points of view.

Two other categories of paper need to be examined before any general conclusions about the role of the press in 1966 can be drawn. The national Sundays, firstly, varied predictably. Neither the *News of the World* (circulation 6,176,000) nor *The People* (5,538,000) devoted much space to the election. The former gave no indication to its readers how they should vote and ran feature-page articles by all three party leaders. *The People* was more partisan, with a long article by the editor entitled 'WHY WILSON MUST WIN' on the Sunday before polling day. At the opposite extreme, the *Sunday Citizen* (232,700) acted in effect as the Labour party's *Daily Worker*. The party slogan 'You know Labour government works' was spread across the front page each Sunday, and much of the paper's resources were devoted to advancing the Labour cause. The *Sunday Mirror* (5,082,000) and *Sunday Express* (4,190,000) reflected the methods and concerns of their daily counterparts. The *Sunday Mirror*'s interest in Europe emerged with a full-page article on the European Economic Community by Lord Gladwyn on March 20th; and on the 27th a front-page comment settled for 'WILSON — WARTS AND ALL!' The Beaverbrook press's policy of promoting suspicion of the polls was reflected in an early *Sunday Express* feature reminding readers that in 1965 'Leyton provided shattering proof of the fallibility of the pollsters' and asking 'Will the voters at Leyton spring another bombshell?' Leading and feature articles were vigorously pro-Conservative.

The three quality Sundays — *Sunday Times* (1,290,000), *Observer* (823,700), *Sunday Telegraph* (650,100) — had the same approach to election coverage as the quality dailies. All of them sponsored polls to which they gave some prominence. In addition, all three papers exploited their position as weeklies to stand back from the campaign and also to attempt reporting in depth. 'How Heath slowly discovered himself' was a typical heading on the *Sunday Times*'s 'Insight' feature. Like the quality dailies, the Sundays carried constituency reports, campaign notebooks and analyses of issues (the *Sunday Telegraph* gave a whole page to immigration on March 20th). Editorially only the *Telegraph* was enthusiastically partisan. Typical of its attitude was its feeling that the Conservative manifesto was suffused with 'the quiet glow of a leader with integrity and knowledge'. The *Sunday Times* rejoiced when Europe became an issue and found it a sufficient reason for supporting the Conservatives. The *Observer*, as ever, sought to make a virtue of indecision.

The provincial morning newspapers treated the campaign much as in 1964.[1] Considerable variations were evident in the extent and sophistication of their coverage. One or two papers, the Darlington *Northern Echo*, for example, and the *Birmingham Post*, ran opinion polls on local seats as well as the usual constituency reports. A few, including the *Echo* and the *Yorkshire Post*, carried reports from constituencies outside their region. Other papers concentrated mainly on reports of speeches by party leaders and local candidates. Nearly all featured discussions on policy, often contributed by outsiders, on a scale larger than most national papers. The Sheffield *Morning Telegraph* carried a series called 'Debate' in which ministers and their shadows wrote about important issues: Mr. Healey and Mr. Powell on defence, Mr. Callaghan and Mr. Macleod on the cost of living, etc. Few papers were at all strident in their partisanship. The *Northern Echo* and the *Morning Telegraph* remained uncommitted as usual. More papers than not supported the Conservatives, though few with the uninhibited vigour of the *Yorkshire Post*, whose centre-page articles, by contrast with the *Morning Telegraph*'s 'Debates', were devoted solely to arguing the Conservative case. Dissatisfaction with the conduct of the campaign was, as in the national press, widespread.

In the light of the 1966 campaign, how important is the press at a British general election? As a medium of communication, of course, newspapers continue to have a depth and range, although not an immediacy, with which television cannot compete; the quality papers, in particular, have become ever more sophisticated in their techniques of reporting and analysis. Even if in 1966 the mechanics of communicating seemed tiresome to the communicators, the importance of the press's communications role remains undiminished. But what remains of the press's role as participant

---

[1] The provincial morning papers were dealt with at some length in *The British General Election of 1964*. See A. J. Beith, 'The Press', pp. 199–200.

in the campaign? Even if election campaigns often change more
votes than is sometimes supposed, there is a great deal of evidence
to suggest that editorial advocacy and scare techniques alike have
no effect whatever. Yet newspapers can influence the electorate,
if only indirectly. For what the press can do, as the 'noose trial' and
Common Market episodes suggest, is to influence the issues that
the parties themselves feel obliged to debate. The *Mirror* and
Guardian may not have influenced what Mr. Wilson said on
Europe; but their strenuous advocacy helped make it difficult for
him to avoid the subject entirely. The press can thus make an
impact on the politicians, as well as deciding, in conjunction with
television, what parts of what the politicians say shall be communicated to the general public.

CHAPTER IX

OPINION POLLS

OPINION polls reached a new level of political importance in the 1964 parliament. Everyone watching to see when Mr. Wilson would decide to call an election knew that Mr. Wilson was watching the polls. The Conservatives' eagerness to harry the government plainly rose as they cut into Labour's poll lead in the summer of 1965; it as obviously ebbed when Labour's lead shot up again in the autumn. Parliamentary and local government by-elections might tell a somewhat different story but plainly opinion polls did most to shape the political climate.

Some commentators credited the polls with a critical influence in Sir Alec Douglas-Home's decision to give up the Conservative leadership. Those who advocated his retirement had long cited the continued low rating he achieved in response to the question 'Do you think he is doing a good job as leader of the Conservative party?' But the *coup de grâce* came in a much-publicised NOP finding published a week before he decided to retire. The British public apparently regarded him as less sincere than Mr. Wilson: this mass failure to appreciate what his intimates would claim to be his greatest quality was deeply wounding.

The influence of the polls was not dimmed by their vagaries. In January 1965 NOP's final forecast for the Leyton by-election gave Mr. Gordon Walker a 20% victory instead of a $\frac{1}{2}$% defeat — the greatest error in prediction ever made by a serious British survey organisation.[1]

Less sensational but more worrying to the pollsters than the Leyton debacle was the discrepancy between the Gallup and NOP findings. All through the parliament NOP tended to show an appreciably bigger Labour lead than Gallup; in five of the first eight months of 1965 Gallup put the Conservatives in the lead, while according to NOP they nosed ahead only in August.

This discrepancy was all the more puzzling since in the last year

---

[1] NOP, as was noted in the previous chapter, defied the trend of newspaper comment by predicting accurately the handsome victory of Labour in Hull North.

before the 1964 election it had been NOP whose findings tended
to be more favourable to the Conservatives. This makes it plain,
if demonstration were needed, that there was no question of
political bias underlying the contrasting findings, only differences
in technique. Different sampling procedures, different interview-
ing instructions and different conventions about pressing 'don't
knows' for their opinions could explain the gap. It is a pity that the

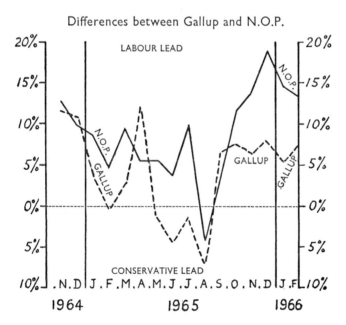

Differences between Gallup and N.O.P.

administration of the polls was not made subject to more constructive outside criticism of a kind that would have elucidated the
facts about these discrepancies and helped to explain them. The
pollsters themselves had no confident answer. It probably lay
partly in the 'don't knows'; Gallup found more than twice as
many as NOP. It may have lain, too, in the two polls' sampling
procedures; Gallup's quota method probably led it to complete
interviews with more of the under-30s and fewer of the very elderly
than NOP's random procedure.

It is worth stressing how difficult it is, in any case, to interpret
short run, and indeed long run fluctuations, in the polls. The polls
after all do not, and cannot be expected to, probe in any detail into

the motives and responses of those they interview. The commercial polls do not normally ask the kind of open-ended questions which would allow the respondents themselves to give shape to the analysis. Even if they did, it would not be worth their while to process their data in the required detail; for one thing, it would take far too long. Academic survey research has pushed the study of voting further, at least in the United States, but even there much remains to be learned about the dynamics of opinion formation. Pronouncements about the state of public opinion by politicians and pundits should thus invariably be treated with caution.

The political importance of polling was advertised by the revelations of the role that Mark Abrams had played in Labour's electoral preparations from 1961 onwards. Paradoxically the Labour party, like the Liberals, sponsored virtually no polling during the 1964 parliament. The Conservatives on the other hand launched the largest effort in private political research ever undertaken in Britain, but, apart from an exaggerated story in December 1964 and a brief report of Humphrey Taylor's activities, little leaked into the press.[1]

The fact that by 1966 polls had become fashionable was shown by the increased newspaper interest in the subject. All those papers which had published polls in 1964 continued to do so as prominently as ever. But the *Daily Telegraph, Daily Mail, Daily Express* and *Observer* were joined this time by the *Guardian, Financial Times, The Economist* and the *Sunday Times*. Provincial papers and the London 'evenings' also gave markedly more space to constituency polls or to regional findings of national polls. It became almost an oddity for a newspaper with any pretensions to be without a poll.

The national polls and their regional offshoots pointed consistently and without exception to a Labour landslide. So did most of the constituency polls. As Mr. Heath remarked they were 'in a groove . . . in a groove . . . in a groove'. But he naturally turned for comfort to the few exceptions, mainly those of A. J. Allen and Associates. This firm produced much publicised polls for *The Economist*, the *Guardian* and the *Birmingham Post*. They were notable for their extraordinarily high 'don't know' rate — averaging well over 20% — and for their method of calculating swing: they compared their findings, not with what actually

[1] See pp. 64–69 above.

happened in 1964, but with how people said that they had voted
in 1964. On this basis (scorned by all established polls) they found
several constituencies moving towards the Conservatives and most
others with swings far below those indicated by the nationwide
polls. On a more conventional method of measuring the swing they
would have been slightly but not much less inaccurate. The firm
also produced some equally unsuccessful constituency forecasts
for the Midlands, not by polling but by an unexplained system of
multiple regression analysis. Finally the day before the poll they
simultaneously, in defiance of all their earlier findings, produced
forecasts of a Labour majority of 'over 100' (*Birmingham Post*) and
162 (*Guardian*). In the *Guardian* they boldly named 88 seats as
probable changes and 24 seats as possible surprises. They were
wrong about 32 of the probables and all of the possibles.

The other constituency polls were of varying accuracy. Anyone
wanting to forecast individual results would have done better to
assume that a uniform national swing would apply to every constituency than to be guided by such polls.[1] The regional and
marginal seat breakdowns of the national polls, published and unpublished, were equally misleading — the suggestions that the
swing would be exceptionally high in the North West (Gallup) or
exceptionally low in the West Midlands (Gallup and NOP) were
falsified by events. So were the suggestions that the swing would
be markedly different in marginal seats or just in Conservative
marginals. When, as in recent British elections, and particularly
in 1966, electoral swings are very uniform, it is not practicable to
conduct polls with samples large enough to detect the minor
variations that may occur in particular constituencies and particular regions.

However, the main importance of polls during the election lay in
their national findings. The fact that the two most regarded polls
agreed in showing Labour 10% or more ahead almost throughout
the campaign took much of the steam out of the contest. The Conservatives were oddly slow to attack the polls. But as time went on
and the polls stayed in their groove, voices began to be raised in

[1] The *Evening Standard* early in the campaign forecast that the Orpington
vote would divide Con. 52·5%, Lib. 28·3%, Lab. 19·2%. In fact it divided
Con. 43·3%, Lib. 46·7%, Lab. 10·0%. This error of 27·6% in the party lead
(admittedly the survey was made four weeks before election day) beat even the
NOP debacle at Leyton. But the other four *Evening Standard* polls showed a
very small average margin of error. The record of the constituency polls was
analysed in the *Sunday Times* 'Insight' feature of April 3rd, 1966.

protest. Mr. Gresham Cooke promised to introduce legislation banning the publication of polls during an election. Mr. A. J. P. Taylor advocated this stridently in a *Sunday Express* article. Mr. Maudling told a meeting that there was a case for an enquiry. And in the correspondence columns of many papers there appeared an increasing flow of letters expressing anxiety about the bandwagon effect of polls and their undemocratic consequences. It was left to Mr. Heath in his first post-election interview to put the other side

Survey	Date of publication	Party percentages ('don't knows' eliminated) *				Don't know %	Labour lead %
		Con. %	Lab. %	Lib. %	Other %		
Gallup quota	Feb. 24th	42	51	6½	½	11½	9
	March 4th	40	51	7½	1½	9	11
	March 13th	41	51	7½	½	9½	10
	March 20th	39	51	9½	—	7	12
	March 27th	42	50½	7	½	6½	8½
Gallup random	March 13th	40½	52½	6½	½	7	12
	March 20th	41½	52	6	—	7	10½
	March 24th	42	50½	7	½	7	8½
Gallup combined	March 31st	40	51	8	1	7	11
NOP	Feb. 17th	39·8	53·8	6·3	0·1	4·0	14·0
	March 3rd	40·1	53·0	6·7	0·2	3·3	12·9
	March 10th	39·4	53·8	6·5	0·3	3·4	14·4
	March 18th	39·2	52·6	7·7	0·5	3·8	13·4
	March 24th	39·5	52·0	7·8	0·7	2·9	12·5
	March 29th	39·6	52·2	7·6	0·6	3·2	12·6
	March 31st	41·6	50·6	7·4	0·4	2·1	9·0
Research Services	March 6th	44·9	49·4	5·2	0·5	12	4·5
	March 13th	41·9	49·6	8·1	0·4	14½	7·7
	March 20th	42·4	49·7	7·4	0·5	16	7·3
	March 27th	41·6	49·7	8·3	0·4	16	8·1
Daily Express	March 7th	39	54	7	—	9½	15
	March 12th	40	54½	5½	(¼)	8¼	14½
	March 19th	37½	55	7½	(½)	8¼	17½
	March 25th	39	53½	7½	—	8½	14½
	March 29th	40	52½	7½	(½)	10½	12½
	March 31st	37·4	54·1	7·7	0·8	7¾	16·7

* All the final polls were published in this form except for the *Daily Express* which excluded the 'Others' from its percentages. The earlier NOP polls have been adjusted to eliminate 'Don't knows'.

of the case: 'Ban polls? Of course not. You can't do that in a free society.' And on April 26th Mr. Wilson in a parliamentary reply flatly refused to consider any restriction on election polls. NOP found that, after the election, 53% of people claimed to have seen poll forecasts and 42% remembered that they had forecast a Labour win. However, there is no evidence that polls had a bandwagon effect. The final Labour majority was less than almost any poll had suggested. The polls' suggestion that the outcome was a foregone conclusion may indeed, by encouraging apathy and abstention, have cut down Labour's share of the vote. The reason why polls attracted so much criticism in this election is that they took the fun out of it by recording the fact that Labour was handsomely ahead. But in four out of five elections from 1950 to 1964 the gap between the major parties was less than the average error of the four major polls in 1966. In other words it has been normal for elections to be decided by margins in which the polls cannot forecast the winner with certainty and in which their findings therefore can only add to the excitement.

Opinion poll fore-casts	Actual result (G.B. only) %	Gallup %	NOP %	Research Services %	Daily Express %
Con. . .	41·4	−1·4	+0·2	+0·2	−4·0
Lab. . .	48·7	+2·3	+1·9	+1·0	+5·9
Lib. . .	8·6	−0·6	−1·2	−0·3	−0·9
Mean error on major parties		1·4	1·1	0·5	3·4
Error in forecast of Labour lead		3·7	1·7	0·8	9·9

In fact the final polls, apart from the *Daily Express*, were within an acceptable margin of error. Research Services came out best although its final interviews must have been a full week before the poll. The comparative accuracy of the four polls was, by some measures, in reverse order to 1964; but no judgment of a polling organisation's merit should be based on a single prediction. The most worrying feature of the national polls was the differing story which they offered about the impact of the campaign. During the month of March Research Services and the *Daily Express* found an increase in the Labour lead. According to Gallup it remained relatively stable. NOP recorded a final falling off and NOP, alone among the polls, re-interviewed at the end of the campaign a sample of the people whom it had talked with earlier. Its final prediction (although this was not given much prominence by the *Daily Mail*) was based on the movement of opinion shown in these re-interviews.

Voting intention in NOP recall survey, March 26th–29th

Voting intention when first inter-viewed earlier in March	Voting intention in recall survey							Total
	Con.	Lab.	Lib.	Other	Would not vote	Un-decided	Re-fused	
Con. . .	556	30	7	—	6	4	4	607
Lab. . .	33	735	16	1	9	13	20	827
Lib. . .	18	22	82	—	2	1	—	125
Other . .	—	2	—	5	—	—	—	7
Would not vote	3	4	2	—	16	4	2	31
Undecided .	24	12	9	1	—	12	7	65
Refused .	9	8	2	—	1	3	8	31
Total .	643	813	118	7	34	37	41	1,693

This table shows absolute numbers not percentages. It does not, of course, represent the final NOP prediction; this coupled the movement shown here with the original intentions of the full samples from which these 1,693 names were drawn for re-interview.

The re-interviews revealed no net shift directly between the two major parties; however, the other movements indicated that on balance the campaign slightly helped the Conservatives, who made net gains from Liberals and 'don't knows'.

The opinion polls had, like British politics, flourished in a hot-house atmosphere for four or five years up to 1966. Public interest had focused overwhelmingly on their latest forecasts of voting intention and, to a much lesser extent, on their ratings of the party leaders. It is to be hoped that the press will now exploit the pollsters' techniques to throw light on opinions and attitudes in more sophisticated ways than hitherto. The Conservative party has, belatedly, found it worth while to invest considerable resources in the collection and analysis of survey data about the British public. If such research is not to be abused, it is desirable that the sort of information which parties may have at their disposal should also be gathered independently — and published.

Politicians, and everyone else, can easily be misled by the apparent findings of polls. The intelligent statesman will neither ignore them nor be intimidated by them. In the short run public opinion sets limits to the politically possible and it is useful to know these limits. But public opinion can be fickle. As Winston Churchill showed before the war, there need be nothing suicidal in defying the opinion of the majority. It is worth remembering that democratic politicians have always conducted affairs with an eye on public opinion. They now have more accurate tools for measuring what public opinion really is. What they still need is education in how to use these tools — and how not to use them.

CHAPTER X

THE CAMPAIGN IN RETROSPECT

To many politicians as well as to newspaper men the 1966 campaign was a great bore. It was a bore because there was so little doubt about the outcome; it was a bore because there had been an election only seventeen months before and electioneering of a sort had hardly stopped for four years; it was a bore because campaign techniques that were new in 1959 had become, on the third time out, established rituals. It is worth reflecting on how far things had changed since 1955: then there were no institutionalised press conferences setting the tone for reporters; then there was no coverage whatever on radio or television; then the party leaders went round the country on whistle-stop tours, and their speeches as reported in the press constituted the national campaign, apart from the few official party broadcasts.

In 1966 there were no visible novelties of a major sort in campaign techniques. It is true that for the first time both the main party leaders stayed in London, substituting day-excursions for campaign tours; yet they were only following the precedent set by Mr. Wilson in 1964. The great bulk of the participants and the observers of the 1966 campaign occupied their time very much as they had seventeen months before. Since they were not on tenterhooks about the result, they were often bored and felt that the whole process was wearisome and repetitious.

Yet the election was far from being a carbon copy of 1964. In style and in substance all three parties were arguing very differently from before. In retrospect some of them were inclined to shrug off their efforts. The Liberals believed they had benefited from the campaign, but in both Conservative and Labour headquarters there were people who said: 'After all, campaigns don't change votes. Nothing we or they could have done could have altered the result.' Such fatalism was, perhaps, the leading myth left by the campaign; for public opinion is not always so stable. It is worth recalling that as late as September 1965 *The Economist* could write, 'Mr. Wilson may be postponing a defeat in order to reap a landslide'. If one looks back over postwar elections, it is plain that a very large swing occurred in the last four weeks of the 1951 campaign and that in 1959 and 1964 there were substantial wobblings. Nor is there much doubt that the level of turnout can be substantially affected by the conduct of the battle. Moreover, in 1966 there plainly was some movement of opinion during the campaign — in contrast to 1955, away from the party in power. If Gallup and NOP on March 10th had been showing a Labour lead of 6% — the actual result on March 31st — instead of the 9% and 14% they did show, the campaign would in fact have been a more tense and exciting affair.

However, it would be wrong to leave the impression that the election was universally seen as dull and unexciting, that people paid no attention to the tedious ritual dance as it drew to its pre-ordained conclusion. 'In short it was a non-election and I am now a non-member,' wrote one defeated Conservative. Yet in fact it was an event which evoked great interest. There is no evidence that the great mass of the public felt less involved than in 1964. Indeed, on March 13th Gallup reported that 42% of voters described themselves as 'very interested' in the outcome of the election compared with 36% in 1964. The television audience did not decline, and when it came to the point the vast majority of electors voted; the apparent certainty of a Labour victory, rather than lack of interest, probably caused the slight decline in turnout. The tedium felt in Smith Square simply did not communicate itself to the country at large.

The Labour party, confident of victory, fought a relatively subdued campaign, giving no hostages to fortune, using few gimmicks, trying in a persistent way to get across the themes 'Thirteen wasted years' and 'You know Labour government works'. This was far from the frenetic activity of 1964. It was a calm unhurried performance without any serious slip. No lapses occurred comparable to Mr. Wilson's Hardy Spicer taunt or Mr. Brown's allusion to 3% mortgages. Mr. Wilson continued to be perceived as prime ministerial throughout the campaign, although he chose to speak from party platforms every night, and although the television news bulletins consistently showed him making party points and responding with relish to heckling. He conveyed a sense of his mastery over affairs by his easy confidence when answering hecklers and by the fatherly common sense of his straight-to-camera appeals. No British party leader can ever have seemed more completely professional at his job.

The Labour strategy was not, even in its own terms, an unalloyed success. The evidence suggests that any movement of opinion during the campaign was against the government, and Labour won by a narrower margin than most polls had predicted. It is doubtful, however, whether any alternative strategy would have boosted Labour's majority. Mr. Wilson was risking his position as a national leader, above politics, by taking such an active part in the campaign; increased partisanship would only have increased the risk. Even more vehement attacks on the Conservatives might have led to a higher Labour turnout, but they would probably also have provoked as many extra Conservatives to go to the polls. An appeal directed largely at the working classes would probably have had a similarly mixed result.

Criticism of Labour during the campaign was focused on the negative tone of its electioneering, and on its persistent harking back to the past. Mr. Heath complained that Mr. Wilson had nothing constructive to say and never spoke about the country's future; the Conservatives maintained that the Prime Minister devoted 27 words to attacking the Conservatives for every word of constructive policy. Such charges were undoubtedly exaggerated, especially in view of the tendency of both television and press to ignore Mr. Wilson's more routine defences of the government's record. Moreover, it is highly doubtful whether a less partisan, more policy-centred campaign would have resulted in a larger Labour majority. Even so, the tone of Labour's campaign — the apparent lack of vision, and the absence of any Gaitskell-like appeal to 'conscience and reform' — undoubtedly dismayed a minority of voters, many of them in Mr. Wilson's own party. If the Labour campaign resulted in victory, it was perhaps less impressive as an exercise in public enlightenment.

The Liberals took reasonable advantage of the enlarged coverage given them by the press and, even more, the television authorities during election campaigns. They put on effective free-wheeling television performances, and the charm and good sense of Mr. Grimond came across in the news bulletins. They were not able, however, to contribute much to what little day-to-day argument there was, and they had the sadness of seeing that the death of their leader's son could attract almost as much attention as the whole of their campaign effort. Nevertheless, within the limits of what a third party can do, they had the satisfaction of producing sympathetically reported press conferences and television shows that were almost universally admired.

Although few people noticed it, the Liberals did try to use the campaign not merely to establish their relevance as a brake on the Labour government's socialist tendencies, but also to put across their more distinctive policies. More than either of the other parties, they used their press conferences as vehicles for policy discussion, inviting a series of Liberal spokesmen to attend in succession in order to make short statements and answer questions in their particular field of responsibility. The intention was to gain coverage, area by area, for Liberal policies, by concentrating on different fields on different days. In fact the strategy, although it contributed something to the interest of Liberal press conferences, was largely a failure: the press paid more attention to Lord Byers' more sparkling quips on the other parties and gave him considerably more coverage than the less obviously newsworthy personalities with less headline-making policies. It was comparatively rare for a policy spokesman to receive anything like as many questions as Lord Byers on any of these days.[1] What the strategy did ensure was that the Liberal press conferences never floundered through lack of material.

The Liberals made another attempt at putting across a strong policy argument in the second of their television broadcasts. Attractively and imaginatively produced, with more visual diversity than any other party political broadcast during the campaign, it concentrated on East of Suez, restrictive practices and European unity. It was well-reviewed the following day, but for style more than content, to which there was little reference. Ludovic Kennedy's first broadcast — attacking Mr. Wilson as a committed believer in nationalisation — attracted far more publicity and, as far as the party could tell, a more favourable public

---

[1] The biggest single effort in this direction was the press conference held to float the interim conclusions of the Liberal committee on regional government — a policy field in which the Liberals had very distinctive views, and which Mr. Grimond in his final message to candidates called one of the most vital issues of the campaign. The interim report was circulated to the press before the conference began (and read with some bemusement and amusement), and Richard Wainwright declared regional government to be a vital and important issue. He managed to provoke questions — mostly conveying an impression of incredulity at the proposals — but the press coverage in the following morning's papers was small, even in the 'qualities'.

N

reaction than the broadcast concentrating on policy. The Liberals may well have succeeded in establishing their electoral relevance, although there is little evidence on this point, but their failure to make any impression with their policies raises the whole question of how far any party can put across policies in the heat of a campaign.

That, indeed, was the problem that faced the Conservatives. Mr. Heath and the men around him wished to persuade the electorate that they had new remedies for the nation's ills. They were indeed putting forward one of the most radical programmes advanced by any party since the war. For better or worse, their advocacy of trade union reform, of the abandonment of agricultural subsidies, and of entry into the Common Market represented sharp breaks with the past. Although constantly goaded by Labour, they managed for the most part to refrain from joining issue on the 'thirteen wasted years'; the Conservatives remained determined to look forward and not hark back. But the task they had set themselves was difficult. They had only a few weeks in which to convey their fresh policies to the electorate, and their proposals, whatever their merits, were not easily reducible to simple slogans — except by their opponents who could see in them 'dear food', 'the means-test state', 'unemployment', and 'union-breaking'. Moreover, any new proposal from a party recently ejected from office after a period of thirteen years was bound to provoke the question, 'Why didn't you do it when you had the chance?'

The Conservatives appreciated these difficulties. Mr. Heath, Mr. du Cann and their immediate colleagues also knew that, in choosing to mount such a campaign, they were running considerable risks. Quite apart from the danger that it might not succeed electorally, a campaign based on positive policies, determined to avoid devoting too much time to defending the Conservatives' record in office and not aimed primarily at destroying Labour's credibility was almost certain to arouse dissent — or at least feelings of unease — within the Conservative party. Many Conservative M.P.s and probably a majority of activists in the country despised the Labour government and loathed Harold Wilson. They might well have been roused to enormous enthusiasm by a campaign directed at destroying both. Moreover, much of the party in the country wished the Conservative leadership to concentrate on issues, notably crime and punishment and resistance to comprehensive schools, which the leadership was largely determined to avoid. Instead Mr. Heath chose to address himself primarily not to committed Conservatives but to opinion leaders and the target voters. In a sense he was trying to do, in the midst of an election campaign and before his leadership had been firmly established, what Hugh Gaitskell had attempted to do with Labour after 1959: to wean the party away from many of its established habits of thought, and to make it come to terms with contemporary realities.

No one ever described an alternative Conservative strategy in any detail. The leadership's critics were expressing more a mood than a developed point of view. But they clearly wished the party to defend its record in office more militantly, to devote more time to cataloguing Labour's broken promises, and above all to try to undermine the political credit of the Prime Minister. Such a strategy was undoubtedly practicable. Attacks on Labour's record and on Mr. Wilson's person could have been pressed even more vigorously than they were; greater efforts could have been made, for example, to link the Prime Minister's Rambouillet charge (see p. 113) with his unfounded allegations against Oliver Poole years before and with the Hardy Spicer affair in 1964. The party might have been less bold and not attempted to put forward such a wide range of new policies. But whether such a strategy could have won the election for the Conservatives, or even substantially reduced Labour's majority, seems doubtful, especially given Mr. Wilson's enormous popularity and the widespread feeling that Labour needed more time in which to prove itself. In any case the strategy was consciously rejected.[1]

Mr. Heath and his colleagues, in addition, had their eye on the future. None of them ever despaired of winning the election — something might always turn up — but all of them knew that the chances of victory were slim. The main lines of Conservative strategy would probably have been the same in any case, but the apparent likelihood of defeat made Mr. Heath particularly concerned with the more distant future. As one Conservative put it after the election: 'We thought we probably couldn't win this

---

[1] It could perhaps be argued that it was rejected partly through lack of adequate advocacy. A few Conservatives felt that their party's strategists were too like-minded and too technocratic: there seemed to be 'no grit in the oyster'.

time, but we were going to make sure we were in a position to win next time.' The Conservatives therefore stuck to their five main themes more closely than they might have otherwise and tried to play on what one Central Office official described as the electorate's 'forward fear' about the economy. Once the campaign was over, it remained to be seen whether the five issues — the economy, Europe, trade union reform, the overhaul of the welfare state and housing — would remain issues from which the Conservatives could benefit in 1970. Some of the issues might have receded in the public consciousness; others might have been pre-empted by Labour. It may only have been Dutch courage that led one Conservative to remark: 'It doesn't matter what you're constructive about as long as people remember that you were constructive.'

Having chosen their strategy, how successful were the Conservatives in carrying it out? The answer must remain a matter of judgment. Apart from Mr. Heath's 'pregnant panda' slip, there were no major gaffes. The party was not deflected more than occasionally from its chosen themes. Three problems, however, were never solved entirely satisfactorily. First, the need to hold the attention of the press and television meant that, despite the party's desire to concentrate on a limited number of issues, it often gave the impression of raising a new issue every day. It is doubtful whether many journalists could have listed the five themes during the campaign, and the result may have been to blur the Conservatives' message to the electorate. Secondly, the campaign, despite major improvements since 1964, was still not fully co-ordinated. Although Mr. Heath and Mr. Macleod communicated frequently, the television broadcasts sometimes seemed to have little to do with the main arguments being advanced by the leader. Mr. Maudling appears to have been left almost entirely on his own. The result was that the Conservatives, as an M.P. put it, seldom 'all fired in the same direction at the same time.' Thirdly, the party seemed to have much to learn about the art of communication generally. Its language was often too abstract, its arguments too abstruse, and its concerns too remote from those of the ordinary citizen. The five themes were never welded into a single, communicable vision.

The main responsibility for the Conservative campaign's taking the form it did lay with their leader. The course followed may have been, objectively, the best possible; it was certainly the one that came most naturally to the policy-minded Mr. Heath, with his great grasp of detail and his intense and genuine pre-occupation with Britain's future. Like Mr. Wilson, he came to the election a wholly professional politician; but unlike Mr. Wilson his skills lay in negotiation and administration rather than in the tactics of mass persuasion. During the campaign Mr. Heath un-doubtedly grew in confidence and in his ability to project himself at press conferences and on the platform. Compared with Mr. Wilson, however, he still had much to learn, and there is, in fact, no evidence that the mass public perceived the growth in his

"Trouble about you, Heath, is you don't look sincere..."

[*Daily Express*, Mar. 23rd, 1966

stature that was so evident to the Conservative élite. The opinion polls after the election gave no sign that Mr. Heath had moved on-to a higher plateau of public esteem. It may be that political leaders take more time than was available to the new Conservative leader to make an impact on the mass consciousness; Conserva-tives after the election recalled that it had taken Harold Macmillan eighteen months to break through. But this ignores the fact that Mr. Wilson — who took over in 1963 after a more contentious election and with more criticism of his past record than Mr. Heath had to suffer — had established himself within a matter of weeks. Obviously the general political climate was more favourable for the

Labour leader in 1963 than for the Conservative leader in the autumn of 1965. Even so, the reasons why Mr. Heath did not become 'established' must be sought as much in his own style and personality as in some natural law of mass communication.

The fact that Mr. Heath felt compelled to dominate the Conservative campaign owed something to his need to secure his hold on his own party. But it owed at least as much to the changing demands of British electoral politics. The gradual growth in the power of the Prime Minister and the dramatic ethos of television both conduce to more 'presidential' campaigns. By now both the public and the parties expect the leaders to conduct campaigns of this type. The time has probably passed when any British party leader could, like Mr. Attlee, tour the country in the family saloon, expecting his colleagues to share equally in the direction of the campaign and in its publicity.

The 1966 campaign also raised in an acute form several questions which have been alluded to already. Do television and the press substitute 'their' campaign for the 'real' one? How far do politicians take the mass media into account in determining the content of their campaigns? Can the parties seriously hope to project detailed policies — as distinct from more diffuse 'images' — during the heat of an electoral contest? Detailed answers to these questions would require a volume by themselves; but certain points can be made, however tentatively.

The Labour party was little concerned with projecting policy in 1966, but Mr. Heath was. Although he attacked Labour's record and defended the Conservatives', the greater part of almost all of his speeches was devoted to expounding policy. Rough estimates of the attention he gave to each issue can be extracted from the press releases of his speeches issued during the campaign:

The economy	30%	Education	3%
Trade union reform	18%	Social services	3%
Europe	9%	Transport	3%
Housing	7%	Defence	2%
Agriculture	6%	Cost effectiveness	1%
Cost of living	4%	Ports, docks	1%
Rates	4%	Other issues	9%

Since agriculture was usually raised in conjunction with Europe and the cost of living together with the economy, it is clear that Mr. Heath did concentrate on four of the Conservatives' five themes. Only the social services were relegated to a lesser position.

Did television and the press, in their coverage of the Conservative leader, pay roughly comparable attention to these same themes? A large part of the answer is to be found in the following table.[1]

Proportion of total coverage of Mr. Heath's campaign devoted to particular issues	The economy %	Trade union reform %	Europe %	Housing %	Social services %
Press releases (from March 5th) . .	30	18	9	7	3
Total press coverage (from March 7th) .	29	6	16	5	2
The Times . . .	33	6	13	1	1
Daily Telegraph . .	25	9	15	5	3
Guardian . . .	29	10	14	2	3
Daily Express . .	31	..	15	10	..
Daily Mail . .	37	4	13	7	..
Sun	25	7	33	2	2
Daily Mirror . .	28	5	22	5	5
Daily Sketch . .	36	7	21	8	..
BBC 8.50 bulletin (from March 11th) . .	29	14	17	..	3
ITN 'Election '66' (from March 14th) . .	22	..	11	18	3

Coverage of particular issues varied widely among different newspapers and between the two broadcasting authorities. The *Sun*, for instance, devoted more than twice as high a proportion of its space as *The Times* or the *Guardian* to Mr. Heath's statements on Europe. The BBC's 8.50 news bulletin rated his views on trade union reform more highly than ITN's 'Election '66' or any national newspaper.

But, at least in terms of quantity, the mass media ranked the Conservative leader's main themes much as he ranked them himself. Only the order of trade union reform and Europe was

---

[1] The information on which the table is based was compiled by Vera King and Colin Seymour-Ure. The dots indicate that a paper's coverage of an issue was negligible. The reader should note that the three sections of the table (press releases, press coverage and television coverage) are not strictly comparable. The totals of press coverage include Mr. Heath's press conferences and other statements in addition to the sections of his major speeches covered by press releases. The totals of television coverage include the same material but refer only to the two news bulletins mentioned. Since this table deals only with Mr. Heath and covers only two news bulletins, there are some discrepancies between it and the one on p. 131.

reversed consistently. Coverage of the Cowley 'noose trial' tended to push Mr. Heath's own pronouncements into the background; in addition, his major speech on trade union reform, at Southampton on March 5th, was reported fully in the Sunday papers of March 6th but not in any of the national dailies covered in the table. The contrast between the 9% of Mr. Heath's press releases devoted to Europe and the higher percentages in the press is accounted for partly by extensive coverage of Mr. Heath's statements and answers at press conferences. Even so, it seems that the whole of the national press was prepared to devote more time and space to Europe than was Mr. Heath himself.

The scale of coverage in the media thus resembled fairly closely what the Conservatives were seeking. Perhaps, however, the Conservatives and the other parties would have sought something different if they had had a different sense of what the press would print and the broadcasters broadcast. Politicians have to respond to the issues being emphasised in the mass media, and also to anticipate the probable reactions of the media to anything they might want to do. The Prime Minister felt compelled to speak out on Europe on March 18th partly because the press was giving the issue such prominence. After the 18th Mr. Heath laid less stress on Europe than before partly because it seemed unlikely that it could go on making headlines for much longer. A Conservative remarked after the election:

> 'In my view, the people who say that we made a mistake in not pushing Europe harder have got to show how it could have been kept in the headlines. I just don't think it was possible. The press was already getting bored.'

This sense of what the media will stand for may influence not merely the handling of a particular issue but the whole tone of a campaign. Mr. Wilson was said to have avoided making major policy speeches in 1966 in part because his detailed expositions of policy during the 1964 election had largely gone unreported.[1] Moreover, as Martin Harrison points out in Chapter VII, the media's insatiable appetite for novelty may force upon one or all

[1] On March 24th *The Times* published a vehement letter from Len Williams, the Labour party's general secretary, complaining that the press often ignored the constructive parts even of the leaders' speeches in favour of the trivial. He was responding to a leading article in *The Times* dismissing the election campaign as 'tawdry'; see above, p. 150.

of the political parties an 'issue-a-day' approach to electioneering. Such an approach may cause the parties to state their policies on issues they might otherwise have avoided; but it may also handicap a particular party and deflect attention from questions of major national importance. At the very least, the demands of the media place a heavy premium on the parties' verbal ingenuity and tactical adroitness.

But undoubtedly the major obstacle standing in the way of the parties' attempts at persuasion is the partisanship and conservatism of the voters themselves. An abundance of communications research, particularly in the United States, testifies to the intractibility of much of public opinion. Most voters ignore the policies of their party if they disagree with them; many unconsciously distort their party's views to make them correspond more closely with their own. Equally important, many voters do not know what the parties' policies are, even on the major election issues, and often do not comprehend the terminology the parties use. During the 1959 campaign Trenaman and McQuail found that none of the mass media significantly influenced either the way people cast their votes or their attitudes on particular issues; television alone increased their knowledge of politics.[1]

Similar data is lacking for 1966, but a small-scale survey conducted at the University of Essex brings out several of the same points. The survey, carried out the day after Mr. Heath's first party political broadcast on March 14th, was designed to test voters' understanding of the issues raised. At two points in the broadcast Mr. Heath referred to 'restrictive labour practices', and respondents were asked what they thought he meant by the phrase. More than 40% of the sample thought it had something to do with trade unions or strikes or workers, but nearly 50% could give no meaning to the term whatever; the proportion of Conservatives among the 'don't knows' was slightly higher than the proportion of Labour supporters.

Mr. Heath also alluded in the broadcast to the desirability of 'remodelling the welfare state'. Respondents were asked whether they thought he was referring to the reintroduction of means tests, the building of more hospitals and the raising of pensions, the paying of additional welfare benefits to the people most in need,

[1] Joseph Trenaman and Denis McQuail, *Television and the Political Image*, Methuen, 1961.

or the restoration of prescription charges. The answers revealed the respondents' partisan inclinations:

	Conservative %	Labour %
Reintroduction of means tests . . .	4	30
More hospitals, etc.	31	13
Additional benefits to those in need . .	48	25
Restoration of prescription charges . .	17	32

Voters may, of course, catch the general drift of a party's policy without understanding it completely. It may be important to a party to be perceived as having positive policies over a wide range of issues. Nevertheless, experience of the 1966 campaign must reinforce doubts about the ability of either the political parties or the mass media to communicate complex ideas to the public at large, at least in a short period of time. An election campaign may launch an educative process, or possibly conclude it; but in three weeks all that a party can reasonably hope to do is to establish in the electorate's mind favourable connections between its own policies and a few broad matters of public concern. This was evidently part of what the Conservatives were trying to do in 1966. Whether they succeeded only time will tell.

CHAPTER XI

ASPECTS OF ELECTIONEERING[1]

At the national level every general election is different. Leaders change, policies change, styles change. But at the local level every general election is basically the same. For, as no local association can hope to change the underlying allegiance of a significant number of electors, it must concentrate on the task of locating its own supporters and getting them to the polls. Naturally it tends to repeat the rituals followed last time — searching for postal votes, canvassing, distributing literature and window bills, preparing the envelopes for sending out election addresses by free post, advertising, arranging meetings and mapping loudspeaker tours.

What is common about all these activities is that they are almost completely 'unpolitical' in nature. Very occasionally, as in Smethwick in 1964 or possibly in Nelson and Colne in 1966, some burning local issue becomes important in the campaign, but normally it is the party headquarters in Smith Square which deal with the presentation of policies and leaders, and the phasing of events. In the constituencies the things to be done are preponderantly administrative: Will there be enough cars on polling day? Have stewards been provided for meetings? Have window-bills been distributed to the branches? Have arrangements been made for the repair of broken loudspeaker equipment? Problems of this kind occupy 95% of the time of the local parties. Thus the skills involved in local campaigning are organisational rather than political, and the election agent is at least as important in the campaign as the candidate himself. Conceivably, the Conservatives have been wrong to worry so much about the lack of political interest and sophistication among their agents; their role is primarily administrative.

A further result of the unpolitical nature of the constituency campaign is that each party proceeds with its own tasks and has little or no contact with its opponents. The illusions, or the blank

---

[1] We should like to acknowledge the very substantial part played by Michael Pinto-Duschinsky in the preparation of this chapter.

ignorance, about what the other side are up to can be staggering: in one marginal seat a very competent Conservative official seriously believed that the other side were quite inactive; in fact there had already been a full Labour canvass and the Labour organisation was among the best in the country.

In a similar way constituency parties have little contact with their national headquarters. Daily notes and advice flow out from Smith Square, but one M.P. commented after the election: 'Constituencies are very much on their own once the campaign begins. National and regional headquarters play a very minor part at our level.' Another M.P. put it more strongly: 'Smith Square might as well be on the moon.'

In spite of the essentially pedestrian nature of campaigning at the local level, one might have expected more innovations than have occurred in recent years. One hundred or so M.P.s and candidates were asked after the 1966 election if there had been any new features in their campaigns. Almost all said 'None' and the most daring exceptions were hardly very radical: 'the use of hats and balloons with the candidate's name'; 'a portable music apparatus on the candidate's car to attract the crowds with martial music'; 'a motorcade'; 'a candidate's promenade across the main shopping centres escorted by Young Conservatives with large badges'.

This lack of innovation has often been blamed on the obstinate traditionalism of party workers; but at least two other factors are as important. The first is the increasingly restrictive limit on expenditure by candidates, laid down in 1948 — in 1966 the maximum permitted ranged between £1,302 (Billericay) and £602 (Glasgow, Kelvingrove). The active constituency parties — the ones most likely to introduce new forms of electioneering — are already near the expenditure limit, and since innovations usually cost money, they are liable to involve breaking or circumventing the law. One candidate reported as a new gimmick the use of a 'do-it-yourself silk-screen printer for posters and window bills', explaining that this was the only way within the expense limit that he could combat 'uninhibited postering' by the opposition.

The other discouragement to innovation is that where it has been tried it has seldom made an impact on the outcome. For example in two London constituencies — Kensington North and Paddington North — energetic young teams of Conservatives, using business methods, analysed and transformed the style of their campaigns. The operations were efficiently executed — but the swings were no different from those in less enterprising neighbouring seats.

The feel of the election at the constituency level is, we hope, conveyed in the brief descriptions of individual contests that fill Chapter XIII. But to give some yardstick for their representativeness we have gathered together here some more general evidence from polls, press and party sources, about the way in which the local battle was fought.

Agents. Less than half the 1,707 candidates had the services of a full-time professional agent. The Conservatives had fairly full coverage: 80 of the 617 seats contested in Britain were dealt with by trainees or volunteer uncertificated agents; the remaining 537 constituencies were dealt with by 499 professional agents; in a number of hopeless seats and a few two-member boroughs these acted for more than one constituency. There had not been time fully to implement the 1965 Chelmer report, which sought to give agents higher pay and, by improving their status to that of managing director of a firm, to attract recruits of a managing director level of ability. While several abler agents had been moved to the new marginals, in scale and quality the full-time staff of the party was much as before.

The Labour party had increased their full-time agents from 193 in 1964 to 202 in 1966, and only three of the seats designated as key marginals by the National Executive were without one. The party tried some limited experiments in getting experienced agents to train two recruits, one being in his own constituency and the other in a nearby marginal. At a higher level the impending election was used to put off still longer the reorganisation of the Greater London Council area which remained divided between four Labour party regions.

The Liberals fielded 60 full-time agents, compared to nearly 80 in 1964. However, in view of the salary scales and promotion prospects, able agents are not easy to come by and, as the Liberal and Labour parties at least have found, constituencies are sometimes better served by part-timers or amateurs than by professionals.

Planning. Since the date of the election was uncertain constituency election plans were less precise than in 1964; but the need for constant readiness, due to the parliamentary situation, meant that most local parties were well enough prepared to go into action, often with an exact repetition of their 1964 operation. In the early stages the preparation of the election address, the detailed arrangements for meetings and the writing of envelopes dominated activity. In all parties there were some complaints about headquarters delay in distributing copies of the manifestos and other centrally prepared documents. There were also a few murmurs about delays in getting from the local authorities copies of the new register that came into force in mid-February.[1]

Marginal seats had extra contact with the higher reaches of their party. Their claims to visits from star speakers and to 'mutual aid' from nearby safe seats had to be assessed. In fact, despite the efforts of headquarters, private contacts between the candidates and the party leaders, or between neighbouring agents and chairmen seemed to underlie a large proportion of such arrangements. Certainly there were key marginals which asked in vain for headquarters to send crowd-drawing speakers or to persuade other constituencies to offer a helping hand. Agents in surprisingly safe seats developed anxieties about whether anyone could be spared and loyal workers were often unwilling to move outside their own neighbourhood.

In the Labour party there was the additional chore of enlisting union co-operation. In a few places local tradition and energetic organisation met with some success. But generally the union contribution in work, if not in money, was limited. Agents spoke bitterly of union officials' inactivity. One Labour regional or-

---

[1] The electoral register, compiled on October 10th, 1965, had only come into force on February 16th. The election was therefore fought on the freshest register since the 1950 contest. There were, indeed, complaints of delays which meant that impatient agents had to wait a week or so for their copy. But these were rare; what were almost universal were protests about errors in the register, which many described as 'the most inaccurate ever'.

The total number of electors was 35,965,000 — 70,000 more than in 1964. But the increase in the adult population was, of course, much greater for the 1964 register had included 330,000 'Y' voters. A similar number were due to be added to the 1966 electorate on October 2nd.

The Speaker's Conference in an Interim Report (Cmnd. 2917/1966) recommended — on the Speaker's casting vote — against a change to two registers annually but it asked the government to make a feasibility study on the use of computer techniques in compiling and keeping up to date the electoral register. Another Interim Report (Cmnd. 2932/1966) made just before the dissolution recommended minor modifications in the law on absent voting, and on the registration of merchant seamen.

ganiser remarked that not a single branch official had heeded a Transport and General Workers' Union circular asking them to get in touch with him. In the business of fighting elections, unions contribute far less to the Labour party's efforts than Conservatives seem to assume.

Publicity. The number of posters was even smaller than in 1964. Apart from the limit on expenses, uncertainty about the election date made it impossible to book sites in advance. However, in a few constituencies there was some effective exploitation of small posters in front gardens. In Cheadle and Orpington, the hard-driving Liberal organisations managed to make a comprehensive visual impact. Advertising in the local press was largely confined to the announcement of meetings — but meetings were often put on to provide the local press with a story. The establishment of a copy-hungry evening newspaper in Reading (where hitherto only weeklies had existed) made it expedient to hold nightly meetings.

Candidates' activities. Every candidate faces the problem of how best to spend his time. Should he try to reach as many electors as possible or should he concentrate on keeping up the spirits of the faithful? How hard should he drive himself?[1] It is rare to find anyone irreverent enough to ask if the candidate is necessary. But a couple of M.P.s who were prevented by illness from doing any campaigning did not seem to suffer in the result. One veteran of hard-fought marginal contests who took over a safe seat was startled to be told: 'your predecessor was very good during elections — he actually gave us four days a week campaigning.'

In order to make an impact, a few candidates turned to newsworthy gimmicks — canvassing on horseback or by rowing boat, ostentatious appearances in shopping centres or travelling on rush hour buses. Local grievances were taken up flamboyantly — there was a notable rush to ask constituency questions in the last days of the old House of Commons, but throughout an electioneering parliament M.P.s, especially for marginal seats, had spent a quite exceptional amount of time in their constituencies.

An increasing number of Conservative candidates experimented with 'impact canvassing' — going out with a team of helpers who drew voters to the doorstep so that the candidate

---

[1] For a very enlightening study of candidates' attitudes and methods, see Richard Rose and Dennis Kavanagh, 'Campaigning for Parliament', *New Society*, July 28th, 1966.

could greet the maximum number in the minimum time. There were stories of people being more offended by the candidate's haste than flattered by his presence. But, if the personal touch matters at all, it is reasonable for candidates to grasp at any opportunity to increase the proportion of electors whom they can encounter.

Conservative candidates may have inflicted an unnecessary handicap on themselves by their traditional Sunday observance, Sunday is the easiest day to find people at home and there is no evidence that the Labour party has caused offence by Sunday electioneering. The argument for taking an occasional day off hardly applies in a three-week campaign.

Canvassing. This most traditional of activities was carried out in the accustomed way: in marginal seats it was sometimes done very efficiently and comprehensively but occasionally in an astonishingly haphazard fashion. In many safe seats it was not even attempted. It was interesting to discover how few constituencies had kept really good records of 1964 so that the 1966 results could be compared with them and reasonable deductions made. Moreover, the information brought back by canvassers often defied systematic analysis: canvass cards marked 'for', 'against' and 'doubtful' offered no scope for analysing Liberal as distinct from Conservative or Labour votes. Agents would answer that their job was not to forecast the election but merely to find out where their supporters were and get them to the polling station: the demands for canvass returns led one very competent agent to a simple answer: 'I'm the last person to see canvass returns. When area office phones up I tell them what they want to know. It stops them pestering me.' Such an attitude might be extreme but it does provide one of the reasons for the failure of the party network to supply headquarters with reliable information. Particularly on the Conservative side of Smith Square there was disillusion with what they were told by the areas: few reports foreshadowed either the general uniformity of swing or the few localised exceptions. Canvassing is of course not only used for gathering information. Liberals in particular believe that the show of interest implied by a call does in fact win support.

The actual extent of canvassing is hard to assess. The great majority of people could not recall having been canvassed when NOP questioned them after the election.

Were you visited by a canvasser? (NOP)	All voters %	Con. %	Lab. %	Lib. %	Other %
Yes, Conservative .	20	26	16	28	15
Yes, Labour . .	15	15	17	12	11
Yes, Liberal . .	5	6	2	22	6
Yes, Other . .	1	1	2	—	2
No . . .	69	61	72	54	66

These figures are slightly below those recorded by Gallup in 1964. Unfortunately NOP did not ask this question in 1964, nor did Gallup in 1966. There are undoubtedly some frailties of memory underlying this evidence: it is hard to believe that Liberal door-steps were quite so exceptionally beset by canvassers. It is also hard to believe the 2% of people who claimed to the Gallup inter-viewers in April 1966 that they had done some canvassing, for this would suggest that twenty calls was the average stint for all can-vassers — hardly a very onerous exercise.

Meetings. Most candidates cut the number of meetings but a majority reported that the attendance held up reasonably well. Conservative candidates were somewhat more prone than Labour ones to admit a falling off. The Gallup poll found a reduction from 8% to 3% in attendance at outdoor meetings but only from 8% to 7% at indoor meetings. But NOP found many fewer claiming to have attended any: such findings, like those on canvassing, must be

Did you go to any political meetings? (NOP)	All voters %	Con. %	Lab. %	Lib. %	Other %
Yes, Conservative .	2	4	1	4	2
Yes, Labour . .	2	1	3	2	1
Yes, Liberal . .	1	1	1	9	—
Yes, Other . .	—	—	—	—	—
Attended no meetings	96	95	96	88	97

a bit suspect, although the detailed figures do suggest a greater political curiosity among Liberals. But it seems plain that about ten times more people watched some at least of the election broad-casts than attended any meeting.

What was the value of visiting speakers? The Labour candidate at Billericay said that the Wilson meeting had made a large impact on the constituency and was repeatedly mentioned to him on the doorstep. The visit of a major personality also gave the local

o

activists a feeling of importance and may have drawn them into keener participation. The large meeting also gave a large audience for once to the local candidate.

There was another side to all this, however. The responsibility of finding a hall, stewards and the like was often a large burden for the local organisation. The meeting itself would normally be geared to a national audience and would have little to do with the local campaign. There was a tendency for quarrels to develop as to who should sit on the platform. Further, the local candidate often faced the humiliation of having to talk immediately after the exit of the star speaker, sometimes to a fast-emptying hall and to the accompaniment of the dismantling of TV cameras. The visits of the more minor cabinet figures, or their shadow opposites, usually failed to muster very substantial audiences.

Addresses. The content of election addresses has been analysed on p. 103. The form was almost as depressing as ever. The Liberals unquestionably had the most eye-catching and original approach; layout and format (and incidentally content) were more ingeniously varied than the addresses of Conservative and Labour, which were usually very dull in presentation — Labour addresses seeming, by a narrow margin, duller and more standardised than Conservative ones. Many of both were identical in format and almost identical in content with 1964. Conservative candidates tended to be more localised in their emphasis and surprisingly often underplayed their party and their leader — only 19% mentioned Mr. Heath compared to the 41% who mentioned Sir Alec Douglas-Home in 1964. The lack of enterprise seems odd in the light of the evidence that the election address reaches far more voters than any other product of local campaigning. According to the Gallup poll, 49% of electors (46% in 1964) claimed to have looked at them.

Almost every major party candidate attempted to distribute an election address to every elector or at least to every household in his constituency — and usually devoted about a quarter of the permitted expenditure to doing so. In addition some sent out introductory leaflets, usually about themselves, and a few sent out last minute messages on some national or local themes. These were often distributed selectively to doubtfuls or to new estates or to marginal areas. There were also a few instances of sectional appeals — to inhabitants of a particular locality or more often to immigrants. In at least one constituency carefully angled leaflets in Urdu prepared with help from Smith Square were distributed to Bengali-speaking Pakistanis. No one seemed to have much confidence in the effectiveness of such efforts.

Morale. It was impossible to move among the parties during the campaign without feeling that the state of morale scarcely coincided with the opinion polls. Labour agents and workers were optimistic and their committee rooms were often more crowded than in 1964 — but few of the senior ones were claiming the gains they actually made, let alone those indicated by the 10–12% lead in the polls of mid-March. Conservatives were frankly incredulous about the polls; even if they conceded that Labour was ahead, they refused to believe it was by as much as the polls were showing. Most of them reported an increase in the numbers and enthusiasm of their workers. Conservative activists, who had been half-hearted in support of the Home administration in 1964, were now united in hostility to Labour and in their dislike of Harold Wilson. The polls were depressing, but the sense of fighting in a common cause buoyed them up. At times they even found reasons why the Conservatives might win:

> 'The postmen all seem very friendly this time; they weren't in '64. My brother on the South Coast writes the same. There must be something in it.'

The great majority of Conservative candidates we consulted spoke of high or 'astonishingly high' morale among their active workers and only a few referred to the opinion polls causing deep depression. The Liberals too tended to claim greater activity and zest than in 1964. Every Labour candidate spoke of increased enthusiasm and usually increased numbers of workers. However, for what it is worth, the Gallup poll found only 3% of all electors claiming to have done party work other than canvassing compared to 8% in 1964.

Local Issues. Even in Scotland a majority of candidates denied that local issues mattered significantly. 'This was a national election fought nationally,' wrote one member for a Scottish county seat. But obviously some national issues had particular local application. Labour's promise of leasehold enfranchisement was particularly important in South Wales, Lancashire and isolated parts of Southern England. Schemes for regional development became more important the further away one got from London.

Rhodesia seemed only to be mentioned as an issue in places with a large body of retired people. Naval cuts were thought to have hurt Labour a little in Portsmouth and Pembroke. The immigration issue, which had receded in prominence to an extraordinary extent, still was mentioned in London and the West Midlands far more than elsewhere. The issue of crime and punishment appeared much more live in Lancashire and Scotland than elsewhere and there was the remarkable effort of Patrick Downey standing for the return of hanging against Sidney Silverman, the leading aboli-tionist, in Nelson and Colne.

The Conservatives promised to develop Portbury as a major dock, which may have won them votes around Bristol but lost them some in South Wales (where fewer marginal seats were at stake). The impact of the TSR-2 cancellation in Preston and of the Highland Development Board in Caithness and Sutherland are discussed on p. 242 and p. 230. A number of M.P.s, Conserva-tive and Labour alike, complained of losing votes because of the activities of local councils which their party controlled; rent and rate increases were announced in a very untimely way in several places. This undoubtedly was the commonest and most emphasised of vote winning or losing local questions. Still more parochial matters such as the closing of a railway line, the reopening of a quarry, or an M.P.'s stand on a police scandal were sometimes mentioned and then dismissed as of trivial effect.

Religion sometimes came into electioneering — and not just in the traditional orange and green battlegrounds of Northern Ireland and Liverpool and Clydeside. In North-east Scotland funda-mentalist Presbyterianism is strong. One candidate wrote:

> ' "Closed" Brethren do not vote and create apathy in villages where they are numerous. "Open" Brethren do not vote unless persuaded by intimate friends. Therefore influential villagers can garner votes on a non-political approach, i.e. "I know you don't care about politics but I do, and you will do me a favour if you vote for Mr. X." The Tory at his prayers is still a formidable opponent in a rural constituency and claims many votes from those who "Fear God and Honour the Queen".'

A Liberal candidate in the West Country complained that the Methodist Church had not supported him as much as he had hoped, 'although it was good', while in a nearby seat the Labour candidate wrote:

'I know of many Labour supporters who send children to Sunday School who were given Liberal window bills to place in their windows. Most of the parents refused but had to give way when the children cried and stated that their Sunday School teacher said they had to do this. This came to light when we observed that many houses had both Labour and Liberal window bills and on enquiry we found this was a compromise solution.'

But such cases were very exceptional.

Polling Day. The weather was reasonable and polling arrangements ran smoothly. There were almost no reports of administrative slip-ups. Cars were more plentiful than ever and in marginal seats the intensity of effort showed no falling off. But the turnout figures, discussed later (p. 262) reflected the concentration on marginals. The Gallup poll figures suggest the diminution in activity.

Did any of the parties call on you or your family on election day itself? (Gallup)	1964 %	1966 %
Yes, Conservative . . .	16	11
Yes, Labour	13	12
Yes, Liberal	2	3
Yes, Other	1	—
No	76	82

The pattern of voting during the day became more even between the parties. Labour supporters still voted later but changes in social habits, as well as in class patterns of party support, seem to be diminishing the Labour party's special vulnerability to bad weather in the evening. NOP found that 45% of Labour supporters voted in the last three hours compared to 39% of Conservatives and of Liberals. In 1964 the Gallup poll in a similar enquiry found 43% of Labour supporters but only 33% of Conservatives voting after 6 p.m.

Postal Votes. Since the election took place on a much fresher register, the opportunities for claiming postal votes were reduced and the number of people who qualified by reason of removal was smaller than in any election since postal votes were introduced in 1948. In the end 617,481 people were granted postal voting facilities and 513,041 of them (86%, the same proportion as in 1964) cast valid votes. Postal votes thus accounted for 1·9% of all votes cast compared to 2·6% in 1964.

According to all reports a heavy majority of postal votes went to the Conservatives. There were 24 seats where the Conservative majority was less than the number of postal votes cast. If the postal vote split 3 to 1 in favour of the Conservatives (and in many constituencies the figure was at least that) the Conservatives owed twelve seats to it. If the split was only 2 to 1, they still owed seven seats to it.[1]

The highest number of valid postal votes came, as usual, from Ulster — Fermanagh and South Tyrone (5,978), Mid-Ulster (5,000), and Londonderry (2,909). In England Dover (2,683) and Buckingham (2,265) again held the record. The Bridgeton division of Glasgow with 87 had the lowest number yet recorded in a general election.[2]

Expenses. The limit on election expenses, unchanged since 1948, had increasingly limited campaign activity — or invited evasion. In 1966 the Speaker's Conference reported a recommendation (voted by 16 to 8) that the maximum should be raised by £300 per constituency.[3]

The actual amount spent by candidates fell. The grand total, about £1,130,000, compared with £1,229,203 in 1964 (when admittedly there were 51 more candidates). But the Conservative total fell from £498,000 to about £480,000 and the Labour total from £472,000 to about £450,000. The fall was concentrated almost entirely in safe seats. In close contests almost everyone returned

---

[1] Seats the Conservatives may have owed to postal votes:

	Con. maj.	Valid postal votes		Con. maj.	Valid postal votes
On a 55–45 split			*On a 75–25 split*		
Peterborough	3	1,358	Norfolk S.W.	775	1,921
Edinburgh,			Holland-with-		
Pentlands	44	793	Boston	316	712
Norfolk S.	119	1,692	Hertfordshire E.	794	1,393
			Southend E.	517	1,050
			Hornsey	615	1,263
			Mid-Ulster	2,560	5,000
On a 66–33 split					
Lowestoft	358	1,569			
Burton	277	1,139			
Plymouth,					
Devonport	319	1,196			
Maldon	506	1,951			

[2] The figures for valid postal votes and spoiled papers are set out in H.C. Deb. 730 c. 886–898 and *149–151*.

[3] Cmnd 2880/1966.

expenses to within £50 of the legal maximum and once again the
number of candidates who went to within a pound or two or even a

	Average £'s per candidate					% of permitted maximum				
	Con.	Lab.	Lib.	Other	All	Con.	Lab.	Lib.	Other	All
England .	786	735	494	376	687	90	84	55	45	63
Wales .	643	743	529	248	565	77	89	61	30	67
Scotland .	714	675	619	348	618	89	84	78	42	77
N. Ireland.	561	310	119	252	357	55	32	10	25	37
U.K. .	766	726	501	338	667	89	84	56	41	77

The average expenditure of the 57 Communists was £354, of the 20 Plaid Cymru candidates
£379, and of the 23 Scottish Nationalists £414.

shilling or two of the maximum underlined the artificiality of much
of the accounting; no one could calculate so closely in advance —
the returns must often have been adjusted after the event. Two
agents miscalculated the legal maximum and had to seek relief in
the courts for presenting returns a few pounds in excess of the
limit.[1]

Because of the increase in his electorate Eric Moonman of
Billericay spent the largest sum, £1,381, of any candidate since the
present limits were set in 1948. Dr. Jane Ellis the Independent in
Scarborough who spent only 30s. achieved a record at the other
extreme. The most economical Labour candidate in Britain was
Mr. Evans who won Islington, South-west on £283, defeating
almost the most economical Conservative candidate, who spent
£291.[2] Once again Mr. Reader Harris was the most frugal of
successful Conservatives, spending only £478 in holding his
marginal seat at Heston and Isleworth.

[1] In Wakefield and in Bodmin. For the Wakefield case see *The Times*, June
28th, 1966. For the Bodmin case see *The Times*, July 7th, 1966.
[2] The only more economical Conservatives were in Rhondda East (£272) and
Rhondda West (£264).

CHAPTER XII

CANDIDATES

THE main interest in the study of the 1966 candidates lies in the new men elected. But the first stress must be on the element of continuity.

The 1966 campaign was fought largely by the same people as in 1964. Of the total of 1,707, 1,087 had been candidates seventeen months previously, 899 in the same seats.[1] Since 41 others had been candidates in earlier contests, there were only 579 absolute beginners. Of the 630 M.P.s elected in 1964, 577 stood again; 38 decided to retire and 15 had already departed — 8 were dead, 6 had been elevated to the House of Lords, and one had been appointed to the Prices and Incomes Board.

All the Labour retirements and all but four of the Conservative involved members over 60 and, with one exception, their withdrawal appears to have been entirely voluntary. Mr. William Warbey's criticism of his leaders had caused some indignation in the Ashfield constituency Labour party and it is doubtful whether he could successfully have sought renomination. But the other cases where M.P.s were publicly challenged by their local supporters all turned in the incumbents' favour. Woodrow Wyatt was attacked by the mining element in the Bosworth constituency party for his lukewarmness towards steel nationalisation, but, after protracted controversy in the first half of 1965, the hatchet was buried.

Early in 1966 Commander Anthony Courtney, the Conservative member for Harrow East, was called upon by his constituency chairman to yield to a candidate who would have a better chance of holding this marginal seat. Commander Courtney had been involved with a woman in Russia in 1961 and scurrilous photographs were being circulated in the constituency, allegedly by the Soviet authorities. Commander Courtney counterattacked strongly, arguing that a British M.P.'s career should not be ter-

---

[1] Most of these were M.P.s but 99 Conservatives, 34 Labour, 113 Liberals and 54 others, unsuccessful in 1964, stayed on to fight the same seat again in 1966.

minated by a Communist plot. The affair, which received very wide coverage, culminated in a full meeting of the constituency association on February 21st, at which Commander Courtney triumphed by 454 votes to 277. All the divisional officers resigned — but the net effect of the row was small: although Commander Courtney was defeated in the election it was on a swing that was about average for that area.

Mr. Paget of Northampton and Mr. Donnelly of Pembroke, two Labour M.P.s who were openly critical of aspects of government policy, both rode fairly easily over constituency grumblings; so did a number of Conservatives who had affronted their more right-wing followers by their support for oil sanctions against Rhodesia. Several, including Richard Hornby and Humphry Berkeley, comfortably survived votes of no confidence but a couple — Angus Maude at Stratford and Terence Higgins at Worthing — were opposed at the general election by protesting Independent Conservatives (who attracted only derisory support).

In the near-marginal seat of Croydon North-east the local Labour party's nominee, John Palmer, was refused endorsement by the National Executive Committee because of his refusal to promise to support party policy on Vietnam, on immigration and on trade unions. The local party persisted in supporting their choice and the NEC finally stepped in to nominate Michael Stewart (a 1964 Labour candidate working in the Cabinet Office). The local party protested but in the end Mr. Palmer did not stand. Despite these ructions, the swing to Labour (3·4%) was just above the average for the area.

There was one other well publicised constituency disagreement early in the parliament. Miscellaneous grievances against Aubrey Jones, mainly about his liberal stands on issues, led the Hall Green Conservative association executive to consider looking for another candidate. In the end a motion of confidence in Mr. Jones was carried by 35 to 19 on January 29th. On March 19th Mr. Jones resigned his seat to take up the chairmanship of the government's new Prices and Incomes Board.

It is worth looking at the fate of the M.P.s defeated in 1964. For almost half of them, defeat meant the end of their electoral efforts. The third who stayed on to fight the same seat again were all unsuccessful. It is significant that, of the 29 Conservative seats that fell vacant after 1964 in a by-election or through the incumbent's decision not to stand again, 13 were taken over by ex-M.P.s and 10 of the remainder by ex-candidates. Only one of the 24 Labour seats vacated went to an ex-M.P. (Mr. Gordon Walker) but only 8 to people without experience as candidates. The 48 other Labour candidates who gained seats in 1966 were similar in

M.P.s defeated in October 1964

	Con.	Lab.	Lib.
Received a peerage	1	2	1
Did not fight in 1966 . . .	26	2	1
Fought a different seat successfully .	11	1	—
Fought the same seat unsuccessfully .	17	—	—
	55	5 *	2

* In 1966 there were 2 Labour ex-M.P.s of an earlier vintage seeking election in hopeless seats — Tom Braddock in Wimbledon and T. C. Boyd in Dumfries. Only two other ex-M.P.s sought election — Dr. McIntyre (Scottish National party) and Sir Oswald Mosley (now Union Movement but first elected as a Conservative M.P. in 1918 and as a Labour M.P. in 1926).

experience; they included no ex-M.P.s but 37 ex-Labour candidates (17 of them trying again in the same seat as 1964) and one who had stood for Plaid Cymru in 1964. Mr. Mackie for the Liberals shared with 8 Conservatives the misfortune of being defeated after sitting only in a single, very short, parliament.

The 1966 election saw an appreciable reduction in the number of long-service M.P.s. While, of the 363 Labour victors, 77 had shared as M.P.s in the party's 1945 triumph, only 17 Labour members had had experience of the pre-war parliament (4 of them as Liberals not as Labour) and only 11 Conservatives. Only 11 Labour and 3 Conservative M.P.s had been in parliament uninterruptedly since the 1930s. Less than two-thirds of the House had served continuously since 1959 (222 Labour, 158 Conservative, 2 Liberal and the Speaker). With the defeat of Mr. Bowen (elected 1945), Mr. Grimond (elected 1950) and Mr. Thorpe (elected 1959) were the only Liberals whose membership reached back more than four years.

As in 1964 the only octogenarian candidate was Mr. Shinwell (81), the chairman of the parliamentary Labour party. But the age balance had shifted. While Labour still had a heavy majority among the old men, their numbers had been reduced appreciably, and at the other end of the scale Labour now had a preponderance of the young men. Thanks to the new blood recruited in 1964 and 1966 the median age of Labour M.P.s had fallen to within eighteen months of the Conservatives'; in 1959 and 1964 the median Labour M.P. had been seven years older. The average age of all candidates, elected and defeated together, was identical for Conservative and Labour. The youngest member, John Ryan of Uxbridge, was still 25 on polling day and there were three more Labour M.P.s within a year of him.

Candidates — Age by Party

Age Jan. 1st, 1966	Conservative		Labour		Liberal	
	Elected	Defeated	Elected	Defeated	Elected	Defeated
21–29 . .	2	54	8	76	1	55
30–39 . .	42	151	77	103	5	124
40–49 . .	93	103	94	49	4	87
50–59 . .	85	53	107	25	1	31
60–69 . .	30	15	61	4	1	1
70–79 . .	1	0	15	1	0	1
80+ . .	0	0	1	0	0	0
	253	376	363	258	12	299
Median age .	48	38	50	34	39	37

Twenty-six women were elected, 19 Labour and 7 Conservative, 2 fewer than the record figure attained in 1964. But only 80 women candidates stood and, as in each election since 1955, the number put up by both the Labour and Conservative parties fell slightly.

Women Candidates 1955–1966

	1955	1959	1964	1966
Conservative . . .	32	27	23	21
Labour	43	34	33	30

The educational pattern remains much as in previous years though the slight decline in Etonian Conservatives continued (there were 84 candidates in 1966 compared to 94 in 1964). Much the most spectacular change was the increase in the number of university-educated Labour candidates (from 281 in 1964 to 330 in 1966).

Education	Conservative		Labour		Liberal	
	Elected	De-feated	Elected	De-feated	Elected	De-feated
Elementary only . . .	1	3	34	7	0	4
Elementary+ [1] . . .	1	2	46	14	0	5
Secondary only . . .	17	63	53	51	2	49
Secondary+ [1]	1	35	40	38	0	30
Secondary and University . .	29	68	124	103	3	84
Public School only . . .	63	81	4	4	0	46
Public School and University .	141	124	62	41	7	81
Total	253	376	363	258	12	299
Oxford	83	64	54	37	3	42
Cambridge	61	57	29	20	3	45
Other Universities . . .	26	71	103	87	4	78
All Universities . . .	170	192	186	144	10	165
Eton	55	29	3	1	2	7
Harrow	14	8	0	1	0	2
Winchester	8	7	2	1	0	2
Other Public Schools . .	127	161	61	42	5	116
All Public Schools . .	204	205	66	45	7	127

[1] The Elementary+ and Secondary+ categories show the numbers whose formal education ended at these stages but who subsequently attended part-time classes or went to adult education colleges.

A classification of the first or formative occupation of each candidate yields much the same proportions as in 1964.

Occupation	Conservative		Labour		Liberal	
	Elected	De-feated	Elected	De-feated	Elected	De-feated
Professions						
Barrister	55	46	36	9	3	20
Solicitor	15	37	18	13	—	23
Doctor, Dentist . . .	2	6	9	2	1	6
Architect/Surveyor . .	2	6	1	5	—	8
Civil Engineer . . .	1	6	3	5	—	3
Chartered Secretary/Accountant	6	25	5	2	1	11
Civil Servant, Local Govt. .	13	17	9	13	—	10
Armed Services . . .	19	16	3	—	—	7
Teaching						
University . . .	1	5	24	9	—	10
Adult	—	2	15	27	—	10
School	3	14	33	45	1	36
Total	117	180	156	130	6	144
Business						
Small business . . .	2	12	2	2	—	9
Company Director . .	40	44	3	3	1	28
Company Executive . .	12	56	11	23	2	27
Commerce, Insurance .	16	25	13	4	—	21
Management, Clerical .	5	7	3	11	—	6
Total	75	44	32	43	3	91
Miscellaneous						
Miscellaneous 'white collar' .	7	7	22	34	—	17
Private means . . .	5	—	—	—	—	—
Politician	2	4	9	7	1	2
Publicist, Journalist . .	17	19	29	14	—	22
Farmer	27	15	2	3	2	13
Housewife	1	1	4	2	—	3
Student	—	—	—	2	—	2
Total	59	46	66	62	3	59

[continued on next page]

Occupation	Conservative		Labour		Liberal	
	Elected	De-feated	Elected	De-feated	Elected	De-feated
Workers						
Railway clerks . . .	—	1	9	—	—	—
Miners	—	—	32	3	—	—
Skilled . . .	2	5	47	19	—	5
Semi- and unskilled . .	—	—	21	1	—	—
Total	2	6	109	23	—	5
Grand total . . .	253	376	363	258	12	299

The nominal religious affiliations of candidates are hard to ascertain let alone the depth of their religious attachment. However, the table which follows presents a fuller picture than ever before, though the Anglican totals may still be too low.

Religion	Conservative		Labour		Liberal		Others		Total
	Elected	De-feated	Elected	De-feated	Elected	De-feated	Elected	De-feated	
Anglican . .	110	144	32	26	2	66	—	2	382
Roman Catholic	12	23	23	8	—	16	1	6	89
Methodist .	2	14	34	6	1	22	—	3	82
Presbyterian .	6	15	8	3	1	13	—	12	58
Baptist . .	2	1	5	—	—	2	—	—	10
Congregational.	1	3	5	1	—	10	—	1	21
Quaker . .	1	1	2	1	—	7	—	—	12
Jew . .	2	6	26	4	—	14	—	—	52
Others . .	1	—	11	15	1	14	—	—	43

Trade unions sponsored the same number of candidates as in 1964 but with even greater success — 96% of them were elected. The pattern of sponsorship changed little.

Sponsored candidates

	1964		1966	
	Total	Elected	Total	Elected
National Union of Mineworkers . . .	28	28	28	27
Transport and General Workers' Union . .	23	21	27	27
Amalgamated Engineering Union . . .	19	17	17	17
National Union of General and Municipal Workers	9	9	10	10
Union of Shop, Distributive and Allied Workers	10	10	8	8
Transport Salaried Staffs' Association . .	7	7	5	5
National Union of Railwaymen . . .	7	6	8	7
Clerical and Administrative Workers' Union .	3	3	4	4
Union of Post Office Workers . . .	3	2	4	4
18 other unions	29	17	27	23
	138	120	138	132

[1] We are much indebted to Rex Walford who collected the data and prepared this table.

The Co-operative party sponsored only 24 Labour candidates compared to 27 in 1964 and 18 compared to 19 were successful. In 1964 we wrote 'the new men coming in to replace the old are surprisingly like them in background'. This could hardly be said in 1966, at least as far as the Labour party is concerned. The 25 Conservatives who were elected in 1966 but not in 1964 included 13 ex-M.P.s and it would be hard to generalise from the remaining 12; but, since 9 of them were public school and 6 Oxbridge-educated and since all had professional or business occupations, no radically new trend seemed to be in the making. However, if we consider the 72 Labour M.P.s who gained or succeeded to seats in parliament after 1964 the contrast is striking. The professional element is greatly increased and the workers' element is vastly reduced while the proportion of graduates is half as high again in the new intake as in the old.

	All Labour M.P.s in 1964 (317) %	Labour M.P.s elected 1965-66 (72) %
Professions	41	57
Business	11	8
Miscellaneous	16	21
Workers	32	14
Elementary	31	14
Secondary	50	67
Public School	17	19
Oxford and Cambridge . . .	19	29
Other University	23	39

There was some speculation whether the new M.P.s would shift the PLP to the left. In the political circumstances of 1966, definition of what is meant by left (or right, for that matter) was unprecedentedly difficult and it was seldom easy to discover where individual candidates stood on the ideological spectrum. Personal impressions suggested that the new men would not alter the balance; a *Sunday Times* enquiry (March 20th) found only 5 out of a sample of 50 in the most winnable seats who could be described as 'strongly left'. Among many there was a strong resistance to ideological description. Their average age, and their professional style of occupation were almost certainly more significant guides to their conduct than their supposed 'leftness' or 'rightness'.

However, it is worth pursuing further the change in the composition of the parliamentary parties, by a comparison with fifteen years earlier. Although there are great difficulties in standardising the classification of occupation and education, the Nuffield election studies have tried to maintain the same criteria, at least since 1951. It is plain that the Conservatives have changed little apart from a decline in the business element and a small increase in professional men and in public school and Oxbridge products.

Background of M.P.s 1951 and 1966

	Conservative M.P.s		Labour M.P.s	
	1951 %	1966 %	1951 %	1966 %
Occupation				
Professions . . .	41	46	35	43
Business . . .	37	29	9	9
Miscellaneous . .	22	23	19	18
Workers . . .	—	—	37	30
Education				
Elementary . . .	1	1	26	22
Secondary . . .	24	18	50	60
Public School . .	75	80	20	18
(Eton) . . .	(24)	(21)	(1)	(1)
Oxford and Cambridge .	52	56	19	23
Other Universities . .	10	10	22	28

The change in the Labour party is not so striking as the 1964–66 developments would suggest; professional people have advanced at the expense of workers and graduates have risen from 41% to 51% of the whole. Within individual occupations the most striking advance is that of the teaching professions: it provided 14% of Labour M.P.s in 1951 but 20% in 1966.[1]

The composition of parliament changes to some extent through the sharp jerks of partisan swings at election — but this affects surprisingly few seats. The number changing hands was only about 25 in the elections of 1951, 1955 and 1959, and about 50 in 1964 and 1966: the great majority of constituencies remained safe. The composition of parliament changes more imperceptibly, but more radically, through the replacement of those who die or retire — there are a dozen or so by-elections each year and at the end of

[1] See *The British General Election of 1951*, p. 41.

each parliament thirty to sixty decisions not to stand again. It is the selection committees of the majority party in these constituencies who do most to determine whether the parliament of the next decade will resemble that of the last. Their standards of judgment are paramount, even though their choice is necessarily limited to those who come forward as candidates. It seems that the Conservatives have gone on choosing the same sort of people, in social and economic terms at least. The Labour party has changed its emphasis more; the result is an intellectually livelier parliament but not necessarily a more representative one.

CHAPTER XIII

CONSTITUENCY CAMPAIGNS

As in past books, we have attempted to convey the feel of electioneering at the local level through a set of constituency studies,
contributed by first-hand observers. But on this occasion we include more constituencies, described more briefly. Instead of providing moderately exhaustive accounts of a few very diverse
constituencies, often typical for their very lack of special features,

we deliberately sought out contests that were of exceptional interest, and asked our contributors to focus upon those aspects
which had rendered them exceptional. Inevitably most of these
seats are marginal but this was never the sole reason for their
selection. Bexley and Huyton sent the leaders of the two main
parties to parliament. Smethwick had produced the most remarkable result in 1964 and Kemptown the narrowest. Billericay had
the largest electorate in the country and one of the most rapidly
expanding. Preston had a special highly publicised local issue.
Chippenham offered an example of a serious Liberal challenge.

Rhondda West posed the problem, with its 8 to 1 majority, of what happens in a purely formal election, while Caithness and Sutherland and Belfast West were illustrations of idiosyncratic contests far from London and quite outside the general pattern. Thus these ten descriptions cannot be claimed as representative. Yet their swings were not untypical and most of their electioneering practices were in line with what was going on all over the country. Although the colour is richer than in past Nuffield studies we do not feel that the overall picture is a misleading one. What goes on even in exceptional constituencies is very ordinary at the grassroots level.

Throughout these studies three themes are dominant: how much difference did organisation make? how much difference did the candidate make? how important were local issues? The constituencies described here differ widely in composition — but only Caithness and Belfast seem seriously to stand outside the national battle, the national issues and the national swing.

Bexley

By William Plowden

1964	1966
64,240 Electors. 84·5% voting	*63,885 Electors. 85·8% voting*
E. Heath (Con.) . 25,716 (*47·4%*)	E. Heath (Con.) . 26,377 (*48·1%*)
L. L. Reeves (Lab.) . 21,127 (*38·9%*)	R. L. Butler (Lab.) . 24,044 (*43·9%*)
P. L. McArthur (Lib.) 6,161 (*11·4%*)	R. F. Lloyd (Lib.) . 4,405 (*8·0%*)
J. Paul (Anti-Common Market) . 1,263 (*2·3%*)	
Conservative majority 4,589 (*8·5%*)	Conservative majority 2,333 (*4·3%*)

In March 1966 the Leader of the Opposition, Mr. Heath, was contesting Bexley for the sixth time. He was one of the more permanent features of a scene where corporate identities change rapidly. He was adopted in 1947, and as a brisk young candidate won the seat in 1950 from Labour, with a majority that grew steadily till it was halved in 1964. By comparison, Bexley itself has grown increasingly indistinct. It doubled its population in the late 1930s and became a municipal borough in 1937. It was dignified with its own constituency in 1944. But the old borough vanished into the Greater London Council and by 1966 there was a Boundary Commission proposal for the drastic rearrangement of the constituency and its neighbours. Bexley's largely middle-income population commutes to London, and in the longer term goes elsewhere altogether, with an annual turnover in the electorate estimated by one local party agent at 10%.

After October 1964 Bexley, wedged between firmly Labour Erith and Crayford and marginally Conservative Chislehurst, was the most solid Conservative property of the three. But it was far from being an impregnable Conservative seat. Mr. Heath's majority would have been wiped out with a 4½% swing to Labour. In the London borough elections of May 1964, only three of Bexley constituency's eight wards returned Conservative councillors.

It was thus a further complication for Bexley Conservatives that Mr. Heath's elevation to the Conservative leadership meant that in 1966 he would spend most of his time stumping the rest of the country. They would have to fight their own campaign virtually without a candidate — as well as trying to exploit his national status without making him seem too big for his local boots. This was not an entirely new situation for them. Mr. Heath had held increasingly prominent government posts for almost his whole time as Bexley's M.P.; and in recent years, for instance, his agent had been filling in for him at his constituency surgeries. Despite this, he had sustained his reputation as a conscientious constituency member, although perhaps arousing more respect than personal affection.

The Bexley Conservative association itself appeared reassuringly solid and permanent — as indeed it was. The agent had taken over in 1949, after four predecessors in as many years. Having established his authority at the centre, he had tended to decentralise, and by 1966 largely independent ward committees handled the bulk of the organisational work. The association aimed to provide the social cohesion that Bexley itself seemed to lack through a network of activities and social groups (ladies, Young Conservatives, Conservative Political Centre, motoring).

Against this formidable team the Labour party, like the Liberals, put up a young and locally unknown candidate. The Labour agent, who had arrived only three months before, had found an association solidly based at the centre in its own freehold villa, and fairly well organised at ward level. For the Liberals, whose campaign was managed from a converted fish-and-chip shop by an energetic shift-worker in his spare time, the problem was to show that they were in the fight at all. (One poll, not quite half-way through the campaign, suggested that nearly half the electors of Bexley did not yet realise this.) For both parties, the strategic decision was how far to try to undermine Mr. Heath by fighting the kind of strictly local campaign that he could not afford to.

In the event, there were in effect three almost entirely separate Conservative campaigns in Bexley. First was Mr. Heath's own very sporadic personal campaign. He visited the constituency for five public meetings — three of them on the final evening — and two whirlwind Saturday tours. With the candidate surrounded by press, television, personal entourage and hangers-on, the circus came briefly to town. On his daytime visits Mr. Heath was given the maximum exposure, driving in a 12-car procession to hand in his nomination paper, walking through the shopping-centres in a hand-shaking presidential-style crowd-bath, getting enough photographic coverage of his short canvassing forays to suggest that he had spent the whole three weeks chatting-up Bexley housewives and jollying Bexley babies. In addition, the national press and the pollsters descended on Bexley to take its temperature about twice a week; two polls forecast a win for Mr. Heath but Marplan (March 11th–14th) saw a 1·7% swing to Labour and Gallup (March 18th–23rd) a 2·8% swing to the Conservatives.

But between these periodic excitements there were long intervals of surprising peace in Bexley. The second campaign consisted of the local Conservatives' valiant efforts to fill these gaps with a continual flurry of activity, aiming with the quickness of the hand to deceive the elector's eye. Mornings and afternoons a formidable team of female canvassers systematically moved through the streets, led not as in other years by Mr. Heath but by Mr. Reginald Watts, himself a former Conservative candidate.

The third campaign was Mr. Heath's own continual evening presence on television. No Conservative candidate can have had more chance of being seen by his electors. Even so, the Marplan survey suggested that 19% of Bexley voters still did not know that Mr. Heath was their candidate.

The content of the collective campaign was unremarkable. The main issues that emerged were national ones. Mr. Heath's own election address was an abridgement of the party manifesto (backed, for good measure, with some personal snapshots and a family tree headed 'From a working-class background came this Tory leader'). Local interest focused particularly on comprehensive schools, rates — the Bexley council announced a 1s. 9d. increase during the campaign — and mortgages; at Mr. Heath's first public meeting the loudest applause, in this constituency of owner-occupiers, came for a demand for economic council rents. The local press reported all three candidates' activities with scrupulous balance and almost without comment.

By polling day, despite the opinion polls, the likely result was far from clear. All parties reported large numbers of doubtfuls. The Conservatives felt encouraged to make a public forecast of an increased majority. To this hopeful atmosphere Mr. Heath returned from the provinces to address three packed-out meetings on the eve-of-poll, noticeably more relaxed and effective with interruptions than three weeks before. His audiences were enthusiastic, although perhaps not all of them fully absorbed, for example, his attack on the government's attitude to the General Agreement on Tariffs and Trade.

On polling day, the Liberal and Labour candidates spent much of their time touring rather mournfully in their loudspeaker vans. Mr. Heath visited various parts of the constituency and generally took things easy. The Labour agent spent most of the day correlating returns telephoned in from the wards; the Conservative agent made periodic spot checks on progress, but did not try to get a comprehensive picture; the Liberals were hopeful but ill-informed.

The result saw Mr. Heath's majority again halved, although he slightly increased his share of the poll, and held the swing to Labour well below the national and Greater London averages; the Liberal vote dropped 3·4%. This should perhaps have held shocks for nobody. But it certainly disappointed the Conservatives, whose confident forecasts had been sincerely meant. With a well-known member of sixteen years' standing, newly elected leader of his party, backed by a long-established and efficient local organisation which had fought a most intensive campaign, they might reasonably have expected to do better than this against an unknown Labour opponent with a new agent and an undramatic, though competent, approach to the campaign. They might not have expected many of the 1,200 votes which in 1964 had gone to the Anti-Common Market candidate, but it was a blow that Mr. Heath had benefited so little from the decline of the Liberals.

On the other hand, there had been little in the Conservative campaign — except perhaps Mr. Heath's continual absence — to suggest that there was anything unusual, still less unique, about the candidate for Bexley. The fact that he was his party's leader was only discreetly mentioned in passing in his election literature.

The result could well be viewed as a classic illustration of the relative unimportance of local factors in British general elections. But in justifying their efforts Bexley Conservatives could fairly point out that while in 1955 and 1959 the Conservatives had held nine of the fourteen surrounding seats, by April 1966 Bexley, snatched from Labour in 1950, was one of the mere three to survive. Nor, with an 85·8% poll, was this survival by default. What will happen when Mr. Heath fights Bexley for the seventh time may never be known; for if the present seat is transformed by the Boundary Commissioners the Conservatives may decide to offer a more expendable candidate in the new and more marginal division.

Billericay

By Michael Pinto-Duschinsky

1964		1966	
96,762 Electors. 82·5% voting		*102,198 Electors. 84·1% voting*	
E. L. Gardner (Con.)	35,347 (*44·3%*)	E. Moonman (Lab.) .	40,013 (*46·5%*)
Mrs. R. A. Smythe		E. L. Gardner (Con.)	38,371 (*44·6%*)
(Lab.)	. 33,755 (*42·3%*)	L. R. Wernick (Lib.)	7,587 (*8·8%*)
P. M. T. Sheldon-			
Williams (Lib.)	. 10,706 (*13·4%*)		
Conservative majority	1,592 (*2·0%*)	Labour majority .	1,642 (*1·9%*)

BILLERICAY achieved national prominence in 1959 as the first constituency to declare its result, and some notoriety in 1964 by the failure of the town clerk's well publicised efforts to repeat the performance. It opted out of the counting race in 1966, but it was still notable for having the largest electorate in Britain — and for the exceptional verve and energy with which the parties carried out the pedestrian jobs of local campaigning. The constituency had swelled from 59,000 at its creation in 1955 to over 100,000 by 1966. It contained at one end Brentwood, a part of the Essex stockbroker belt, and at the other the new town of Basildon, inhabited mostly by former East Enders; the smaller towns of Billericay and Wickford lay in between.

The contests in 1959 and 1964 had been very close and the Conservatives had won both times. Encouraged by their successes, they had developed one of the most efficient campaign machines in the country. By 1966 their energetic agent Ian Greer was supported by a 9,000-strong Conservative association and by a number of sympathetic local newspapers.

The Conservative campaign was off to an early start. Already in January the job of addressing envelopes was begun. When the new electoral register came out, personally topped letters went out to the 20,000 new electors. Another 20,000 letters went to households shown on existing marked registers to be Conservative; these concerned postal votes. Other letters were sent to the 9,000 party members asking for their help during the expected campaign. And when rumours about an imminent election intensified in February, Mr. Greer decided it was time for Edward Gardner, the Conservative M.P. for Billericay, to launch a petition appealing for a better bus service in the area. Advertisements were put in the local papers and names were solicited at bus stops and later, a few days before the election, letters were sent to all those who had signed the petition. The Labour party challenged the sincerity of this 'stunt', but not its effectiveness.

By the time the election date was announced, Conservative plans had mostly been completed. Only one or two branches were without working committees and *ad hoc* election committees were assigned to these.

The response of helpers was better and the efficiency of the organisation even smoother than it had been in 1964. Coach loads of Young Conservatives and of Conservative women descended on the constituency from Chigwell, Southend West and South-east Essex. The canvass was completed (it indicated a Conservative majority of 2,000) and personalised letters were then sent to the 6,000 marked in the returns as 'don't knows'. The candidate spent most of his time canvassing and speaking and was normally accompanied by a team of knockers-up (the Labour party used their candidate in exactly the same way). An information caravan was sited regularly in Basildon and six vehicles were fitted with public address systems. At the central committee rooms, a team of ladies was permanently on hand to answer questions and the whole operation was co-ordinated with the aid of radio-telephones fitted to the cars of the candidate, agent and their assistants. The main problem for the Conservatives was that the election law restricted total expenditure to about £1,300. They decided to economise chiefly by sending only one copy of the election address to each household, even if it contained several electors. They held a large number of meetings with a string of shadow ministers. The attendance was about the same as 1964 but there was little excitement. It was generally agreed that the main value of the visits of distinguished speakers was the spur they offered to active party workers. On election day itself, the Conservatives had about 1,000 tellers and 700 cars, and all in all it is difficult to see how they could have done more in their campaign if they were to keep within the legal limit.

The most important source of organisational strength for the Conservatives was that they had built up their association, had made their candidate known, had booked poster sites, had cultivated good relations with the press and had set their campaign in motion before the election was announced.

By contrast, the Labour party were still without an agent, without an office and without a telephone a few weeks before polling day, and, to make things worse, their candidate was new and almost totally unknown. An emergency arrangement was made whereby Leslie Bridges, the assistant regional organiser, came from Ipswich to act as agent. He was shocked by what he found in Billericay: the local Labour party seemed to have 'an obsession with the Tory organisation and with Gardner'. He said that he had never known such a feeling of defeatism among a party because of their opponents.

However, his task was made easier by the large influx of volunteers after the campaign started. He also had a good deal of help from Stepney and Poplar and from neighbouring Thurrock. Still, it was a considerable achievement that the Labour party managed, in total contrast to their weak effort of 1964, to carry out a virtually complete canvass. There were also visits from several cabinet ministers and the Prime Minister himself started his national campaign with a speech in Billericay. Eric Moonman, the Labour candidate, was left to speak to a fast emptying hall and to the accompaniment of the noise of TV cameras being dismantled.

The Liberals had a lively candidate, a local company director who had previously belonged to the Labour party. But the Liberal campaign was very rudimentary — there was almost no canvassing and some meetings had to be cancelled for lack of support. The Liberals were strongest in the Brentwood area and they left Basildon completely untouched.

In spite of the emphasis on the purely organisational aspects of the struggle in Billericay, it would be wrong to omit all mention of the political decisions that had to be taken by the respective parties. The main decision that the Conservatives took was to play down national issues and, in the words of their agent, 'to emphasise local issues to the nth degree'. This was done because the sitting member was Conservative and was better known than his opponent. It was also done because the polls showed Labour well in the lead and Wilson ahead of Heath in the leadership ratings to such an extent that it seemed foolish to emphasise the 'presidential' aspect of the election. Accordingly, the election address had on its front page three pictures of the M.P. and the words 'Edward Gardner' with no mention of the fact that he was the Conservative candidate. The other handouts were concerned almost exclusively with local issues.

The Labour party was put out by these tactics at first. They wanted to concentrate on national affairs, but they did not want to leave Conservative claims on local affairs unanswered. Their election address put a considerable degree of emphasis on local matters, and during the first few days of the campaign the agent spent a good deal of time doing homework on local issues. As the campaign progressed, however, Labour realised that local issues were proving less pressing than had been thought. Mr. Moonman summed up Labour tactics when he said at a press conference:

> 'I think it would be very dishonest for a candidate just to concern himself with the parish pump. You are on the platform to defend the manifesto.'

Both major parties also had the problem of how to deal with the Liberals. It was made more difficult by the lack of any indication of the way Liberal defectors would be likely to turn. In the event, both parties simply ignored them.

On election day, a record 84·1% of the electorate, 85,951 people, went to the polls in Billericay. There was a small swing to Labour of 1·9% — slightly less than in most neighbouring seats but enough to add Billericay to the mass of marginals lost by the Conservatives.

The Conservatives explained their defeat by the fact that (in their view) the majority of the new electors who had moved into the constituency since 1964 were Labour. The Labour and Liberal parties thought that the swing was lower than might have been expected and both attributed this to the success of the Conservatives in projecting Mr. Gardner. Although local issues were not important in themselves, it was maintained that they were useful as a means of putting over the name 'Gardner' to the electorate, and this paid its dividends.

A closer examination of the figures suggests that all three parties were wrong in their conclusions. An analysis of the electoral register shows that the new voters were fairly evenly split between the Basildon housing estates and the Brentwood 'executive belt'. This means that they probably divided evenly between the two parties. Furthermore, the swing to Labour in Billericay did not differ significantly from the regional average.

This leads to the not unfamiliar conclusion that, apart from increasing turnout and apart from the undoubted advantage of a few hundred votes gained by the Conservatives in their postal votes campaign, the hectic efforts of the thousands of helpers on both sides had a negligible net effect on the votes cast for each party.

Brighton, Kemptown

By Daniel Snowman

	1964		1966	
	61,820 Electors. 72·2% voting		*61,250 Electors. 80·1% voting.*	
D. Hobden (Lab.) .	22,308 (*50·001*%)	D. Hobden (Lab.) .	24,936 (*50·8*%)
D. James (Con.) .	22,301 (*49·999*%)	A. Bowden (Con) .	24,105 (*49·2*%)
Labour majority .	7 (*0·002*%)	Labour majority .	831 (*1·6*%)

In 1964 Brighton, Kemptown became the most marginal constituency in the country. After seven recounts, Councillor Dennis Hobden was declared the winner by seven votes. Mr. Hobden was the first Labour M.P. Sussex had ever had. The Brighton area had traditionally been considered particularly safe territory for the Conservatives. Prior to its division into Pavilion and Kemptown in 1948, the old two-member constituency of Brighton had regularly sent two Conservatives to Westminster. Despite the initial hopes of some Labour supporters at the time, the new Kemptown constituency returned Conservatives by comfortable and gradually increasing majorities throughout the 1950s.

Kemptown resembles most other resort constituencies in containing a disproportionate number of elderly people and women. Along the seafront it tends to be solidly Conservative; Pier Ward is full of genteel guest-house proprietresses, while the Regency terraces of King's Cliff and Rottingdean's expensive bungalows house many of Brighton's successful solicitors, estate agents and antique dealers. But, hidden away from the casual glance of most holidaymakers, Kemptown also contains several large council estates. Since there is very little industry in Brighton, many of the inhabitants of these estates (in the Whitehawk estate in the north of King's Cliff Ward and in much of the housing in Falmer Ward, for instance) are concerned, directly or indirectly, with servicing the town. Their political sympathies tend to be with Labour. The job facing 'Nobby' Clarke, Mr. Hobden's laconic and efficient agent, was to get these people to the polls on the day. Mr. Clarke knew that many potential Labour supporters in Kemptown had not bothered to vote in 1964; he was painfully aware that Labour support tended to be much higher among Kemptown's more apathetic voters than among people who definitely intended to vote. In the event, there was a very large turnout on polling day (80·1% — a bigger increase over the 1964 turnout than in any other constituency in the country) and the Labour majority went up to the still marginal (but, to Hobden supporters, heroic) figure of 831. How and why had this result come about?

For many years Mr. Hobden had been an active and outspoken member of the left wing of the Labour party. Indeed, so critical was he of Transport House that in 1961 the Labour party NEC had refused his application to have his name included on the 'B' list of eligible candidates; in 1964, he was adopted by the Kemptown party in defiance of the wishes of Labour headquarters. Once in parliament, he criticised his party on its immigration white paper, on its support of American policy on Vietnam, and on many other issues — hardly the sort of candidate, one might think, to appeal to the hitherto staunch Conservatives of Brighton. But Mr. Hobden had also been a Brighton councillor for ten years and had become an expert in the myriad of local problems that preoccupied the people of Kemptown. At the beginning of the 1966 campaign, the Brighton *Evening Argus*, which found his left-wing views unpalatable, admitted that 'throughout his short term in parliament, he has kept the interests of Kemptown firmly to the fore' — a wise enough precaution for any marginal M.P.

Hobden's opponent, 35-year-old Andrew Bowden, had been a founder-member of the Brighton Young Conservatives and, in 1960–61, was the national chairman of the YCs. Like Mr. Hobden, he was selected in unusual circumstances. After a distasteful squabble over the original short-list, Mr. Bowden was eventually adopted, despite the candidature of two former M.P.s for the division, in February 1965, at an open meeting of the entire Kemptown constituency association — one of the very few instances in which Britain has seen something approaching a genuine primary election. Mr. Bowden was anxious to adopt new streamlined tactics in this, his third, constituency. From May 1965 onwards, he and his youthful agent, Charles Constance, and a committee including nine 'campaign directors', met every two or three weeks to discuss their plans. One 'director' was to be in charge of the postal vote, another was to mobilise cars, a third had the job of ensuring that wealthy Brightonians with two residences would, if they could, vote in Kemptown. On the day the dissolution was announced, the Conservatives were in the field immediately; by that evening, the Bowden organisation had delivered glossy little introductory leaflets to some 60% of the constituency. At the Hobden headquarters, all this fanfare of early activity was watched with quiet scorn. By March 14th, both parties had announced their campaign plans. Mr. Hobden, following tradition, would hold at least one public meeting every night (four of them with well-known speakers — Ian Mikardo, Michael Foot, Lord Sorensen and the Minister of Health, Kenneth Robinson) as well as an eve-of-poll rally at the Brighton Dome. Mr. Bowden, the professional salesman, made it clear that he would avoid wasting too much time preaching to the converted; he would hold a few 'frank get-togethers', invite no 'big-guns' to speak for him, and spend the great majority of his time — and even election eve — canvassing on the doorsteps.

Outwardly the election in Kemptown seemed a rather dull affair, though the two protagonists did all in their power to enliven it. Just as Mr. Heath tried to blow up the Cowley 'noose trial' and the Common Market into exciting and divisive issues, Mr. Bowden tried to get some mileage out of an accusation that Labour canvassers had intimidated known Conservative voters. Mr. Hobden, for his part, tried to identify his opponent with the notorious Sussex Racial Preservation Society. But, as at the national level, none of these potentially explosive issues ever caught fire. Even Mr. Hobden's arrest in February on a charge (from which he was later acquitted) of drunken driving, which some people feared might dominate the campaign in the form of insidious whispers, seemed to be of no major concern to Kemptown voters except, perhaps, to the extent that it reinforced the predispositions of a handful of rock-ribbed Tories and, possibly, alienated a few of Mr. Hobden's Methodist supporters in Warren Ward. Mr. Bowden gave his workers strict orders never to mention the drink charge. The only occasions on which it was mentioned publicly during the campaign were when Mr. Hobden himself made jokes at his own expense; for example, he started an address at the University of Sussex with the words 'Fellow members of Alcoholics Anonymous!'

As in the nation as a whole, the only serious issues that seemed to bother the electorate — and the ones that were persistently brought up by the candidates and their questioners at meetings — were the relatively undramatic bread-and-butter ones: the cost of living, the national economy, and (particularly important in many South East towns like Brighton) pensions and housing. The latter was a subject on which Mr. Hobden was known to be an expert.

One or two local issues did enter the campaign to a limited extent. Mr. Bowden, in answer to a questioner, mentioned that he opposed the proposal to build a costly Marina in Kemptown, thus annoying a few normally Conservative fishermen who had been promised concessions there. Then there was Mr. Hobden's continuing clash with the Minister of Health. In the House of Commons he had requested an inquiry into the conditions at Bevendean Hospital in Brighton where a patient had recently died in unusual circumstances, and his request had been refused. When the Minister of Health (a strange choice by Transport House) came to speak on Mr. Hobden's behalf, he was given a very rough passage both on account of the Bevendean affair and for other reasons. After Mr. Robinson's departure, the Labour candidate endeared himself to all elements in the very diverse audience by apologising for the Minister's attitude.

As the campaign progressed, both sides concentrated on building up their forces for the big day. The Bowden headquarters thought that one reason for Labour's 1964 victory in Kemptown was that a large number of complacent Conservatives did not vote. Mr. Bowden, accordingly, devoted most of his abundant energies to the job of activating the entire 'natural' Conservative vote. In particular, he spent a great deal of time patiently talking to people who, according to canvassing returns, preferred the Conservatives but had only a weak preference. The Labour campaign, also concerned with persuading the apathetic to vote, spoke with several voices. Sometimes Mr. Hobden's literature emphasised, in a tone resembling an SOS message, the importance of increasing the precarious 1964 majority in Kemptown (one election notice was dominated by a huge figure 7 and the words: 'It depends on YOU'); more often the Labour campaign had an air of workmanlike practicality. But there were also times when some of Mr. Hobden's eager helpers from the University (whom Mr. Bowden repeatedly branded as dangerous Communists) gave the Labour campaign something of the aura of a religious crusade.

Polling day arrived at last. 'Nobby' Clarke, the impassive sergeant-major, felt throughout the day that Mr. Hobden had a good chance of winning, though there were some anxious moments in the mid-afternoon when the 400 or 500 Conservative cars and the ubiquitous Young Conservatives from all over the South East were particularly busy. By the early evening, it was becoming fairly clear to both sides that Labour would win again. After only one recount, the result was declared; the winner and loser made gentlemanly speeches about each other while, in the packed galleries of the Dome, some of their supporters started some rather less gentlemanly brawls.

Mr. Hobden won Kemptown primarily for the reasons that Labour won nationally. Kemptown's voters admired Mr. Wilson more than Mr. Heath and, to the extent that they had opinions about policies, were more impressed by Labour's domestic programme than by any of the policies proposed by the Conservatives. But in two respects the constituency did not follow the national pattern: the increase in turnout (7·9%) was by far the greatest in the country, while the swing to Labour (0·8%) was well below the national average. The extra voters were drawn in largely by the frantic activity and publicity resulting from the super-marginality of the seat and also, to some extent, by the thoroughly professional organisation of both sides: these factors, it should be noted, helped both parties, and not just the winner, to increase their turnout dramatically. It would seem that this large and very similar increase in turnout by both parties — coupled with the fact that the swing to Labour in 1964 had been a very large one (6·4%) — explains why the 1966 swing was so small.

Caithness and Sutherland

By Ian Grimble

1964	1966
27,291 Electors. 80·1% voting	*26,781 Electors. 79·2% voting*
G. Y. Mackie (Lib.) . 7,894 (*36·1%*)	R. A. R. Maclennan
J. B. Urquhart (Lab.) 6,619 (*30·3%*)	(Lab.) . . . 8,308 (*39·1%*)
P. Maitland (Con.) . 4,550 (*20·8%*)	G. Y. Mackie (Lib.) . 8,244 (*38·9%*)
J. M. Young (Ind. C.) 2,795 (*12·8%*)	J. M. Watt (Con.) . 4,662 (*22·0%*)
Liberal majority . 1,275 (*5·8%*)	Labour majority . 64 (*0·2%*)

CAITHNESS and Sutherland is bounded by the entire north coast of Britain from Cape Wrath to John O'Groats, falling about fifty miles from there to the Dornoch Firth in the east, and about as far in more crumpled fashion among the mountains of the west. Alone in all Britain, this constituency bestrides the Celtic West and Germanic East; it is as though England possessed a single constituency stretching from Wales to East Anglia. The language barrier remains where it stood a thousand years ago, at the still Gaelic-speaking village of Portskerra, facing Dounreay. The people still bestride the two worlds. A daily bus service carries workers to Dounreay from the hills to the west as well as from the plains to the east. Soon after the election men coming off night shift in a nuclear reactor were delivering lambs on their crofts at Melvich and Bettyhill. The postman milks the cows before starting on his rounds.

Sir Archibald Sinclair, now Lord Thurso, was member of parliament for decades until his defeat in 1945. His great castle dominated the little town of Thurso in those distant times; his vast estate filled the surrounding horizon. There are those who still remember how people were astonished by the lack of respect when somebody had the temerity to question him at a political meeting in Bettyhill. Today the castle is a ruin and Thurso has grown round it, engulfing its home-acres. Sir David Robertson has come and gone, a radical Conservative who tried from 1950 until 1964 to persuade his government to take a greater interest in the Highlands, and who ended by forsaking his party. In 1964 he supported John Young, a Caithness farmer, against the official Conservative, and the rival Unionist candidates landed at the bottom of the poll. George Mackie recovered the seat for the Liberals with a 1,275 majority, a large one by local standards. The entire northern Highlands turned Liberal at the same time, leaving only Argyllshire in Tory hands.

England's Celtic West has long been overwhelmingly Labour. Why has Scotland's Celtic West — apart from the Western Isles — been so different in its voting pattern from Wales? Why in 1966 did Caithness and Sutherland become the first Highland constituency to follow the Welsh trend?

The Welsh have not abandoned Wales: the Gaels have deserted or been driven from the greater part of the Scottish Highlands, leaving it largely in the hands of mammoth absentee landlords. Of all the nineteenth-century clearances, those of Sutherland are rightly the most notorious. The Hebrides suffered equally, but their largest, northernmost island, Lewis, was notable for its resistance. Today it provides the most numerous, the most vital and perhaps the most viable Gaelic society left.

Where did the revolt occur that produced the almost unparalleled drop of 36% in Unionist votes on the northern mainland between 1955 and 1966, and at last aligned it with the Western Isles? It seems to have occurred mainly in the scattered Celtic West, where deference for landlord and Calvinist minister is at last almost dead. For instance, the children in Bettyhill school's secondary class held a mock election in which there were 31 Labour votes, 9 Liberal, one Conservative, and one spoilt ballot paper. The ballot box revealed how closely the children reflected the affiliations of their parents.

While about two-thirds of Sutherland is thought to be owned by six landlords, Caithness is largely in the hands of working farmers. These were offered a choice of two farmers to vote for, in the Conservative and Liberal candidates. Absentee landlordism has no more defenders in Caithness than in Sutherland, and the Liberal and Conservative candidates were as outspoken in their condemnation as the Labour one. But perhaps this issue, though it might require a Labour government for its solution, was not such a live one in Caithness, particularly in Thurso and Wick. Yet these towns, the only two of any size in the constituency, have been asylums for over a century for refugees and emigrants bringing long memories from the West. Since the first reactor came to Dounreay these towns have recruited a well-educated population from the South and given them an opportunity to explore this corner of Europe in which feudalism has not yet vanished. It was in these towns that the only virulent meetings of the campaign occurred, and it was the presence of Sir Alec Douglas-Home that occasioned them in each case. In Wick he was asked 'Where are your ghillies?' No such outbursts greeted him in the Ross-shire towns of Tain and Dingwall, where his reception was tepid and well-behaved.

Since 1964, Grampian Television had increased its transmission coverage to include the constituency's largest town of Thurso, which had hitherto only received the BBC. The number of viewers throughout the constituency had increased greatly, and far more electors must have watched the political debates on television than ever before. This may have operated in favour of George Mackie, who was the Liberal spokesman in both BBC and Grampian Television discussions.

Perhaps television played some part, also, in bringing the constituency closer to the political pattern of the rest of Britain. But perhaps the visit of two cabinet ministers of the Labour government, Tom Fraser and William Ross, was more important — particularly the brilliant performances of the Scottish Secretary of State. Again, comparison with neighbouring Ross-shire is suggestive. Here there were no equivalent *tours-de-force* by Labour cabinet ministers, no such television appearances by the Liberal candidate. The Conservative organisation was at least as impressive as in Caithness, and Sir Alec was more kindly received. Yet the Unionists for the first time sank to the bottom of the poll, their vote slumping almost as dramatically as in Caithness and Sutherland. The Liberal, a popular local resident, was returned.

The simplest explanation for the different results is the siting of the new reactor at Dounreay. Obviously this was an important factor, but it would be an over-simplification to accept it as decisive in a constituency so vast and diverse. Mr. Maclennan won

Q

by a handful of votes, such as the candidates might win or lose in tiny scattered townships during an electoral tour of nearly 400 miles. Mr. Maclennan polled 1,700 votes more than the Labour candidate in 1964, and over a thousand more than any previous Labour candidate. The Dounreay votes (about 3,000 in this election) had been available for the past three elections, but previous Labour candidates did not harvest them, and it has been reckoned that 500 potential Labour voters left the area between 1964 and 1966. However, while the 1964 Labour candidate was a member of the Electrical Trades Union, Mr. Maclennan was a barrister-at-law in London; perhaps this contrast was as decisive as the siting of the new reactor.

The winning formula for a Labour candidate in this constituency may have become increasingly refined since the first of them won his twelve votes in it. He should not be a carpet-bagger, but someone with sufficient local affiliations to convince the electorate that the Labour party is looking to the constituency for more than a vote in parliament. Yet he must possess a social background such as to reassure a rural population long accustomed to see authority exercised from a big house. Robert Maclennan happened to combine his professional skill with long association with the little Sutherland village of Rogart: and to these was added titled parentage, through recognition of talent, not accident of descent. The last and most difficult requirement was to demonstrate that a Labour candidate really could defeat his Liberal and Conservative opponents at the polls. Maclennan's outstanding ability, fighting his first election at the age of 28, was reinforced by the best Labour party organisation yet seen in the constituency. A large number of quite independent factors thus contributed to give the Scottish Highlands their first Labour M.P.

It ought to be arguable that the creation of the Highland Development Board assisted the Labour candidate in every Highland constituency. But it is doubtful whether it was worth a vote, while in some constituencies it may have been an actual embarrassment. When William Ross expounded his new creation during his speech in Thurso, it was the only subject he mentioned to be received in icy silence. For the Board was not in itself a solution to the Highland problem, and Highlanders had seen many before this one that provided well-paid jobs and thick reports and not much else. It was remarked that the Highland Development Board's unprecedented powers could, in the wrong hands, achieve as much harm as any factor to an absentee landlord. William Ross explained that the Board was in exactly the right hands, but people in the Highlands, knowing some of its members as well as he did, could judge for themselves.

The principal issue facing the candidates in Sutherland and Caithness, in connection with the Board, was that of agriculture versus forestry. Agriculture is still the major industry of the constituency and before the nineteenth-century clearances the Highlands were predominantly cattle country. Today there is a Forestry Commission with a planting target imposed by parliament, and a new pulp mill at Fort William, hungry for fast-growing soft woods. The Forestry Commission has compulsory powers of purchase which it has not exercised. Landlords need no compulsion to surrender their agricultural land for forestry, especially when this helps to protect the higher ground, on which trees ought to be grown, for sport. Nor is it the responsibility of the Forestry Commission to incur greater expense than necessary in the long-range interests of proper land use. It remained to be seen whether the Highland Development Board would remedy this situation, or would merely rush in with increased planting targets, without carrying out any capability surveys. Kildonan in Sutherland became one of the target areas, the Island of Mull another.

'Rivals support Kildonan Crofters' ran the headline in Sutherland's newspaper on election day, carrying the issue above party. Although Mull soon became the subject of more public controversy, the issue would perhaps be fought to a conclusion in the valley of Kildonan, with the remaining native population, the landlords, the Forestry Commission and the Board, as the parties involved. It was a remarkable paradox that at a time when this constituency had just returned its first Labour member of parliament, and a Labour government had erected a body with powers to expropriate the absentee landlords, no one was certain whence salvation would come to the man-made wildernesses of Sutherland — from the Board, or from the proprietors. But the issue now joined in Kildonan should be decided long before the next election, and it is unlikely that any other new member with such a slender majority as Robert Maclennan will be more difficult to unseat. This may sound surprising in a constituency that has returned candidates under four different labels in four successive elections.

But in fact the seat has hitherto been occupied alternately by Liberals and Unionists. No previous change was revolutionary, as the Labour victory was; revolutions in rural areas are slow to arrive, but they generally come to stay.

Chippenham

BY WILLIAM WALLACE

1964		1966	
55,071 Electors. 81·1% voting		*54,717 Electors. 82·8% voting*	
D. E. Awdry (Con.) . 18,089 *(40·4%)*		D. E. Awdry (Con.) . 18,275 *(39·6%)*	
Hon. C. Layton (Lib.) 16,546 *(37·0%)*		Hon. C. Layton (Lib.) 17,581 *(38·1%)*	
G. H. Radice (Lab.) . 10,086 *(22·6%)*		G. H. Radice (Lab.) . 10,257 *(22·3%)*	
Conservative majority 1,543 *(3·4%)*		Conservative majority 694 *(1·5%)*	

THE 1966 election was Chippenham's third in four years; in effect the campaign had been in progress since the 1962 by-election which transformed Chippenham from a safe Conservative seat to a Liberal-threatened marginal. Two of this election's candidates had fought here on all three occasions, and the third was fighting for the second time; all had local bases in the constituency area, from which they had been working to prepare for the expected early election.

Chippenham constituency covers 1,600 square miles of northwest Wiltshire. The bulk of its population lies in an inverted 'L' along its southern edge and up its eastern border, from the outskirts of the Bristol–Bath area in the west to the suburbs of Swindon. More than a quarter of its electorate lives in Chippenham itself, a market town dominated by the Westinghouse brake factory, employing over 6,000 men. Calne, its second largest town, five miles away, relies for its prosperity on the Harris bacon factory. Its northern area is prosperous farming and hunting country; Malmesbury, similarly dependent on a single factory, is its only town, though some areas look to Cirencester, across the border, as their natural centre.

It is not a naturally cohesive constituency; the towns around its edges exert their influence and circulate their newspapers, and to be known in Chippenham is not necessarily to be treated as a local in Malmesbury or Cricklade. Nor is it mainly a collection of rural communities, insulated by an element of stability from the shifting currents of national opinion. Half of its labour force works in industry, only 12% in farming; and although the population in the villages is fairly stable, there is considerable mobility in the urban areas — accentuated by the constant turnover of RAF personnel at its several air bases. There are local issues, but few of these are peculiar to north-west Wiltshire: the need for alternative industries, slum conditions in local schools, the lack of rural transport and the congestion which through traffic brings to the centres of its towns. Traditional and local ties matter, but are not of overwhelming importance. In almost every respect, Chippenham is a 'mixed' constituency; politically this is perhaps best demonstrated in its local politics, where the parties all contest the borough and county council elections, but where Independents still survive alongside them, and where a strong or a popular personality often outweighs the importance of a party label.

The Liberals had great hopes of Chippenham in 1966, considering it one of their likeliest gains. They had achieved a close second place in the 1962 by-election, their vote leaping from 16·9% to 32·5%. It increased to 37·0%, mainly at Labour's expense, in a much higher poll at the 1964 election. 1966, they hoped, would be 'This time Layton'.

Yet Chippenham is no more naturally a Liberal stronghold than the adjacent Wiltshire seats of Westbury and Devizes. Like them, it had been frequently held by Liberals until the slaughter of 1924; like them, it saw the Liberals slip into third place in 1945. The association survived the early 1950s with difficulty, regaining some support in the 1959 election, and beginning to have some successes in local elections in 1960 and 1961. The memory of a Liberal tradition had survived strongly enough to leave many people favourably disposed to voting Liberal if a sufficiently good opportunity offered; Chippenham and Calne still had active Liberal workingmen's clubs, which were to be 'reclaimed' by the association as it recovered strength. But very few of the leading members of the revived association were local in origin; more often they had followed their jobs to Chippenham, and had adjusted as best they could to the few survivals of old-style Liberalism in the villages where committees still met after chapel. The key to Liberal strength lay in the luck of a by-election falling in the immediate aftermath of Orpington, at a time when unexpected lay-offs from Westinghouse had caused some local discontent. The by-election allowed the establishment of a position which had since been strengthened, with the expansion of membership and organisation, and through the efforts of an energetic candidate. By the end of 1965, aided by help from outside and from headquarters, the Chippenham Liberals had built up a membership of over 1,500, covering organisationally most of the division; and their finances, though still far from strong, were sufficient to support their activities and to retain the full-time agent they had had since mid-1963.

Their candidate, Christopher Layton, was an economist who had worked for a while as personal assistant to Mr. Grimond. Coming into the constituency a few months before the 1962 by-election, he had worked hard and continuously since then, achieving considerable publicity and popularity by his espousal of local issues, from rents and roads to drains and primary schools — 'headline-seeking gimmicks' to his opponents, but winning headlines and support. The son of a peer, 'he always seemed to be having tea in the council houses', as a Conservative complained; he had also organised groups in the factories and the towns to discuss Liberal policies for industry, agriculture and regionalism. By this election he was probably the best known of the three candidates, and according to a local opinion poll was also the one who most often attracted favourable personal comment.

For the Conservatives the by-election result on Sir David Eccles' departure was less of a shock than the failure to recover votes in 1964; since then a major membership drive had raised their numbers from four to over six thousand. Strongest in the rural north, weakest in numbers in Chippenham and Calne, they had a firm organisation throughout the constituency, headed by an experienced agent and two other staff, and markedly superior in manpower and financial resources to the other two parties'. The present member, Daniel Awdry, had been chosen in 1962 in response to a demand for a local man; the son of a mayor of Chippenham, he had himself been mayor in 1958, while serving on the borough council as an Independent. He had kept up his solicitor's practice in the town since his election, and was well known and liked in the Chippenham area; but his work as a constituency M.P., though diligent, had been less directed to cultivating publicity than Mr. Layton's efforts, and was therefore less well known.

Labour's strong period had been in the post-war years; in the 1950s their association and their vote had been slowly declining. With few large union branches in the area, and little help from these, their finances had been doubtful, and their membership small; their organisation was confined to the urban areas. In 1964, with a raw candidate, a piecemeal organisation and a weak campaign, they had lost votes heavily to the Liberals; since then they had tried, without professional or outside help, to regain some of the lost ground. Giles Radice, the youngest of the three candidates, distantly related to Mr. Awdry by marriage, and like him a Wykehamist, had been little known in the constituency in 1964; since then he had been working at week-ends to help rebuild the Labour organisation and to establish for himself a local base in the constituency.

There could be few new issues in a campaign that had been brewing for such a long period; on national issues the candidates, all on the 'modernising' wings of their parties, were seldom in serious disagreement. The lines of battle had been laid down long before: the crucial struggle was to be for the non-Conservative vote, with the Liberals hoping to win by adding to the Labour defections of 1964, and Labour fighting to retain and regain its vote, and so to maintain its long-term prospects in the constituency. The Liberal attack was two-pronged: a strongly personal campaign to 'Get Chris Layton In' — as thousands of orange and black posters proclaimed in front gardens throughout the division — built around the local issues he had championed; and a 'radical' appeal which, repeating his tactics of 1964, aimed at winning the anti-Conservative vote for 'the best chance in a generation to get a change in Chippenham'. The importance which the Liberals attached to Chippenham was underlined by visits from Mr. Grimond and Mr. Thorpe, by outside assistance from university students and non-fighting constituencies, and by Mr. Layton's frequent television appearances as a party spokesman. The Labour defence was to assert the national against the local; Mr. Radice, compensating for the weakest organisation with the loudest loudspeaker, repeated constantly that 'a vote for Giles Radice is a vote for Harold Wilson and the Labour government'.

The Conservatives found themselves in an odd position; as Mr. Awdry later remarked, although they were the incumbents, 'nobody was attacking us'. Left largely to themselves, they pursued an efficiently conventional campaign of meetings and canvassing, rounded up the postal votes and quietly hoped that the other parties would divide evenly enough to save their majority; their posters, dominating the rural hedgerows, mixed Daniel Awdry's local appeal with that of 'the Alternative Government'.

The result fulfilled Conservative hopes; though Chris Layton gathered a thousand extra votes, Labour support held steady and denied him the victory which a 'Lib–Lab' appeal had seemed to promise. In part this reflected the greater energy of the 1966 Labour campaign. Fighting more determinedly with a more familiar candidate, Labour made its presence felt and heard through wider areas of the constituency, concentrating its efforts in the Liberals' wake on rallying Labour waverers; the fully stretched Liberal organisation lacked the manpower, in a general election, to re-canvass and was insufficiently powerful to generate the sort of bandwagon effect which would sweep waverers along. But most of all the result reflected the changed national circumstances under which this local campaign had to be fought. The 1964 appeal to 'get the Conservatives out', so successful then in attracting Labour voters to the Liberals, had a much weaker impact when there was no longer a Conservative government in office. In this campaign, as in his many television appearances, Chris Layton was competing less against Giles Radice than against Harold Wilson. The local and personal appeal which Mr. Layton had built up, though strong enough to maintain his vote, was insufficient to carry him forward against a Labour tide in the country. That the Liberals came so close to success is a mark of how much can be achieved through hard work, the use of local issues and the exploitation of favourable opportunities. That they nevertheless failed to gain the seat is an indication of how hard it is, even under the most favourable circumstances, to insulate a constituency from the blasts of national politics.

Huyton

By Robert Taylor

1964	1966
86,129 Electors. 76·7% voting	*88,288 Electors. 70·1% voting*

J. H. Wilson (Lab.) .	42,213 (*63·9%*)		J. H. Wilson (Lab.) .	41,122 (*66·4%*)
H. Tucker (Con.) .	22,940 (*34·7%*)		T. L. Hobday (Con.)	20,182 (*32·6%*)
M. Baker (Communist Anti-Revisionist) . . .	899 (*1·4%*)		D. E. Sutch (Nat. Ind. Teenage) .	585 (*1·0%*)
Labour majority .	19,273 (*29·2%*)		Labour majority .	20,940 (*33·8%*)

FOR most of the campaign, there was little evidence to suggest that an election was taking place in the Prime Minister's constituency of Huyton. Until the last week-end of the campaign, Mr. Wilson paid only two fleeting visits to his constituency, for his adoption and to hand in his nomination papers. Yet television and press coverage of the national campaign ensured that the electors of Huyton would not forget who their Labour candidate was. In a sense, the Prime Minister was campaigning throughout the election in every home in Britain, and his actual appearances in the constituency were superfluous. In the 1964 general election, Mr. Wilson had trebled his majority which now stood at over 19,000. There was no serious danger that he would lose it. Yet the Huyton Labour party had constructed an elaborate and efficient machine to ensure that the maximum support would be gathered in on polling day — an organisation which would have been more characteristic of a marginal seat. Mr. Wilson's energetic and amiable agent, Arthur Smith, presided for electoral purposes as over-all controller of the five local Labour parties in Huyton organised in a federal structure. He appointed group leaders in each of the five areas, who were responsible to him for the running of the campaign in their particular districts. The whole constituency had been canvassed by the beginning of the campaign.

Before the Prime Minister's arrival in the final week-end, the Huyton campaign revolved round his two opponents. Dr. Thomas Hobday, a lecturer in public health at Liverpool University, a qualified barrister and a Lieutenant Colonel in the Territorial Army, stood for the Conservatives. Since fighting Rochdale as a Liberal in 1964, he had left the party, convinced that Mr. Grimond's repudiation of the independent nuclear deterrent indicated a lurch to the left. Crime was the issue he stressed most frequently. Just before the campaign a petition had been sent to the Prime Minister by a number of residents from the Kirkby district of his constituency, expressing concern at the rise in crime and violence in the area. Mr. Wilson's reply had clearly not satisfied Dr. Hobday, who forcefully expressed his views on the subject in the press and on the hustings. As he put it during the campaign, 'the rope used at BMC [Oxford] to terrorise honest workmen should be used round the necks of murderers and on the backs of thugs and vandals'. The Huyton Conservatives did not have the services of Mr. Martell's Freedom League in the campaign, as they had had in 1964. They put a greater effort into winning support in Kirkby, which had a 100% Labour council and which had been left almost untouched by the Conservatives in previous elections. The agent claimed that there would be a noticeable abstention in the election. Apparently there were Labour voters in Kirkby who thought they would be able to continue voting for their old M.P., Bessie Braddock, as they had done when living in Liverpool Exchange, and disliked the idea of supporting someone unknown called Wilson.

Screaming Lord Sutch, the pop singer, also stood as an Independent National Teenage party candidate. He campaigned for the creation of a Beatles' Memorial College and a foreign policy of 'enforced birth control' to combat the population explosion. As he put it, 'we just want to restrict the product, not the pleasure'. Press coverage at the local level was almost entirely devoted to Mr. Sutch's misadventures. He was turned out of his committee rooms in a deserted house and tried to make the Huyton council find him alternative accommodation by parking his campaign van in the council car park in the place allotted to the chairman.

The Prime Minister arrived on the Friday evening before polling day to address six meetings in the constituency. In his speeches and in the question and answer sessions which followed, Mr. Wilson tended to deal primarily with 'bread and butter' issues, which affected his working-class constituents. Old age pensions, prescription charges, redundancy payments and the repeal of the Rent Act were emphasised. Perhaps most of all, the Prime Minister stressed his achievement in maintaining full employment, a matter of considerable importance on Merseyside, where the above-average swing of 8% to Labour in 1964 owed much to the 1962–64 depression in the area. Mr. Wilson spoke to his constituents as their representative and not as a national leader. Clearly he aroused greater interest and larger attendances at his meetings because of his elevation to high office. As he pointed out to a crowded gathering in the Conservative district of Eccleston, at past elections he had only spoken to a handful in a cold school-room. A woman passer-by commented, 'look what happens when someone gets power'. Yet there was no sign of sycophantic or obsequious cap-touching to the Prime Minister, nor did he seek it, despite his formidable entourage of press men and police cars. He never gave the impression to his audiences of benevolent aloofness or calculated ambivalence. The only unfavourable comment was from someone who thought 'he sounded more like Ramsay MacDonald every day'.

In the national campaign Mr. Wilson's emphasis lay, perhaps, more heavily on the need for strong government and a national purpose to overcome economic difficulties. The search for consensus was not nearly so evident in his constituency campaign, particularly in the solid Labour areas. Mr. Wilson stood as the compassionate defender of his constituents against Conservative attempts to 'dismantle' the welfare state. Only hostile questioning on Vietnam shattered the harmony of his gatherings. In his question and answer sessions, many constituents brought up their own personal problems, which Mr. Wilson promised his readiness to deal with. He had always stressed his desire to help Huyton as their local M.P. Before 1964 he had taken great pride in his constituency work, and he still did, even when as Prime Minister he had heavy demands on his attention. His agent looked after his constituency business, but he still tried to manage a monthly surgery in Huyton and eagerly took up local problems. His support and sponsorship of an unsuccessful private member's bill in 1959 to give local authorities the power to provide free or cheap-rate bus passes to old age pensioners came directly from his constituency experiences. Many of his constituents, being old and poor, found difficulty in visiting friends and relatives, still living in Liverpool. Mr. Wilson was appreciatively applauded by his audiences during the campaign when he emphasised that this measure was one of the first he acted on in October 1964.

The Prime Minister gave the impression that he was able to identify himself with the emotions and needs of his constituents. Whether he was shaking hands with housewives shopping in

Kirkby, having tea with old age pensioners, or playing football with schoolboys, Mr. Wilson appeared as the simple man of the people filled with compassion and a desire for social justice. His solid presence and avuncular expression gave his audience the feeling that they could depend on him to look after their interests. His position as Prime Minister had not divorced him from his other work as Labour candidate for Huyton. His constituency party had clearly benefited from his national position. In Eccleston the local Labour party had increased its support considerably since 1964, and the Labour agent claimed that a deferential vote for Mr. Wilson had been built up in the Conservative districts. Yet the local party did not seem over-enthusiastic at attempts to personalise politics in the constituency. It had been a traditionally left-wing party and solidly supported Mr. Wilson during his Bevanite days. Much unease had been created, particularly over foreign policy. At one of the Prime Minister's meetings, the chairman, a local schoolmaster, stressed that the election was about the Labour party and socialism and proceeded to give a shortened version of its history to a bemused audience — an incongruous build up for Mr. Wilson's performance.

The count and declaration lacked the dramatic atmosphere of 1964. The campaign had been mere shadow-boxing for the most part, and a procession for the rest of the time. Commenting on the result Mr. Wilson claimed that, 'the more he stayed away from his constituency the larger his majority became'. The swing (2·3%) was smaller than average, presumably because the turnout was down by 6·6%. The turnout was down not because Mr. Wilson was less active or less popular than in 1964 but because in 1964 he was defending a 6,000 majority which some people misguidedly thought was vulnerable. In 1966 no one could imagine that a 20,000 lead was in danger. However, Mr. Wilson is unlikely to get such a large absolute majority again for the Boundary Commissioners must divide up Huyton before 1970, leaving him a more compact but perhaps even safer seat.

Preston North and South

BY RODERICK MARTIN

Preston North

1964	1966
52,233 Electors. 78·7% voting	*50,140 Electors. 81·1% voting*
J. Amery (Con.) 20,566 (*50·002%*)	R. H. Atkins (Lab.) . 21,539 (*53·0%*)
R. Kerr (Lab.). 20,552 (*49·998%*)	J. Amery (Con.) . 19,121 (*47·0%*)
Conservative majority 14 (*0·004%*)	Labour majority . 2,418 (*6·0%*)

Preston South

1964	1966
48,685 Electors. 78·8% voting	*48,343 Electors. 80·0% voting*
P. Mahon (Lab.) . 19,352 (*50·5%*)	P. Mahon (Lab.) . 20,720 (*53·6%*)
A. Green (Con.) . 19,004 (*49·5%*)	A. Green (Con.) . 17,931 (*46·4%*)
Labour majority . 348 (*1·0%*)	Labour majority . 2,789 (*7·2%*)

THE election campaign in Preston was conducted under a glare of publicity; special reports on the campaign in the city appeared in at least three London newspapers, and one agent complained mildly of over-much national attention. Front-bench speakers appeared regularly, including the Prime Minister, Mrs. Castle, Mr. Jenkins, Mr. Hogg and Mr. Macleod. But despite all this coverage, the political temperature remained low; attendance at meetings was small, while the campaign only caught alight on one occasion — characteristically when Quintin Hogg addressed a cheering and jeering crowd of 'Bonkers' fans. (On another occasion the Young Conservatives were alleged to be planning to disrupt the Prime Minister's meeting, but the threat failed to materialise.) As the local evening paper, the *Lancashire Evening Post*, commented two days before polling day, it had been 'the dullest election so far' in Preston.

The main significance of the campaign in Preston lay in the impact which the cancellation of the TSR-2 aircraft might have had upon Labour's chances of winning Preston North and retaining Preston South, both highly marginal constituencies. The results in the borough council elections the previous May, when the Conservatives won every seat they contested and the swing against Labour was 16·6%, compared with a national swing against the government of only 10·0%, suggested that the Preston seats might swing against the national trend. Throughout the campaign Julian Amery in Preston North, a former Minister of Aviation, and Alan Green in Preston South concentrated their attack upon the Labour government's betrayal of Preston aircraft workers and failure to fulfil election promises. Every lunchtime Mr. Amery, occasionally accompanied by one or two shop stewards, addressed aircraft workers outside the main British Aircraft Corporation factory in his constituency, while a leaflet distributed outside the Prime Minister's meeting effectively quoted a pamphlet issued by the Labour party in Preston North in 1964 explicitly promising that a Labour government would not cancel the TSR-2. The Prime Minister was forced to meet the issue head on when he spoke in the town; he departed from his set speech more than anywhere else in his campaign to do so.

The attention devoted to the cancellation of the TSR-2 during the campaign was misplaced. The number of workers directly affected by the cancellation was small, and it had provided no more than a temporary jolt to those not directly concerned. Although the British Aircraft Corporation was alleged to have laid off nearly 2,000 men when the aircraft was cancelled, few of them remained out of work for long. The total number of unemployed men in Preston rose from 698 in May 1965 to 809 the following month; it reached its peak in August — 873 — but it soon dropped to below 800 again.[1] The number directly affected by the cancellation cannot have exceeded 200, and may well have been less. Nor did the cancellation remain like a festering sore in the minds of Preston's inhabitants. In a poll conducted on behalf of the *Sunday Times* ten days before polling day only three people, out of a sample 607, gave it as a reason for switching from Labour; an equal number said they were switching because of Labour's failure to do much for the old age pensioners. The cancellation of the TSR-2 was an individual tragedy for one or two of the older workers who were unable to find work elsewhere, but it was not an important political liability for the Labour party in the borough.

Preston's continued prosperity mattered more. According to figures announced during the campaign, unemployment was lower in Preston in March 1966 than it had been twelve months

[1] I am grateful to the Ministry of Labour Employment Exchange, Preston, for these figures.

earlier, when work on the TSR-2 was still in progress. Even the British Aircraft Corporation was working at full stretch, and advertising for skilled workers to help build Lightning jet fighters for Saudi Arabia; the Prime Minister triumphantly pointed out that the BAC would not have been able to accept the order if work had continued on the TSR-2. In March 1966 Preston was booming; in addition to the aircraft industry and its satellites, large commercial-vehicle (Leyland Motors), artificial-fibre (Courtaulds) and carpet (Cyril Lord) factories were all working at capacity. (Paradoxically, some workers who had not been declared redundant were grumbling because they had not received windfall redundancy payments; a Liberal progress chaser at BAC complained: 'It's the payment the redundant workers got that makes me hesitate to vote again. They got the lucky ticket, say £700, and then got their jobs back; those who weren't redundant got nothing.') Labour speakers concentrated upon contrasting the city's continued prosperity under the Labour government with the large-scale unemployment which had followed the decline of the cotton industry under Conservative rule.

The major issues in Preston, as elsewhere, were the cost of living, pensions and housing. In the *Sunday Times* poll over 37% spontaneously mentioned pensions and the same number housing. Yet the Conservative candidates, distracted by TSR-2 and in Mr. Amery's case by Rhodesia, failed to ram home the issues. In any case, all three subjects posed difficulties for the Conservatives. Pensions and the cost of living were, like the weather, constant problems, and Conservative criticism of Labour was always countered by Labour criticism of Conservative failures to act when in power. Mr. Green initially hoped that the young married couples buying new houses on mortgages in the expanding suburb of Walton-le-Dale (which accounted for over 10,000 votes in Preston South) would vote against the Labour government for their failure to provide the promised cheaper mortgages. But houses were comparatively cheap in Preston — small semi-detacheds could be bought for under £3,000 — and council flats were not as difficult to obtain as elsewhere, while wages were higher than in other parts of north Lancashire. Peter Mahon had used bread and butter issues effectively to oust Alan Green in 1964; with the additional advantage of seventeen months' careful nursing of the constituency his touch remained sure.

Neither comprehensive education nor immigration, two issues which had hit the headlines in Preston before the campaign, seemed to play any part during it. Plans for comprehensive education in Preston were still in the melting pot, and although the headmaster of the main local grammar school had expressed public doubts about going comprehensive, his protest was not taken up during the election campaign. Mr. Mahon very delicately avoided the issue in his election address, calling for 'full and equal educational opportunity irrespective of creed or class . . . the abilities of no single child should be wasted because of the financial position of its parents'. One complication, which could affect Mr. Mahon's own position in the future, was the role of the three Catholic selective entry schools in the city. Like Liverpool, Preston had a substantial Catholic minority, mainly of Irish origin, and Mr. Mahon, himself a Catholic, went out of his way to commend the government's increased grants to denominational schools. The future of Preston's Catholic schools remained uncertain.

There was also a substantial Pakistani minority. Certain jobs at Courtaulds were already recognised as 'non-English', and there had already been one strike there with racial overtones. However, immigration was scarcely mentioned during the campaign, and few interviewees in the *Sunday Times* survey raised the subject.

The candidates themselves seem to have made little difference to the result. Despite their distinctiveness and varying abilities, standing and local connections, the swing to Labour in both constituencies was virtually identical — 3%. Nearly everyone in Preston agreed that Mr. Green deserved well of the borough, while feelings towards Mr. Amery were cooler and his Rhodesian stand aroused only a committed minority. Similarly, Mr. Mahon had always lived in north Lancashire, had many trade union contacts in the area, and had worked hard for his constituents during his short stay in Westminster, while Mr. Ron Atkins, a teacher from Essex with no previous connection with Preston, had only been adopted a short time before the election. (Mr. Amery wryly commented on the failure of Labour candidates to stand against him twice. The candidate in 1964, Mr. Russell Kerr, had originally promised to fight against Mr. Amery a second time, but changed his mind and became candidate for the safer, and more convenient, Feltham constituency.)

The campaign was really fought in the sitting rooms and on the door step, not on the platform. Here the traditional Conservative advantage in organisation told less than usual. The local Conservative machine had only just recovered from being shaken up after the comparatively poor showing in 1964, and although the new Conservative agent, Harry Booth, was generally highly thought of, he lacked the personal experience of the constituencies of his opposite number, Mr. Harry Jackson. The Labour organisation, buoyed up by the prospects of winning (and dislike for Mr. Amery) and helped by more cars than usual, went into the campaign with high morale. Better Labour organisation and the interest attached to marginal — and still more to super-marginal — constituencies, may explain the increases in turnout, 1·2% in Preston South, and 2·4% in Preston North.

Despite Conservative hopes and Labour fears, the election campaign and the result in both Preston constituencies fitted in with the national pattern. The much-publicised cancellation of TSR-2 had little impact upon the campaign, its edge blunted by the town's continued prosperity. A few designers and engineers may have left the constituency, a few workers may have voted against the Labour government because of broken promises; but the main issues in Preston were national, not local.

Rhondda West

By Kenneth O. Morgan and Peter Stead

1964	1966
32,401 Electors. 80·7% voting	*31,189 Electors. 80·3% voting*
I. R. Thomas (Lab.). 20,713 (79·3%)	I. R. Thomas (Lab.). . 19,060 (76·1%)
N. Lloyd-Edwards	V. Davies (Plaid
(Con.) . . 2,754 (10·5%)	Cymru) . . 2,172 (8·7%)
V. Davies (Plaid	B. Sandford-Hill
Cymru) . . 2,668 (10·2%)	(Con.) . . . 1,955 (7·8%)
	A. C. True (Comm.). 1,853 (7·4%)
Lab. maj. over Con . 17,959 (68·8%)	Lab. maj. over P.C. . 16,888 (67·4%)

'North of Pontypridd, they've just stopped thinking', a disconsolate Conservative agent complained. He probably had Rhondda West in mind. Not since 1931 had the Conservatives saved their deposit there. In 1966 their candidate polled a mere 7·8% of the votes, and finished third, just above the Communist. The Labour candidate, I. R. Thomas, gained over 76%, confirming

R

Rhondda West as just about the safest Labour seat in the British Isles.

Rhondda West consisted mainly of the more westerly of the two Rhondda valleys, some twenty miles north-west of Cardiff. Its six wards comprised a series of small mining townships, winding along the bleak sides of the valley, from Tonypandy up to Treorchy. It formed the very heart of the South Wales coalfield, and symbolised the bitter passions of two generations of industrial conflict. The Tonypandy riots took place here, around the Cambrian colliery and in Pandy Square, back in 1910. In the 1920s, there were violent strikes and protest marches; the red flag flew at pitheads. In the thirties came crushing unemployment; there were 24,352 on the dole in the Rhondda in 1932. After the war, nationalisation brought a new deal for the Rhondda miner, but it also speeded up pit closures. There were now only 4,000 miners in the constituency, as compared with 20,000 fifty years earlier. The Rhondda West electorate had fallen by 1,200 since the 1964 election.

Gwyn Thomas has written of 'the psychoses of poverty and dread' in the Rhondda of his youth. Since 1945, they had largely disappeared. Nearly thirty standard factories had been introduced, notably a clothing factory which employed over 1,500. People still lived in the drab, terraced houses of the last century, but everywhere there were symbols of a new and unfamiliar prosperity. In particular, there was an immense array of social clubs of all kinds, monuments to eighty years of Sunday closing. As one disillusioned socialist veteran reflected, 'We were out to build the new Jerusalem, and all we've got is a fairground.'

The politics of Rhondda West had always been dominated by the miners. Since the Rhondda first returned an M.P. in 1885, the area had only three members, William Abraham (1885–1920), Will John (1920–50), and now I. R. Thomas, all miners. The sitting member, 'Iorrie' Thomas, had represented the division since 1950. He was a 70-year-old veteran of strikes and lock-outs, who had spent some months in gaol in the 1920s. He was sponsored by the NUM who paid 80% of his election expenses. But by 1966 only a few of the local Labour party executive were miners; unions like the AEU and the Tailors and Garment Workers were increasingly active in the local organisation. Mr. Thomas therefore presided over a constituency socially much more complex than ever before.

Labour was all-powerful in the politics of the Rhondda. Thirty of the borough council of 32 were Labour members, even though in so highly unionised an area individual party membership was traditionally low. The changing industrial pattern had made little difference to Labour's overwhelming dominance. Rhondda people moving up the social scale preserved their old political loyalties.

By comparison, the other parties were mere splinter groups. The Conservatives barely existed in their own right. Their main organisational base lay in the seven Conservative clubs in the division. However, the stimulation sought was evidently liquid rather than political, since their membership was many times greater than the total Conservative vote. Only a glamorous club at Treorchy even tried to make party loyalty a test of membership, and, as one member ambiguously remarked, 'It's going the way of all flesh like the rest.' The Conservative candidate, Dr. Sandford-Hill, a 31-year-old doctor, was imported from Cardiff, like his agent and many of his helpers, just before the campaign began.

The Communists were fighting Rhondda West for the first time since 1931. However, they had a base from which to build, since many lodges had a long Marxist tradition, and often elected Communist agents. In neighbouring Rhondda East, the Communists had always maintained a high poll, since Harry Pollitt's campaigns in the thirties. Like Plaid Cymru, they regarded the election as a recruiting drive for future municipal contests. Their candidate was Arthur True, a 45-year-old ETU official and ex-miner.

The Welsh Nationalist party, Plaid Cymru, had fought the seat before; in 1959 they had gained 17% of the poll. They relied traditionally on an older Liberal chapel vote, but claimed new support from schoolteachers and students. Their candidate, Victor Davies, was backed by three local branches of his party. A local lecturer and a former AEU shop steward, he was clearly trying to broaden Plaid Cymru's support among trade unionists disillusioned with the Labour government. In addition, his party regarded Mr. Thomas as a marked man, since he was a caustic and frequent critic of the nationalist spirit in Wales.

There was a brief, abortive threat of a fifth candidate, Mr. D. T. Davies of Chalfont St. Peter, who had fought Smethwick on an anti-immigration platform in 1964. He claimed to stand as a 'Welsh Progressive Labour' candidate on the issue of pit closures, and promised to donate his parliamentary salary to the miners.

Mr. Thomas dismissed him as a 'political adventurer' and urged him to 'take his thirty pieces of silver' elsewhere. After this harsh criticism, Mr. Davies did not in fact contest the seat.

The campaign followed the time-honoured pattern. Labour held no meetings and conducted no canvass. The election addresses were delivered by hand so that the free postage was not used. Mr. Thomas spent his evenings visiting social clubs and giving a brief invocation to the faithful before the evening's bingo and dancing began. There were twenty such visits, and all candidates testified to their value. During the day, Mr. Thomas toured the constituency by car, equipped with loudspeaker and tape-recorded speeches. These set addresses were occasionally interrupted by live 'greetings' to passers-by and irreverent children. The main feature of Labour's campaign, in fact, was the help given to neighbouring marginal seats. Many Rhondda party workers went to Cardiff North, where the Conservative, Donald Box, was a well-known critic of trade unionists, and the Labour candidate, Edward Rowlands, an ex-resident of the Rhondda. They had the satisfaction of seeing Mr. Box ousted on a 4·4% swing.

The other candidates in Rhondda West followed much the same approach as Mr. Thomas. The Conservative made nine club visits, and also placed prominent advertisements in the local journal, the *Rhondda Leader*. The Communists alone held meetings. All these were badly attended, save for one addressed by John Gollan, but the Communists' club visits aroused more discussion than those of other candidates. The Communists attributed this interest in their policies to the impact of Mr. Gollan's television broadcast. For Plaid Cymru, Mr. Davies took only one day off from lecturing and concentrated on leaflets and loudspeaker work. His young supporters were severely handicapped by the proximity of school examinations.

Mr. Thomas fought solely on the Labour government's record. 'A vote for I. R. Thomas is a vote for Harold Wilson.' Many houses and even shops displayed Harold Wilson posters. The other three candidates fought on local issues. The Conservatives ignored Mr. Heath; they stressed the need for more doctors in the Rhondda valleys. As Mr. Hill was a doctor, he laid himself open to the obvious retort that it would help if he came to live there himself. The Communist and Plaid Cymru candidates, both of whom advocated Welsh home rule, emphasised the industrial future of the Rhondda. The main issue here was obviously that of pit closures. The largest colliery in the division, the Parc and Dare, had closed down in December 1965, and there was great uncertainty about the future. Mr. Davies and Mr. True both demanded an end to closures and a national fuel policy. But Mr. Thomas was well armed with pre-recorded replies: he pointed out that the Labour government had written off £415 m. of the NCB debt.

As polling day approached, Mr. Wilson's record seemed virtually the only theme. The Conservatives appeared almost an irrelevance. There had been some Labour concern at the possible size of the Communist vote, which some forecast might be as high as 3,000. In fact, however, Mr. True took only 1,853 from Mr. Thomas's crushing majority. These votes presumably came mainly from miners or ex-miners disillusioned with Labour, and from those who felt Mr. Thomas ought to retire. There was the traditionally high poll of over 80%; psephological purists could note a 0·3% swing against Labour. Once again, the Conservatives found they had no hope of any progress in this area; they contested the seat presumably to swell their national vote and to curb the flow of Labour workers into more marginal seats. Plaid Cymru — as the Carmarthen by-election was to show in July 1966 — continued to form a useful refuge for older Liberals and for young romantic idealists, disillusioned with one-party government. Labour, however, remained utterly impregnable in an old mining area where to vote Labour was less a political act than a pledge of loyalty to your own community, its memories, its values and its way of life.

Smethwick

By James Byrne

1964		1966	
47,305 Electors. 74·1% voting		*44,960 Electors. 75·4% voting*	
P. H. S. Griffiths (Con.) . . .	16,690 (47·6%)	A. M. W. Faulds (Lab.) . . .	18,440 (54·4%)
P. Gordon Walker (Lab.) . . .	14,916 (42·6%)	P. H. S. Griffiths (Con.) . . .	14,950 (44·1%)
D. Hugill (Lib.) .	3,172 (9·1%)	R. Stanley (B.N.P.) .	508 (1·5%)
D. T. Davies (Ind.) .	262 (0·7%)		
Conservative majority	1,774 (5·0%)	Labour majority .	3,490 (10·3%)

IN the general election of 1964 Smethwick returned its first Conservative M.P. since the war, Peter Griffiths, and sent Patrick Gordon Walker, who had represented the constituency since 1945, on his catastrophic journey to the Leyton by-election of January 1965. This one result, therefore, cost the Labour government two seats and a Foreign Secretary.

Mr. Griffiths — a headmaster who had sat on the council since 1955 before contesting the division unsuccessfully in 1959 — had made his mark in 1964 (and for the previous two years) as an outspoken advocate of strict immigration control. Smethwick, said Mr. Griffiths, had rejected the idea of becoming a multi-racial society. Furthermore, he declared loudly and often, the immigrants had lowered the moral standards of the town, created slums, indulged in criminal activities and brought about problems in the fields of housing and education. That immigrants had come to Britain (and to Smethwick in particular) in large numbers, he argued, was the fault of the Labour government of 1945–51 in which Mr. Gordon Walker — 'the architect of Labour's let them all come policy' — had served. The fact that Mr. Gordon Walker had opposed the introduction of the 1962 Commonwealth Immigrants Act was frequently stressed.

Immigration had been a matter of political dispute in Smethwick since 1960. Mr. Griffiths did not create the issue; but he recognised its electoral possibilities and campaigned accordingly. The manner in which Mr. Griffiths achieved his success infuriated the Labour party — the Prime Minister suggested that the new member for Smethwick might serve his term at Westminster as a 'parliamentary leper' — and made clear the potentialities of immigration as a vote-winning factor.

By 1966 Mr. Griffiths' position had been weakened considerably: immigration had been allowed to go off the boil in Smethwick (the issue had lost some of its novelty and Mr. Gordon Walker had disappeared from the scene); one of his most angry anti-immigration supporters, Donald Finney, a former Conservative councillor, had turned his attention to West Bromwich in the hope of ousting Maurice Foley; and both Mr. Heath and Mr. du Cann had made it clear that the Conservative party would not tolerate any candidate who attempted to exploit the immigration issue. Another factor which suggested that Mr. Griffiths might be defeated was the selection of Mr. Andrew Faulds, a television and film actor, as the Smethwick Labour candidate.

Mr. Faulds, who had fought Stratford in the by-election of 1963 and again in the general election of the following year, brought enthusiasm and confidence to the jaded and disheartened local party organisation. It was obvious that he, unlike his predecessor, would not allow Mr. Griffiths to make all the running.

A late arrival on the scene was the third candidate, Mr. Roy Stanley of the British National party, who campaigned without equivocation on the issue of 'the coloured invasion', with the re-introduction of capital punishment as a second string to his bow. His leaflets and posters — 'KEEP BRITAIN WHITE and to hell with Wilson's RACE LAW' — ran true to expectation; but the impact of his intervention was negligible.

The real contest, clearly, was to be between Mr. Faulds and Mr. Griffiths, each of whom, as is customary, predicted his own comfortable victory. A more objective analysis, however, suggested that the outcome would be close indeed. For although the February elections for the town council of the new county borough of Warley — an amalgamation of Oldbury, Rowley Regis, and Smethwick — had indicated a swing to the left in Smethwick, there still remained the possibility that Mr. Griffiths, playing heavily on his local knowledge and as heavily as he dared on immigration, might retain the seat.

That Smethwick needed a Smethwick man to represent it in the House of Commons had been one of Mr. Griffiths' major themes in 1964. And having reached Westminster Mr. Griffiths was careful never to stray far from the comforting shadow of the parish pump. Swift personal attention to the wants of his constituents was one of the main ingredients in his formula for continued success. He was proud of his record both as a councillor and as an M.P. Mr. Faulds, like Mr. Gordon Walker before him, was a carpet-bagger, a stranger to the town.

The matter of immigration, however, presented Mr. Griffiths with a problem of some delicacy. There was no question but that he should criticise the Wilson administration and applaud the Conservative manifesto; nor was there any reason why he should not underline his local knowledge — but how much should he emphasise immigration when the party leadership had made its views so abundantly clear on this subject? Would he, if less impassioned than in 1964, lose votes to the BNP candidate? The BNP candidate thought that he would. Mr. Griffiths in his seventeen months at Westminster had sought to convince friend and foe alike that he was a reasonable man, a middle-of-the-road Tory; and his 1966 campaign platform was graced by the presence of three Conservative M.P.s, Selwyn Lloyd, Jasper More and Sir John Eden, all of whom had come to praise him without stint.

Rather than risk the loss of this mantle of respectability, therefore, Mr. Griffiths campaigned on 'the bread and butter issues', one of which, immigration, was a diluted version of the 1964 model. None the less, if his statements were less angry than in the previous campaign, his attitude had not softened. He favoured a complete ban on immigration, although he was willing to make allowance for businessmen and students. It was a 'major problem' in Smethwick and one which it would be 'hypocritical to ignore'. His attitude was summed up by a phrase in his election address: he would 'stand firm on immigration'. And it was this message which was singled out for special attention in a leaflet distributed in the town on March 29th: 'Peter Griffiths has ALWAYS stood firm on immigration'. He was loudly applauded at each of his three public meetings when he declared that this was an issue on which he 'would not budge one inch'. The excitement and enthusiasm of 1964, however, were conspicuous by their absence. Gone were the old ladies who objected vigorously to having 'them' for neighbours; gone, also, were the cries of 'send them all back on the next banana boat'. The temperature had dropped considerably.

Mr. Griffiths devoted much of his time to housing, pensions, leasehold reform, education, prices, taxation and rents. He was particularly worried about the problem of crime and punishment. He had voted against the abolition of capital punishment, favoured the use of corporal punishment in certain circumstances, and thought it time 'we showed more sympathy for the victim of the crime than for the criminal'. Reducing the issues on which he spoke to the local context, he campaigned on 'A Policy For All Smethwick People'; he was 'Smethwick's Own Peter Griffiths'.

Mr. Faulds came to the battle with many advantages: he had a ready charm, he was well known — he had 'made over 30 films and dozens of television appearances', his election address reminded the electorate — and his candidature had brought into the constituency willing helpers from as far afield as Blackpool,

Sheffield and Oxford. But he had one potential weakness: his attitude towards immigration control. He had, at first, supported the government's white paper on immigration; then, at the Labour party conference of 1965, he had attacked it vigorously. During the campaign, however, he came into line once more: 'The Labour government is imposing controls on all immigration as part of the necessary planning of our economic and social development.' Immigration, he said, was not the main issue in Smethwick in 1966; and it had been an issue in 1964 only as the result of 'an artificially stimulated campaign'. It was a subject which, as far as possible, he preferred to play down.

Keeping in close touch with the Labour party manifesto throughout, Mr. Faulds emphasised the National Plan, housing, education and the welfare state. Sometimes stern, but never unbending, he sought, not always successfully, to convey to his audience an understanding of the principles of modern socialism. Always on the offensive, he defined Mr. Griffiths as a candidate of the extreme right, a supporter of Mr. Ian Smith, and one who had been warned by the leadership of the Conservative party 'to behave himself this time or he will get a wigging'. He rallied his followers with the demand that they 'split their collective guts to ensure a thumping Socialist majority'. His victory, he informed the electorate, would bring to a close 'an unhappy chapter in Smethwick's political history' — a reference to the argument that Mr. Griffiths' activities in 1964 had earned the town a 'bad name'.

Mr. Faulds' margin of victory was surprisingly large and it was clear that the intervention of the BNP candidate had played almost no part in Mr. Griffiths' defeat. Two factors had undermined Mr. Griffiths' position: the fact that he was obliged to play the immigration issue *pianissimo*; and the fact that in campaigning so insistently on immigration in 1964 he had raised high hopes which, as an M.P., he was unable to satisfy. If he had claimed (as well he might have done) that his efforts had contributed to the introduction of strict immigration controls by the Labour government, Mr. Griffiths could have improved his chances. However, he chose to argue that under the Labour government immigration was on the increase, which suggested that his anti-immigrant crusade had been less than effective.

In Smethwick the wheel had come full circle. Immigration, as an election-winning issue, was dead — possibly for all time.

Belfast West

BY CORNELIUS O'LEARY[1]

1964	1966
69,399 Electors. 74·7% Voting.	*67,588 Electors. 74·8% Voting.*
J. A. Kilfedder (Un.) 21,337 *(41·2%)*	G. Fitt (Rep. Lab.) . 26,292 *(52·0%)*
H. Diamond (Rep. Lab.) . . . 14,678 *(28·3%)*	J. A. Kilfedder (Un.) 24,281 *(48·0%)*
W. R. Boyd (Lab.) . 12,571 *(24·3%)*	
L. McMillan (Rep.) 3,256 *(6·2%)*	
Unionist majority . 6,659 *(12·9%)*	Republican Labour majority . . 2,011 *(4·0%)*

THE most remarkable thing about Belfast West is that a constituency as unmistakably working-class as Bermondsey or the Gorbals should also be a marginal seat. However, the structure of politics in Ulster is peculiar. The two parties, Unionist and Nationalist, which between them control forty-five of the fifty-two seats in the local parliament at Stormont are not essentially British parties but rather survivors of nineteenth-century Irish parties. The Unionists were the issue of a marriage in 1886 between the upper-crust Irish Conservatives and the Orange Order, a classless and aggressively Protestant organisation. The Nationalists, lineal descendants of the Irish parliamentary party, resemble them in unflinching devotion to the ideal of a united Ireland and a dislike of rigid organisation. Splinter groups, variously named Socialist Republican, Republican Labour, Irish Labour and Independent Labour, have competed for the support of the 'nationally-minded' (a section of the electorate loosely identifiable with the Roman Catholic 35%) with both the official Nationalists and the non-parties, Sinn Fein and the Republicans, who refuse to recognise either state established in Ireland in 1921. From this *damnosa hereditas* the Northern Ireland Labour party has never really managed to escape. Though founded in 1923 it has never won a Westminster seat or more than four Stormont seats.

In Belfast West the religious distribution is about equal — two of the four Stormont constituencies have overwhelmingly Catholic majorities and two are correspondingly Protestant. In the 1961 census the Protestants were in a majority of 4,600. Since the 1930s Belfast West has oscillated between Unionist and Anti-

[1] Mr. Gerald F. Loughran helped greatly in the preparation of this study.

Partitionist Labour. Sinn Fein intervention in the elections of 1955 and 1959 helped give the Unionists large majorities. In 1964 a member of the NILP stood in addition to Republican Labour and Sinn Fein; the Irish tricolour adorning the Sinn Fein headquarters was seized by the police following threats by Protestant extremists and for three nights rioting followed which the police were barely able to control. The anti-Unionist vote was split but the Unionist share went down by 12·9%.

When the 1966 election approached fewer candidates seemed likely. The withdrawal of a 'National Democratic Candidate', Mr. Joseph Lavery, left Mr. Gerard Fitt 'Republican Labour' as the only opponent to the Unionist. A former merchant seaman and insurance agent he had been a member of Dock Ward on the city council since 1957 and Stormont M.P. for Dock since 1962 — in 1965 he increased his majority by 8% despite an overall swing of 6% to the Unionists in Belfast, making his constituency the only one to go against the tide. But Dock is in Belfast East. Mr. Fitt's only contact with West lay in the fact that Mr. Diamond, the elderly Republican Labour member for Falls had in 1964 joined forces with Mr. Fitt (then labelled Irish Labour) thus converting two one-man parties into one two-man party.

Mr. Fitt at once started to distribute his election literature, not only to the converted but throughout the constituency — another innovation. His election address dealt very briefly with his republicanism: the main emphasis was on his role as 'the standard bearer of Labour' — the 'new British Government' would have respect only for a Labour man. Unlike his rival he had 'no extremist support' — a reference to Ulster Protestant Action, an obscure sectarian group which comes to life only during elections and which during the 1964 campaign had circulated leaflets with the Smethwick-type question, 'Do you want Roman Catholics in your street?' (In 1966 UPA circulated pro-Unionist leaflets merely attacking Fitt's republicanism.)

Mr. Fitt's machine[1] was largely imported from Dock — some thirty youthful workers operating from an upstairs room in a Catholic club who might be jostled on the stairs by uninterested

[1] It is difficult to get exact statistics for the number of part-time election helpers or canvassers. Mr. Fitt claimed that he had between 120 and 500 out every night, the Unionists claim 780. But these figures seem exaggerated. From personal inspection on a number of nights there did not appear to be more than 50 people helping Mr. Fitt.

citizens coming in for bingo sessions, as they returned breathlessly for forays into enemy territory armed with Fitt literature. His election address was still being distributed a few days before polling, but Mr. Fitt's confidence never wavered. The Protestant working-man would, he felt sure, vote for him, and his majority would lie between 2,000 and 3,000.

The Unionist campaign was directed from their Northern Ireland headquarters, a large house in Belfast West equipped with a canteen and committee rooms. Its full-time staff[1] of six is reinforced during election times by hundreds of volunteer canvassers. The Unionist candidate for Belfast West was Mr. Kilfedder, a barrister born in the Irish Republic and formerly practising in London. Together with the other eleven Unionist candidates, he circulated a common manifesto (on March 14th) which was criticised by the pro-Unionist *Belfast Telegraph* as 'unduly parochial'. Each candidate also was entitled to issue a personal message to the electors. Mr. Kilfedder's was composed after nomination day (March 21st) and was still being distributed up to polling day. For Mr. Kilfedder there was clearly but one issue — the Ulster constitution. But having asserted that the constitutional question was settled forty-five years ago he proceeded to re-open it by asking for a new demonstration of belief in the role of Ulster as an integral part of the United Kingdom. Some statistics were adduced: a list of social benefits in the Republic 'which Mr. Fitt is so anxious to join' was contrasted unfavourably with Northern Ireland services.

The subject of sectarianism was bound to recur during the campaign. At the outset Mr. Robert Chichester-Clark, speaking for the twelve Unionists, refused to accept the support of anyone 'who was prepared to stir up sectarianism in the election'. But Mr. Kilfedder, while deploring sectarianism, refused to condemn the anti-Catholic organisations.

In 1951 the open-air meeting was still the main feature of Ulster electioneering. By 1966 it had been replaced by block canvassing and TV confrontations. No public meetings were held in Belfast West until the last days of the campaign and, as had been traditional with the block canvass, the meetings were confined to friendly areas. Mr. Fitt's procession started from his Dock strong-

---

[1] There were only three full-time agents — in the rural constituencies. The secretary of the party directed the campaign for Belfast constituencies.

hold and moved from there into the Falls Road, the main artery of the Catholic sector, ending up in the poorest streets where penurious nineteenth-century builders had erected houses like barracks with no back access. In their republican fervour Mr. Fitt's speeches made up for the perfunctoriness of his election address; the loudest cheers were evoked whenever he referred to the Easter rising of 1916. Otherwise he adhered closely to the themes of working-class interest and anti-sectarianism.

Mr. Kilfedder's meetings were more like constituency tours. Two nights before polling a flag-bedecked lorry preceded by a loudspeaker van and followed by two bands and a crowd of excited children paraded through the Sandy Row and Shankill areas — as typically Protestant as the Falls is Catholic and lying uncomfortably close to the latter. From his position on the front of the lorry the candidate waved discreetly to the bystanders while the loudspeaker blared: 'This is Jim Kilfedder, the Unionist and Loyalist candidate. Protestant and Loyalist voters are asked to vote for the Unionist and Loyalist candidate. We are the people and Jim Kilfedder is the people's candidate. Vote Unionist and keep the Republicans out of West Belfast.' The world of Mr. Wilson and Mr. Heath seemed far away.

On polling day the main concern of both parties was to minimise the inroads on their electoral strength likely to be caused by personation, a malpractice which, though uncommon in the rock-ribbed Unionist constituencies, is endemic to Belfast West — after every election since 1950 a few voters have been prosecuted. Mr. Fitt had publicly announced his precautions: a personation agent furnished with a list of 411 'Unionists' (i.e. Protestants) who had died since the register was compiled, would be stationed at each of the 102 ballot boxes in the twenty-six polling places.

But personation of dead voters can be more easily guarded against than personation of the living. In the early afternoon Mr. Fitt complained that eighty of his supporters had been personated by Unionists at a station where his agents had failed to arrive on time. The Unionist party secretary repudiated this claim as 'wild and unsubstantiated'. Eventually three people were arrested, pleaded guilty and fined — one, an unemployed shipyard worker, received the maximum fine of £50. When the election was over Mr. Kilfedder alleged widespread personation of *his* supporters. The police made numerous enquiries, particularly in the Falls

Road area, and eventually (as in 1964) reported back to the Attorney General for Northern Ireland. No further action was taken.

Polling began slowly and was not encouraged by the rain which fell continuously from 4 o'clock. By 6 o'clock barely a third of the electorate had polled at a representative selection of polling places, but the pace then quickened and by the close of poll the turnout, 74·8%, was a shade above the 1964 level and was 9·2% above the 1966 average of the other Belfast constituencies. Up to the last the pro-Unionist newspapers predicted a Kilfedder victory, but with a smaller majority, and a local bookmaker was offering 7 to 2 on him. After 9 o'clock a cheerful Unionist crowd gathered outside the Clarence Place Hall, the scene of the count, and were regaled by Orange songs. When the news of Mr. Fitt's victory was brought out by a leading Unionist — results are never publicly announced in Belfast — it was greeted, according to the *Belfast Telegraph*, by 'a deafening silence'. Then Mr. Kilfedder appeared and said a few words ending: 'Friends, before we depart in peace, let us sing the National Anthem.' The second part of the injunction was obeyed more readily than the first. Scarcely had Mr. Kilfedder made a dignified withdrawal than Mr. Fitt appeared and the crowd 'pounded down on him'. But police skilfully whisked him into his car while a woman uttered the poignant cry: 'God, we are now represented by a Republican.'

Why was the West won? The answer lies in Mr. Fitt's ability to hold all the Nationalist votes and to gain a fair slice of the support which had previously gone to the constitutionalist N.I. Labour party. In Stormont elections Mr. Fitt had already proved his ability to win Protestant working-class votes. But there was also an exceptional turnout in Catholic areas, due perhaps to a singular polling day incident. The 4 p.m. *Belfast Telegraph* carried a photograph of two nuns being jeered outside the polling place in a strongly Protestant area — and this was also reported in the 1 o'clock radio news. The psychological impact of this on Catholic voters may have contributed powerfully to the peculiar blend of religious and political loyalties which carried Gerard Fitt to Westminster.

CHAPTER XIV

THE OUTCOME

THE polls closed at 9 p.m. on March 31st after a calm mild day in which there had been no more than a trace of rain anywhere except in the North of Scotland. At 10.04 p.m. Cheltenham once again won the race to be the first constituency to declare. The 2·9% swing to Labour there indicated that the opinion polls had not been wrong and that a massive Labour victory was in the making. Results from Salford and Wolverhampton soon confirmed the trend. When at 10.51 p.m. it was announced that Labour had gained Exeter any lingering doubt disappeared.

The early returns, quickly analysed by computers and commentators on television and radio, pointed to a Labour majority over all parties of around 120. But the rural returns on the second day were less favourable and the final majority was 97.

More constituencies than ever before counted on the night. By 4 a.m. 460 results were in (in 1964 the figure had been 430 and in 1950 only 270). But the drama was continued on the Friday. It was not until just after noon that the 315th Labour victory was announced. Mr. Heath, who had declined to make any statement the previous night, at 11.15 a.m. conceded defeat from his Albany flat. In the afternoon he held a press conference at Conservative headquarters. He handled the situation gracefully. He had no regrets: the Conservatives had fought the election in exactly the right way and would now offer vigorous constructive opposition; people had wanted to give the Labour party a longer period of trial. Mr. Wilson, travelling south from Liverpool during the morning, was less graceful in victory. His publicised refusal to grant a BBC interview on the journey, or to appear in the evening round-up programmes, managed to divert some press attention from his victory and to provoke some rather disproportionate editorial homilies on the arrogance of office.

Labour won 363 seats in all; the Conservatives got 253 and the Liberals 12; the Speaker, retaining his once-Labour seat of Itchen, and Mr. Fitt, who gained Belfast West under the title 'Republican

Labour', completed the House. The parliamentary balance was almost the mirror image of 1959.

1959   Con. 365   Lab. 258
1966   Lab. 363   Con. 253

Compared to 1964 Labour's total vote rose by three quarters of a million while the Conservatives' fell by over half a million. Labour's percentage margin (47·9% to 41·9%) was the greatest for any victorious party since 1945.

The Conservatives suffered some notable casualties. Henry Brooke, who two years earlier had been sitting on a 12,000 majority, lost Hampstead and Peter Thorneycroft lost Monmouth. Christopher Soames, Sir Martin Redmayne, Peter Thomas and Julian Amery were also defeated, together with such veterans as

SEATS CHANGING HANDS   SEATS WHERE LIBERALS
1964–66   WON OR CAME SECOND

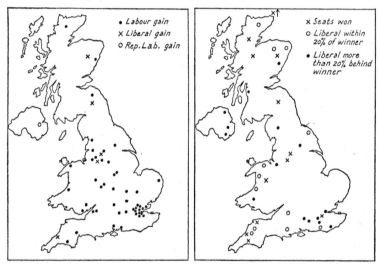

Sir William Anstruther-Gray and Dame Patricia Hornsby-Smith, and such younger hopefuls as Humphry Berkeley, Christopher Chataway, Charles Longbottom and Geoffrey Howe.

Patrick Gordon Walker enjoyed a double revenge; he recovered Leyton from Ronald Buxton and he saw Peter Griffiths defeated at Smethwick. Among the seats gained by Labour were eleven they had never held, even in the high tide of 1945: Aberdeen South, Caithness and Sutherland, Cardigan, Exeter, Hampstead, High

Peak, Lancaster, Middleton and Prestwich, Monmouth, Oxford, and Sheffield, Heeley. But they failed to win back a few they had not lost until 1955 (Maldon and Devonport), 1959 (Lowestoft and Brierley Hill) or even 1964 (South-west Norfolk).

The Liberals, although losing strength in 251 of the 278 seats they fought both in 1964 and 1966, managed to gain four new seats to compensate for the loss of George Mackie, their Scottish whip, in Caithness and Sutherland and of Roderic Bowen, their senior member, in Cardigan. The victories of Dr. Michael Winstanley in Cheadle and Richard Wainwright in Colne Valley greatly broadened their regional base; now only two-thirds of the parliamentary party came from the Celtic fringe. Given the existing electoral system, the luck of the draw had, for once, favoured the Liberals: 10 of their 12 M.P.s had majorities under 2,500, while only 5 of their defeated candidates came as near to victory.

The vote for Nationalist candidates held steady in Wales but rose appreciably in Scotland (where they secured three good second places). Apart from the Nationalists, the only 'other' candidate to save his deposit was Mr. Downey in Nelson and Colne, with his call for the return of hanging. There was, incidentally, no evidence that this theme reaped any benefit for the scattering of Conservative candidates who specifically exploited it. Minor parties stressing the immigration issue fared worse than in 1964: the highest vote (for the British National party in Southall) was 7·4%, a fall of 1·7% from 1964. Sir Oswald Mosley won only 4·6% of the vote for the Union Movement in Shoreditch and Finsbury. The Communists fared badly; in seats fought in 1964 their support fell slightly and the average vote for their 57 candidates was only 2% — but in one constituency, Hornsey, they secured enough to cost Labour the seat.

The most notable feature of the results was the uniformity of the swing to Labour. In almost half the seats the swing was within 1% of the national average of 3·5%. The Conservatives did not gain a single seat; their most remarkable feat was to hold the ever-fickle South-west Norfolk with an increased majority. It was one of only 8 seats that swung clearly against the tide (the others included Mr. Cousins' Nuneaton and Mr. Brown's Belper). Labour lost only Colne Valley — and that was only through a switch of Conservative votes to the Liberal.

Area by area the results varied little. The map showing regional

s

swings which has been used in past Nuffield studies is omitted here because almost all the regions would have been shaded alike. Only the North and East Ridings of Yorkshire (5·1%), the West Midlands (3·9%), Lincolnshire (3·7%) and the North East of England (3·7%) had swings markedly above the average and only Wales (2·2%), Scotland (2·1%) and Severn (2·1%) had swings markedly below — though the swing over the whole of the South and East (the London area excepted) was measurably less than the swing in the Midlands and North.

All the large cities swung more to Labour than the rest of their regions — most notably Hull (7·5%), Birmingham (6·6%), Belfast (6·1%), Newcastle (5·7%) and Bradford (5·1%). But even so the variations were very much smaller than in 1959–64.

The proportion voting fell to the lowest level since the war. Only 75·8% of registered electors cast their ballots. The registers were said to be exceptionally imperfect, but they were six months fresher than in 1964. However, the drop was heavily concentrated in safer seats where it could make no difference. In marginal constituencies, turnout was slightly above the 1964 figure and in the super-marginals it rose appreciably.

Once again Michael Steed has examined the results in great detail in an Appendix. Here, for the less statistically minded, is a summary of his main conclusions.

1. The turnout dropped by 1·3% but, because the register was newer, the real drop in participation must have been at least 4%.

2. Because the fall in turnout over the years has been mainly in strong Labour areas around mines and city centres, the Labour share of the national vote now under-represents the total Labour strength in the country by about 1%. In addition there is evidence that in 1966 Labour suffered a little more than the Conservatives from abstention.

3. The average swing, 3·5%, is, if anything, an underestimate of the direct movement from Conservative to Labour. It was a very uniform movement and there is little evidence that low swings in 1964–66 compensated for high swings in 1959–64, or *vice versa*.

4. Liberal candidates lost ground, on average by 3·1%, but there were wide variations. In seats where Liberals still stood, voters deserting the Liberals seem to have split evenly between Conservative and Labour.

5. At least a quarter and perhaps more of Liberals who had no

candidate abstained — a substantially larger number than in previous contests. Those who voted seem to have favoured the Conservatives by a small margin, but not enough to have had a significant effect on seats.[1]

6. In an election of uniform movements, large cities differed most from the national pattern, with a markedly higher average swing to Labour (4·6%) and an exceptional drop in participation. Mining seats also had a large drop in turnout but their swing was slightly lower than average. Otherwise voting differed little between urban and rural areas.

7. The only marked divergent trends at a regional level were the exceptional swing to Labour on Humberside and the Liberal advance in Northern Scotland.

8. Marginal seats behaved distinctively. In seats hovering between Labour and Conservative, about 5% of those who would normally have voted Liberal switched to one of the two major parties. In seats where the Liberals had a chance, the squeezing of the vote for the party that lay third probably accounts for the four Liberal gains. But there is no evidence of voting generally being affected by which party held second place.

9. In constituencies which had been named in advance by regional party officials as having notably improved organisation, the swing was no more favourable to the party concerned than in neighbouring seats.

10. There is no evidence that capital punishment, immigration or any local issue had significant effects.

11. In constituencies where the sitting M.P. withdrew there is some evidence of a small personal vote for the former Conservative

---

[1] It is plain that a limited number of Liberals did decide to spoil their ballot papers. The total number of spoiled ballots, 49,899, was almost 9,000 greater than in 1964: the number classified as 'unmarked or void for uncertainty' jumped from 15,486 to 27,794 and the increase was overwhelmingly concentrated in seats where no Liberal stood. There were 59 constituencies where over 100 ballots were disallowed under this classification; in not one of these constituencies did a Liberal stand in 1966 — and in 35 of them a Liberal had stood in 1964. But in only 10 seats did the figure exceed 200, the highest being 271 in Henley (apart from 409 in Mid-Ulster where nationalism rather than Liberalism was probably at issue). 271 represents only 3·0% of the 1964 Liberal vote in Henley and only 0·5% of the total of all 1966 votes there. The total number of spoiled ballots in all categories averaged 79 per constituency. There were only two seats where the number of spoiled ballots exceeded the majority Peterborough (38, majority 3) and Edinburgh, Pentlands (51, majority 44).
For full details of spoiled ballots see H. C. Deb. 730 c. 887–898 and c. 149–151.

M.P.s but none of one for former Labour M.P.s; among the Conservative M.P.s who may have held their seats because of a personal vote was Mr. Heath.

12. The former bias in the electoral system against the Labour party has now disappeared in favour of one against the Conservatives; the growth of abstention in safe Labour seats is the main reason for this and the anti-Labour bias would return if turnout returned to the same level as fifteen years ago.

How is Labour's victory in 1966 to be explained? Any answers given on the basis of the fragmentary evidence now available must be tentative. They are unlikely to be wholly wrong, but they may overlook factors of importance and get others out of perspective. It is hoped that the research described on p. x will make it possible to set the 1966 election, and that of 1964, in the context of longer-term historical change.

As in 1964, NOP combined the findings of their pre-election polls to produce a demographic profile of voting in 1966.

	All	Men	Women	Age					
				21–24	25–34	35–44	45–54	55–64	65+
	%	%	%	%	%	%	%	%	%
Con. .	41·4	37·7	44·7	40·6	37·1	37·9	41·8	44·8	47·4
Lab. .	48·7	52·4	45·4	51·2	54·6	51·2	47·0	45·9	43·2
Lib. .	8·6	8·3	8·9	8·2	7·3	9·6	9·8	8·2	7·8
Other	1·3	1·6	1·0	—	1·0	1·4	1·4	1·2	1·6
Swing	2·7	3·1	2·4	0·7	4·6	1·4	2·5	1·2	4·7

	All	Social class			
		Middle class AB (12%)	Lower middle C1 (22%)	Skilled working C2 (37%)	Unskilled 'very poor' DE (29%)
	%	%	%	%	%
Con. .	41·4	72·2	58·8	32·4	26·3
Lab. .	48·7	15·5	29·9	58·5	65·2
Lib. .	8·6	11·4	10·7	8·0	6·6
Other .	1·3	0·9	1·0	1·0	1·8
Swing .	2·7	4·6	3·7	2·8	5·4

The swings are based on a comparison between NOP results in 1964 and 1966 weighted to fit the actual voting results. But, of course, owing to deaths, ageing and changes in social class, like is not being compared exactly with like. In particular, a reduction in the number rated as C2 (the largest class category) explains the apparent paradox of the swing in every class being greater than the total swing.

Certain features of the tables are worth noting at once. Probably for the first time since the war, more women intended to vote Labour than Conservative; even so, the margin was narrow, and Labour's dominance among men was even more marked than in 1964. The 25–34 age group, which seems to have swung less to Labour than the groups above it in 1964 (no precise figures are available), now swung more than any age group except the over-65s. The swing among the over-65s may owe something to Labour's increases in pensions, but, since it is notoriously difficult to obtain an accurate sample of the older age groups, the figures must be treated with caution. As in 1964, a high swing to Labour was registered at the top of the social scale. This may be part of a long-term phenomenon since other evidence suggests that the Labour supporters in the AB social classes are disproportionately young. An even higher swing was registered among unskilled manual workers and the very poor. These groups, like the 25–34 age group, had swung less than others in 1964. Labour made gains in all social classes; the class polarisation of the British electorate was perhaps fractionally reduced.

Two short-term explanations for the swing to Labour, current during the election, find some support in NOP and Gallup data. The first was the widespread belief that the Conservatives were to blame for the country's economic difficulties, and that Labour deserved a further period in which to prove itself in office. Early in March, according to NOP, only 16% of a sample blamed the Labour government for Britain's economic troubles; fully 42% blamed the Conservatives (a higher figure even than six months before). Enthusiasm for the government was not enormous — the proportion expressing satisfaction with Labour was only a little higher than the proportion satisfied with the Conservatives just before the 1964 election — but the opinion poll data suggests a feeling of mild relief that the Conservatives' dire prophecies of 1964 had not been fulfilled, and also the feeling that Labour had done its best in a short period of seventeen months. In particular, individual prosperity was maintained.

The second short-term reason, though it might remain a factor for some time to come, was the contrast between Mr. Wilson and Mr. Heath. The Gallup poll during the campaign asked voters which of certain qualities they would ascribe to the two men. The results were almost uniformly unfavourable to Mr. Heath. The proportion thinking that Mr. Wilson had a 'strong, forceful personality' (54%) was nearly double that for Mr. Heath (28%). More voters regarded the Prime Minister as sincere, warm and friendly, and a man who could be trusted. Nearly four times more respondents attributed a 'weak personality' to Mr. Heath than to Mr. Wilson (15% to 4%). According to NOP, the percentage even of Conservative voters satisfied with Mr. Heath never rose above 70 during the campaign; the proportion of Labour voters approving of Mr. Wilson was regularly about 95%. In Lewisham North voters were asked which man they thought would make the better Prime Minister; 20% of Conservatives opted for Mr. Wilson compared with only 2% of Labour supporters for Mr. Heath.[1]

Too much weight should not be assigned to these short-term factors alone. The standings of both party leaders were liable to substantial short-term fluctuations (see chart p. 2) as were the electorate's attitudes towards the Labour government. The view that the Labour party, having won in 1964, was certain to win the next election, whenever it came, will not stand up to close scrutiny. The government was unpopular and held increasingly to blame for the country's economic difficulties in the summer of 1965; it might well have been again later in 1966 or in 1967. Moreover, these short-term attitudes themselves require explanation; the belief that Labour deserved another chance, for example, may only have been a neat rationalisation for some other, more diffuse sentiment.

Although the Conservative defeat in 1966 was not inevitable, the Conservatives were undoubtedly handicapped by another, medium-term, factor. For reasons that are still not entirely clear, the Conservatives in the early 1960s came to be regarded in the eyes of many voters as antipathetic: tired, out of touch with ordinary people, too much dominated by the upper classes. These attitudes were not suddenly dispelled, even by the election of Mr. Heath to the Conservative leadership. They persisted through the 1964 parliament and, although difficult to explain, could be de-

---

[1] Mr. Wilson's fear that the electorate would react against whichever party forced an election proved unfounded (though of course it might not have proved unfounded if the election had been held earlier). As late as mid-February exactly 75% of an NOP sample thought the election should be held in the autumn of 1966 or later; only 24% wanted it in the spring. Yet as soon as the campaign began 68% said they approved of the decision to hold an election; only 20% disapproved.

tected easily enough. Even at moments of declining Labour popularity, the Conservatives' standing in the opinion polls was slow to recover. Perhaps more significant, a high proportion of Conservative voters remained dissatisfied with their own party. In answer to almost every general question put to the electorate by the opinion polls, the proportion of Conservatives sympathising with Labour was substantially higher than the number of Labour supporters leaning towards the Conservatives. For example, during the campaign NOP asked a sample, 'Do you think the Conservatives are ready to return to power, or do they need longer in opposition?' Only 8% of Labour voters thought the Conservatives were ready to return; fully 25% of Conservatives thought that they were not. To this extent, at least, the 1966 election can be regarded as part of a continuous process that began in 1961 or 1962, perhaps before.

To these short- and medium-term factors should be added at least one important long-term consideration. It is a truism of electoral research that most voters acquire an identification with one or other political party at a fairly early age and that, in the absence of major political upheavals, they tend to retain this identification throughout their lives. From this point of view, it is important that Labour is a relatively young party which is still in the process of building up its electoral strength. The older age groups, who entered the electorate when Labour was still in its infancy and who cannot in most cases have had Labour parents, are still in the 1960s disproportionately pro-Conservative. But these groups are gradually being replaced by younger voters, a much higher proportion of whom have Labour parents and all of whom are entering the electorate with Labour well established as one of the two major parties. The process is slow and uneven, and may be overlaid at any particular election by influential short- or medium-term factors. It does not follow from this that Labour is bound to become the permanent party of government in Britain. It does mean, however, that the Conservatives in the late 1960s and 1970s may well suffer from a handicap from which they were free in the 1940s and 1950s.

The press in its comments on Labour's victory focused less on its causes than on the fact itself and its consequences. The opinion polls having eliminated the element of surprise from the results, the press's moralising was less extensive and less interesting than usual.

Certain themes were dominant: acknowledgment of Mr. Wilson's tactical skill and timing, speculation about his vulnerability to new left-wing pressures, tributes to Mr. Heath in defeat, relief that three years of electioneering were at an end, and anxiety about the economic future.

'Labour has won an impressive vote of national confidence and a victory that the party tacticians can be proud of.' (*Western Mail*)

'There is a clear danger that [Mr. Wilson's] tactical skills will now increasingly be employed in humouring and appeasing the more extreme sections of the Labour majority carried to Westminster by this high tide.' (*Glasgow Herald*)

'Mr. Heath has lost a gallant fight. After an uncertain start his stature as Conservative leader has remarkably increased. He has established himself as a national figure and the right leader of his party.' (*Daily Mail*)

'The single most important result of the election is that for the first time for three years Britain has a government which can afford to judge issues on their merits rather than on short-term political considerations.' (*Financial Times*)

'Mr. Wilson has won a famous victory. Labour's decisive majority gives him all the authority he needs to attack Britain's economic problems.' (*Sun*)

Like most elections, the general election of 1966 will be judged by historians mainly in the light of its consequences over a period of years. It did not mark a moment of abrupt change like the elections of 1906 and 1945 but found Britain in the midst of attempting to solve problems — economic, social, educational, political — which had been with her for many years, and would be with her for many years to come. It also found both major political parties, more perhaps than at any time since the war, in the course of evolving new attitudes towards the electorate and new philosophies. The election accelerated the process in both parties, but it did not begin it in either.

Two possibilities raised by the 1964 election receded into the background in 1966. The first was that questions of colour and immigration might become major issues in British national politics. Indeed immigration remained one of the chief topics of political debate until well into 1965, and it seemed for a time that the Conservatives would try to make it an issue at the next election. But the government's immigration white paper in August removed all plausibility from the argument that Britain was about to be flooded with coloured people, and the Conservatives under Mr. Heath largely chose to leave the issue to one side. It remains to be seen whether friction between the white and coloured communities, perhaps erupting in some sudden riot, will once more cause race to become a factor in politics.

The other possibility was that, owing to the success of the Liberals, Britain might be entering an era of genuine three-party politics. The Liberals certainly exercised an influence over the Labour government, especially in connection with steel nationalisation, and if Labour had ever lost its majority in the House of Commons the attitude of the Liberals would have become crucial. But their moment passed, at least for the time being. Labour's comfortable victory in 1966 meant that the Liberals, although both their voting strength and their parliamentary representation had increased since Mr. Grimond became leader, had made no real strategic advance. In the weeks after polling day in 1966 it was no clearer than it had been ten years before how the Liberals were going either to form a new radical coalition with elements from both the Conservative and Labour parties, or to supplant Labour as the chief opposition to the Conservatives. The circumstances of the 1964 parliament did not present the Liberals with as great an opportunity as was often imagined; at no stage did they hold the balance of power. Nevertheless, to the extent that an opportunity existed, the Liberals failed to seize it.

The 1966 election left the Labour party as completely in command of British politics as the Conservatives had been after 1959. In the aftermath of victory it seemed possible that Labour — led by a man who openly boasted of his pragmatic approach to politics, and of his success in capturing the crucial centre ground from the Conservatives — might be about to enter into a long hegemony. In every election from 1859 to 1951 the pendulum had swung in some measure against the previously victorious party. Now for the third time in the last four elections the trend had been reversed. The power of governments to command publicity and to control the level of economic activity had grown steadily. It seemed possible that the alternation of parties in power in Britain, frequent in the past, might be less frequent in future.

Yet, like the Conservatives after 1959, Labour faced the prospect that its moment of triumph might be followed by its bitterest disappointments. The larger Labour majority enhanced the possibility of party divisions, while Britain's economic problems seemed as insoluble as ever. In 1964 the Labour party had entered into power eager and filled with confidence that it could succeed where the Conservatives had failed. By 1966 Labour had indisputably asserted its will to govern; but the eagerness of the first few weeks had largely vanished, and so had much of the confidence.

AN ANALYSIS OF THE RESULTS

By Michael Steed

Press comment on the results of the 1966 election focused on the apparent uniformity of behaviour throughout the country; the 1959 and 1964 contests had led people to expect that there would again be spectacular exceptions to the national pattern. But a detailed analysis of the figures reveals conflicting currents beneath the surface. The first part of this Appendix explores the three main movements and how they were interrelated. The next part explores points peculiar to each of these movements — the swing, the drop in Liberal support, and the increase in abstentions. Following this, factors underlying the variations in the results are examined — principally how far different types of constituency, region or tactical situation show differences in voting behaviour. This arrangement of the material means there is no complete discussion of, for example, swing on its own: there is a short section on the variation of swing but it is also discussed wherever it is relevant to other points. The minor parties and voting in Northern Ireland are covered separately and the Appendix ends with a section on the working of the electoral system.

The changes between 1964 and 1966 can be expressed in different ways. Here are three statements of the overall result in the United Kingdom.[1]

	% of registered electorate		% of total votes cast		% of two-party vote	
Conservative .	31·7	−1·7	41·9	−1·5	46·7	−2·9
Labour . .	36·6	+2·3	47·9	+3·8	53·3	+2·9
Liberal . .	6·5	−2·1	8·5	−2·7		
Others . .	1·3	+0·3	1·7	+0·4		
Non-voters .	24·2	+1·3				
'Swing' to Labour	2·0		2·7		2·9	

These global figures, however, shed no light on how far the swing was due to direct switching between the two main parties or how far it was affected by the other changes. Using the global figures it could be argued

[1] These figures are for the United Kingdom; all other figures quoted in this Appendix, unless otherwise stated, refer only to the 617 constituencies in Great Britain excluding the Speaker's seat (Itchen).

that Labour's gain came almost wholly from the former Liberals while the former Conservatives moved to non-voting. In fact the reverse is true: the direct movement from Conservative to Labour was substantially greater than the overall swing figures suggest.

This is reflected in the difference between the average of the two-party swing[1] in individual constituencies (3·5%)[2] and the overall swing in the national vote (2·9%). The main reason for this discrepancy is to be found in the continued decline in turnout in safe Labour seats. The following table shows how far turnout is now lower in Labour-held seats:

Turnout	Con. seats	Lab. seats	Lib. seats	Total	U.K. total
Below 60% . .	1	23	0	24	28
60–65% . .	5	17	0	22	24
65–70% . .	10	38	1	49	52
70–75% . .	49	80	2	131	132
75–80% . .	106	128	1	235	236
Above 80% . .	71	77	8	156	158
Total . . .	242	363	12	617	630

The average turnout in Labour seats was 2·7% lower than in Conservative ones. This is a striking contrast with the position fifteen years ago; in 1950 the turnout was 1% higher in Labour than in Conservative seats and the highest turnout was in the safest Labour seats.[3] The consequence of this change is that the national totals of votes now underestimate Labour's potential strength and render comparisons with national totals in the past somewhat misleading. If with identical party percentages in each constituency the 1966 turnout had been at the 1950 level, the Labour share of the national vote would have been about 1% higher than it was. While turnout trends are so uneven, it is misleading to use measures of overall swing that are based on the national totals of votes cast; both for prediction and as a yardstick for the movement between the main parties, the average of the individual constituency swings is more accurate.

[1] In this Appendix swing is defined on the basis of the two-party vote. For the difference between this and the more conventional method of averaging the Conservative and Labour percentage change see *The British General Election of 1964*, pp. 337–8. For the predictive value of the two methods see below, p. 293n. A striking instance of the advantage of the two-party swing occurred in 1966 in Barnsley where the Conservative vote rose by 3,039 and the Labour vote by only 1,494. This is measured as a swing to Labour of 0·7% by averaging, but as a swing of 4·1% to Conservative on the two-party basis.

[2] The mean swing was 3·48% and the median 3·49%. The standard deviation from the mean was 2·1% (1964 3·1%).

[3] See *The British General Election of 1950*, p. 339.

The Swing: in relation to changes in turnout, in Liberal candidatures* and in the Liberal vote

	To Con.	Swing 1964–66 To Lab.					Total seats	Mean swing
		Up to 1·9%	2·0–3·4%	3·5–4·9%	5·0–6·9%	Over 7·0%		
A. Increase in Turnout .	10	13	51	51	30	10	163	−3·7%
B. Decrease in Turnout up to 2·9% . . .	10	57	104	74	63	16	324	−3·5%
C. Decrease in Turnout over 3·0% . .	12	20	29	40	23	4	130	−3·1%
D. No Liberal candidate 1964 or 1966 . .	1	36	70	63	42	11	223	−3·7%
E. Liberal intervention .	2	0	8	8	9	4	31	−4·7%
F. Liberal withdrawal .	11	14	26	16	11	6	84	−2·7%
G. Increase in Liberal vote	4	9	6	1	3	2	25	−2·4%
H. Decrease in Liberal vote up to 4·9% . .	7	29	63	62	28	2	191	−3·1%
I. Decrease in Liberal vote over 5·0% . .	7	2	9	15	22	5	60	−4·3%
J. All seats . . .	32	90	184	165	116	30	617	−3·5%

Effect of Liberal candidatures* on turnout

	Change in turnout 1964–66 Increase	−0·0% to −1·4%	−1·5% to −2·9%	Over −3·0%	Total seats	Mean change
K. Liberal intervention .	19	8	4	0	31	+0·7%
L. Increase in Liberal vote .	11	7	7	0	25	−0·0%
M. Decrease in Liberal vote	89	91	53	19	251	−0·5%
N. No Liberal candidate 1964 or 1966 .	35	41	73	74	223	−1·9%
O. Liberal withdrawal .	7	18	22	37	84	−2·6%
P. All seats . . .	161	167	159	130	617	−1·2%

* Three seats complicated by Independent Liberal candidates are omitted from the breakdown by Liberal candidatures.
We are deeply indebted to Honeywell Data Control for providing the raw material for this table and other parts of the Appendix. In particular we would like to thank L. R. Price for permission to use Honeywell equipment in the preparation of these tables, and also Allan Fletcher, Arthur Tulip and Jim Wheatley for their assistance.

The relationship between the swing, the changes in turnout and the Liberal vote. The table above shows how far the swing was affected by the decrease in turnout and the changes in the Liberal vote. It is plain from lines A to C that the swing was higher where turnout increased. The extent of this relationship is masked in two ways: by the link between turnout and the Liberal vote and because in the large cities both the swing and the drop in turnout were high. But though measurement is thus difficult, Labour clearly suffered more than the Conservatives from abstention.[1]

The effect of the Liberal vote on the swing is more complex. The difference in the swing of 2·0% between seats where Liberals intervened (E) and seats where they withdrew (F) suggests very strongly that the Liberal vote was more pro-Conservative at this election. In fact this partially reflects that fact that these changes in Liberal candidatures were concentrated in Labour-held seats, where a Liberal candidate took proportionately more votes from the Conservatives. Nevertheless, in more marginal seats Liberal intervention was associated with an average swing of 4·0% and withdrawal with one of 3·1%. This suggests that, in 1966, a Liberal withdrawal was worth a swing of about 0·5% to the Conservatives.[2]

In seats with Liberal candidates at both elections, the effect of the drop in the Liberal vote appears fairly complex. Lines G to I of the table suggest that where Liberals managed to improve their vote against the national tide it tended to be at Labour's expense and that Labour benefited more than the Conservatives from a marked drop in the Liberal vote. This seems to fit the theory, advanced before the election, that the Liberal party would suffer and the Labour party benefit from a squeeze on the votes of third place radical candidates.[3] Yet if this was so, the swing should have been high wherever the Liberal vote dropped; in fact it was below average in seats where the Liberal vote was decreasing by a normal amount (line H). The explanation which most easily fits the figures in the table is: (i) that, despite many local variations, the other two parties gained very equally from a normal drop in the Liberal vote of 3·1%, (ii) that where the Liberal vote held it was the more pro-Labour Liberal voters who remained, and (iii) that where the Liberal vote was squeezed most heavily the more pro-Conservative Liberal voters were likeliest to stay Liberal. The net effect on the national swing was probably almost nil.[4]

From this it would seem that the net direct movement from Con-

---

[1] Apathy among Labour supporters may have lost Burton and Pentlands for Labour and increased turnout may have given Labour its gain at Bedford; the most unexpected Labour gain (Conway) was very probably the result of a marked increase (3·4%) in turnout.

[2] There are no seats where the Conservatives could have won through Liberal withdrawal and (except conceivably Aberdeen South) none where Liberal intervention produced a Labour victory. However, local evidence suggests that Labour won Cardiff North through Liberal withdrawal.

[3] See, for instance, *The Economist*, March 5th, 1966, p. 873.

[4] In terms of seats, Labour may owe Bedford to a large squeeze on the Liberal vote and may have been baulked at Lowestoft because the Liberal vote was nearly held. However, the most plausible case for the effect of former Liberals is the Conservative victory in Hendon North (Liberal −5·4%; swing to Labour −0·8%); there is other evidence that the slight rightward shift of the Liberal vote since 1964 was more marked in Greater London.

servative to Labour was in fact higher, but not substantially higher, than the average swing figure. The mean swing in seats with no Liberal candidate at either election, and with an increased turnout, was 3·7%. This may well be the best available estimate of this direct movement; if so, Labour attracted some 7½% of those who voted Conservative in 1964. However, a very small element of the figure probably reflects deaths and comings of age as distinct from individual conversions.

The relationship between the change in turnout and the Liberal vote is, however, refreshingly clear. Lines K to P of the table on page 273 show that the extent of the drop in turnout was fairly exactly determined by what the Liberal party did. This reflects an increased tendency for Liberal voters without a candidate to stay at home. Taking seats with no Liberal candidate in 1964, turnout fell 2·6% less in the 31 where a Liberal intervened in 1966 than in the 223 where there was again no Liberal candidate. 2·6% of the electorate represents 3·4% of those who voted; as the Liberal vote in these seats averaged 10·6%, the implication is that nearly one-third of Liberal voters abstained if denied a candidate. Unfortunately these 31 seats cannot be relied on as a representative sample and one-third may be an overestimate. But it seems likely that at least one-quarter of the Liberal vote would have abstained in this situation, in contrast to the estimate for 1964 of about one-fifth. About 0·5% of the national decrease in turnout can thus be ascribed to the decrease in Liberal candidatures; if the Liberal party had fought every seat, national turnout would have increased.

The Swing. The diagram overleaf shows how uniform was the movement from Labour to Conservative between 1964 and 1966. Nearly three-fifths of the individual constituency swings were within 1·5% of the average compared with under two-fifths in 1959–64. Extreme swings, too, were less common; only one in ten constituencies had swings more than 3·5% away from the average compared with one in five in 1959–64. In fact nearly half these extreme swings were probably due to Liberal or Nationalist behaviour rather than to unusual movements between Conservative and Labour. Ignoring such cases, there were only 8 constituencies which showed a significant (over 0·5%) swing to the Conservatives[1] although there were 22 with swings to Labour of more than 7%. However all but 4[2] of these 22 were in large cities.

This swing of 3·5% could be regarded as the second instalment of a total swing of 7·0% to Labour between 1959 and 1964. Several of the anomalous swings in 1964–66 merely compensated for anomalous

---

[1] Belper, South Dorset, Faversham, Lichfield & Tamworth (where the size of the electorate had risen by a record 14%), Newton, South-west Norfolk, Nuneaton, and Torrington.

[2] Blackpool North, Middleton & Prestwich, Smethwick, and Willesden East.

Variations in constituency swings, 1964–66

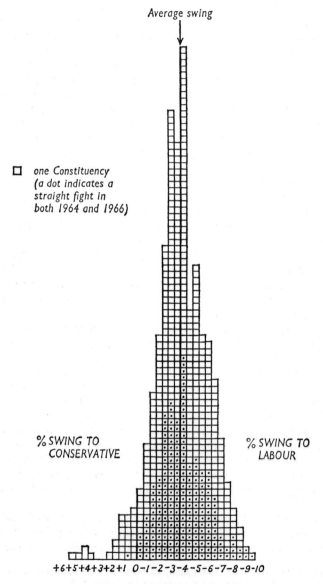

Average swing

one Constituency
(a dot indicates a
straight fight in
both 1964 and 1966)

% SWING TO
CONSERVATIVE

% SWING TO
LABOUR

+6 +5 +4 +3 +2 +1 0 -1 -2 -3 -4 -5 -6 -7 -8 -9 -10

The extreme swings in Colne Valley (−11·7%), Ladywood (−14·0%),
and Paisley (+7·9%) are not marked.

swings in 1959–64; South Dorset, Dudley, Peckham, and Smethwick provide examples. Yet there is little evidence that such compensatory movements were the general pattern. In those constituencies which in 1959–64 had swung, against the tide, to the Conservatives, the 1964–66 swing was 3·4% to Labour; those which had swung by more than 7% to Labour in 1959–64 still managed a further 3·1% swing in 1964–66. Over the lifetime of the two parliaments together there were, accordingly, more extreme swings than in either, even ignoring those special cases which were probably by-products of Liberal or Nationalist behaviour. Between 1959 and 1966 Hampstead swung by 18·0% to Labour; it was followed by Springburn (16·4%), Middlesbrough West (15·3%) and five others over 14%. At the other extreme 1959–66 saw rightward movements in three constituencies — Falmouth & Camborne (1·7%), South-west Norfolk (1·2%), and George Brown's Belper (0·4%).

The swing of 3·5% applied surprisingly evenly to safe Conservative, marginal and safe Labour seats. In constituencies where the Conservative vote in 1964 was more than twice the Labour vote, the swing still averaged 3·5%; in the seats where Labour outnumbered the Conservatives by two to one the swing was lower (2·9%) but, if the mining seats are omitted, the swing, once more, was 3·5%. Clearly the size of the movement from Conservative to Labour was not significantly related to the number of Conservatives available for conversion.[1]

The drop in the Liberal vote. The average drop in Liberal support (3·1%) meant that the Liberal party lost about three-quarters of the support it had gained between 1959 and 1964. In seats comparable with 1959, the Liberal vote was on average up by 1·0% in 1966. On the basis of comparable seats, the Liberal party did better in 1966 than in any of the four general elections of the 1950s but worse than in 1964, 1945 or any earlier election.

But these average changes hide considerable individual variations; in more than one-fifth of the comparable constituencies the Liberal share of the vote either fell more than twice the average or increased. Clearly the change in Liberal support was more subject to factors operating at constituency level than was the movement of votes between the two main parties. It seems that to a much larger extent than with the other two parties, the size of the Liberal vote depended on the Liberal candidate or on local organisational strength or on both.

The biggest drops in Liberal support reflected the withdrawal of a strong candidate; among the seven drops of more than 10%, four — West Derbyshire, Ipswich, Paisley, and Tiverton — had had Liberal

---

[1] H. B. Berrington in 'The General Election of 1964' (*The Journal of the Royal Statistical Society*, Series A, Vol. 128, 1965) argues that the swing should be related to the original share of the vote obtained by the party losing support.

T

candidates in 1964 who had built up support on the basis of a previous by-election, one — Bolton West — had had a retiring M.P. and another — Western Isles — a former Conservative candidate who had carried much of his Conservative vote with him. The eight constituencies where the Liberal vote rose by more than 4% included three contiguous ones in North-east Scotland and three with very close results in 1964. One more, Cheadle, linked with the remaining case of a very large drop — in Stretford — since the victor, Michael Winstanley, had fought Stretford in 1964. This leaves the Isle of Wight, where the Liberal vote rose by 7·5%, as one of the most surprising results of the election.

The increase in abstention. A fall in the percentage turnout (the total vote as a percentage of the registered electorate) need not be the same as an increase in abstention (failure to vote on the part of those able to do so). There is every reason to believe that the increase in abstention between 1964 and 1966 was about four times as big as the decrease in turnout (1·3% for the United Kingdom). The 1966 election was held on a register six and a half months newer than that in 1964; approximately 1% more of the registered electorate must have died by October than by March. The proportion affected by moving house is more problematical. From the census migration tables[1] it is possible to estimate the proportion of the electorate who move house within a given period. It is likely that 2·9% fewer of the electorate had moved within their local authority area in March 1966 than in October 1964 and 2·8% fewer had moved out of their local authority area;[2] the first group would not normally be entitled to a postal vote but the second group would. The proportion of people who, because they have moved, do not exercise their right to vote — either in person or by post — is a matter for guesswork. It seems reasonable to suppose that at least one-third and at most two-thirds of the first group and that at least two-fifths and at most three-quarters of the second group are so affected. On the minimum assumptions, the real increase in abstention at the 1966 election was 4·4%; on the maximum assumptions it was 6·3%. It is plain that there was a striking increase in abstention; allowing for the system of registration and of postal voting, there was more apathy in 1966 than in any previous general election — with the possible exceptions of 1918 and 1935.

Turnout increased in 163 constituencies but, allowing for the fresher register, in most of these there was no increase in the proportion of those able to vote who actually did so. On the minimum assumptions about the effect of mobility, in only 14 of these 163 was there an in-

---

[1] *Census 1961 Migration National Summary Table,* HMSO, 1965, Table 4, pp. 35–57.
[2] This calculation assumes that no seasonal or demographic bias in mobility nor any change in mobility rates since 1961 materially affected the situation.

creased readiness to vote.[1] But precise calculations can only be based on the change in turnout, so that in effect 'increased turnout' normally means a below average decline in participation.

In the Appendix analysing the results of the 1964 general election it was stated that the variation in the drop in turnout at that election did not seem related to weather conditions on polling day.[2] There is some evidence now to suggest that the conclusion drawn from this may have been wrong. The areas which suffered worst from rain in 1964 increased their turnout in 1966. Clearly any effect of rainfall in 1964 was masked by regional movements of turnout. One cannot be sure, therefore, whether the increase in turnout in 1966 in the South-west peninsula (+2·0%) or in the Southern third of England as a whole (+0·1%) — in contrast to the decrease in the rest of the country (−1·9%) — was due to the weather in 1964 or to independent regional behaviour. At any rate, there is no evidence that, apart from the snow-fall in Orkney & Zetland, weather affected turnout in 1966.

Voting according to type of constituency. The table set out below shows how, by five different measures, voting behaviour differed according to types of constituency. Although most of the figures show

Voting according to type of constituency

No. of seats	Type	Average swing since %		Average change in turnout since %		Average drop in Liberal vote since 1964 %
		1959	1964	1955	1964	
146	Large cities	9·4	4·6	−3·6	−1·3	3·0
249	Other urban	7·4	3·4	−0·9	−0·9	3·5
82	25–50% rural	5·7	3·3	+0·1	−1·2	2·2
64	50–75% rural	4·7	2·7	+2·0	−0·9	2·9
28	Over 75% rural	4·3	3·1	+1·2	−1·3	3·2
46	Partly mining	5·2	2·4	−1·8	−2·4	2·7
27	Mining	3·8	2·7	−3·8	−3·0	—
617	All seats	7·0	3·5	−1·2	−1·2	3·1

Definitions: Rural and mining categories (which overlap) are defined as in *The British General Election of 1964* (p. 341). The term 'urban' is used for constituencies falling outside any rural or mining category. Large cities are the former County of London and the eighteen provincial cities with more than 200,000 population.

little variation certain tendencies are clear. The drop in the Liberal vote was particularly even; in only one group did the fall differ by

[1] Conway, Exeter, Hampstead, Ladywood, North Norfolk, Norwood, Reading, Tavistock, West Bromwich, North Cornwall, Eton & Slough, Falmouth & Camborne, Kemptown, and Leyton. In the last five seats there was real increase in participation even on the maximum assumptions about the effect of mobility.

[2] *The British General Election of 1964*, p. 344.

more than 0·5% from the average. The change in turnout since 1964 was similarly even except in mining seats; however, since the changes in the efficiency of the register vary in different types of constituency, a comparison is also made with 1955, the last general election to take place in the spring. It is clear that the change in turnout patterns since then was systematic. Rural seats displayed greater readiness to vote and most urban seats some increase in apathy. But the shift to abstention in the mining areas and in large cities is very striking.

In the 471 seats outside large cities, the swing was very even, averaging 3·2%; mining seats had slightly lower swings but there was little difference between rural areas and urban seats away from the cities. This is somewhat surprising as a large proportion of the 'other urban' seats are in the suburban rings of conurbations. Despite this, such suburban seats usually had swings more in line with the rest of the country than with their metropolitan cities.

All but two of the nineteen large cities had swings of more than 3·2% — and these two, Portsmouth and Glasgow, had had very large swings between 1959 and 1964. Among large cities, the size of swing in 1966 did seem to compensate for the abnormal variations of 1964. In 1959–64 the range among the nineteen cities had been 1·7% to 8·6%; in 1964–66 it was 2·4% to 7·8%. But the combined 1959–66 swing only ranged from 6·5% (Bristol) to 12·0% (Liverpool). Despite their geographical scatter, it was within 1·5% of the average (9·4%) in fourteen of them. This total movement in the large cities from 1959 to 1966 was almost half as great again as that in the rest of the country (6·4%).

The internal consistency of the swing among the cities, together with the consistent differences between their swings and those in neighbouring suburban and rural areas, argues that there was some common cause underlying their behaviour. Population changes were perhaps partially responsible — the movement of middle-class city residents into the outer commuting areas and their replacement by more working-class inner city residents. Yet, although some of the more central middle-class constituencies, such as Handsworth, Streatham or Withington, have seen a large drift to Labour, the biggest movements have generally been in slum or near-slum city centre working-class districts, such as Newcastle Central, Paddington North or Small Heath. It may be that there has been a largely unnoticed switch of working-class Conservative voters to Labour in such areas.[1]

The high swing in cities might also be related to issues specifically

[1] The table of NOP's breakdown of voting by social class (see page 264) shows the largest swing to Labour in poorest (DE) class; hitherto Conservative strength in the semi- and unskilled working-class had only been a little less than in the skilled (C2) category.

affecting the central areas of conurbations — particularly housing and rents. If so, it should be apparent in London with its numerous constituencies and diverse housing conditions; but in fact the swing was not higher in boroughs with poorer housing conditions or more dwellings let by private landlords. The simplest explanation may be the real one: that opinions are more fluid in large urban communities.

Whatever the reasons, the low rural swing in 1964 combined with the high city swing in 1966 have shifted the relative political strengths of the two large parties. The Labour party is now more dependent on the large industrial cities and relatively weaker in rural areas than at any time since the war. This shift can be seen by comparing the seats Labour would have gained on a uniform 7% swing from 1959 with those it actually gained. The 22 seats Labour should have won but did not, and the 25 extra seats won although needing more than a 7% swing are distributed thus:[1]

	Lab. failures	Lab. extra seats
Large cities . . .	1	8
Other urban . . .	5	14
25–75% rural . . .	10	3
Over 75% rural . .	6	0

Regional voting. Political awareness of regional differences within Great Britain increased markedly in the 1960s and was accompanied by a greater consciousness of regional variations in electoral behaviour. This probably led to some exaggeration of the role of regional behaviour at the 1964 election. When the swing in a particular geographical area differs from the national average, the contrast often reflects the urbanisation of the region rather than any distinctively regional behaviour. Thus in 1966 average swing in the South Western region (2·9%) was 0·6% below the national average; but the urban seats within the region had a swing of 3·7%, only 0·1% away from the national average for urban seats. The low swing in the South West reflected, therefore, the fact that more people there live in the countryside, not any tendency for people to behave differently because they lived in that region. Truly regional behaviour, extending to all types of constituency within a region, was a marked feature of the 1959 election but was much less common in 1964 and in 1966.

The one clearly regional swing at this election was on Humberside. The lowest swing in the three Hull seats was 7·0% and essentially rural

---

[1] Labour parliamentary representation from the rural areas of Scotland and Wales has held up but the proportion of the parliamentary Labour party sitting for English rural or partly rural seats has declined from 11% in 1945 and 10% in 1955 to 8% in 1966.

constituencies such as Gainsborough and Howden had swings as high as 5·5%. Every seat in the East Riding of Yorkshire and the Lindsey division of Lincolnshire surpassed the national average; the mean swing in these eleven seats was 5·9%. Other neighbouring seats with high swings, such as Holland-with-Boston or York, may have been part of the same regional pattern. This Humberside area had hardly

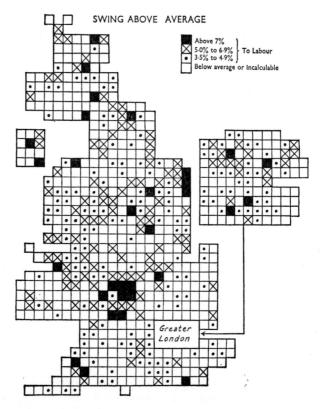

SWING ABOVE AVERAGE

Above 7%
5·0% to 6·9% } To Labour
3·5% to 4·9%
Below average or Incalculable

Greater
London

been recognised as a region until the last few years.[1] Traditional regional boundaries were ignored when the Department of Economic Affairs united the two sides of the Humber to form part of the Yorkshire and Humberside Economic Planning Region in 1964. During 1964–65, with discussion of a Humberside New City by the Minister of Housing and of a Humber road bridge by the Minister of Transport, the regional needs of a hitherto neglected (though fairly prosperous) part

[1] Thus regions in the Appendix recognise only a Lincolnshire region and an East and North Riding region, each of them having an above average swing because it includes part of Humberside.

of the country were given more recognition than before. The Hull
North by-election and reports of gas discoveries in the North Sea
focused more political attention on the region. May not Humberside's
political behaviour in March 1966 have sprung from the sense of regional
identity that the period of Labour government had given it?

The other strong swing to Labour in a large city, Birmingham, was

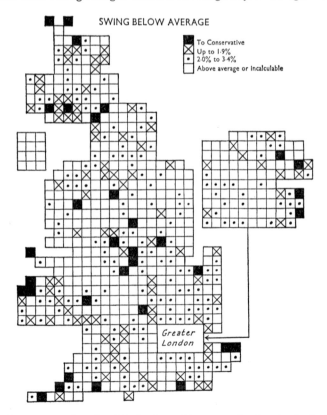

SWING BELOW AVERAGE

To Conservative
Up to 1·9%
2·0% to 3·4%
Above average or incalculable

Greater
London

clearly not part of regional behaviour. Every seat in the city had a high
swing but only three of the eight seats surrounding it followed suit; the
average swing in the three neighbouring counties was, at 3·7%, almost
precisely the national average. Birmingham was once more demonstrating
that, of the big provincial cities, it has been supremely capable of following its own inclinations despite the national tide.[1] The only entire
conurbations to go their own way were Clydeside, which swung by

[1] Birmingham ignored the Liberal landslide in 1906 and swung heavily to
Labour against the national tide in 1924; in 1931, 1945 and 1959 as in 1966 it
went with the national swing but more than doubled it.

only 2·2%, and Greater Manchester where the Liberal vote fell sharply.[1]

Only one region moved against the national trend in any respect; in the North of Scotland the Liberal vote rose slightly overall and in some seats in the North East jumped dramatically. In fact the region is really two: the six Highland and Island constituencies and the seven seats in North East Scotland. The Liberal party put a concerted regional effort into North East Scotland after 1964; a candidate stood in every seat for the first time in forty years; a regional organisation was formed and a policy for the region produced. As in Humberside, the Liberal success was probably the result of the identification of regional consciousness with one political party.[2] In the Highlands themselves, the Liberal vote rose slightly and the swing was average. However, this further Conservative loss means that the Conservative party has now sunk to the status of a third party for the first time in any region outside Wales:

Results in High- lands and Islands	1945		1955		1966	
	Votes	Seats	Votes	Seats	Votes	Seats
Conservatives .	44·1%	5	49·7%	4	30·0%	1
Labour . .	34·9%	1	30·2%	1	32·8%	2
Liberal* . .	21·0%	0	20·1%	1	37·2%	3

* Only five Liberal candidates stood in 1945 and only three in 1955.

Some of the social developments behind this dramatic change have been discussed in Chapter XIII by Ian Grimble.

Otherwise, the country behaved with general uniformity as the maps of the swing show; the only exceptions[3] were low swings to Labour in two areas where Labour had done relatively well during the 1950s, East Kent (1·4%) and Cornwall (0·7%), a marked switch from Liberal to Labour in East Devon, and a generally good Liberal performance throughout Hampshire, Kent, Surrey and Sussex (an average drop of only 1·7%).

Marginal seats. In 1966 British electors showed a greater awareness than before of the significance of living in a marginal seat. In marginals, apathetic voters were much more likely to turn out and all voters were less likely to vote for a party in third place. The following table shows the effect on turnout and the Liberal vote in constituencies fought in close competition between the two main parties:

[1] It is remarkable that this included Cheadle which went even more against the regional trend than against the national trend. The Liberal vote fell by 7·0% in the other twelve Manchester region seats but rose by 7·6% in Cheadle.

[2] An interesting account of how the Liberal party fought North East Scotland appeared in the *Scotsman*, March 14th, 1966.

[3] But see p. 279 for the possibly regional pattern in the change in turnout and p. 290 for the essentially regional concentration of the Scottish Nationalist vote.

Type of marginal seat	Average change in turnout	Average decline in Lib. vote	No. of seats
1964 Shares of two-party vote:			
Con. 47½–50% Lab. 50–52½%	+0·1%	3·8%	40
Con. 50–52½% Lab. 47½–50%	+1·3%	5·1%	39
Con. 52½–55% Lab. 45–47½%	+0·1%	3·2%	34
New marginal seats . . .	+1·4%	6·7%	10
Super-marginal seats . . .	+2·3%	5·1%	20
All constituencies . . .	−1·2%	3·1%	617

The response of those wavering on the brink of abstention was most clearly seen in the 'super-marginals', those where a majority of less than 1% at the 1964 general election had brought home the situation with special drama;[1] the response of those wavering about voting Liberal was clearest in the 'new' marginals, seats with a majority of over 15% in 1959 but under 5% in 1964, where electors were adapting their behaviour in the light of changed circumstances. The change in turnout seems to have been very closely related to the size of the majority at the previous election: the 1964 repetition of a 1959 majority of under 100 votes in Eton and Slough brought yet another increase in turnout, whereas in seats which ceased to look marginal after 1964, such as Edmonton or Edge Hill, there were often large drops in turnout.

The Liberal party, however, fared relatively badly in any marginal situation as in 1959 and 1964. The extent of this cumulative squeeze can be seen by a direct constituency by constituency comparison with the 1950 general election; since then there has been a fall in the Liberal vote in 1964 marginals (0·3%) but a rise in 1964 non-marginals (4·1%). As the 1966 Liberal vote in marginals averaged 10% this estimate suggests that nearly a third of the potential Liberal vote could be squeezed into voting for another party.

Similar calculations can be applied to those wavering between voting and non-voting. The 1966 turnout in super-marginals (81·7%) was 5·7% higher than the national turnout; direct comparison with the 1950 election shows that the drop was 4·7% less in super-marginals than it was nationally. Most of this difference seems to have arisen between 1964 and 1966 when the turnout rise in super-marginals (2·3%) contrasts with a 1·2% national drop. In contrast to the steady build-up of the squeeze on Liberals, a marginal situation had a marked effect on apathy only in 1966.

Taken together these estimates indicate that some 10% of electors

---

[1] The effect on turnout of the smallest majority was dramatically evident in Kemptown; see pp. 226.

decided either on whether to vote or on how to vote simply by virtue of living in a marginal constituency. This remarkable instance of adaptation in electoral behaviour suggests that sophistication about the working of the electoral system has increased notably in a few years. In part this sophistication may be indirect; differing behaviour in marginal constituencies may partly reflect the extra organisational effort put in by local parties. But the recent trends in turnout in safe and marginal seats do suggest that the public was increasingly aware of where votes count; what had the most direct effect was a cliff-hanger result when a few hundred or a few dozen votes separated the candidates.

However, the extra effort of this 10% appears to have been of little political avail. The swing in marginal seats has remained obstinately similar to the national average: in 1964 it was 3·8% and in 1966 3·3% compared to national figures of 3·5% in both years. The extra voters and the erstwhile Liberals appear to have split between the two main parties in such equal numbers as to cancel each other out.

Other tactical voting. The Liberal party, before the election, placed some trust in a rather similar example of electoral sophistication: it believed that people would vote increasingly according to which party held second place. But this did not happen. The Liberal vote declined in seats where Liberals held second place at almost the same rate as nationally (−2·8% against −3·1%); 28 of the 54 Liberals second places were lost. But in fact the electorate displayed considerable sophistication in such seats. Most of the Liberal second places were in seats held safely by one part and in these the electorate took little notice of which losing party happened to have had a narrow lead over the other. In those Conservative-held seats where a Liberal candidate had led Labour by less than 10% the Liberal vote dropped 2·9%; it dropped by 3·4% where a Labour candidate had a similar lead over a Liberal.

However, in marginal seats where the Liberal party was a serious competitor for victory, the electorate did take notice. There were six seats[1] where the Liberal party had been within 10% of victory in 1964; the turnout increased in each (on average by 2·2%) and so did the Liberal share of the vote in five (on average by 3·4%); in all six the third-place party lost ground, regardless of the national swing. Similar behaviour occurred in two seats where Liberals were 10–15% off victory in 1964 (West Aberdeenshire and Cheadle), but not in six others. But the positive instances of a marginal constituency pattern of behaviour certainly had a considerable effect on Liberal fortunes; without the decision of voters in these few seats to ignore national trends and to behave according to the local situation, the number of Liberal seats

---

[1] A seventh seat where the Liberal party was within 10% of victory is excluded as a very special case: Huddersfield West was marginal as between all three parties.

in the House of Commons would have declined, in concert with the fall in the Liberal vote.

The role of the candidate. The table below explores how various groups of candidates fared. There is little evidence that any particular type of candidate votes. If we consider the largely left-wing Labour

	Mean swing	Weighted Mean swing*	No. of seats
Con. M.P. 1964; Lab. M.P. 1966 .	4·1%	3·8%	53
Con. M.P. replaced . . .	4·1%	4·1%	18
Lab. M.P. replaced . . .	4·0%	3·8%	16
Lab. M.P. pro-arms cut . .	3·4%	3·3%	69
Con. Rhodesia rebel M.P. (for) .	3·3%	3·5%	27
Con. Rhodesia rebel M.P. (against)	3·6%	3·6%	44
Con. woman 1964; man 1966 .	3·3%	3·3%	10
Con. man 1964; woman 1966 .	3·4%	3·7%	6
Lab. woman 1964; man 1966 .	4·3%	4·3%	7
Lab. man 1964; woman 1966 .	4·0%	4·0%	9

* The swing in any group could reflect the distribution of the seats in it between large cities and the rest of the country rather than the influence of the candidate. Therefore large city constituencies have been weighted to one quarter of each group to produce the 'weighted mean swing'.

M.P.s who advocated reduced defence expenditure[1], the mainly left-wing Conservative M.P.s who in defiance of their leader's advice voted for oil sanctions against the rebel regime in Rhodesia, and their more right-wing colleagues who rebelled to vote against such sanctions we find that their electoral fate was almost identical with that of members who did none of these things. This underlines how little concern (or indeed knowledge) there is among the electorate about the particular political views of their M.P. There is no positive evidence that the electorate paid much attention to whether Conservative or Labour candidates were women. However, as in 1964, there is clear evidence that Liberal women do worse than men. The Liberal vote dropped 6·5% where a woman candidate replaced a man but 3·0% where the replacement was the other way round.

Among Conservative candidates fighting constituencies in place of sitting M.P.s who had withdrawn, the above average swing suggests that the former M.P. had built up a small personal vote (averaging about 250) — but the evidence on the Labour side suggests the reverse. The high swing in seats where a Conservative M.P. was defeated in

[1] In *Tribune* (July 23rd, 1965) 73 Labour M.P.s published a statement calling for defence expediture to be reduced by at least a quarter.

1964 and which had a sitting Labour M.P. in 1966 provides some confirmation that M.P.s may draw a few personal votes. A few Conservative M.P.s may therefore have survived the swing to Labour at the last two elections because of an above average personal vote built up over the years. Possible claimants to this distinction are Raymond Gower (Barry), Brian Harrison (Maldon), Geoffrey Hirst (Shipley), Sir Harmar Nicholls (Peterborough), David Price (Eastleigh), James Prior (Lowestoft) and Dame Joan Vickers (Devonport). But perhaps the best claimant of all is the leader of the Conservative party. When Edward Heath won Bexley in 1950, it was as marginal as nearby Chislehurst and Woolwich West and much more marginal than Lewisham North, Lewisham West and Norwood. Now Labour has gained these five while Bexley, where Mr. Heath has improved on the national swing at every election he has fought there, has a fair Conservative majority.

Other local effects. There is little evidence that local organisation had any effect as far as the two main parties were concerned. During the campaign the authors of this book again asked Conservative area agents and Labour regional organisers to name the seats where they expected a better than average result because of improvements in local party organisation since 1964. In the seats spotted by the Conservatives the average swing was 3·3% in those spotted by Labour organisers it was 3·7%. This barely significant difference is still less if allowance is made for large cities. Organisation may have helped slightly to bring out voters: the turnout increased on average by 1·0% in the seats named by one or other of the parties. But since most of these seats were also marginals, it is difficult to judge whether organisation or public awareness of a close fight was the primary cause.

Local issues can hardly have played much part. Despite the way in which the 1965 agricultural price review had been greeted, the swing in agricultural areas was much more favourable to Labour than in 1964. Nor was there much sign of any reaction to government's defence cuts (for Preston, see p. 244) except possibly for the low swing in naval Portsmouth; nor did constituencies particularly affected by local rows over comprehensive schools or by projected steel nationalisation swing distinctively.

During the campaign there were reports of strong feeling over crime in general and the restoration of capital punishment in particular. Several Conservative candidates, mainly in North-western England and on Clydeside, reacted by advocating capital or corporal punishment.[1] Only in Nelson & Colne did the Independent candidate tap this strong

---

[1] At the beginning of the campaign Gallup asked which party could best handle a series of issues. 'Hanging and Capital Punishment' was the only one of twenty-two issues mentioned on which the Conservatives had improved their standing compared to 1964. *Gallup Political Index*, no. 71, pp. 36–37.

feeling with a vote of 13·7% (see p. 261). The swing was low in Glasgow compared with other large cities but higher than in nearby areas of Western Scotland; it was relatively high in the North West and particularly so in some constituencies, such as Ashton-under-Lyme and Moss Side, where Conservative candidates had given the issue prominence.

Immigration similarly seems to have affected pre-election commentators much more than voters. The return of Smethwick to its previous allegiance had been foreshadowed by the Warley borough elections earlier in the year and may have owed something to the Conservative Council in Smethwick's handling of local housing problems as well as to the cooling of feelings on immigration. The swing to Labour in areas with concentrations of immigrants was above average; but not necessarily owing to popular acceptance of the government's policy. Mr. Freeson, one of the leading critics of that policy, secured one of the highest swings to Labour in Willesden East with its high concentration of immigrants, and a free-lance anti-immigrant candidate polled a derisory 1·4%.

By-elections and the general election. By-elections during the 1964–66 parliament presented some contrast to the 1966 general election. The average swing in all thirteen contests was 2·5% to the Conservatives; even the three that took place after the government's recovery in early autumn of 1965 showed a swing to Labour of only 1·2%. Probably the best measure of the difference between a government's performance in by-elections and in the subsequent general election is the difference between the individual by-election results and the subsequent general election results in the same constituencies. By this measure the average swing to the government in 1966, compared to the three by-elections of the previous six months, was 3·1%, only a little more than at other post-war general elections.[1] The Hull North by-election turned out to have been an extremely misleading guide; the large swing to Labour then was still 3·8% less than in March. A January by-election in a constituency typical of the national swing in March would presumably therefore have shown practically no swing.[2]

The Liberal party, despite the drop in its vote, fared better than had seemed likely from by-elections. Although the average Liberal vote remained unchanged in the ten by-elections during the first year of the 1964–66 parliament, it plunged by 7·2% in the last three contests from November 1965 on. Liberal candidates stood again in each of

---

[1] The pro-government swing compared to immediately preceding by-elections has ranged from 1·6% (1955) to 3·1% (1959); including 1966, the average swing to the government has been 2·4%.
[2] See pp. 41–42 for the influence of Hull North on timing of the general election.

these three at the general election and in each their vote recovered compared to the by-election, on average by 2·0%. As in 1964 and several earlier general elections, the Liberal party was able to improve in general election conditions on the immediately preceding by-elections.

Minor parties. Of the other groups contesting the election, the Communists and Welsh Nationalists more or less held their own, the Scottish Nationalists advanced to their strongest electoral position ever while various anti-immigrant groups lost ground. This was despite the fact that the Communist party, the Scottish Nationalists, the British National Party and the Union Movement all put up more candidates than in 1964.

Of the forty-five Communist candidates standing in seats fought by their party at any time since the war, 19 improved on their party's previous vote while 26 lost ground; on average there was a drop of 0·5% since 1964. The Communist vote averaged 4·7% in South Wales, 3·8% in the former County of London, 3·6% on Clydeside and 2·2% in the rest of the country; overall their 57 candidates averaged 3·0% compared with 3·4% in 1964.

The Welsh Nationalists fought 19 seats they had contested in 1964 and one new one; in the comparable 19, ten candidates gained and nine lost support, the average change being a drop of 0·1%. Liberal intervention halved the Nationalist vote in Wrexham while an increased Nationalist vote in Anglesey and Llanelly reflected Liberal withdrawal. The only other large changes in 1964 votes were the continued decline in Merioneth and the continued build-up of strength in Carmarthen. The overall average vote was 8·7% compared to 8·4% in 1964.

The Scottish Nationalists achieved their first major electoral advance. Thirteen nationalists stood in seats fought in 1964 and twelve of them improved their vote; in these thirteen seats the average rise was 3·2%. The average vote for all 23 candidates standing was 14·1%, compared with 10·7% in 1964. However, most of their success was concentrated in one part of Scotland, a region around the Forth and Tay.[1] In this area the SNP fought every seat and saved every deposit; it polled an average of 18·7% and improved its vote by 4·6%. In the rest of the country, the party only put up twelve candidates for sixty seats and lost desposits in ten of them with an average vote of 10·7% and an average improvement of 1·5%. Their challenge was especially weak in Northern Scotland and in the capital city, Edinburgh.

It is very difficult to understand why this Forth–Tay area should be so much more Nationalist than the rest of Scotland; it is a very varied region of both Labour industrial areas (including West Lothian with its

[1] The administrative counties of Clackmannanshire, Fife, Kinross-shire, Midlothian, Perthshire, Stirlingshire, and West Lothian.

remarkable Nationalist vote of 35·3%[1]) and Conservative rural strong-holds. It is certainly no coincidence that the Liberal upsurge in Northern Scotland has not affected this region; although discussion in both the Liberal and Scottish Nationalist Parties about a pact led nowhere, the two parties avoided fighting each other[2] and it is quite likely that their respective successes in different parts of Scotland reflect some common causes.

Thirty-six other candidates stood,[3] fewer than in 1964. Nine can be grouped as anti-immigrant: including four Union Movement (average 3·7%, compared with 5% for three Union Movement candidates standing in 1959–62) and three BNP (average 4·5% compared with the 6% for the anti-immigrant candidates standing in the same seat in 1964). The other 27 included one outstanding personal success for Mr. Downey in Nelson & Colne (see p. 261); his 13·7% was higher than any vote for an Independent who was neither a former M.P. nor someone standing on a split in a local political association since 1945. Although most of the rest secured derisory votes, six[4] polled over 4% on a variety of platforms.

Northern Ireland. Perhaps the most interesting feature of the election in Northern Ireland was the way in which non-Unionist candidates avoided splitting the non-Unionist vote. By and large this seems to have been achieved informally as in Belfast West (see p. 255) where it led to the first defeat for a Unionist in Northern Ireland since 1955. Where two non-Unionists competed (in South Down, Fermanagh & South Tyrone and Londonderry) it was noticeable that the more moderate candidate pushed the Republican into third place. Comparison with the 1964 election is misleading since most of the non-Unionist candidates improved their vote through lack of competition; the Unionist share of the total vote dropped only slightly from 63·0% to 61·8%. However, it is clear that there was a marked movement from the Unionists to the Northern Ireland Labour party: the swing averaged 8·2% in the four seats fought by the latter.

The electoral system. Under the British electoral system, argument about vote-splitting is inevitable. There is bound to be constant speculation about what would have happened in a straight fight or, more hypothetically, what would have happened under the alternative vote

---

[1] This was the highest vote for any candidate in Great Britain not supported by one of the three main parties since 1945.

[2] Together the two parties fought forty-four seats in Scotland but fought each other only in three of them.

[3] Not including Itchen where no party political candidates stood and the Speaker defeated an Independent opponent who barely saved his deposit.

[4] Bootle (Ind. Lab. 6%). Bristol Central (5·1%), Dearne Valley (4·8%), Islington South-West (5·1%), Stratford-upon-Avon (Ind. Con. 4·0%) and Tyne-mouth (Ind. Lib. 6·5%).

system. In either case the assumptions involved are similar and mainly revolve around Liberal candidates who take third place.

The evidence of the effect of Liberal intervention and withdrawal in marginal seats (see p. 274) suggests that, on average, Liberal withdrawal was worth a swing of 0·5% to Conservative: equivalent to 55:45 split of Liberal votes in such seats in favour of the Conservatives. However, it is clear that the ratio of such a split would vary regionally: in a Southern English rural seat Labour would probably still have been the net loser.[1] A further complication peculiar to the 1966 general election is that, whereas there were seven seats won by Labour which even a 60:40 split of the Liberal vote would have given to the Conservatives, there were no less than 22 where a similar split of a Liberal vote in favour of Labour would have enabled Labour candidates to win Conservative seats. It is doubtful whether the Conservatives would, on balance, have gained from Liberal withdrawal for although the Liberal vote would probably have split more often in their favour, there were nearly four times as many seats where Labour could have benefited from a locally favourable split. If in every seat the Liberal vote had split uniformly 55:45 in favour of the Conservatives the Conservatives would have retained four seats gained by Labour (Bedford, Croydon South, Harrow East, and Rushcliffe). But in four Southern English rural, or partly rural, seats (Lowestoft, Maldon, South Norfolk, and Peterborough) Labour would have won on a split of 55:45 or less. In the circumstances, perhaps the most sensible assumption is that neither party would have benefited significantly from the withdrawal of all Liberal candidates in marginal seats, or from the transfer of their votes.

There is less room for arguments about other cases where M.P.s were elected on minority votes. Communist candidates cost Labour Hornsey, and possibly Mitcham. It is reasonably certain that the Liberals would have won East Aberdeenshire, Banff, Caithness & Sutherland, Cardigan, Chippenham, Denbigh and Scarborough & Whitby in a straight fight, or with the alternative vote; it is probable in Torrington and possible in North Dorset and Eastbourne.[2] The only other constituency possibly affected was Merioneth, but it is very uncertain how Welsh Nationalist votes would split between Labour and Liberal.

In the table below these probable cases (but not the possible ones)

---

[1] See *The British General Election of 1964*, p. 349, for an estimate of the regional variations in 1964; the evidence in 1966 is more scanty but by and large confirms the same pattern except for some indications that in the Greater London area the Liberal vote may have since become more pro-Conservative.

[2] It is assumed that a Liberal could be reasonably certain of a 60% net transfer (equivalent to an 80:20 split) from a third place Labour, Conservative or Scottish Nationalist vote; could probably count on 70% and possibly on 80%.

are allowed for in a calculation of what the result of the 1966 general election might have been under the alternative vote system; it involves the unavoidable but very dubious assumption that a change in the electoral system would not itself change voting behaviour. A similar assumption is also necessary in calculating what the result might have been under the single transferable vote system (the form of proportional representation favoured by the Liberal party). This estimate is made by combining the present constituencies into multi-member seats of three to seven M.P.s each.[1] The figures are necessarily approximate as they involve assumptions about the allocation of second and lower preferences and about a party's strength in seats it has not fought. But the two estimates may serve to indicate the sort of results that a different electoral system might produce:

	Labour	Con-servative	Liberal	Others*
Actual result . . .	364	253	12	1
Alternative vote . .	363	246	20	1
Single transferable vote .	320	265	39	6

* The Speaker is included with Labour. The six others under the STV system are two Scottish Nationalists, one Welsh Nationalist and three assorted Irish Nationalists (presumably one Republican Labour, one orthodox Nationalist, and one Republican).

The relationship between seats and votes 1966. The electoral system actually in use continued to work with fairly predictable regularity. On a uniform two-party swing of 3·5% Labour should have won 52 seats which had elected a Conservative in 1964;[2] in fact Labour took 47 such seats. Only two Conservative seats fell to a swing of more than 4·5% (Cardiff North and Conway), but six vulnerable to a swing of 2·5% were saved — Ayr, South Dorset (where following their 1962 by-election gain, the 1964 result had overstated Labour's strength), Eastleigh, Hendon North, Maldon, and the perennially perverse South-west Norfolk. On the 1959–66 comparison, the regularity is more striking: if the 7·0% swing had been completely uniform Labour would have gained 100 seats from the Conservatives; in fact the net Labour gain from Conservative was 103.

[1] The STV system is the more proportional the larger the number of M.P.s per constituency. The Electoral Reform Society has published an estimate using smaller constituencies of 328 Labour, 265 Conservative, 33 Liberal and 4 Others (*Representation*, April 1966).

[2] Defining swing by averaging the percentage gain and loss of the two parties, the mean swing of 3·1%, uniformly applied, would have meant 51 such Labour gains. The values of the two versions of swing for prediction is much the same.

U

The table below shows the relationship of seats and votes after the 1966 election; to retain consistency with similar tables in the past the same definition of swing is used (based on percentages of the total votes as in the full tables starting on p. 313). The table shows that the bias against the Labour party, evident during the 1950s, has now been replaced by an apparent bias in favour of Labour. If by a uniform swing, the Labour and Conservative votes were made equal, Labour would still have an overall parliamentary majority of eight seats — or a lead of twenty-two over the Conservatives.

Seats and votes 1966*

Swing to Conservative				Swing to Labour		
Con.	Lab.	Con. lead over Lab.		Lab.	Con.	Lab. lead over Con.
253	364	−111	Actual result	364	253	111
272	345	−73	1%	386	231	155
279	337	−58	2%	405	211	194
297	319	−22	3%	422	194	228
316	304	12	4%	450	165	285
337	284	53	5%	471	144	327
381	242	139	7½%	511	105	406
426	196	230	10%	539	75	464

* In this table allowance is made for seats that would be lost or gained by the Liberal party as a consequence of uniform swings between the two main parties; hence the total of seats won by the two parties varies slightly. The Speaker's seat is included with Labour.

In 1950 the bias against Labour, in terms of a likely Conservative lead of seats for an equal division of the vote, amounted to 35 seats.[1] An equivalent bias would operate in 1966 if, with the actual distribution of seats, the Labour lead in votes had been 9% instead of the actual 6%. Earlier (see p. 272) it was estimated that the drop in turnout in safe Labour seats meant that Labour's share of the national vote was about 1% less than it would otherwise have been; on this estimate the Labour lead would be about 8%.[2] It is therefore evident that the major part, and perhaps the whole, of the disappearance of the bias reflects the drop in turnout in safe Labour seats.

[1] See *The British General Election of 1950* by H. G. Nicholas, p. 330.
[2] In *Parliamentary Affairs*, vol. XIX, 1966, no. 3, p. 340, Peter Bromhead estimated what the 1966 division of the national vote would have been with turnout at the 1951 level: his estimate amounts to a Labour lead of 8·7%. However, he later argued (p. 342) that the population shift and consequent maldistribution of seats was 'probably a more important' factor than the turnout in Labour seats.

Another possible reason why Labour no longer appeared so handi-capped by the electoral system is that the electorate had fallen in most Labour seats but risen in most Conservative ones since the last redistri-bution in 1954. Certainly in 1966 the electoral boundaries favoured Labour and the Conservatives now stand to benefit from the impending redistribution. However, to argue that the shifts of population had affected the relationship of seats and votes, one must find the seats which changed hands as a consequence; the mere transfer of Labour voters across constituency boundaries could not otherwise affect the bias. In fact Labour gains attributable to an influx of new voters were few in number and there were as many which population changes may have saved for the Conservatives.[1]

Impending redistribution considerably reduces the value of the table above showing the likely effect of swings from the 1966 result. How far the precise figures in this table will be applicable to the next election will depend on the new constituency boundaries. They presumably underestimate Conservative and overestimate Labour strength. But once an adjustment for redistribution effects has been made, a regular relationship between seats and votes should still be evident.

[1] The only plausible such Labour gains since 1954 are Heeley, Middleton & Prestwich, Monmouth and Putney; population shifts may equally have saved Barry, Brierley Hill, Chigwell, Eastleigh, and South Gloucestershire for the Conservatives.

The National Results, 1945–1966

	Electorate and turnout	Votes cast	Conservative	Labour	Liberal	Nationalist†	Communist	Others
1945*	73·3% 32,836,419	100% 24,082,612	39·8% 9,577,667	48·3% 11,633,891	9·1% 2,197,191	0·6% 138,415	0·4% 102,760	1·8% 433,688
1950	84·0% 34,269,770	100% 28,772,671	43·5% 12,502,567	46·1% 13,266,592	9·1% 2,621,548	0·6% 173,161	0·3% 91,746	0·4% 117,057
1951	82·5% 34,645,573	100% 28,595,668	48·0% 13,717,538	48·8% 13,948,605	2·5% 730,556	0·5% 145,521	0·1% 21,640	0·1% 31,808
1955	76·8% 34,858,263	100% 26,760,493	49·7% 13,311,936	46·4% 12,404,970	2·7% 722,405	0·9% 225,591	0·1% 33,144	0·2% 62,447
1959	78·7% 35,397,080	100% 27,859,241	49·4% 13,749,830	43·8% 12,215,538	5·9% 1,638,571	0·6% 182,788	0·1% 30,897	0·2% 61,619
1964	77·1% 35,892,572	100% 27,655,374	43·4% 12,001,396	44·1% 12,205,814	11·2% 3,092,878	0·9% 249,866	0·2% 45,932	0·2% 53,116
1966	75·8% 35,964,684	100% 27,263,606	41·9% 11,418,433	47·9% 13,064,951	8·5% 2,327,533	1·2% 315,431	0·2% 62,112	0·3% 75,146

* University seats are excluded: other 1945 figures are adjusted to eliminate the distortions introduced by double voting in the 15 two-member seats then existing.
† Including all types of Irish Nationalist.

The House of Commons, 1945–1966

	1945	1950	1951	1955	1959	1964	1966
Conservative	213	298	321	345	365	304	253
Labour	393	315	295	277	258	317	363
Liberal	12	9	6	6	6	9	12
Others	22	3	3	2	1	0	2
Total	640	625	625	630	630	630	630

Regional Results

Most areas in the tables are self-explanatory. There is no overlapping between sub-areas, and no overlapping between areas into which sub-areas are grouped. But the following sub-areas seem to require further definition:

Area	Sub-area	Constituencies included
County of London	East End	Bethnal Green, N. Hackney and Stoke Newington, Central Hackney, Poplar, Shoreditch and Finsbury, Stepney.
	Business and Residential	Chelsea, Westminster, Hampstead, Kensington, Paddington, St. Marylebone.
	Remainder	Baron's Court, Fulham, N. Hammersmith, Islington, Holborn and St. Pancras S., St. Pancras N.
Suburban Boroughs	Middlesex,	All constituencies in the former county of Middlesex.
	Kent, Surrey, Essex	All boroughs in Kent, Surrey, and Essex on the fringe of London and the Dartford division of Kent.
South-east England	Kent, Surrey	All constituencies in Kent and Surrey not included in suburban boroughs.
	Sussex	All constituencies in Sussex.
Wessex	Hampshire Ports	Portsmouth, Gosport and Fareham, Southampton.
	Remainder	The rest of Hampshire, Dorset and the Salisbury and Westbury divisions of Wilts.
Severn	Glos. and N. Wilts.	All Glos. (except Bristol), Swindon and the Chippenham and Devizes divisions of Wilts.
Outer Essex	Outer Essex	All constituencies in Essex except for the boroughs on the fringe of London.
West Midlands	Black Country	All boroughs in S. Staffordshire and N. Worcestershire.
	Potteries	Newcastle-under-Lyme and Stoke on Trent.
	Salop, Herefordshire, Worcs.	All constituencies in these counties except Dudley, and Oldbury and Halesowen.
North-east Midlands	Leics., Notts., Northants.	The cities of Nottingham and Leicester are not included.
Lancashire	N. Lancashire	S. Fylde, Clitheroe, and all constituencies to their north.
	S. Lancashire	The rest of Lancashire, except for Liverpool and Manchester.
North and East Riding	Counties and York	All constituencies in the N. and E. Ridings of Yorkshire, together with York, except for Hull and Middlesbrough.
North-east England	Boroughs	Middlesbrough, all boroughs in Durham (except Jarrow), Blyth, Tynemouth, Wallsend and the Morpeth division of Northumberland.
	Durham Counties	All county constituencies in Durham and the borough constituency of Jarrow.
Border	Border	Cumberland, Westmorland and the Berwick and Hexham divisions of Northumberland.
Wales	Industrial Wales	Glamorgan, Monmouth and the Llanelly division of Carmarthenshire.
	Rural Wales	The remainder of Wales
Scotland	Highlands	Perth and Kinross, Argyll, Inverness and all the constituencies to their north.
	North-east	Moray and Nairn, Banff, Aberdeenshire, Angus and Kincardine.
	Clyde	Dunbartonshire, Renfrewshire and Lanarkshire (except the Lanark division).
	Forth	Fife, Stirling and Clackmannan, West Lothian and Edinburgh.
	Lowlands	Ayrshire, the Lanark division of Lanarkshire, the county division of Midlothian and all constituencies to their south.

Regional Results

THE WHOLE COUNTRY	Electorate (in '000s)	% voting	Change in % voting 1964–1966	Members Elected				Votes (as % of votes cast in constituencies where the party concerned put up candidates)				Swing (Average of Con. and Lab. % gain and Lab. % loss)	
				Con.	Lab.	Lib.	Total	Con.	Lab.	Lib.	Other‡	1964–1966	1959–1964
UNITED KINGDOM .	35,964	75·8	−1·3	253	363	12	630*†	629 41·8	621 48·7	311 16·1	125 8·6	−3·1	−2·9
GREAT BRITAIN England . . .	29,900	75·9	−1·1	219	285	6	511*	510 42·8	510 47·9	273 15·6	62 3·0	−2·8	−3·0
Wales . . .	1,802	79·0	−1·1	3	32	1	36	27·9	60·7	11 19·5	23 8·6	−2·2	−2·9
Scotland . . .	3,361	75·9	−1·7	20	46	5	71	37·6	49·9	24 22·2	34 11·0	−2·1	−4·0
Total . . .	35,063	76·0	−1·2	242	363	12	618*	617 41·5	617 48·8	308 16·1	119 6·4	−2·7	−3·2

* Includes the Speaker. † Includes 1 Republican Labour. ‡ Throughout this column the votes cast in Southampton, Itchen, are ignored.

The small figures above the percentages indicate the number of seats fought by Liberals and others and by Conservative and Labour in the few cases when they did not fight every seat. The Conservatives fought every seat except Southampton, Itchen. Labour fought every seat in Great Britain except Southampton, Itchen, but only 4 of the 12 seats in Northern Ireland.

AREAS OF ENGLAND	Electorate (in '000s)	% voting	Change in % voting 1964–1966	Members Elected				Votes (as % of votes cast in constituencies where the party concerned put up candidates)				Swing (Average of Con. % gain and Lab. % loss)	
				Con.	Lab.	Lib.	Total	Con.	Lab.	Lib.	Other	1964–1966	1959–1964
ENGLAND													
London Area	5,231	71·5	+0·2	34	66	—	100	40·7	49·9	[64] 11·5	[22] 3·3	−3·1	−4·2
South and East	9,485	78·7	−0·4	106	37	4	148*	[147] 47·4	[147] 38·8	[115] 17·2	[9] 1·7†	−2·1	−3·1
Midlands	5,805	76·1	−1·6	35	61	—	96	43·2	51·5	[33] 14·4	[12] 2·5	−3·4	−1·8
North	9,378	75·2	−2·4	44	121	2	167	38·8	54·3	[61] 17·0	[19] 3·4	−3·3	−3·4
Total	29,900	75·9	−1·1	219	285	6	511*	[510] 42·8	[510] 47·9	[273] 15·6	[62]† 3·0	−2·8	−3·0
LONDON AREA													
County of London	2,080	64·9	+0·2	6	36	—	42	36·9	56·7	[20] 10·5	[13] 4·2	−3·5	−4·3
Suburban Boroughs	3,151	75·8	+0·1	28	30	—	58	42·9	46·0	[44] 13·9	[9] 2·4	−2·8	−4·3
Total	5,231	71·5	+0·2	34	66	—	100	40·7	49·9	[64] 11·5	[22] 3·3	−3·1	−4·2
SOUTH AND EAST													
South-east	2,410	77·7	−0·1	30	5	1	36	50·6	33·1	[30] 19·1	[13] 1·6	−2·2	−3·6
Wessex	1,355	75·5‡	−1·7‡	18	2	—	21*	[20] 49·3	[20] 35·1	[17] 17·6	—†	−1·1‡	−4·1
West of England	836	80·9	+2·0	9	3	3	15	45·7	31·3	[13] 27·2	—	−2·3	−2·7

Severn	1,298	79·2	-0·6	14	8	—	22	44·3	43·9	[14] 17·2	[3] 2·4	-2·0	-2·5
South-central . .	1,766	81·1	-0·1	16	9	—	25	46·5	42·9	[20] 13·7	[1] 1	-2·8	-3·6
Outer Essex . .	852	80·0	+0·2	9	3	—	12	46·4	42·9	[12] 13·7	1·2	-2·3	-3·0
East Anglia . .	964	80·4	+0·2	10	7	—	17	46·8	46·1	[9] 12·1	[2] 1·1	-2·6	-1·0
Total . .	9,485	78·9	-0·4	106	37	4	148*	[147] 47·4	[147] 38·8	[115] 17·2	[9†] 1·7	-2·1	-3·1
MIDLANDS													
West Midlands .	3,243	74·8	-1·2	22	32	—	54	44·7	50·8	[15] 15·5	[10] 2·6	-3·9	-1·6
North-east Midlands	2,041	78·2	-2·3	7	26	—	33	40·3	53·7	[14] 13·3	[2] 1·8	-2·7	-2·0
Lincolnshire .	521	75·8	-1·5	6	3	—	9	45·8	47·8	15·2	—	-3·7	-4·5
Total . .	5,805	76·1	-1·6	35	61	—	96	43·2	51·5	[33] 14·4	2·5	-3·4	-1·8
NORTH OF ENGLAND													
Cheshire . .	979	78·7	-2·0	9	6	1	16	45·3	41·0	[10] 20·4	[1] 1·5	-3·0	-4·5
Lancashire . .	3,406	73·2	-2·7	14	48	—	62	40·1	53·6	[22] 14·7	[0] 4·0	-3·2	-4·7
West Riding .	2,410	75·7	-2·2	9	33	1	43	35·0	58·3	[15] 18·4	[5] 3·2	-3·5	-2·6
East and North Riding	690	75·1	-1·5	6	5	—	11	43·9	43·7	[8] 16·9	[1] 0·9	-5·1	-3·1
North-east . .	1,557	75·2	-3·2	2	26	—	28	33·7	65·3	[2] 8·7	[3] 4·0	-3·7	-2·7
Border . .	336	78·9	-2·9	4	3	—	7	45·3	44·1	[4] 18·9	—	-2·9	-2·9
Total . .	9,378	75·2	-2·4	44	121	2	167	38·8	54·3	[61] 17·0	[19] 3·4	-3·4	-3·4

* Includes the Speaker. † The votes in Southampton, Itchen, are ignored in this column. ‡ See note on next page.

Sub-areas of England	Electorate (in '000s)	% voting	Change in % voting 1964-1966	Members Elected Con.	Lab.	Lib.	Total	Votes (as % of votes cast in constituencies where the party concerned put up candidates) Con.	Lab.	Lib.	Other	Swing (Average of Con. gain and Lab. % loss) 1964-1966	1959-1964
COUNTY OF LONDON													
South of Thames . . .	996	69·1	−0·1	1	19	—	20	37·5	57·9	10·2 [7]	4·0 [4]	−3·4	−4·5
East End . . .	322	55·4	−1·0	—	6	—	6	21·0	71·5	13·7 [2]	5·3 [3]	−4·8	−2·5
Business and Residential .	391	63·9	+1·8	5	3	—	8	49·6	39·3	10·8 [8]	1·1 [2]	−3·7	−6·6
Remainder . . .	371	63·0	+0·5	—	8	—	8	33·7	60·4	8·5 [3]	5·5 [4]	−3·6	−4·0
Total . . .	2,080	64·9	+0·2	6	36	—	42	36·9	56·7	10·5 [20]	4·2 [13]	−3·5	−4·3
SUBURBAN BOROUGHS													
Middlesex . . .	1,532	75·9	+0·2	15	14	—	29	43·8	44·6	14·2 [22]	3·3 [5]	−3·1	−4·2
Kent and Surrey . .	857	78·5	+0·8	11	4	—	15	47·2	40·0	14·1 [13]	1·2 [2]	−2·5	−6·0
Essex . . .	762	72·8	−0·6	2	12	—	14	36·0	56·2	12·5 [9]	1·9 [2]	−2·7	−4·1
Total . . .	3,151	75·8	+0·1	28	30	—	58	42·9	46·0	13·9 [44]	2·4 [9]	−2·8	−4·3

	Votes	% voting	±				Total						
SOUTH-EAST ENGLAND													
Kent	921	78·7	−0·1	9	4	1	14	48·0	39·7	16·9 [10]	—	−1·8	−3·0
Surrey	659	78·8	−0·3	10	—	—	10	51·3	28·3	20·4 [10]	—	−2·2	−3·5
Sussex	830	75·6	+0·1	11	1	—	12	53·1	29·4	20·2 [10]	1·6 [3]	−2·4	−4·4
Total	2,410	77·7	−0·1	30	5	1	36	50·6	33·1	19·1 [30]	1·6 [3]	−2·2	−3·6
WESSEX													
Hampshire Ports	418	70·4‖	−4·7‖	3	2	—	6*	50·0 [5]	40·9 [5]	12·7 [3]	—†	+0·5‖	−5·3
Remainder	937	77·8	−0·4	15	—	—	15	49·1	33·1	18·9 [14]	—	−2·0	−3·4
Total	1,355	75·5‡	−1·7‡	18	2	—	21*	49·3 [20]	35·1 [20]	17·6 [17]	—†	−1·1‡	−4·1
WEST OF ENGLAND													
Cornwall	248	82·2	+2·8	2	1	2	5	41·4	27·8	30·9 [5]	—	−0·8	−0·5
Devon (except Plymouth)	456	81·1	+1·5	6	1	1	8	47·5	27·4	25·1 [8]	—	−2·6	−2·1
Plymouth	133	77·7	+2·4	1	1	—	2	47·6	53·4	—	—	−4·9	−4·1
Total	836	80·9	+2·0	9	3	3	15	45·7	31·3	27·2 [13]	—	−2·3	−2·7

* Includes the Speaker. † The votes cast in Southampton, Itchen, are ignored in this column. ‡ If Southampton, Itchen, is excluded these figures would read: % voting 77·0% (−0·2%), Swing −2·1%. ‖ If Southampton, Itchen, is excluded these figures would read: % voting 74·9% (−0·2%), Swing −2·3%.

SUB-AREAS OF ENGLAND (contd.)	Electorate (in '000s)	% voting	Change in % voting 1964–1966	Members Elected Con.	Members Elected Lab.	Members Elected Lib.	Members Elected Total	Votes (as % of votes cast in constituencies where the party concerned put up candidates) Con.	Lab.	Lib.	Other	Swing (Average of Con. % gain and Lab. % loss) 1964–1966	1959–1964
SEVERN													
Somerset, Glos. and N. Wilts. (exc. Bristol)	431	82·2	+0·1	7	—	—	7	45·8	38·1	16·7 (7)	—	−2·3	−2·3
	538	79·5	−0·6	6	3	—	9	43·7	43·5	18·2 (6)	1·8 (1)	−1·4	−2·5
Bristol	329	74·9	−1·4	1	5	—	6	43·3	53·1	19·6	2·6 (2)	−3·0	−3·1
Total	1,298	79·2	−0·6	14	8	—	22	44·3	43·9	17·2 (14)	2·4 (3)	−2·0	−2·5
SOUTH-CENTRAL													
Oxon., Berks., Bucks.	917	80·0	+0·1	9	4	—	13	47·4	40·6	14·7 (11)	—	−2·9	−3·1
Beds. and Herts.	849	82·0	−0·6	7	5	—	12	45·5	45·2	12·5 (9)	1·2 (1)	−2·8	−4·1
Total	1,766	81·1	−0·1	16	9	—	25	46·5	42·9	13·7 (20)	1·2 (1)	−2·8	−3·6

OUTER ESSEX .	852	80·0	+0·2	9	3	—	12	46·4	42·9	13·7 (12)	—	−2·3	−3·0
EAST ANGLIA													
Norfolk .	391	81·1	+0·5	3	5	—	8	47·7	51·0	10·8 (1)	—	−2·2	−1·2
Suffolk, Ely, Hunts., Cambs. .	573	80·0	+0·1	7	2	—	9	46·1	42·7	12·3 (8)	1·1 (2)	−3·0	−0·9
Total .	964	80·4	+0·2	10	7	—	17	46·8	46·1	12·1 (9)	1·1 (2)	−2·6	−1·0
WEST MIDLANDS													
Birmingham .	672	69·1	−0·3	4	9	—	13	41·6	53·6	14·1 (4)	2·4 (1)	−6·6	−2·5
Coventry .	202	79·1	−0·4	—	3	—	3	38·2	58·3	7·0 (1)	2·3 (1)	−4·4	−3·4
Black Country .	682	72·9	−0·5	2	9	—	11	43·6	56·3	—	1·5 (1)	−3·8	+0·6
Potteries .	239	72·7	−4·0	—	4	—	4	33·5	65·8	—	5·1 (1)	−4·6	−1·8
Staffs. and Warwick. Counties .	891	78·8	−1·6	7	6	—	13	48·3	45·7	15·3 (5)	2·5 (2)	−2·3	−2·1
Salop, Hereford, Worcs. .	557	77·0	−2·2	9	1	—	10	50·6	40·6	19·3 (5)	2·7 (1)	−3·2	−2·7
Total .	3,243	74·8	−1·2	22	32	—	54	44·7	50·8	15·5 (15)	2·6 (10)	−3·9	−1·6

Sub-areas of England (contd.)	Electorate (in '000s)	% voting	Change in % voting 1964–1966	Members Elected				Votes (as % of votes cast in constituencies where the party concerned put up candidates)				Swing (Average of Con. % gain and Lab. % loss)	
				Con.	Lab.	Lib.	Total	Con.	Lab.	Lib.	Other	1964–1966	1959–1964
North-East Midlands													
Nottingham . . .	238	74·0	−3·3	—	4	—	4	42·6	56·8	—	2·1 [1]	−4·2	−4·1
Leicester . . .	188	74·0	−2·9	1	3	—	4	44·4	52·9	11·8 [1]	—	−4·4	−2·6
Leics., Notts., Northants.	1,006	80·2	−1·6	5	10	—	15	41·3	50·2	13·2 [9]	1·3 [1]	−2·4	−1·5
Derbyshire . . .	610	77·9	−2·8	1	9	—	10	36·4	58·8	13·8 [4]	—	−2·2	−1·7
Total . . .	2,041	78·2	−2·3	7	26	—	33	40·3	53·7	13·3 [14]	1·8 [2]	−2·7	−2·0
Lincolnshire . . .	521	75·8	−1·5	6	3	—	9	45·8	47·8	15·2 [4]	—	−3·7	−2·6
Cheshire . . .	979	78·7	−2·0	9	6	1	16	45·3	41·0	20·4 [10]	1·5 [1]	−3·0	−4·5

LANCASHIRE												
Liverpool	446	64·5	−4·1	2	7	—	9	42·2	55·2	¹17·2	¹3·9	−2·7	−9·0
Manchester	440	67·8	−2·8	2	7	—	9	36·8	55·7	⁴12·4	²3·7	−4·5	−3·7
South Lancashire	1,976	73·1	−5·4	4	30	—	34	37·9	56·3	¹²14·1	4·6	−3·0	−4·3
North Lancashire	54ɔ	76·4	−0·5	6	4	—	10	49·1	41·3	⁵17·4	¹1·8	−3·8	−4·3
Total	3,406	73·2	−2·7	14	48	—	62	40·1	53·6	²²14·7	⁹4·0	−3·2	−4·7
WEST RIDING												
Sheffield	341	71·0	−1·9	1	5	—	6	33·7	62·7	¹16·2	²3·1	−4·8	−4·5
Leeds	338	70·2	−3·2	2	4	—	6	41·8	55·7	¹11·7	¹2·1	−4·0	−2·5
Bradford	198	74·3	−1·8	—	4	—	4	40·2	56·2	¹12·1	—	−5·1	−2·7
Remainder	1,533	78·2	−2·1	6	20	1	27	33·2	58·1	¹²19·7	²3·6	−3·0	−2·1
Total	2,410	75·7	−2·2	9	33	1	43	35·0	58·3	¹⁵18·4	⁵3·2	−3·6	−2·6
NORTH AND EAST RIDING												
County Divisions and York	498	75·4	−2·4	6	2	—	8	48·8	36·9	⁶19·2	¹0·9	−4·4	−3·7
Hull	192	74·3	−0·0	—	3	—	3	30·8	61·8	²10·4	—	−7·5	−3·4
Total	690	75·1	−1·5	6	5	—	11	43·9	43·7	⁸16·9	¹0·9	−5·1	−3·1

SUB-AREAS OF ENGLAND (contd.)	Electorate (in '000s)	% voting	Change in % voting 1964–1966	Members Elected				Votes (as % of votes cast in constituencies where the party concerned put up candidates)				Swing (Average of Con. % gain and Lab. % loss)	
				Con.	Lab.	Lib.	Total	Con.	Lab.	Lib.	Other	1964–1966	1959–1964
NORTH-EAST ENGLAND													
Newcastle . . .	189	74·8	−2·6	1	3	—	4	38·0	59·7	9·5[1]	1·6[1]	−5·7	−3·1
Boroughs . . .	821	75·8	−2·9	1	13	—	14	36·3	62·4	8·2[1]	4·6[2]	−3·8	−4·5
Durham County Divisions .	547	74·5	−3·8	—	10	—	10	28·1	71·9	—	—	−2·9	−0·9
Total . . .	1,557	75·2	−3·2	2	26	—	28	33·7	65·3	8·7[2]	4·0[3]	−3·7	−2·7
BORDER . . .	336	78·9	−2·9	4	3	—	7	45·3	44·1	18·9[4]	—	−2·9	−2·9

Areas of Wales	Electorate (in '000s)	% voting	Change in % voting 1964–1966	Members Elected				Votes (as % of votes cast in constituencies where the party concerned put up candidates)				Swing (Average of Con. % gain and Lab. % loss)	
				Con.	Lab.	Lib.	Total	Con.	Lab.	Lib.	Other	1964–1966	1959–1964
WALES													
Rural Areas . . .	611	81·0	−0·6	2	10	1	13	30·5	45·8	[9] 22·0	[13] 7·8	−1·9	−2·6*
Industrial Wales . .	1,191	78·0	−1·4	1	22	—	23	26·5	68·6	[2] 10·6	[10] 9·8	−2·4	−3·3
Total . . .	1,802	79·0	−1·1	3	32	1	36	27·9	60·7	[11] 19·5	[23] 8·6	−2·2	−2·9
INDUSTRIAL WALES													
Cardiff, Swansea, Newport .	363	77·8	−1·2	—	6	—	6	37·8	59·6	[1] 7·4	[1] 9·1	−2·9	−5·2
Remainder . . .	828	78·1	−1·5	1	16	—	17	21·6	72·5	[1] 14·1	[0] 9·9	−1·6	−2·5
Total . .	1,191	78·0	−1·4	1	22	—	23	26·5	68·6	[2] 10·6	[10] 9·8	−2·4	−3·3

* Because Conservatives left two seats unfought in 1959, this figure may overestimate the swing to Labour by about 1%.

x

Areas of Scotland	Electorate (in '000s)	% voting	Change in % voting 1964–1966	Members Elected				Votes (as % of votes cast in constituencies when the party concerned put up candidates)				Swing (Average of Con. % gain and Lab. % loss)	
				Con.	Lab.	Lib.	Total	Con.	Lab.	Lib.	Other	1964–1966	1959–1964
SCOTLAND													
Highlands	275	71·5	−1·3	3	2	3	8	39·0	30·1	37·2 (6)	17·5 (2)	−1·8	−6·4
North-east	475	74·7	−1·6	5	4	1	10	42·3	40·1	20·0 (8)	3·7 (8)	−2·4	−2·4
Clyde	1,295	74·8	−2·1	3	24	—	27	35·5	58·0	17·2 (3)	6·9 (16)	−1·7	−6·1
Forth	751	77·3	−1·5	5	10	—	15	34·9	50·0	10·9 (4)	17·8 (10)	−3·0	−3·9
Lowlands	565	80·1	−1·1	4	6	1	11	41·5	48·3	21·7 (3)	12·9 (3)	−1·6	−3·2
Total	3,361	75·9	−1·7	20	46	5	71	37·6	49·9	22·2 (24)	11·0 (34)	−2·1	−4·0
CLYDE													
Glasgow	636	71·1	−1·7	2	13	—	15	35·0	60·2	—	6·4 (10)	−2·2	−6·8
Lanark, Renfrew, Dunbarton	659	78·3	−2·7	1	11	—	12	35·9	56·0	17·2 (3)	7·4 (6)	−1·2	−5·4
Total	1,295	74·8	−2·1	3	24	—	27	35·5	58·0	17·2 (3)	6·9 (16)	−1·7	−6·1
FORTH													
Edinburgh	330	76·8	−1·9	4	3	—	7	46·0	47·4	11·4 (3)	4·7 (2)	−3·0	−4·6
Fife, Stirling, W. Lothian	421	77·6	−1·3	1	7	—	8	26·4	52·1	9·5 (1)	20·4 (8)	−2·8	−3·4
Total	751	77·3	−1·5	5	10	—	15	34·9	50·0	10·9 (4)	17·8 (10)	−3·0	−3·9

NORTHERN IRELAND	Electorate (in '000s)	% voting	Change in % voting 1964-1966	Members Elected				Votes (as % of votes cast in constituencies where the party concerned put up candidates)				Swing	
				U.U.	N.I. Lab.	Lib.	Total	U.U.	N.I. Lab.	Lib.	Other	1964-1966	1959-1964
NORTHERN IRELAND Northern Ireland .	902	66·1	−5·5	11	—	—	12*	61·8	39·3	20·6	39·2	—	—

* Includes 1 Republican Labour.

Large Cities	Electorate (in '000s)	% voting	Change in % voting 1964–1966	Members Elected Con.	Lab.	Lib.	Total	Votes (as % of votes cast in constituencies where the party concerned put up candidates) Con.	Lab.	Lib.	Other	Swing (Average of Con. gain and Lab. % loss) 1964–1966	1959–1964
Greater London	5,415	71·9	+0·3	37	65	1	103	41·1	48·5	[67] 14·2	[22] 3·3	−3·0	−4·0
Glasgow	636	71·1	−1·7	2	13	—	15	35·0	60·2	—	[10] 6·4	−2·2	−6·8
Birmingham	672	69·1	−0·3	4	9	—	13	41·6	53·6	[4] 14·1	[4] 2·4	−6·6	−2·5
Liverpool	446	64·5	−4·1	2	7	—	9	42·2	55·2	[1] 17·2	[1] 3·9	−2·7	−9·0
Manchester	440	67·8	−2·8	2	7	—	9	36·8	55·7	[1] 12·4	[2] 3·7	−4·5	−3·7
Edinburgh	330	76·8	−1·9	4	3	—	7	46·0	47·4	[1] 11·4	[2] 4·7	−3·0	−4·6
Bristol	329	74·9	−1·4	1	5	—	6	43·3	53·1	[1] 19·6	[2] 2·6	−3·0	−3·1
Leeds	338	70·2	−3·2	2	4	—	6	41·8	55·7	[1] 11·7	[1] 2·1	−4·0	−2·5
Sheffield	341	71·0	−1·9	1	5	—	6	33·7	62·7	[1] 16·2	[1] 3·1	−4·8	−4·5
Belfast	242	70·9	−0·4	3	—	—	4*	55·7	41·1	—	52·0	−6·1†	−0·4*
Bradford	198	74·3	−1·8	—	4	—	4	40·2	56·2	[1] 12·1	—	−5·1	−2·7
Leicester	188	74·0	−2·9	1	3	—	4	44·4	52·9	[1] 11·8	[1] 1·6	−4·4	−2·6
Newcastle	189	74·8	−2·6	1	3	—	4	38·0	59·7	[1] 9·5	[1] 2·1	−5·7	−3·1
Nottingham	238	74·0	−3·3	—	4	—	4	42·6	56·8	—	—	−4·2	−4·1
Cardiff	182	77·7	−1·3	—	3	—	3	41·2	56·1	[1] 7·4	[2] 2·3	−3·2	−6·5
Coventry	202	79·1	−0·4	—	3	—	3	38·2	58·3	[1] 7·0	—	−4·4	−3·4
Hull	192	74·3	−0·0	—	3	—	3	30·8	61·8	[2] 10·4	—	−7·5	−3·4
Portsmouth	196	73·7	−0·2	2	1	—	3	51·5	41·2	[1] 14·8	[1] 5·1	−2·1	−6·3
Stoke-on-Trent	175	70·6	−4·1	—	3	—	3	31·3	66·9	—	—	−4·8	−1·7

* Includes 1 Republican Labour. † Swing for the 3 seats fought by N.I. Lab. in 1959 and 1966.

CONSTITUENCY RESULTS

London Boroughs

Constituency	% voting 1966	Change since 1964	Con. %	Lab. %	Lib. %	Other %	Lib. 1964–1966	Swing 1964–1966	Swing 1959–1964
Barons Court . .	75·2	+2·3	41·1	51·7	7·2	—	−1·2	−3·6	−2·9
Battersea, North .	63·2	−2·5	24·9	72·1	—	Cm 3·0	[9·3]	−4·2	−1·6
South . .	73·0	+0·7	38·3	52·9	8·8	—	−3·8	−4·2	−6·1
Bermondsey . .	60·9	−2·4	19·4	80·6	—	—	—	−1·3	−2·5
Bethnal Green . .	57·7	−1·5	17·0	69·7	13·3	—	−3·9	−3·1	−1·1
Camberwell, Dulwich.	73·7	−0·0	38·6	51·9	9·5	—	−2·3	−3·7	−5·1
Peckham . .	55·6	−2·5	28·0	72·0	—	—	—	−8·0	+1·2
Chelsea . . .	63·1	+0·4	59·9	28·1	12·0	—	−1·3	−2·2	−5·6
Cities of London and Westminster .	60·0	+0·3	54·7	35·1	10·2	—	−0·9	−4·1	−6·4
Deptford . . .	60·1	−0·0	26·2	66·7	—	BNP7·1	—	−3·6	−4·7
Fulham . . .	76·4	+3·2	38·0	58·3	—	2·1, 0·5, 0·4, Cm 0·7	—	−3·1	−3·3
Greenwich . .	67·7	−3·9	35·1	64·9	—	—	[12·8]	−2·3	−6·4
Hackney Central .	57·5	+0·4	22·1	63·8	14·1	—	*	−4·5	−4·8
Hammersmith North .	63·9	+0·8	31·2	68·8	—	—	—	−5·9	−3·5
Hampstead . .	72·4	+4·8	42·2	46·8	10·6	0·4	−6·8	−4·3	−10·6
Holborn & St. Pancras South . .	65·5	−2·0	40·5	59·5	—	—	—	−4·8	−5·8
Islington, East . .	57·1	−0·0	28·9	57·9	8·8	New Lib 4·4	−2·6	−2·5	−4·4
North . .	54·2	−0·5	30·7	59·4	9·9	—	−3·1	−2·6	−6·1
South-west .	50·9	−0·6	23·7	64·9	—	Ind 5·1 UM 3·3 Cm 3·10	—	−2·9	−2·7
Kensington, North .	62·1	+0·8	36·8	54·8	8·4	—	−0·7	−5·0	−2·8
South . .	58·1	+1·3	65·1	19·8	15·1	—	−0·4	−3·0	—
Lambeth, Brixton .	57·0	−0·0	38·7	61·3	—	—	—	−3·2	−5·0
Norwood . .	71·8	+4·0	42·9	48·8	8·3	—	−1·8	−3·5	−7·5
Vauxhall . .	58·6	−0·6	33·4	66·6	—	—	—	−2·5	−2·1
Lewisham, North .	77·4	+2·8	46·9	53·1	—	—	[10·1]	−3·5	−5·0
South . .	75·1	+0·3	30·3	56·9	12·8	—	−2·1	−3·4	−6·3
West . .	75·7	+0·9	47·5	52·5	—	—	[12·6]	−3·6	−6·1
Paddington, North .	66·4	+1·3	32·3	58·4	9·3	—	*	−5·2	−6·5
South . .	62·4	+4·0	48·3	41·5	10·2	—	−0·9	−4·9	−6·5
Poplar . . .	57·7	−0·6	15·5	84·5	—	—	—	−6·8	−0·5
St. Marylebone . .	65·1	+0·7	56·7	30·5	10·6	1·4, 0·8	−4·2	−0·6	−6·9
St. Pancras, North .	63·4	+0·8	32·0	64·2	—	Cm 3·8	—	−3·4	−5·1
Shoreditch & Finsbury	53·5	−2·2	24·3	71·1	—	UM 4·6	—	−5·0	−1·3
Southwark . .	54·0	−1·9	21·7	73·6	—	Cm 4·7	—	−4·7	−5·5
Stepney . . .	50·7	−0·6	16·6	76·1	—	Cm 7·3	—	−4·4	−1·3
Stoke Newington & Hackney North	55·8	−2·4	28·5	67·4	—	Cm 4·1	[14·0]	−5·1	−4·7
Wandsworth, Central .	74·2	−0·0	38·9	52·9	8·2	—	−1·9	−4·4	−4·6
Clapham . .	73·1	+0·8	40·6	51·6	7·8	—	+1·0	−4·8	−3·0
Putney . .	78·9	+1·9	41·9	48·3	9·8	—	−2·7	−2·0	−6·4
Streatham . .	70·4	−1·4	54·6	45·4	—	—	[14·1]	−2·0	−6·4
Woolwich, East .	67·0	−2·0	28·3	71·7	—	—	—	−3·4	−4·4
West . . .	81·4	+0·0	44·3	53·6	—	2·1	—	−2·6	−6·1

Notes for all constituency tables.

The swing (the average of the Conservative % gain and the Labour % loss) is given only where the two main parties shared the top two places in the poll in both elections. Where there was a straight fight in both years, the swing is printed in italic type.

The Liberal 1964–66 column shows the increase or decrease in the Liberal % of the total vote. The 1964 Liberal vote is given in brackets where Liberals withdrew in 1966. An * denotes Liberal intervention in 1966.

The party labels of other candidates are given for Communists and where any candidate polled over 5%.

English Boroughs

Constituency	% voting 1966	Change since 1964	Con. %	Lab. %	Lib. %	Other %	Lib. 1964– 1966	Swing 1964– 1966	Swing 1959– 1964
Accrington . .	83·1	−1·4	36·1	53·0	10·9	—	−2·8	−1·9	−5·9
Acton . . .	73·9	−3·5	42·3	57·7	—	—	[8·8]	−3·9	−5·0
Altrincham & Sale .	78·0	−3·2	48·0	34·7	17·3	—	−7·9	−2·8	−5·4
Ashton under Lyne .	73·7	−3·7	41·3	58·7	—	—	—	−4·2	−1·7
Barking . . .	72·0	−1·2	21·8	66·2	12·0	—	−2·8	−2·1	−5·4
Barnsley . . .	73·4	−6·6	24·3	75·7	—	—	[14·3]	−0·7	−1·3
Barrow-in-Furness .	76·8	−1·2	39·7	60·3	—	—	—	−5·2	−0·4
Bath . . .	80·5	−0·2	43·0	41·2	15·8	—	−3·4	−3·3	−2·7
Batley & Morley .	75·3	−3·4	29·0	56·2	14·8	—	−2·2	−2·5	−2·8
Bebington . .	79·8	−1·1	48·0	52·0	—	—	[13·1]	−3·8	−6·8
Beckenham . .	77·9	+0·4	51·5	26·8	21·7	—	−1·1	−2·5	−4·6
Bexley . . .	85·8	+1·3	48·1	43·9	8·0	—	−3·4	−2·1	−3·6
Bilston . . .	73·2	−1·0	43·1	56·9	—	—	—	−3·8	+0·4
Birkenhead . .	72·8	−1·6	38·4	60·1	—	Cm 1·5	—	−3·9	−3·2
Birmingham, All Saints .	65·1	−1·0	41·5	58·5	—	—	—	−7·7	−0·8
Aston . .	64·2	−1·2	39·1	60·9	—	—	—	−6·2	−1·6
Edgbaston .	67·8	+1·3	53·9	32·3	13·8	—	*	−6·6	−2·3
Hall Green .	73·6	−2·2	47·4	39·7	12·9	—	−2·7	−6·5	−4·4
Handsworth .	63·2	−3·4	49·9	46·0	—	UM 4·1	[17·6]	−5·0	−6·3
Ladywood .	59·7	+6·0	17·4	58·9	23·7	—	*	—	+0·5
Northfield .	75·1	−2·1	39·7	58·7	—	Cm 1·6	[12·4]	−6·1	−2·6
Perry Barr .	76·2	+2·1	45·0	55·0	—	—	—	−5·4	+0·6
Selly Oak .	66·4	+0·0	45·2	43·0	11·8	—	*	−5·8	−3·2
Small Heath .	59·6	−1·3	28·7	69·5	—	Cm 1·8	—	−8·3	−4·7
Sparkbrook .	66·7	−1·6	39·4	60·6	—	—	—	−8·6	−3·3
Stetchford .	70·3	−0·7	33·2	64·2	—	Cm 2·6	—	−8·7	−3·2
Yardley .	77·6	+0·6	43·7	56·3	—	—	—	−6·1	−1·7
Blackburn . .	79·2	−1·8	41·7	58·3	—	—	—	−0·8	−4·7
Blackpool, North .	72·9	−1·8	47·1	34·0	18·9	—	−8·6	—	—
South . .	70·5	−0·6	54·3	45·7	—	—	—	−4·0	−7·6
Blyth . . .	74·4	−3·9	21·8	78·2	—	—	—	−2·3	−1·3
Bolton, East .	77·0	−3·4	40·8	59·2	—	—	[14·4]	−5·9	−6·1
West . . .	78·3	+0·0	37·7	50·6	11·7	—	−13·4	−2·7	—
Bootle . . .	68·2	−2·7	33·6	60·4	—	Ind Lab 6·0	—	−1·4	−8·3
Bournemouth, East .	74·7	+0·0	55·9	26·1	18·0	—	−3·6	−2·3	−4·1
West . .	73·4	−0·3	50·1	31·7	18·2	—	−4·4	−2·6	−6·1
Bradford, East .	65·1	−2·1	30·5	69·5	—	—	—	−7·7	−3·8
North . .	77·7	−2·7	44·7	55·3	—	—	[16·2]	−3·6	−4·8
South . .	75·7	−2·9	35·4	52·6	12·0	—	−4·0	−4·3	−1·0
West . .	76·6	−0·2	48·0	52·0	—	—	—	−6·0	−2·2
Brentford & Chiswick.	82·1	+3·0	45·7	47·6	6·7	—	−3·0	−1·8	−3·6
Brighouse & Spenborough .	84·0	−1·3	45·2	54·8	—	—	[13·7]	−3·8	−0·9
Brighton, Kemptown .	80·1	+7·9	49·2	50·8	—	—	—	−0·8	−6·4
Pavilion .	70·3	+0·2	58·1	41·9	—	—	[18·6]	−4·3	−7·6
Bristol, Central .	69·9	−2·0	36·0	58·9	—	Ind 5·1	—	−3·7	−4·1
North-east .	77·0	−0·1	45·8	54·2	—	—	—	−5·4	−1·4
North-west.	82·0	−1·1	48·7	50·1	—	Cm 1·2	[12·0]	−1·8	−0·9
South . .	69·5	−3·3	32·9	67·1	—	—	—	−3·6	−2·7
South-east .	76·2	−1·7	38·6	61·4	—	—	—	−1·2	−4·0
West . .	72·2	−0·9	56·7	23·7	19·6	—	−0·5	—	—
Bromley . .	77·7	−0·1	52·3	26·7	21·0	—	−1·4	−1·9	−5·4
Burnley . .	80·0	−1·7	27·7	60·4	11·9	—	−3·5	−1·9	−7·5
Bury & Radcliffe .	81·2	−1·1	41·5	49·8	8·7	—	−5·3	−3·1	−4·8
Cambridge . .	80·0	+0·9	43·4	45·5	10·2	0·9	−6·0	−2·5	−5·7
Carlisle . .	83·5	−2·1	43·9	56·1	—	—	[11·0]	−3·6	−5·0
Cheltenham . .	77·2	−0·3	53·4	46·6	—	—	[18·1]	−2·8	−4·5
Chesterfield . .	76·7	−2·1	26·2	61·6	12·2	—	−2·6	−3·8	−1·5
Coventry, East .	77·3	−0·6	29·9	69·8	7·0	Cm 2·3	*	−4·7	−4·1
North . .	78·7	−2·7	40·7	59·3	—	—	—	−5·4	−2·6
South . .	80·2	+0·4	45·1	54·9	—	—	—	−3·3	−3·3
Crosby . . .	72·2	−4·5	54·1	45·9	—	—	[19·4]	−4·2	−8·6
Croydon, North-east .	76·3	+1·3	43·5	42·2	14·3	—	−1·1	−3·8	−5·3
North-west.	74·4	−0·0	45·4	38·8	15·8	—	−3·8	−3·4	−4·7
South . .	76·1	+1·8	44·6	44·7	10·7	—	*	−2·8	−5·5
Dagenham . .	67·4	−3·6	22·4	74·7	—	Cm 2·9	[14·4]	−3·1	−4·1
Darlington . .	82·3	−0·7	41·3	50·5	8·2	—	−5·4	−2·6	−6·4

English Boroughs—continued

Constituency	% voting 1966	Change since 1964	Con. %	Lab. %	Lib. %	Other %	Lib. 1964–1966	Swing 1964–1966	Swing 1959–1964
Derby, North	70·8	−3·6	38·2	61·8	—	—	[12·5]	−2·7	−6·4
South	72·6	−2·2	31·8	57·5	10·7	—	*	−5·2	−3·7
Dewsbury	78·0	−1·5	28·7	53·6	17·7	—	+0·3	−5·3	−3·1
Doncaster	81·2	−1·5	43·3	56·7	—	—	−0·1	−5·5	−4·8
Dudley	73·9	−2·6	40·9	59·1	—	—	[12·0]	+0·0	−4·1
Ealing, North	82·1	+1·0	43·4	48·7	7·9	—	−5·7	−2·6	−4·2
South	73·3	+3·2	50·5	36·9	12·6	—	*	−4·3	−4·2
East Ham, North	64·7	−2·7	34·1	65·9	—	—	—	−5·5	−3·6
South	65·7	−2·2	30·1	69·9	—	—	—	−3·9	−4·5
Eccles	74·1	−3·6	37·5	59·5	—	Cm 3·0	—	−3·7	−5·3
Edmonton	72·2	−4·8	41·4	58·6	—	—	[11·9]	−3·4	−4·8
Enfield, East	75·2	−1·1	32·9	54·9	12·2	—	−4·1	−1·8	−4·3
West	80·1	−0·9	53·8	27·4	18·8	—	−4·6	—	—
Erith & Crayford	81·7	+2·1	34·4	55·5	8·8	Cm 1·3	−5·6	−0·2	−3·6
Eton & Slough	85·3	+5·4	45·2	54·8	—	—	—	−4·8	+0·1
Exeter	83·6	+3·3	40·7	48·6	10·7	—	−9·6	−5·5	−4·9
Feltham	77·3	+0·1	33·5	53·9	12·6	—	−2·2	−3·2	−4·4
Finchley	75·3	−2·9	46·5	28·1	25·4	—	−4·5	—	—
Gateshead, East	75·7	−4·2	30·4	69·6	—	—	—	−5·1	−5·6
West	70·1	−4·8	25·2	74·8	—	—	—	−5·8	−4·1
Gillingham	78·5	+0·5	49·5	41·8	8·7	—	−1·6	−3·3	−2·1
Gloucester	77·5	−1·0	36·3	48·5	15·2	—	−2·5	−1·4	−1·6
Gosport & Fareham	75·4	−0·6	51·7	34·3	14·0	—	−4·7	−2·5	−3·4
Grimsby	74·2	−1·7	41·1	58·9	—	—	—	−4·6	−4·2
Halifax	80·5	−1·6	39·0	50·3	10·7	—	−3·7	−4·6	−3·2
Harrow, Central	80·2	+1·6	45·1	40·5	14·4	—	−5·6	−3·9	−6·7
East	82·8	+2·8	43·5	44·4	12·1	—	*	−3·4	−4·3
West	80·2	+0·4	53·1	28·9	18·0	—	−3·1	−2·3	−6·5
The Hartlepools	78·5	−3·4	40·7	59·3	—	—	—	−6·4	−3·1
Hastings	76·4	+0·1	40·3	34·1	25·6	—	−0·0	−4·3	−5·0
Hayes & Harlington	72·8	−0·5	35·7	62·2	—	Cm 2·1	—	−3·2	−4·5
Hendon, North	80·0	+1·5	46·3	44·9	8·8	—	−5·4	−0·6	−4·8
South	73·2	−0·5	45·3	34·6	20·1	—	−1·9	−3·8	−5·5
Heston & Isleworth	79·9	+1·6	44·4	42·1	13·5	—	−2·0	−3·1	−5·6
Hornchurch	81·1	−0·8	47·9	52·1	—	—	[17·1]	−2·2	−4·9
Hornsey	72·8	+2·4	44·1	42·9	10·5	Cm 2·5	−1·9	−3·6	−7·1
Hove	72·1	+2·5	57·2	25·7	16·0	1·1	*	−2·6	−6·4
Huddersfield, East	77·9	−0·7	28·2	55·8	16·0	—	−2·6	−3·5	−6·6
West	82·3	+0·7	33·0	43·9	23·1	—	−9·6	—	—
Ilford, North	76·2	−0·2	46·5	39·9	13·6	—	−7·2	−4·0	−5·5
South	76·9	+2·2	41·8	47·6	10·6	—	−9·1	−4·7	−5·9
Ipswich	77·5	−1·5	38·6	49·9	10·2	1·3	−13·6	−3·7	+0·6
Jarrow	76·7	−3·3	32·4	67·6	—	—	—	−3·4	−1·5
Keighley	83·5	−2·1	45·0	55·0	—	—	[20·6]	−1·8	−3·4
Kingston upon Hull,									
East	73·4	−1·4	21·6	65·5	12·9	—	−5·0	−7·0	−3·8
North	79·0	+1·8	37·0	55·2	7·8	—	−8·1	−7·8	−2·0
West	70·4	−0·5	35·2	64·8	—	—	—	−7·9	−4·4
Kingston upon Thames	77·0	−0·1	51·3	33·6	15·1	—	−2·1	−2·5	−5·9
Leeds, East	72·7	−3·4	38·5	61·5	—	—	—	−3·6	−3·4
North-east	68·1	−3·0	56·8	43·2	—	—	—	−3·9	−3·4
North-west	73·1	−4·1	55·6	44·4	—	—	[15·2]	−4·0	−5·9
South	68·1	−3·9	29·1	68·8	—	Cm 2·1	—	−5·4	−0·6
South-east	61·5	−2·8	28·1	71·9	—	—	—	−4·2	−3·5
West	72·0	−2·5	32·0	56·3	11·7	—	−3·3	−4·1	−3·2
Leicester, North-east	75·4	−2·1	34·2	54·0	11·8	—	−5·3	−5·0	−3·1
North-west	73·7	−2·5	39·1	60·9	—	—	—	−5·1	−3·7
South-east	73·3	−3·4	59·9	40·1	—	—	[17·3]	−2·7	−2·9
South-west	74·0	−3·5	41·3	58·7	—	—	[13·3]	−2·7	−2·4
Leigh	74·3	−3·3	31·3	68·7	—	—	—	−1·2	−2·3
Leyton	76·1	+5·9	36·9	54·4	7·8	0·9	−8·4	−0·4	−4·7
Lincoln	78·7	−1·6	41·7	58·3	—	—	[15·8]	−2·6	−0·6
Liverpool, Edge Hill	60·5	−5·1	36·9	63·1	—	—	—	−4·1	−8·1
Exchange	50·7	−3·7	26·3	73·7	—	—	—	−3·6	−8·8
Garston	68·2	−4·7	54·4	45·6	—	—	[13·8]	−2·3	−7·8
Kirkdale	65·7	−3·4	40·7	59·3	—	—	—	−3·8	−8·8
Scotland	51·7	−7·9	24·0	72·1	—	Cm 3·9	—	−3·8	−8·5
Toxteth	65·8	−1·7	43·4	56·6	—	—	—	−2·2	−9·9

See notes on p. 313.

English Boroughs—continued

Constituency	% voting 1966	Change since 1964	Con. %	Lab. %	Lib. %	Other %	Lib. 1964–1966	Swing 1964–1966	Swing 1959–1964
Walton	71·2	−4·4	42·7	57·3	—	—	—	−3·7	−8·1
Wavertree	71·0	−2·7	48·6	34·3	17·1	—	−3·8	−2·7	−9·4
West Derby	67·6	−5·8	43·1	56·9	—	—	—	−2·2	−8·7
Luton	79·2	−0·6	43·6	48·8	6·4	Cm 1·2	*	−1·8	−5·9
Manchester, Ardwick	59·1	−4·2	33·9	63·2	—	UM 2·9	—	−3·5	−3·1
Blackley	75·5	−4·0	37·1	52·4	10·5	—	−5·2	−6·3	−6·1
Cheetham	57·0	−3·1	29·1	70·9	—	—	—	−4·6	−2·0
Exchange	53·7	−2·1	26·5	73·5	—	—	—	−4·4	−4·5
Gorton	72·6	−3·8	39·9	60·1	—	—	—	−5·0	−4·2
Moss Side	65·4	−0·0	45·4	41·8	12·8	—	−9·4	−4·6	−5·9
Openshaw	65·9	−5·4	30·7	64·9	—	Cm 4·4	—	−4·9	−2·0
Withington	71·2	−1·1	42·9	41·3	15·8	—	−8·1	−5·4	−4·7
Wythenshawe	74·8	−4·8	35·9	53·1	11·0	—	−2·0	−4·4	−5·5
Merton & Morden	81·2	−1·1	50·5	49·5	—	—	[14·1]	−2·9	−6·1
Middlesborough, East	68·3	−4·6	24·9	75·1	—	—	—	−5·6	−8·0
West	81·5	−2·6	45·5	54·5	—	—	[13·1]	−3·2	−11·0
Mitcham	79·4	+0·2	45·8	44·8	8·3	Cm 1·1	−4·4	−3·2	−4·9
Nelson & Colne	80·9	+0·1	37·0	49·3	—	Ind 13·7	—	−2·6	−2·0
Newcastle under Lyme	79·9	−2·3	38·2	61·8	—	—	—	−3·8	−2·4
Newcastle upon Tyne, Central	65·9	−3·2	21·8	76·6	—	Cm 1·6	—	−5·6	−6·0
East	80·5	−2·9	40·2	59·8	—	—	—	−7·8	−2·1
North	75·0	−0·7	49·6	40·9	9·5	—	*	−6·5	−4·0
West	75·8	−3·6	37·3	62·7	—	—	—	−4·4	−3·6
Northampton	76·4	−3·3	43·3	56·7	—	—	[9·5]	−2·9	−1·6
Norwich, North	74·2	−0·3	34·4	65·6	—	—	—	−4·7	−0·7
South	83·2	+0·5	45·2	54·8	—	—	—	−3·9	−4·0
Nottingham, Central	67·7	−3·7	41·1	58·9	—	—	—	−6·2	−5·0
North	74·0	−3·8	37·1	60·7	—	Cm 2·2	—	−3·1	−3·7
South	75·6	−2·6	49·7	50·3	—	—	[13·0]	−2·8	−4·6
West	78·3	−3·5	42·0	58·0	—	—	—	−5·4	−2·8
Oldbury & Halesowen	76·7	−2·2	46·8	53·2	—	—	[20·6]	−2·4	+1·3
Oldham, East	72·7	−4·1	35·1	50·5	14·4	—	−4·6	−2·8	−2·8
West	72·4	−2·7	38·8	61·2	—	—	—	−2·4	−3·8
Oxford	79·3	+2·0	41·8	46·5	11·7	—	−5·3	−3·7	−6·7
Plymouth, Devonport	76·2	+2·6	50·4	49·6	—	—	—	−3·6	−2·4
Sutton	78·9	+2·2	45·5	54·5	—	—	[13·1]	−4·9	−5·5
Pontefract	77·3	−0·3	23·3	76·7	—	—	—	−0·5	+0·2
Poole	79·0	−1·0	47·6	36·7	15·7	—	−7·5	−2·4	−3·5
Portsmouth, Langstone	74·0	−1·2	48·4	36·8	14·8	—	−7·9	−1·0	−8·2
South	70·7	−0·3	60·6	39·4	—	—	—	−3·1	−6·3
West	76·5	+1·7	48·3	51·7	—	—	—	−2·4	−7·0
Preston, North	81·1	+2·4	47·0	53·0	—	—	—	−3·0	−5·1
South	80·0	+1·2	46·4	53·6	—	—	—	−3·1	−4·2
Pudsey	83·3	−1·2	44·6	39·6	15·8	—	−3·0	−3·4	−1·3
Reading	84·0	+4·2	42·7	51·0	6·3	—	−5·9	−4·2	−4·0
Richmond	79·4	+2·9	49·5	35·4	15·1	—	−2·6	−2·2	−5·7
Rochdale	79·0	−3·3	28·3	52·4	19·3	—	−9·6		
Romford	75·4	−2·4	42·6	57·4	—	—	[14·2]	−2·1	−4·9
Rossendale	80·4	−1·4	44·6	55·4	—	—	—	−1·4	−1·1
Rotherham	68·7	−2·9	30·3	69·7	—	—	—	−3·2	−3·7
Rowley Regis & Tipton	69·2	−1·2	34·2	65·8	—	—	—	−5·6	+1·0
Ruislip-Northwood	81·7	+0·3	51·4	33·4	15·2	—	−4·2	−3·1	−3·8
St. Helens	68·6	−3·7	29·2	70·8	—	—	—	−3·8	−4·9
Salford, East	61·1	−5·7	32·8	67·2	—	—	—	−6·1	−6·5
West	67·1	−6·0	40·8	59·2	—	—	—	−3·7	−2·2
Sheffield, Attercliffe	67·6	−4·4	22·7	77·3	—	—	[10·6]	−5·1	−3·4
Brightside	66·2	−4·1	21·3	75·9	—	Cm 2·8	—	−4·9	−3·4
Hallam	75·0	+0·9	51·3	32·5	16·2	—	−1·9	−4·6	−4·3
Heeley	78·7	+2·7	46·0	54·0	—	—	—	−5·5	−7·5
Hillsborough	70·3	−4·2	32·1	67·9	—	—	—	−5·5	−5·9
Park	64·9	−3·7	16·4	80·3	—	Cm 3·3	—	−6·3	−4·5
Smethwick	75·4	+1·3	44·1	54·4	—	BNP1·5	[9·1]	−7·6	+7·2
Southall	68·9	−1·3	40·2	54·9	—	BNP4·9	—	−4·8	+0·2
Southampton, Itchen	49·0	−27·1	Speaker, 85·6,			Nat Dem 14·4	—	—	−5·7
Test	78·1	+1·4	43·6	48·4	8·1	—	*	−2·7	−6·0
Southend, East	76·9	+0·7	45·3	44·1	10·6	—	−4·2	−3·4	−5·3

See notes on p. 313.

English Boroughs—continued

Constituency	% voting 1966	Change since 1964	Con. %	Lab. %	Lib. %	Other %	Lib. 1964–1966	Swing 1964–1966	Swing 1959–1964
West .	78·4	−0·4	50·9	27·4	21·7	—	—	−7·1	—	—
Southgate .	75·1	−1·3	53·5	24·6	21·9	—	—	−1·7	—	—
Southport .	72·7	−3·8	51·0	29·3	19·7	—	—	−3·3	—	—
South Shields .	68·7	−5·4	35·3	64·7	—	—	[14·5]	−2·3	−4·6
Stockport, North	79·1	−2·4	45·8	54·2	—	—	[15·4]	−2·0	−5·9
South .	76·7	−5·1	44·2	55·8	—	—	[18·9]	−1·8	−7·4
Stockton on Tees	77·4	−4·4	38·4	59·9	—	Cm 1·7	[14·1]	−3·2	−3·9
Stoke on Trent,									
Central .	68·3	−4·0	31·9	68·1	—	—	—	−3·9	−3·1
North .	72·4	−3·8	28·5	71·5	—	—	—	−6·8	−0·7
South .	71·0	−4·7	33·2	61·7	—	Cm 5·1	—	−3·6	−1·3
Stretford .	77·1	−2·1	40·7	47·1	12·2	—	−11·3	−5·0	−6·6
Sunderland, North	74·5	−1·8	39·2	60·8	—	—	—	−4·0	−4·4
South .	75·5	−0·3	42·5	57·5	—	—	—	−5·9	−2·5
Surbiton .	77·0	+1·6	57·9	42·1	—	—	—	−2·7	−6·8
Sutton & Cheam	76·4	+2·1	51·1	30·3	18·6	—	−1·6	−2·3	−3·7
Sutton Coldfield	76·3	−2·0	52·5	24·6	22·9	—	−2·6	—	—
Swindon .	73·7	−1·3	36·7	61·3	—	Cm 2·0	—	−1·2	−6·8
Torquay .	77·4	+2·4	49·4	28·6	22·0	—	−2·8	—	—
Tottenham .	59·8	−4·1	34·7	65·3	—	—	[12·7]	−4·2	−3·9
Twickenham .	78·6	+0·9	47·7	34·0	18·3	—	−3·7	−4·0	−3·7
Tynemouth .	78·4	−0·6	49·6	43·9	—	Ind Lib 6·5	—	−3·4	−5·7
Wakefield .	73·4	−4·6	34·6	65·4	—	—	[14·2]	−2·8	−2·9
Wallasey .	76·1	−0·5	43·7	42·6	13·7	—	−5·7	−5·1	−7·7
Wallsend .	77·5	−4·0	34·8	65·2	—	—	—	−4·8	−3·9
Walsall, North .	70·9	−1·0	34·9	65·1	—	—	—	−3·7	−0·4
South .	77·2	−1·9	53·4	46·6	—	—	—	−3·7	−1·3
Walthamstow, East .	80·1	+0·8	42·3	47·9	9·8	—	−5·5	−3·4	−3·5
West .	71·0	−1·1	24·8	61·2	14·0	—	−3·3	−3·3	−0·9
Wanstead & Woodford	76·8	−2·5	56·1	25·8	18·1	—	−7·0	—	—
Warrington	68·9	−2·5	26·3	64·6	9·1	—	−2·4	−6·3	−6·6
Watford .	82·9	−0·7	45·6	54·4	—	—	[12·9]	−2·7	−4·9
Wednesbury	72·0	+0·8	41·2	58·8	—	—	—	−5·1	+3·5
Wembley, North	80·9	+0·3	48·1	36·5	15·4	—	−3·0	−2·8	−5·5
South .	79·3	+0·9	45·3	41·8	12·9	—	−3·7	−4·6	−3·9
West Bromwich.	68·8	+4·1	42·1	57·9	—	—	—	−2·8	+2·3
West Ham, North	61·8	−1·0	16·7	65·6	17·7	—	−2·3	—	—
South .	61·8	−2·1	11·5	77·2	11·3	—	−2·2	—	—
Wigan .	76·0	−3·4	25·0	75·8	—	Cm 2·2	—	−3·3	−3·3
Willesden, East .	71·1	+2·3	37·1	54·6	6·9	—	*	−6·5	−4·9
West .	63·6	+0·1	28·4	68·5	—	Cm 3·1	—	−5·7	−5·7
Wimbledon .	75·0	+0·0	50·3	31·5	18·1	—	−0·9	−2·1	−5·3
Wolverhampton,									
North-east .	69·3	+1·3	38·1	61·9	—	—	—	−5·9	−0·9
South-west .	73·6	−1·7	59·1	40·9	—	—	[11·2]	−3·9	−0·9
Wood Green .	67·3	−3·0	39·2	60·8	—	—	—	−4·2	−5·3
Worcester .	77·9	−1·4	53·5	46·5	—	—	[13·5]	−4·1	−0·1
Worthing .	75·7	−0·5	59·6	20·5	17·8	2·1	−5·1	—	—
York .	82·7	−0·3	44·8	55·2	—	—	[12·7]	−6·2	−2·4

See notes on p. 313.

English Counties

Constituency	% voting 1966	Change since 1964	Con. %	Lab. %	Lib. %	Other %	Lib. 1964–1966	Swing 1964–1966	Swing 1959–1964
Bedfordshire, Bedford	81·5	+1·1	44·5	45·2	10·3	—	—6·0	—3·7	—4·0
Mid . . .	82·3	—0·7	46·0	40·0	14·0	—	—4·9	—2·4	—0·3
South . .	83·7	+2·9	41·9	47·8	10·3	—	*	—3·2	—4·0
Berkshire, Abingdon .	82·5	+1·9	46·3	40·8	12·9	—	—2·6	—3·0	—4·9
Newbury . .	79·1	—0·2	45·3	38·0	16·7	—	—3·5	—1·8	—4·6
Windsor . .	76·3	—0·0	47·6	33·5	16·9	—	—5·7	—3·5	—3·8
Wokingham .	79·2	+0·0	47·9	34·4	17·7	—	—3·6	—4·6	—3·5
Buckinghamshire, Aylesbury .	79·9	—0·0	44·9	37·5	17·6	—	—2·7	—3·6	—3·0
Buckingham .	85·8	—0·7	43·1	47·5	9·4	—	—1·7	—0·7	—3·3
South . .	80·3	+1·4	51·3	25·6	23·1	—	—2·0	—	—
Wycombe . .	80·7	—0·6	49·2	38·2	12·6	—	—2·6	—2·0	—1·9
Cambridgeshire . .	79·2	—0·6	47·7	38·0	14·3	—	—3·7	—2·2	—0·9
Cheshire, Cheadle .	82·4	—1·2	41·5	16·2	42·3	—	+7·6	—	—
City of Chester .	78·0	—1·6	46·1	40·1	13·8	—	—2·2	—3·8	—4·6
Crewe . .	75·6	—3·5	39·0	61·0	—	—	—	—3·8	—2·7
Knutsford .	79·1	—1·2	51·5	23·6	24·9	—	+0·0	—	—
Macclesfield .	81·7	—2·4	46·8	38·9	14·3	—	—2·9	—2·1	—3·5
Nantwich . .	79·3	—2·2	43·8	37·9	18·4	—	—4·9	—5·0	—1·3
Northwich .	82·3	—0·6	45·1	43·1	11·8	—	—5·5	—5·0	—4·7
Runcorn . .	82·1	—1·5	48·4	36·7	14·9	—	—4·0	—2·6	—7·4
Stalybridge & Hyde	73·6	—5·0	43·1	56·9	—	—	—	—2·9	—2·5
Wirral . .	79·7	—1·6	48·1	33·1	18·8	—	—3·9	—3·9	—6·5
Cornwall, Bodmin .	84·4	+1·7	41·4	12·0	46·6	—	—2·0	—	—
Falmouth & Camborne	82·5	+4·9	39·7	46·8	13·5	—	—4·4	—0·1	+1·3
North . .	87·5	+4·4	44·5	7·0	48·5	—	+4·7	—	—
St. Ives . .	77·9	+2·8	41·4	30·9	27·7	—	—1·6	—	—
Truro. . .	79·2	+0·0	40·4	37·0	22·6	—	—5·3	—2·8	—0·6
Cumberland, Penrith & the Border .	78·7	—1·9	52·7	30·3	17·0	—	—5·6	—1·9	—4·4
Whitehaven .	78·8	—3·2	38·0	62·0	—	—	—	—1·9	—2·3
Workington .	80·4	—3·1	36·7	63·3	—	—	—	—1·2	—1·9
Derbyshire, Belper .	84·1	—2·0	46·7	53·3	—	—	[15·2]	—2·2	—1·2
Bolsover . .	74·6	—4·3	18·5	81·5	—	—	—	—2·2	—1·1
High Peak .	84·2	—1·1	39·2	41·3	19·5	—	—7·5	—2·6	—4·4
Ilkeston . .	76·2	—5·8	29·9	70·1	—	—	[15·8]	—2·0	+0·5
North-east .	73·8	—4·1	33·1	66·9	—	—	—	—2·7	—1·3
South-east .	81·8	—1·0	45·4	54·6	—	—	—	—3·9	—0·8
West . .	83·4	—2·4	49·6	37·2	13·2	—	—17·2	—	—
Devon, Honiton .	78·6	—0·2	54·4	26·8	18·8	—	—6·9	—	—
North . .	85·3	+1·0	40·5	15·9	43·6	—	—7·1	—	—
Tavistock .	81·4	+3·1	49·2	20·2	30·6	—	—3·6	—	—
Tiverton . .	80·7	+0·6	48·6	27·0	24·4	—	—10·1	—	—
Torrington .	85·8	+0·7	47·0	15·5	37·5	—	—2·0	—	—
Totnes . .	79·4	+0·6	47·8	31·5	20·7	—	—2·9	—2·3	—3·3
Dorset, North .	81·3	—0·4	48·2	16·6	35·2	—	—0·9	—	—
South . .	81·0	—0·0	46·0	42·3	11·7	—	—2·9	+0·9	—6·6
West . .	80·9	—0·8	47·7	31·6	20·7	—	—1·7	—1·8	—1·6
Durham, Bishop Auckland .	73·4	—2·8	35·2	64·8	—	—	—	—3·0	—1·3
Blaydon . .	77·4	—2·6	30·8	69·2	—	—	—	—2·5	—1·3
Chester-le-Street .	74·9	—4·5	23·0	77·0	—	—	—	—1·8	+0·6
Consett . .	73·5	—3·2	26·7	73·3	—	—	—	—5·2	—1·3
Durham . .	74·7	—4·1	29·4	70·6	—	—	—	—2·3	—1·9
Easington . .	70·5	—4·7	18·6	81·4	—	—	—	—1·0	—0·6
Houghton-le-Spring .	73·9	—4·8	22·5	77·5	—	—	—	—2·7	+1·1
North-west. .	73·4	—4·6	26·4	73·6	—	—	—	—3·9	—1·6
Sedgefield .	76·0	—3·5	35·3	64·7	—	—	—	—4·0	—2·2
Isle of Ely .	75·9	+2·2	46·2	42·4	11·4	—	*	—4·3	—0·9
Essex, Billericay .	84·1	+1·6	44·6	46·5	8·8	—	—4·6	—2·0	—2·8
Chelmsford. .	82·5	—0·3	47·2	38·9	13·9	—	—2·3	—2·0	—3·8
Chigwell . .	81·3	—0·6	47·3	41·4	11·3	—	—2·6	—1·3	—2·5
Colchester . .	82·3	+0·2	45·6	43·7	10·7	—	—4·2	—2·5	—4·4
Epping . .	82·4	—0·9	39·0	48·4	12·6	—	—2·7	—2·6	—5·2
Harwich . .	74·4	—0·7	47·5	34·9	17·6	—	—2·1	—3·9	—3·4
Maldon . .	83·2	+0·0	45·4	44·5	10·1	—	—2·4	—1·1	—0·9

See notes on p. 313.

English Counties—continued

Constituency	% voting 1966	Change since 1964	Con. %	Lab. %	Lib. %	Other %	Lib. 1964–1966	Swing 1964–1966	Swing 1959–1966
Saffron Walden .	82·5	+0·1	47·4	39·9	12·7	—	−0·5	−2·1	−2·7
South-east .	77·3	+2·3	48·5	39·8	11·7	—	*	−2·6	−4·0
Thurrock .	72·7	−1·5	26·7	60·7	12·6	—	−2·6	−2·1	−3·4
Gloucestershire, Cirencester & Tewkesbury .	74·9	−3·1	58·2	41·8	—	—	[16·2]	−1·5	−3·7
South .	84·4	+0·2	45·2	42·9	11·9	—	−3·0	−2·1	−1·6
Stroud .	85·0	−0·4	43·2	40·2	16·6	—	−1·1	−1·4	−2·3
West . .	78·0	−1·6	34·5	51·8	13·7	—	−2·3	−0·7	−1·8
Hampshire, Aldershot.	75·4	+0·4	48·9	32·0	19·1	—	−1·2	−3·7	−2·8
Basingstoke .	78·6	+0·5	45·9	39·4	14·7	—	−1·5	−4·2	−4·2
Eastleigh .	83·7	−0·2	45·4	44·1	10·5	—	−2·5	−1·3	−1·5
New Forest .	74·2	−1·7	51·2	26·7	22·1	—	+0·0	−2·1	−4·4
Petersfield .	75·7	+0·3	52·3	23·8	23·9	—	−2·0	—	—
Winchester .	77·9	−1·9	51·6	30·4	18·0	—	+1·9	−0·6	−6·2
Herefordshire, Hereford .	77·3	−1·8	44·6	37·6	17·8	—	−6·0	−3·9	—
Leominster .	75·2	−1·9	51·5	22·3	26·2	—	−3·7	—	—
Hertfordshire, Barnet.	80·5	−1·1	47·1	36·7	16·2	—	−2·8	−2·7	−4·7
East . .	80·1	−0·9	46·6	38·4	15·0	—	−1·3	−2·3	−3·0
Hemel Hempstead .	84·7	+0·2	44·4	41·6	14·0	—	−3·3	−2·1	−3·3
Hertford .	83·7	−0·9	50·6	49·4	—	—	[13·8]	−2·5	−5·1
Hitchin .	82·3	−2·2	43·5	56·5	—	—	[12·9]	−4·3	−5·7
St. Albans .	83·0	+0·4	47·7	41·6	10·7	—	−5·0	−2·8	−3·9
South-west .	83·1	+0·1	45·7	40·5	13·8	—	−4·4	−2·3	−3·8
Huntingdonshire .	77·6	−1·2	49·2	36·6	14·2	—	−3·4	−3·6	−1·1
Kent, Ashford .	75·4	−2·1	49·9	31·1	19·0	—	−3·4	−1·1	−2·3
Canterbury .	76·1	−0·2	49·8	28·2	22·0	—	+3·4	−0·4	−4·9
Chislehurst .	84·3	+1·4	43·5	45·1	11·4	—	−3·1	−2·4	−5·0
Dartford .	80·8	−0·7	38·2	49·8	12·0	—	−3·4	−1·7	−3·0
Dover .	84·2	+1·5	43·5	49·3	7·2	—	−3·7	−2·6	−3·5
Faversham .	79·9	−1·8	47·5	52·5	—	—	[9·9]	+1·6	−3·8
Folkestone & Hythe .	70·6	−0·4	59·6	40·4	—	—	—	−2·6	−3·9
Gravesend .	82·0	+1·6	41·9	49·7	8·4	—	−2·1	−3·3	−2·8
Isle of Thanet .	75·7	+1·5	47·5	39·6	12·9	—	−4·2	−2·3	−4·8
Maidstone .	74·3	−3·7	54·7	45·3	—	—	[21·0]	−2·7	−3·1
Orpington .	86·9	+1·6	43·3	10·0	46·7	—	−1·8	—	—
Sevenoaks .	79·2	−0·9	50·5	32·3	17·2	—	−3·7	−3·4	−1·5
Tonbridge .	77·3	−1·4	46·7	34·9	18·4	—	+1·3	−1·8	−2·2
Lancashire, Chorley .	81·1	−3·5	45·2	54·8	—	—	[10·4]	−1·1	−3·0
Clitheroe .	83·5	−1·8	46·1	40·1	13·8	—	+0·1	−2·7	−2·5
Darwen .	82·6	−1·1	42·2	38·7	19·1	—	−6·9	−3·1	−4·1
Farnworth .	74·8	−4·0	33·8	66·2	—	—	—	−4·1	−3·5
Heywood & Royton .	79·7	−3·1	37·7	49·0	13·3	—	−6·8	−4·8	−3·0
Huyton .	70·1	−6·6	32·6	66·4	—	0·9	—	−2·3	−9·7
Ince .	75·4	−4·2	26·4	73·6	—	—	—	−1·6	+0·3
Lancaster .	79·2	−0·5	47·4	52·6	—	—	—	−6·1	−4·2
Middleton & Prestwich .	77·9	−1·5	37·5	44·8	17·7	—	−5·9	−5·6	−7·8
Morecambe & Lonsdale .	76·5	−0·6	51·9	29·8	18·3	—	*	−2·4	−4·5
Newton .	78·0	−4·0	37·2	62·8	—	—	[13·5]	−0·1	−5·3
North Fylde .	73·4	+1·2	53·7	31·1	13·4	1·8	*	−4·0	−5·2
Ormskirk .	73·9	−1·9	58·8	41·2	—	—	—	−3·8	−6·7
South Fylde .	74·6	−2·4	54·4	24·6	21·1	—	−0·6	—	—
Westhoughton .	78·8	−3·1	35·0	65·0	—	—	—	−3·3	−0·5
Widnes .	72·8	−5·1	39·6	60·7	—	—	—	−3·9	−4·8
Leicestershire, Bosworth .	79·8	−3·0	36·0	50·2	13·8	—	−5·4	−1·9	−3·9
Harborough .	81·6	−1·8	36·1	36·2	17·7	—	−2·6	−4·4	−1·6
Loughborough .	82·3	−1·6	37·0	50·2	12·8	—	−1·3	−1·8	−0·6
Melton .	80·5	−2·1	48·0	36·2	15·8	—	−2·1	−4·5	−0·8
Lincolnshire, Brigg. .	72·4	−5·1	39·9	60·1	—	—	[12·0]	−4·3	−3·8
Gainsborough .	75·8	−2·4	37·5	37·1	15·3	—	−6·9	−3·9	+0·3
Grantham .	80·5	+1·7	47·7	43·6	8·7	—	*	−3·8	−0·9

See notes on p. 313.

English Counties—continued

Constituency	% voting 1966	Change since 1964	Con. %	Lab. %	Lib. %	Other %	Lib. 1964–1966	Swing 1964–1966	Swing 1959–1964
Holland with Boston . .	75·0	+1·1	50·3	49·7	—	—	—	−5·1	−4·9
Horncastle . .	75·9	+1·2	46·7	30·0	23·3	—	−1·9	—	—
Louth . .	74·4	−3·5	46·4	36·8	16·8	—	−1·5	−3·4	−3·0
Rutland & Stamford .	77·6	−1·7	53·4	46·6	—	—	—	−2·1	−1·9
Middlesex, Spelthorne.	80·9	+0·8	45·8	40·7	13·5	—	−4·0	−3·2	−3·9
Uxbridge . .	82·6	+1·8	43·6	45·5	10·9	—	−3·2	−1·6	−0·8
Norfolk, Central .	79·8	−1·7	54·3	45·7	—	—	[13·9]	−1·7	−1·9
King's Lynn .	82·9	+2·4	47·7	52·3	—	—	—	−2·2	−2·2
North . .	83·2	+3·5	49·1	50·9	—	—	—	−0·8	+0·7
South . .	81·4	−1·3	44·8	44·4	10·8	—	−2·2	−2·7	−0·9
South-west . .	84·0	+2·0	51·1	48·9	—	—	—	+1·0	+0·2
Yarmouth . .	79·9	−0·4	49·1	50·9	—	—	[10·8]	−3·1	−2·0
Northamptonshire, Kettering . .	81·3	−0·2	35·6	52·6	11·8	—	*	−3·3	−2·4
Peterborough .	81·4	−0·4	46·0	46·1	7·9	—	−4·1	−2·0	−2·0
South . .	82·2	−0·8	52·8	47·2	—	—	—	−1·5	−2·7
Wellingborough .	86·5	−0·6	47·6	52·4	—	—	[15·6]	−2·3	−0·7
Northumberland, Berwick-upon-Tweed . .	76·6	−2·9	47·6	33·1	19·3	—	−4·9	−4·7	−1·1
Hexham . .	78·5	−3·4	48·1	37·1	14·8	—	−2·6	−3·9	−3·6
Morpeth . .	76·9	−3·9	25·6	74·4	—	—	—	−1·7	−0·8
Nottinghamshire, Ashfield . .	73·3	−3·9	26·4	73·6	—	—	—	−0·8	−2·1
Bassetlaw . .	73·3	−3·7	38·4	61·6	—	—	—	−2·6	−1·0
Carlton . .	82·5	−0·9	45·6	39·2	15·2	—	−1·7	−2·1	−2·3
Mansfield . .	74·8	−3·1	22·3	64·2	12·2	Cm 1·3	−2·3	−0·2	−3·0
Newark . .	81·1	−2·0	43·3	56·7	—	—	—	−2·3	−2·5
Rushcliffe . .	85·4	+2·0	45·1	45·8	9·1	—	*	−2·9	−1·8
Oxfordshire, Banbury.	81·9	−0·5	47·5	40·3	12·2	—	−1·4	−0·8	−2·0
Henley . .	75·2	−3·1	55·4	44·6	—	—	[17·9]	−2·8	−2·1
Shropshire, Ludlow .	73·9	−3·6	54·9	45·1	—	—	[23·8]	−4·0	−1·4
Oswestry . .	73·3	−3·3	48·2	35·4	16·4	—	−6·4	−2·4	−5·2
Shrewsbury .	76·5	−1·7	45·2	37·6	17·2	—	−1·5	−3·8	−3·8
Wrekin . .	81·3	−0·7	49·1	50·9	—	—	[8·6]	−3·9	−0·6
Somerset, Bridgwater.	80·2	−0·1	44·4	38·1	17·5	—	−1·9	−3·5	−2·5
North . .	85·3	−0·1	46·4	42·7	10·9	—	−2·9	−1·4	−3·0
Taunton . .	85·3	+0·6	47·5	40·8	11·6	—	−5·7	−1·8	−1·9
Wells . . .	81·5	−0·9	43·0	35·6	21·4	—	−3·9	−2·1	−1·3
Weston super Mare . .	79·1	+0·0	52·1	28·8	19·1	—	−3·9	−3·0	−2·8
Yeovil . .	83·6	+0·3	43·2	39·2	17·6	—	−6·5	−2·6	−1·5
Staffordshire, Brierley Hill .	79·0	−1·0	51·2	48·8	—	—	—	−2·2	−0·1
Burton . .	78·7	−1·5	50·3	49·7	—	—	—	−2·9	−2·8
Cannock . .	73·7	−2·5	40·2	59·8	—	—	—	−2·3	−0·7
Leek . . .	78·8	−2·5	43·8	56·2	—	—	—	−2·9	−2·4
Lichfield & Tamworth .	78·8	−2·1	46·0	54·0	—	—	[11·2]	+0·1	−2·2
Stafford & Stone .	79·4	−1·6	49·4	39·6	11·0	—	−2·0	−1·8	−4·2
Suffolk, Bury St. Edmunds	78·8	−3·4	54·6	45·4	—	—	[9·6]	−0·4	−3·9
Eye . . .	81·5	−1·0	44·6	37·0	18·4	—	−1·7	−1·9	+3·1
Lowestoft .	83·1	+0·6	46·0	45·4	8·6	—	−1·2	−2·4	+1·1
Sudbury & Woodbridge .	80·2	−1·6	50·2	37·0	12·9	—	−2·5	−1·6	−1·8
Surrey, Carshalton .	79·4	+0·8	47·0	35·8	17·2	—	−3·8	−3·8	−2·4
Chertsey . .	78·0	+0·2	48·4	34·8	16·8	—	−2·4	−1·9	−3·4
Dorking . .	79·0	−0·4	53·8	28·4	17·8	—	−2·6	−3·7	−2·0
East . . .	79·3	+0·1	54·5	16·5	29·0	—	+0·8	—	—
Epsom . .	79·2	−0·7	54·6	24·0	21·4	—	−2·7	—	—
Esher. . .	78·0	−1·2	55·4	25·5	19·2	—	−1·5	−1·6	−4·1
Farnham . .	80·0	+1·3	48·8	23·2	28·0	—	−0·4	—	—
Guildford . .	78·7	+0·1	50·4	32·9	16·7	—	−4·4	−2·7	−2·8
Reigate . .	80·1	+0·4	47·4	32·6	20·0	—	−1·9	−1·9	−3·3
Woking . .	77·1	−1·0	51·4	30·8	17·8	—	−0·9	−0·8	−6·4

See notes on p. 313.

English Counties—continued

Constituency	% voting 1966	Change since 1964	Con. %	Lab. %	Lib. %	Other %	Lib. 1964–1966	Swing 1964–1966	Swing 1959–1964
East Sussex,									
Eastbourne.	77·2	+0·5	46·3	22·4	29·7	1·6	+1·1	—	—
East Grinstead .	76·8	−1·2	55·3	20·9	23·8	—	−3·2	—	—
Lewes . .	76·3	−0·1	53·5	28·3	18·2	—	−0·3	−1·9	−4·9
Rye . . .	75·7	−1·8	58·6	19·8	21·6	—	−1·0	—	—
West Sussex, Arundel									
& Shoreham .	75·8	−0·7	55·5	28·3	16·2	—	−1·9	−3·0	−4·4
Chichester . .	73·2	−0·8	57·2	25·1	17·7	—	−5·1	—	—
Horsham . .	79·0	−0·5	45·8	37·2	17·0	—	−1·4	−2·9	−3·6
Warwickshire,									
Meriden .	85·7	+2·2	46·4	53·6	—	—	—	−3·3	−0·6
Nuneaton . .	79·7	−0·4	31·5	54·0	14·5	—	−3·6	+0·6	−1·9
Rugby .	84·9	+0·3	49·1	50·0	—	0·9	[13·0]	−2·4	+1·3
Solihull .	74·8	−5·7	65·7	34·3	—	—	[18·6]	−3·1	−5·1
Stratford .	78·0	−2·0	51·3	29·7	15·0	4·0	−1·9	−1·4	−6·3
Warwick &									
Leamington .	78·9	−1·5	51·6	36·1	12·3	—	+0·2	−2·1	−2·8
Westmorland .	75·5	−3·3	50·5	23·9	25·6	—	−4·4	—	—
Isle of Wight .	75·0	+0·7	48·6	29·0	22·4	—	+7·5	−1·1	−2·0
Wiltshire,									
Chippenham .	82·8	+1·6	39·6	22·3	38·1	—	+1·1	—	—
Devizes .	81·0	−0·4	44·7	39·2	16·1	—	+0·9	−1·7	−0·4
Salisbury .	76·2	−2·4	55·0	45·0	—	—	[17·3]	−1·9	−2·9
Westbury .	82·5	−0·3	43·6	37·8	18·6	—	−5·7	−2·4	−1·2
Worcestershire,									
Bromsgrove .	79·9	−3·0	53·0	47·0	—	—	[14·0]	−2·7	−2·4
Kidderminster .	75·6	−3·8	52·0	45·3	—	2·7	[12·1]	−3·7	−3·1
South .	75·6	−1·7	51·7	28·0	20·3	—	−4·5	—	—
Yorks, East Riding,									
Bridlington. .	71·5	−1·3	54·6	29·6	15·8	—	−5·3	−4·6	−6·2
Haltemprice .	76·5	−2·9	54·5	27·8	17·7	—	−3·8	−3·6	−1·9
Howden .	71·8	−4·1	50·6	26·9	22·5	—	−2·4	—	—
Yorks, North Riding,									
Cleveland .	81·1	−2·5	35·1	53·6	11·3	—	−6·5	−5·8	−4·9
Richmond . .	71·3	−4·3	56·6	24·6	18·8	—	−1·6	−3·1	−6·3
Scarborough &									
Whitby .	74·1	−0·8	43·1	24·2	31·8	0·9	+1·9	—	—
Thirsk & Malton .	70·3	−3·5	61·6	38·4	—	—	—	−4·8	−2·6
Yorks, West Riding,									
Barkston Ash .	79·8	−1·6	56·3	43·7	—	—	—	−2·5	+0·4
Colne Valley .	86·2	+1·4	8·3	43·1	48·6	—	+6·9	—	—
Dearne Valley .	76·7	−2·4	13·6	81·6	—	4·8	—	−3·2	−3·1
Don Valley .	78·3	−2·5	25·1	74·9	—	—	—	−3·0	−1·0
Goole .	73·1	−4·3	34·0	63·7	—	Cm 2·3	—	−3·1	−0·3
Harrogate .	74·5	−2·5	55·0	22·2	22·8	—	+0·8	—	—
Hemsworth .	76·0	−2·8	14·6	85·4	—	—	—	−2·3	−0·9
Normanton. .	74·3	−3·2	23·6	76·4	—	—	—	−3·9	+0·2
Penistone .	78·9	−2·2	23·4	62·3	14·3	—	−2·0	−3·2	−5·2
Ripon .	78·9	−1·7	52·2	25·9	21·9	—	−1·2	—	—
Rother Valley .	73·5	−3·9	23·2	76·8	—	—	—	−2·4	−0·3
Shipley . .	86·6	−0·1	46·5	42·7	10·8	—	−2·2	−2·5	−2·6
Skipton . .	82·0	−2·0	45·1	34·1	20·8	—	−3·8	−3·0	−2·4
Sowerby . .	77·7	−1·8	43·1	56·9	—	—	—	−2·7	−2·0

See notes on p. 313.

Welsh Boroughs

Constituency	% voting 1966	Change since 1964	Con. %	Lab. %	Lib. %	Other %	Lib. 1964–1966	Swing 1964–1966	Swing 1959–1964
Aberdare . . .	77·0	−2·1	11·7	73·3	—	WN 8·6 Cm 6·4	—	+0·2	−1·3
Cardiff, North . .	79·0	−1·7	49·3	50·7	—	—	[16·0]	−4·4	−7·1
South-east . .	78·9	−1·0	35·8	56·8	7·4	—	*	−3·0	−6·7
West . . .	75·1	−1·3	39·0	61·0	—	—	—	−1·8	−5·9
Merthyr Tydfil . .	73·9	−2·4	14·0	74·5	—	WN11·5	—	−0·3	−2·9
Newport . . .	78·8	−0·2	40·2	59·8	—	—	—	−2·3	−4·4
Rhondda, East . .	78·5	−1·0	6·7	77·4	—	Cm 8·4 WN 7·5	—	—	—
West . . .	80·3	−0·4	7·8	76·1	—	WN 8·7 Cm 7·4	—	—	—
Swansea, East . .	73·8	−2·5	15·5	75·4	—	WN 6·9 Cm 2·2	—	−2·7	−4·5
West . . .	80·4	−1·0	43·6	56·4	—	—	[9·7]	−3·6	−3·2

Welsh Counties

Constituency	% voting 1966	Change since 1964	Con. %	Lab. %	Lib. %	Other %	Lib. 1964–1966	Swing 1964–1966	Swing 1959–1964
Anglesey . .	73·2	−5·4	35·4	55·0	—	WN 9·6	[20·4]	+1·8	−0·6
Brecon & Radnor .	80·5	−2·3	36·5	57·5	—	WN 6·0	—	−0·2	−3·0
Caernarvonshire,									
Caernarvon. .	78·4	−2·0	22·2	56·1	—	WN21·7	—	−1·9	−3·5
Conway . .	83·7	+3·4	45·9	47·4	—	WN 6·1	—	−5·5	−1·3
Cardigan . .	81·0	+2·1	19·3	37·2	35·4	WN 8·1	−3·0	—	—
Carmarthenshire,									
Carmarthen .	82·6	−1·9	11·6	46·2	26·1	WN16·1	−6·2	—	—
Llanelly .	76·2	−3·2	15·1	71·4	—	WN10·9 Cm 2·6	[12·2]	−1·6	−2·9
Denbighshire,									
Denbigh .	80·6	+0·1	39·4	25·6	28·9	WN 6·1	−1·7	—	—
Wrexham .	77·2	−1·5	24·5	58·6	12·4	WN 4·5	*	−4·4	−0·7
Flintshire, East .	86·5	−0·4	33·5	51·3	13·3	WN 1·9	*	−4·7	−4·1
West . .	81·9	+1·2	43·2	36·0	17·0	WN 3·8	−1·5	−2·8	−3·2
Glamorgan,									
Aberavon .	78·3	−2·6	20·9	75·5	—	Cm 3·6	—	−1·5	−6·7
Barry .	83·6	+1·3	51·3	48·7	—	—	—	−2·7	−5·3
Caerphilly .	76·8	−1·6	14·6	74·3	—	WN11·1	—	−2·2	−0·6
Gower .	77·9	−1·9	22·8	77·2	—	—	—	−2·9	−2·8
Neath .	78·7	−1·5	16·1	79·7	—	Cm 4·2	—	−5·4	−2·7
Ogmore .	78·4	−1·3	14·6	71·3	14·1	—	*	−2·8	−0·9
Pontypridd.	74·7	−2·1	25·1	74·9	—	—	—	−3·6	−3·1
Merioneth. .	85·8	+2·7	8·9	44·2	35·5	WN11·4	+2·8	—	—
Monmouthshire,									
Abertillery .	73·4	−2·1	11·9	88·1	—	—	—	−2·2	−0·9
Bedwellty .	76·7	−2·4	13·8	86·2	—	—	—	−2·7	−1·7
Ebbw Vale .	79·3	−0·2	14·9	85·1	—	—	—	−1·5	−2·6
Monmouth .	84·3	−0·1	47·3	52·7	—	—	[13·2]	−3·4	−6·3
Pontypool .	75·4	−2·4	20·5	77·0	—	Cm 2·5	—	−1·9	−2·9
Montgomery .	82·8	−1·3	27·4	23·8	41·4	WN 7·4	−0·8	—	—
Pembroke. .	79·8	−1·7	36·2	48·1	10·7	WN 5·0	−8·4	+2·5	−3·4

See notes on p. 313.

Scottish Burghs

Constituency	% voting 1966	Change since 1964	Con. %	Lab. %	Lib. %	Other %	Lib. 1964–1966	Swing 1964–1966	Swing 1959–1964
Aberdeen, North	72·1	−2·8	20·6	67·5	10·2	Cm 1·7	*	−4·6	−1·6
South	81·3	+0·3	42·5	46·0	11·5	—	*	−5·7	−4·7
Coatbridge & Airdrie	77·0	−4·2	35·8	64·2	—	—	—	−2·1	−11·2
Dundee, East	78·9	−1·1	43·7	56·3	—	—	—	−1·5	−0·5
West	79·9	−1·6	36·9	53·7	6·9	Cm 2·4	*	−3·8	−3·9
Dunfermline	76·3	−0·9	26·6	58·4	—	SN 15·0	—	−4·3	−0·2
Edinburgh, Central	68·9	−2·9	41·4	58·6	—	—	—	−4·6	−2·9
East	77·4	−3·6	39·5	60·5	—	—	—	−4·4	−5·8
Leith	76·1	−1·8	42·2	56·8	—	Cm 1·0	—	−1·8	−0·6
North	73·9	+0·3	50·3	39·2	10·5	—	*	−2·7	−5·8
Pentlands	80·5	−1·1	44·9	44·8	10·2	—	−3·1	−2·7	−7·6
South	77·6	−2·7	53·2	39·5	—	SN 7·3	[13·1]	−2·9	−4·8
West	78·7	−2·2	48·3	39·0	12·8	—	−1·3	−3·0	−5·4
Glasgow, Bridgeton	58·8	−4·8	25·7	74·3	—	—	—	−2·7	−8·2
Cathcart	79·7	+0·4	50·7	48·3	—	1·0	—	−1·7	−6·3
Central	58·7	−3·7	25·2	74·8	—	—	—	−4·7	−5·5
Craigton	80·4	−0·5	32·7	57·9	—	SN 9·4	—	−4·2	−7·6
Gorbals	61·7	−2·8	22·8	73·1	—	Cm 4·1	—	−0·9	−8·0
Govan	67·5	−2·8	28·1	67·9	—	Cm 4·0	—	−2·7	−4·5
Hillhead	73·5	−1·2	62·9	37·1	—	—	—	−1·1	−4·3
Kelvingrove	66·3	−1·1	42·2	57·8	—	—	—	−3·8	−6·3
Maryhill	68·5	−2·0	20·7	67·8	—	SN 11·5	—	−3·2	−6·4
Pollok	79·0	+1·2	47·6	52·4	—	—	[11·5]	−2·1	−9·2
Provan	70·8	−4·9	30·8	66·9	—	Cm 2·3	—	−2·2	−10·2
Scotstoun	74·3	−2·9	32·8	61·8	—	Cm 5·4	—	−2·9	−7·9
Shettleston	68·6	−2·8	22·3	65·6	—	SN 12·1	—	−3·7	−7·2
Springburn	66·6	−2·6	19·1	67·8	—	SN 9·4 Cm 3·7	—	−2·6	−10·7
Woodside	73·0	−0·9	41·8	50·6	—	SN 7·1 0·5	[8·3]	−1·7	−5·7
Greenock	73·6	−2·9	17·6	57·1	23·2	Cm 2·1	−2·2	—	—
Kirkcaldy	75·4	−1·8	27·0	59·6	—	SN 13·4	—	−0·9	−2·6
Paisley	76·3	−3·5	23·2	60·0	16·8	—	−17·1	—	—
Stirling & Falkirk	77·1	−2·8	31·2	52·7	—	SN 14·4 Cm 1·7	—	−3·3	−4·5

See notes on p. 313.

Scottish Counties

Constituency	% voting 1966	Change since 1964	Con. %	Lab. %	Lib. %	Other %	Lib. 1964–1966	Swing 1964–1966	Swing 1959–1964
Aberdeenshire, East .	68·2	−1·8	41·6	22·1	27·7	SN 8·6	+4·4	—	—
West . . .	76·3	−1·1	39·8	17·1	43·1	—	+9·9	—	—
Angus, North & Mearns . .	76·2	−0·7	50·4	20·2	29·4	—	−4·7	—	—
South . .	71·2	−4·4	70·4	29·6	—	—	[19·2]	+2·6	—
Argyll . . .	72·3	+2·0	43·2	30·1	26·7	—	+2·8	−2·6	−7·1
Ayrshire, Ayr .	85·4	+2·4	50·6	49·4	—	—	—	−1·6	−2·5
Bute & North Ayrshire . .	76·0	+1·4	48·7	40·7	10·6	—	−3·4	−2·8	−5·6
Central . .	82·1	−2·1	42·3	57·7	—	—	—	−1·3	−4·4
Kilmarnock .	79·0	−3·8	31·5	68·5	—	—	[11·0]	−0·7	−5·1
South . .	75·1	−2·5	32·8	67·2	—	—	—	−0·5	−3·0
Banff . . .	65·1	−2·7	41·4	24·2	34·4	—	+8·8	—	−10·0
Berwick & East Lothian . .	85·3	+0·3	48·1	51·9	—	—	—	−2·6	−2·7
Caithness & Sutherland .	79·2	−0·9	22·0	39·1	38·9	—	+2·8	—	—
Dumfries . . .	80·2	−1·4	45·6	35·9	5·9	SN 12·6	*	+0·1	−3·7
Dunbartonshire, East.	80·6	−1·1	36·4	52·2	—	SN 9·0 Cm 2·4	—	−1·3	−3·5
West . . .	81·9	−0·2	33·1	52·3	—	SN 14·6	—	−2·8	−4·3
Fife, East . . .	76·1	−1·7	51·5	24·6	9·5	SN 14·4	−3·6	−1·0	−5·4
West . .	76·8	−1·8	19·3	63·1	—	SN 14·0 Cm 3·6	—	−2·6	−3·6
Galloway . . .	66·6	−7·2	62·0	38·0	—	—	[24·0]	−2·8	—
Inverness . .	72·1	+0·7	32·9	27·7	39·4	—	−0·4	—	—
Lanarkshire, Bothwell . .	77·8	−2·6	36·4	60·9	—	Cm 2·7	—	−1·9	−5·7
Hamilton . .	73·3	−4·2	28·8	71·2	—	—	—	−0·2	−1·8
Lanark . .	83·7	−2·3	38·2	51·7	—	SN 10·1	—	−1·9	−4·3
Motherwell .	74·4	−4·5	35·2	60·8	—	Cm 4·0	—	−2·1	−5·4
North . .	78·8	−3·2	39·1	60·9	—	—	—	−0·3	−1·9
Rutherglen. .	84·2	−1·8	39·5	54·1	—	SN 6·4	—	−2·4	−7·0
Midlothian . .	77·5	−1·4	27·1	56·6	—	SN 16·3	—	−3·5	−1·1
Moray & Nairn .	68·0	−1·4	48·1	34·1	17·8	—	−4·1	−4·8	−2·0
Orkney & Zetland	65·2	−7·5	22·3	18·6	59·1	—	−3·5	—	—
Perthshire, Kinross & West . .	73·5	−2·4	60·8	18·7	—	SN 20·5	—	—	−1·8
Perth & East .	72·3	−3·3	56·5	27·9	—	SN 15·6	—	−2·3	—
Renfrewshire, East	79·9	−2·7	53·2	33·1	13·8	—	−2·6	−0·7	−4·3
West . .	81·6	−1·3	45·7	54·3	—	—	[10·1]	−3·1	−4·7
Ross & Cromarty .	71·2	+1·8	27·6	30·3	42·1	—	+1·9	—	—
Roxburgh, Selkirk & Peebles . .	84·8	+2·6	40·7	13·6	45·7	—	+6·8	—	—
Stirlingshire, Clackmannan & East	77·5	−2·3	24·6	55·3	—	SN 20·1	—	−2·0	−4·0
West . .	82·4	+1·2	25·4	48·6	—	SN 26·0	—	—	−1·3
West Lothian . .	79·6	+0·0	11·2	52·4	—	SN 35·3 Cm 1·1	—	−4·4	—
Western Isles . .	61·5	−5·4	20·2	61·0	18·8	—	−12·1	—	—

See notes on p. 313.

Northern Ireland

Constituency	% voting 1966	Change since 1964	Con. %	Lab. %	Lib. %	Other %	Lib. 1964– 1966	Swing 1964– 1966	Swing 1959– 1964
Belfast, East . .	68·2	−4·3	54·7	45·3	—	—	—	−6·3	−0·5
North : :	65·5	−4·0	57·4	42·6	—	—	—	−4·9	−0·4
South : :	63·3	−5·0	65·4	34·6	—	—	[4·9]	−8·3	−0·4
West . . .	74·8	+0·1	48·0	—	—	Rep. Lab 52·0	—	—	—
Antrim, North . .	56·7	−6·6	78·1	—	21·9	—	*	—	—
South .	55·9	−8·4	64·3	35·7	—	—	—	−8·5	—
Armagh . . .	63·3	−11·2	72·0	—	—	IR 28·0	—	—	—
Down, North .	48·9	−14·2	78·5	—	21·5	—	+15·3	—	—
South .	65·8	−6·3	64·0	—	18·6	IR 17·4	+8·6	—	—
Fermanagh & South Tyrone . .	86·1	+0·5	54·0	—	—	NU 26·9 IR 19·1	[11·0]	—	—
Londonderry . .	76·4	−0·1	58·1	—	—	IN 37·1 IR 4·8	—	—	—
Mid-Ulster . .	83·8	−1·2	52·2	—	—	IR 47·8	—	—	—

See notes on p. 313.

	% Highest Swings		% Highest Turnouts		% Biggest Turnout Increase
−8·7	Birmingham, Stechford	87·5	Cornwall, North	+7·9	Brighton, Kemptown
−8·6	Birmingham, Sparkbrook	86·9	Orpington	+6·0	Birmingham, Ladywood
−8·5	Antrim, South	86·6	Shipley	+5·9	Leyton
−8·3	Birmingham, Small Heath	86·5	Flintshire, East	+5·4	Eton & Slough
		86·5	Wellingborough	+4·9	Falmouth & Camborne
−8·3	Belfast, South	86·2	Colne Valley	+4·8	Hampstead
−8·0	Camberwell, Peckham	86·1	Fermanagh & S. Tyrone	+4·4	Cornwall, North
−7·9	Kingston upon Hull, West	85·8	Bexley	+4·2	Reading
		85·8	Buckingham	+4·1	West Bromwich
−7·8	Kingston upon Hull, North	85·8	Merioneth	+4·1	Paddington, South
		85·8	Torrington	+4·0	Norwood
−7·8	Newcastle-on-Tyne, East	85·7	Meriden	+3·5	Norfolk, North
−7·7	Birmingham, All Saints				
−7·7	Bradford, East				
−7·6	Smethwick				

	% Lowest Swings		% Lowest Turnouts		% Biggest Turnout Decrease
+2·6	Angus, South	48·9	Down, North	−27·1	Southampton, Itchen
+2·5	Pembroke	49·0	Southampton, Itchen	−14·2	Down, North
+1·8	Anglesey	50·7	Stepney	−11·2	Armagh
+1·6	Belper	50·7	Liverpool, Exchange	−8·4	Antrim, South
+1·6	Faversham	50·9	Islington, South-west	−7·9	Liverpool, Scotland
+1·0	Norfolk, South West	51·7	Liverpool, Scotland	−7·5	Orkney & Zetland
+0·9	Dorset, South	53·5	Shoreditch & Finsbury	−7·2	Galloway
+0·6	Nuneaton	53·7	Manchester, Exchange	−6·6	Antrim, North
+0·2	Aberdare	54·0	Southwark	−6·6	Barnsley
+0·1	Dumfries	54·2	Islington, North	−6·6	Huyton
+0·1	Lichfield & Tamworth	55·6	Camberwell, Peckham	−6·3	Down, South
+0·0	Dudley	55·8	Stoke Newington & Hackney North	−6·0	Salford, West

Y

BY-ELECTIONS 1964–1966

Constituency	Date	% voting	Con. %	Lab. %	Lib. %	Other %	Swing '64 By-election	Swing '66 By-election
Nuneaton	*1964*	*80·1*	*29·1*	*52·8*	*18·1*	—	—	—
	21/1/65	60·8	34·9	48·9	16·2	—	+4·9	—
	1966	*79·7*	*31·5*	*54·0*	*14·5*	—	—	−4·3
Leyton	*1964*	*70·2*	*33·5*	*50·3*	*16·2*	—	—	—
Conservative gain	21/1/65	57·7	42·9	42·4	13·9	0·4, 0·4	+8·7	—
	1966	*76·1*	*36·9*	*54·4*	*7·8*	*0·9*	—	−9·1
Altrincham & Sale	*1964*	*81·2*	*46·8*	*28·0*	*25·2*	—	—	—
	4/2/65	62·0	50·0	29·0	19·4	1·6	+1·1	—
	1966	*78·0*	*48·0*	*34·7*	*17·3*	—	—	−3·6
East Grinstead	*1964*	*78·1*	*53·2*	*19·8*	*27·0*	—	—	—
	4/2/65	64·5	55·0	13·5	31·5	—	—	—
	1966	*76·8*	*55·3*	*20·9*	*23·8*	—	—	—
Salisbury	*1964*	*78·6*	*48·3*	*34·4*	*17·3*	—	—	—
	4/2/65	69·1	48·2	37·4	12·9	1·5	−1·6	—
	1966	*76·2*	*55·0*	*45·0*	—	—	—	−0·4
Saffron Walden	*1964*	*82·4*	*49·3*	*37·4*	*13·3*	—	—	—
	23/3/65	76·6	48·5	39·6	11·9	—	−1·5	—
	1966	*82·5*	*47·5*	*39·8*	*12·7*	—	—	−0·6
Roxburgh, Selkirk &	*1964*	*82·2*	*42·8*	*15·8*	*38·9*	SN 2·5	—	—
Peebles.	24/3/65	81·6	38·6	11·3	49·2	0·9	—	—
Liberal gain	*1966*	*84·8*	*40·8*	*13·6*	*45·6*	—	—	—
Abertillery	*1964*	*75·5*	*14·1*	*85·9*	—	—	—	—
	1/4/65	63·1	14·3	79·0	—	WN 6·7	+3·6	—
	1966	*73·4*	*11·9*	*88·1*	—	—	—	−5·8
Birmingham, Hall Green	*1964*	*75·8*	*52·5*	*31·8*	*15·7*	—	—	—
	6/5/65	52·3	54·9	28·7	16·4	—	+2·8	—
	1966	*73·6*	*47·4*	*39·7*	*12·9*	—	—	−9·3
Hove	*1964*	*69·6*	*68·4*	*31·6*	—	—	—	—
	22/7/65	58·1	62·2	20·6	16·9	0·3	+2·4	—
	1966	*72·1*	*57·3*	*25·7*	*16·0*	—	—	−5·0
Cities of London and	*1964*	*59·7*	*58·4*	*30·6*	*11·0*	—	—	—
Westminster.	4/11/65	41·8	59·5	32·9	6·3	1·3	−0·6	—
	1966	*60·0*	*54·7*	*35·1*	*10·2*	—	—	−3·5
Erith, Crayford	*1964*	*79·6*	*32·5*	*53·1*	*14·4*	—	—	—
	11/11/65	72·8	37·5	55·4	7·1	—	+1·4	—
	1966	*81·7*	*34·4*	*55·5*	*8·8*	Cm 1·3	—	−1·8
Kingston upon Hull,	*1964*	*77·2*	*40·8*	*43·3*	*15·9*	—	—	—
North	27/1/66	76·3	40·8	52·2	6·3	0·6, 0·1, 0·1	−4·5	—
	1966	*79·0*	*37·0*	*55·2*	*7·8*	—	—	−3·4

INDEX

Printed in Great Britain by
Richard Clay (The Chaucer Press), Ltd,
Bungay, Suffolk